Genealogies of Legal Vision

It was the classical task of legal rhetoric to make law both seen and understood. These conjoint goals came to be separated and opposed in modernity and a degree of blindness ensued. Legal reason was increasingly deemed to be a purely textual enterprise. Against this constraint and in furtherance of an incipient visual turn in legal studies, *Genealogies of Legal Vision* seeks to revive the classical *ars iuris* and, to this end, traces the history of regimes of visual control.

Law always relied in significant measure upon the use of visual representations, upon pictures, architecture, costume and statuary to convey authority and sovereign norm. Military, religious, administrative and legal insignia found juridical codification and expression in collections of signs of office, in heraldic codes, in genealogical devices, and then finally in the juridical invention in the mid-sixteenth century of the legal emblem book.

Genealogies of Legal Vision traces the complex lineage of the legal emblem and argues that the *mens emblematica* of the humanist lawyers was the inauguration of a visiocratic regime that continues into the multiple new technologies and novel media of contemporary governance. Bringing together leading experts on the history and art of legal emblems, this collection provides a groundbreaking account of the long relationship between visibility, meaning and normativity.

Peter Goodrich is Professor of Law at Cardozo Law School and Director of the Program in Law and Humanities and is author of *Legal Emblems and the Art of Law* (2013).

Valérie Hayaert is a researcher at the Fondation Bodmer, Cologny, Geneva and author of Mens emblematica *et humanisme juridique* (2008).

Discourses of Law

Series editors: Peter Goodrich, Michel Rosenfeld and Arthur Jacobson
Benjamin N. Cardozo School of Law

This successful and exciting series seeks to publish the most innovative scholarship at the intersection of law, philosophy and social theory. The books published in the series are distinctive by virtue of exploring the boundaries of legal thought. The work that this series seeks to promote is marked most strongly by the drive to open up new perspectives on the relation between law and other disciplines. The series has also been unique in its commitment to international and comparative perspectives upon an increasingly global legal order. Of particular interest in a contemporary context, the series has concentrated upon the introduction and translation of continental traditions of theory and law.

The original impetus for the series came from the paradoxical merger and confrontation of East and West. Globalization and the internationalization of the rule of law has had many dramatic and often unforeseen and ironic consequences. An understanding of differing legal cultures, particularly different patterns of legal thought, can contribute, often strongly and starkly, to an appreciation if not always a resolution of international legal disputes. The rule of law is tied to social and philosophical underpinnings that the series has sought to excoriate and illuminate.

Titles in the series:

Nietzsche and Legal Theory: Half-Written Laws
Edited by Peter Goodrich and Mariana Valverde

Law, Orientalism, and Postcolonialism: The Jurisdiction of the Lotus Eaters
Piyel Haldar

Endowed: Regulating the Male Sexed Body
Michael Thomson

The Identity of the Constitutional Subject: Selfhood, Citizenship, Culture, and Community
Michel Rosenfeld

The Land is the Source of the Law: A Dialogic Encounter with Indigenous Jurisprudence
C.F. Black

Shakespearean Genealogies of Power: A Whispering of Nothing in Hamlet, Richard II, Julius Caesar, Macbeth, The Merchant of Venice, *and* The Winter's Tale
Anselm Haverkamp

Visualizing Law in the Age of the Digital Baroque: Arabesques and Entanglements
Richard K. Sherwin

The Scene of Mass Crime
Peter Goodrich and Christian Delage

Novel Judgments: Legal Theory as Fiction
William Macneil

Sex, Culpability and the Defence of Provocation
Danielle Tyson

Wickedness and Crime: Laws of Homicide and Malice
Penny Crofts

Shakespeare's Curse
Björn Quiring

Exemplarity and Singularity: Thinking through Particulars in Philosophy, Literature, And Law
Edited by Michèle Lowrie and Susanne Lüdemann

Law and Enjoyment: Power, Pleasure and Psychoanalysis
Daniel Hourigan

Genealogies of Legal Vision
Edited by Peter Goodrich and Valérie Hayaert

Forthcoming:

Crime Scenes: Forensics and Aesthetics
Rebecca Scott Bray

The Rule of Reason in European Constitutionalism and Citizenship
Yuri Borgmann-Prebil

Varieties of Liberalism: Nineteenth Century Contract Between Literature, Law and History
Anat Rosenberg

The publisher gratefully acknowledges the support of the Jacob Burns Institute for Advanced Legal Studies of the Benjamin N. Cardozo School of Law to the series *Discourses of Law*.

Genealogies of Legal Vision

Edited by
Peter Goodrich and Valérie Hayaert

Routledge
Taylor & Francis Group
LONDON AND NEW YORK

First published 2015
by Routledge
2 Park Square, Milton Park, Abingdon, Oxon, OX14 4RN

and by Routledge
711 Third Avenue, New York, NY 10017

Routledge is an imprint of the Taylor & Francis Group, an informa business

British Library Cataloguing in Publication Data
A catalogue record for this book is available from the British Library

Library of Congress Cataloging-in-Publication Data
Genealogies of legal vision / edited by Peter Goodrich, Valérie Hayaert.
pages cm
Includes bibliographical references and index.
ISBN 978-0-415-74907-7 (hardback) — ISBN 978-0-415-74906-0 (pbk) —
ISBN 978-1-315-77426-8 (ebk) 1. Symbolism in law. 2. Devices (Heraldry)
3. Emblems. 4. Law and art. I. Goodrich, Peter, 1954- editor. II. Hayaert, Valérie, editor.
KB78.G46 2015
340'.1—dc23

ISBN: 978-0-415-74907-7 (hbk)
ISBN: 978-0-415-74906-0 (pbk)
ISBN: 978-1-315-77426-8 (ebk)

Typeset in Minion
by FiSH Books Ltd, London
Printed in Great Britain by Ashford Colour Press Ltd,
Gosport, Hants

MIX
Paper from responsible sources
FSC www.fsc.org FSC® C011748

Contents

List of figures

Contributors

Christian Biet is Professor of the History and Aesthetics of Theatre at the University of Paris Ouest-Nanterre, and Senior member of the Institut Universitaire de France. He has published numerous works on issues relating to law, history, performance and theatrics. Amongst his many books are *Œdipus in Monarchy, tragedy and early modern theory of Law* (1994); *Law and Literature in the Ancien Regime* (2004); *The Theatre of Cruelty in 16th and 17th Century France* (2006) and *Tragedy* (2010).

Dennis Curtis is Clinical Professor Emeritus of Law at Yale Law School, where he teaches courses on sentencing and professional responsibility and directs a clinical course in which students work with Connecticut's State Disciplinary Counsel to prosecute lawyers who violate rules of professional conduct. Professor Curtis has written extensively on clinical education and the legal profession, and on sentencing and post-conviction justice. His most recent book, *Representing Justice: Invention, Controversy, and Rights in City-States and Democratic Courtrooms*, co-authored with Professor Judith Resnik, addresses the relationship between adjudication and democracy. In 2011, *Representing Justice* was selected by the *Guardian* newspaper as one of the year's ten best legal reads and, in 2014, it won the Order of the Coif award.

William Egginton is Andrew W. Mellon Professor in the Humanities and

Vice Dean for Graduate Education at the Johns Hopkins University, where he teaches Spanish and Latin American literature, literary theory and the relation between literature and philosophy. He is the author of *How the World Became a Stage* (2003), *Perversity and Ethics* (2006), *A Wrinkle in History* (2007), *The Philosopher's Desire* (2007), *The Theater of Truth* (2010), and *In Defense of Religious Moderation* (2011). He is also the translator of Lisa Block de Behar's *Borges, the Passion of an Endless Quotation* (2003, second edition 2014) and coeditor of *The Pragmatic Turn in Philosophy* (2004) and *Thinking With Borges* (2009).

Peter Goodrich embarked upon his ontological journey as a fetus in India and then a child in Singapore. His epistemological trajectory was triggered by encountering the work of the philologist jurist turned Lacanian legal theorist, Pierre Legendre. While this could well have led to the demise of his career, he picked up the pieces, kept quiet, and published his thesis, *Legal Discourse*, and then a latter-day enchiridion, *Reading the Law*, in quick succession. Working to expand his conusances and the amplitude of theoretical jurisdictions, later works combined semiotics, history and psychoanalysis, and *Languages of Law and Oedipus Lex* vied (largely unsuccessfully) for shelf space beside the Latin American bibliomysteries and Nordic existential noir that you were reading back then. The inevitable emotional crises engendered by being English resulted in works on *Law in the Courts of Love* and *Laws of Love*, and departure to the United States in the hope of irritating a larger cohort of complacent academic lawyers than are available targets in the shrinking United Kingdom. Things are different in the United States. You teach cases and publish exclusively in law reviews. Despite these distractions, Goodrich, *bonus dives*, has adapted and refused in equal measure. He publishes regularly, which is to say not very often, in *Critical Inquiry*, and an erudification, under the snappy title *Legal Emblems and the Art of Law*, appeared in stylish print, much to the surprise of his colleagues, in 2014.

Agnès Guiderdoni is Research Associate of the Fonds National de la Recherche Scientifique (Belgium) and Professor of Early Modern Literature at the Université Catholique de Louvain, where she is the director of the Centre for Early Modern Cultural Analysis. Originally a specialist in seventeenth-century French literature, she more particularly studies emblematic literature and the field of figurative representations (*imago figurata*). She has recently worked on Francis de Sales's beatification and canonization's feasts; she is preparing a monograph on this topic. Among her publications are *Emblemata sacra. The Rhetoric and*

Hermeneutics of Illustrated Sacred Discourse, co-edited with R. Dekoninck in 2007, *Ut pictura meditatio. The Meditative Image in Northern Art, 1500–1700*, co-edited with W. Melion and R. Dekoninck, in 2012, and *Fictions sacrées. Esthétique et théologie durant le premier âge moderne*, co-edited with R. Dekoninck and E. Granjon, in 2012. A monograph, *Emblematics and Spirituality*, is to appear in 2015.

Piyel Haldar teaches legal history at the School of Law, Birkbeck, University of London, where, despite his efforts to achieve honourable oblivion, he is a senior lecturer. Under pressure and general demand he has published numerous papers on the history of evidence and its relationship to law. He is currently researching the relationship between rhetoric and logic and its impact on the juridical and social thought of early modern common lawyers. He is the author of *Law, Orientalism and Postcolonialism; the Jurisdiction of the Lotus Eaters* (2008).

Valérie Hayaert is a classicist, historian, linguist and humanist researcher of the early modern European tradition. Her particular interest lies in the *mens emblematica*, the humanist lawyers' invention of woodcut depictions of legal and theological themes, in the tradition of *serio-ludere* or playful seriousness. Her book of that title, Mens emblematica *et humanisme juridique* is the definitive study of the genesis of the emblem tradition and was published in 2008. Her subsequent work has added dexterous particulars to the tracing of the key figures and works of the legal humanists and has also looked at the aesthetics of justice in the early modern period and *Allégories de justice: le décor de la Grand' chambre du Parlement de Flandre*, co-authored with Antoine Garapon, was published in 2014. Valérie has taught in Cyprus, Tunisia, England and France. She is now a researcher at the Fondation Bodmer in Geneva.

Anselm Haverkamp has been teaching literature and philosophy in New York, Berlin and Munich for the last decades and has published, among other things, *Shakespearean Genealogies of Power* (2011).

Alick M. McLean's scholarship and teaching focus on the urban history of Italian city-states in relation to the longer term history of architecture, settlement, and sustainability in the Mediterranean basin. A common thread linking his studies to legal history is the visual and spatial construction of political institutions and their underlying mentalities. His publications include *Prato: Architecture, Piety, and Political Identity in a Tuscan City-State* (2008), a series of articles on Italian Romanesque,

Gothic and Renaissance architecture and urban design for the German publishing house Könemann Verlag and book reviews. McLean teaches courses on *Florence The Mediterranean City*, *'Renaissance' Architecture*, and the travelling seminar *The Greek Odyssey: The Origins of Western Myth, Architecture, and Politics* for Syracuse University in Florence. He is currently an architectural and urban history consultant for two new museums in Tuscany, the Museo delle Terre Nuove in San Giovanni Valdarno, and the Museo Palazzo Pretorio in Prato.

Paul Raffield is Professor of Law at the University of Warwick, where he teaches tort law, origins, images and cultures of English Law, and Shakespeare and the law. After graduating from Cardiff University with a degree in Law, Paul went to drama school and subsequently worked for twenty-five years as an actor, before being appointed at Warwick. While an actor, Paul studied for his PhD at Birkbeck Law School. He has subsequently published extensively in the fields of law and literature and legal history. He is the author of *Shakespeare's Imaginary Constitution: Late Elizabethan Politics and the Theatre of Law* (2010) and *Images and Cultures of Law in Early Modern England: Justice and Political Power, 1558–1660* (2004). He is founding co-editor of the journal *Law and Humanities*, and a member of the Italian Cultural Association for the Study of Law and Literature. Paul is a National Teaching Fellow and a Fellow of the UK Higher Education Academy.

Judith Resnik is the Arthur Liman Professor of Law at Yale Law School, where she teaches about federalism, procedure, courts, prisons, equality and citizenship. Her books include *Representing Justice: Invention, Controversy, and Rights in City-States and Democratic Courtrooms* (with Dennis Curtis, 2011) and *Migrations and Mobilities: Citizenship, Borders, and Gender* (co-edited with Seyla Benhabib, 2009). In 2011, *Representing Justice* was selected by the *Guardian* newspaper as one of the year's ten best legal reads and in 2014, the book won the Order of the Coif award. Recent articles include 'The Privatization of Process: Requiem for and Celebration of the Federal Rules of Procedure at 75' (*University of Pennsylvania Law Review*, 2014); 'Fairness in Numbers' (*Harvard Law Review*, 2011); and 'Detention, The War on Terror, and the Federal Courts' (*Columbia Law Journal*, 2010).

Introduction: the emblematic cube

Peter Goodrich and Valérie Hayaert

In an engaging and provocative account of movies and spectators after cinema, the light-lipped Gabriele Pedullà asserts intriguingly that 'in the twentieth century, the auditorium was the true blind spot of film theory'.[1] Even though art historians had developed complex theories of the gallery device, the 'white cube' as constitutive of the aesthetic experience, film theory remained recalcitrantly blind to the omnipresent yet paradoxically invisible role of the cinematic auditorium, the dark cube, as an intrinsic dimension of what was unique about the affective impact of films. Darkness, separation, immobility, serial intensity and duration were all linked to the distinctive architecture and scenography of the movie theatre. In sum, the critical focus on the film, *diegesis*, the narrative on screen, distracted from the role played by the movie theatre, the setting, the *mise en scène*, in producing the high cathartic impact of classical cinema.

Genealogies of Legal Vision traces a similar and not unrelated blindness in the modern theory of law. The courtroom, the emblematic cube, the imagistic and theatrical setting of law, the art and now also the cameras, have played only a very minor role in jurisprudential accounts of governance, justice and the rule of law. The focus on legal texts, upon the Code, or in common law upon the books, the precedents and *rationes decidendi* of case law, have largely obscured the crucial role played by visual depictions, by cameras, portraiture, architectural symbols, statuary, costumes and other modes of monumental inscription, as primary tools of access to and relay of law. Judicial robes, for instance, are dismissed by the American legal realist Jerome Frank as archaic and obstructive 'priestly flutterings'.[2] And if the

1 Gabriele Pedullà, *In Broad Daylight. Movies and Spectators After the Cinema* (London: Verso, 2012), 7.

2 Jerome Frank, 'Cult of the Robe,' in *Courts on Trial: Myth and Reality in American Justice* (Princeton, NJ: Princeton University Press, 1973), 255; and, for recent and insightful commentary, see Michelle Castaneda, 'Priestly Flutterings: Sacred Time and the Performance of Judicial Authority' (ms). See further Antoine Garapon, *Bien juger: Essai sur le rituel judiciaire* (Paris: Odile Jacob, 2001).

robes, judicial costume and *dramatis personae* are dismissed as archaic vestiges, as irrelevant relics, the analysis will likely be even more oblivious to the symbolic dimensions of the immoveable environment, the architecture as also the monumental inscriptions and installations by means of which law is first visible in the public sphere. By the same token, the study of the theatrical dimensions of law, of the scene of trial, of *in vivo* enactment, of the rendering – which is also to say the painting – of judgment, and the performance of governance, are relegated to the non-legal disciplines, to the lower status of the humanistic and merely scholarly domains of study. The visual domain of legal performance, the ornate and distinctive filigree of law's social presence has been treated as profoundly secondary and marginal to the business of rationalizing doctrine and cohering texts, and yet, as this study evidences, which is to say makes visible and shows, the image is the mode of law's opening to the social and simultaneously the medium of its transmission.

The history of law's resistance to analysis of its own spectacular rites, its manipulation of images, the symbolic valence of its settings and its theatrocratic modes of its promulgation is a lengthy one and will not be rehearsed here.[3] The *muta eloquentia* of images and *emblemata*, the desiderata of gesture and delivery, the figurations of text and enunciation all fall within the domain of rhetoric and have only recently come to be deemed worthy of serious study as topics of juristic and doctrinal significance. The essays collected in *Genealogies of Legal Vision* begin the labour of retracing, augmenting and correcting this jurisprudential blindspot and of potentially furthering a visual return in legal studies comparable to the 'linguistic turn' that dominated the critical movements of the last half-century. To dismiss the visual and spectacular as merely rhetorical, as weakness, lamentable art or boundless poetry, misses the crucial and distinctive character and role of the image and, for the purposes of the present volume, the emblem, the visual depiction inserted into the text, which both opens and undoes the fiction of law's purity, the belief in a closed textual system of rules, and gives the lie to the dissimulation of law's visual rule.

Inaugurating law

Texts are inert. The *Corpus iuris* is not simply a body of law, its sibylline leaves capture the corpse of long dead jurists and the expression of antique

3 For a recent and powerful account of legal theatrocracy, see Julie Stone Peters, 'Theatrocracy Unwired: Legal Performance in the Modern Mediasphere', 26/1 (2014) *Law and Literature*, 31.

rules. These dead letters of governance, the *ipsissima verba* of rule, the printed norms, have to emerge from the book, come to life, be animated and put into play. This simple yet profound dysfunction of the textual and scriptural tradition has always required the figure of the sovereign and the delegated roles of judge and jurist to bring the text to life and implement the imaginary, the principle that drives the rule. At a most basic level of governance, the image of the animator of the rule, the depiction, often in the frontispiece of the compilations of laws, will be that of the handing down of the tables and, latterly, the books of law from a figure above to scribes or citizens below. The threshold of the text, the first encounter is with the image of the collection, of the tablets, tables or library of law, and then and more specifically with the boards and clasps of the individual volume. The frontispiece of the law book will classically have heavy letters, often in gothic typeface, coloured ink and an emblematic image, a frontispiece that forms the *facies* or face of the work.[4]

The frequently majestic, classically constructed entry to the courthouse, via the columns and steps, the bifold doors and ornamented foyer, often with painted scenes, statuary and Latin inscriptions, introduces the other space of trial. So, too, the frontispiece of the early law book will portray a columned and classically constructed scene of foundation or of mythic lawgiving and will act in its turn as the threshold to the legal text. Here, we will find images and inscriptions that indicate the descent of *nomos* from the heavens to the earth and, in return, the passage from the tellurian to the eternal, from the image to the invisible realm of the soul – *hac itur in astra*; this is the path to the heavens, as one common motto relays it. The examples are numerous and some have not been entirely forgotten in the race to reason that for so long pretended to ban images from law and figures of speech from legal texts. As if. The portal to the law is itself an emblem, an image of entry, an opening of the curtain on to the tableau and stage of the juridical. Thus, the figure of law that inaugurates the body of laws is that of a higher power, a super-terrestrial image, such as that of Leviathan for Hobbes or that of the divinity, depicted as a crescendo of light, handing the laws to Moses, to Solon, to Homer or some further figure of mythological or Christian rule. The frontispiece depicts the face, often the Janus face of entry into a sacral space, another scene, the emblematic cube of law.

Pause on the frontispiece as face of the laws. In the classical idiom of legality, the visage is *index animi*, the sign of the soul, as well as being the transitional site of the living in relation to the eternal. The face is an opening;

4 Marc Fumaroli, *L'Ecole du silence* (Paris: Flammarion, 1998).

it is the conduit in Augustinian terms of *pneuma*, of breath and of all the other insufflations that are marked by the diverse facial orifices that allow for the passage from external to internal and from visible to invisible. There is, importantly, a dual relay connected to the face in that it opens to and simultaneously or also lets in, imbibes and exhales. If the face is an image, a mobile site of identity and difference, the image is equally a face and, in the case of law, it is explicitly *facies altera*, the mark of time and judgment. The face opens and in meeting, encounter, it is precisely the face to face, the *osculum pacis*, the kiss of brotherhood, the caress of the lips or touching of cheeks, that signals the dissolution of boundaries and the advent of the animated, meaning the shift from distance and separation to contact, exchange and being together that law both demarcates and identifies.[5] The kiss is a flag, a vexillological expression, and it allows for both the exchange of breath and the touching that mingles and so obliterates the boundaries of the solipsistic individual. The body opens to the other. Breath intermingles and, in classical theological terms, souls are mixed.

The face of the book, the frontispiece emblem, plays a similar role. The book has to incite and seduce the lector into opening it. It needs a face that will beckon, entice, attract and move to action. The image that opens the book is there to open the reader, so as to lead the *lector* into opening the book. The image, as Didi-Huberman has so persuasively argued, is always a species of incarnation; the image gives birth, it begins, it opens up and, hence, the importance of the frontispiece as portal and threshold into another domain, a *ius quaesitum alteri*, which is most directly marked by the *facies altera* that has to be excavated, broken into, opened or disinterred.[6] There is a backface of law, an umbrageous history, the tenebrous imprint of the past, of the immemorial which is only and can never be other than a mythography, an image of an expanding and contracting history, the living presence of the long dead. The law that opens up through the portal, beyond the threshold, shares thus with the image the dual character of absence and presence, of death and desire, past and present which finds expression in the ambiguity of the Latin of the *desiderium*, referencing an approach that both lusts for and mourns. The French idiom captures this well in the phonetic play of *deuil* and *seuil*, a duality that neatly encompasses the juristic ambivalence toward the image and the figure. It has to be renounced, discarded, eschewed as mere ornament, as an idol, a dead thing (*idolum nihil est*) and so the image can only be incidental and exterior to the text. The image, therefore, can neither directly evince nor expressly represent doctrine but then,

5 John Selden, *Jani Anglorum facies altera* (London: Helme, 1610).
6 Georges Didi-Huberman, *L'Image ouverte* (Paris: Gallimard, 2007), 31–7.

and at the same time, the lawyer, the ambulant image of the human subject, variously becomes *anima legis*, *lex loquens*, *viva vox iuris*, and must open the book, must enter the domain of the imaginary that the inke divinities and printed pictures encode and transmit. The lawyer becomes an image and walks among the spectres that the print releases from their atemporal interment in the tomes.

There is a certain humour in the legal ambivalence, in the play of dissimulation that governance, which is to say the *œconomy* of practice requires. The rhetorical figure of law is *allegoria*, extended metaphor, irony and dissimulation. One thing is said, another is meant or, in the baroque maxim that Agamben has recently revived, *rex regnat sed non gubernat* – the sovereign, *Deus otiosus*, rules but does not govern.[7] Administration, governance and practice are a separate and in many respects undisclosed or symptomatic sphere. They are hidden by images as much as they are expressed through them and it is precisely to this two-way street, this opening out and drawing in, this dilation and insufflation of the image as Huberman defines it, this institutional desire *aperire imagines*, that attracts, threatens and at times undoes the fictional security and putative certainty of Code and rule, law book and judgment. Recollect that the emblems were explicitly enigmas, and so acted as the opaque and polysemic representations of law's spectacular, which is to say visible presence, while also conveying an esoteric and paradoxically inaccessible content that related as much to governance as to law, as much to practice as to rules. The emblem, as image, as an independent and yet correlative expression of doctrine as practised, as enacted and made visible, is both an aspect of law's presence, often embedded in the legal text, and at the same time it escapes the law and plays another and less fettered role as an expression of the juridical imaginary. As Hayaert has amply shown, and as Drysdall has also adumbrated, emblems were in many senses hieroglyphs of law and proceeding according to a symbolic logic that was more *ad apparentiam* than *ad similia*, could play with law, poke fun at rules, ridicule practices and even defame lawyers.[8]

The latter point deserves a certain elaboration. The tradition of legal emblems falls squarely within the humanities and expresses a *mens emblematica*, an appreciation of the rhetorical and literary, the humorous and satirical that accompany what are the forbidding, resistant and frequently unpleasant seeming texts of the wizened figure of the *corpus iuris*

7 Giorgio Agamben, *The Kingdom and the Glory* (Palo Alto, CA: Stanford University Press, 2011).

8 Valérie Hayaert, Mens emblematica *et humanisme juridique* (Geneva: Droz, 2008); Denis L. Drysdall, 'Hieroglyphs, Speaking Pictures and the Law: The Context of Alciato's Emblems', *Glasgow Emblem Studies*, 16, (2014).

depicted by Placentinus as *ager vetus iuris nostrae*.[9] Accede for the moment to a certain sense of the festive and satirical in the circulation and insertion of images in laws and, as Hayaert has shown, these range from specific and personalized responses to and critiques of colleagues, to the more generally recognized although often uncomprehended references to classical literary and legal sources.[10] In the latter aspect, as references to other disciplines, to satirical texts, to the symbolic and figurative dimensions of legality, the emblematic exceeds and to a degree potentially undoes the law. Specifically, in entering the domain of images, in drawing law out of its prominent seclusion and making manifest the spectacular and often absurd dimensions of rule, emblems were archetypical normative depictions of the interstices of law made visible. The lustful lawyer, the sleeping judge, the greedy and corrupt advocate, the overbearing sovereign, the repentant counsellor, the licit and illicit causes of dispute, the excesses of the tongue, the crimes of the eyes, are all variously depicted and inserted into texts that will generally relate but not fully accord or mirror what the image shows. The imaginary plainly attaches to but also exceeds the similar and the symbolic.

There is a certain humour, both critical and conservative to the emblematic depictions, to these alien insertions or other faces that merits a momentary mention. The backface, in Selden's terminology, or the other face in Octavio Paz's brilliant rendition, is also of course the backside, the ass.[11] Such a reference is self-consciously irreverent and intentionally playful and allows us to draw out the role of humour and the sting of many satirical, obscene or simply visceral and surprising *emblemata*. The depiction, and specifically so, meaning the image, the portrait, the *actio*, shows too much, reveals or uncovers the corporeal and all too human substrate of the order of honour and the echelons of dignity. In showing engorged tongues with wings, gaping mouths on mortal stomachs, naked women, grasping sovereigns, illicit love, blind lawyers, ruined polities, the emblems not only bring the law to life with all the blemishes and frailties that living concatenates but also expose the human dimensions of judgment and the venal limitations upon office. At one level, the emblem shows that the mystery of law has always to be constructed, created, fabricated by lawyers and politicians and it shows this process of the delivery of law *in actu*, in flashes or glimpses of the *œconomy* practice. At a more profound level, humour is

9 Placentinus, *Sermo de legibus* ed. Kantorowicz; François Hotman, *Anti-Tribonian* (Paris).

10 V. Hayaert, '*Calumnia, De famosis libellis* et ripostes aux attaques injurieuses: la verve satirique de l'emblème', *textimage*, 7 (2010), 2. Available online at www.revue-textimage.com/05_varia_2/hayaert.pdf (accessed 8 January 2015).

11 Octavio Paz, *Conjunctions and Disjunctions* (New York: Viking, 2004).

arguably the *punctum* of the emblematic depiction as is most obviously the case with the blindfold or band on the face of justice, as also with handless lawyers, trees of jurisdiction lodged on the antlers of satyrs, or skeletons representing the fate of monarchy. Humour, in woodcut form, transforms the subject and forces thought, reaction, change of view. The point is that emblems in juristic texts necessarily unsettle and not only by virtue of being images – classically ornaments but also prototypes – in texts, by dint of their form but also because of the liberality of their substantive representations, the freedom and, at times, abandon of their content. If, as the rhetoricians like to expound, figures of speech, metaphor in particular, transports and transforms, the emblem is a double metaphor in being not only an appearance within the linearity of printed discourse but also in being an enactment of the norm in a non-normative, quasi-juridical and often humorous or satirical modality.

Humour attaches to the mood and mobility of thought and so to the order of action and, specifically, to the hierarchy, the roles and offices of the theatrical *dramatis personae* who perform the law. The last inaugural dimension of the image, embedded in the emblematic cube as also in the variety and complexity of apparent and published *emblemata* lies in their role as mediators of the order of honour upon which the specular dimension of law depends. The aspects of pleasure and pain, the *obiter dicta* or indeed *obiter depicta* of the image, exercise their power both positive and critical most immediately within the scopic regime of law as a system and hierarchy of honour. The spectacular order of the visual, of the sovereign and of lawmaking, the *vim et potestatem* of text and promulgation belong within a seldom explored order of dignity and its echelons and other titles of spectacularity and honorific valence. The depiction of law is embedded in a visual code of statuses and offices, *personae* and masks, theatrical positions and dramatic displays that make up the first order and edifice of justice and its sovereign display. It is within that order of titles, of administrative and military codes, that the emblems are inserted so as to mediate between, to express and deflect the various sites of authority and institutional relays of power.[12] At the same time, the visual escapes strict confinement and these foreign insertions also act to criticize and to solemnize, to question and to transmit in variant forms and with divergent degrees of transformational revelation, be it abasement, obscenity, absurdity, punning or reverence, the practices that the honorific norms and titles so cunningly both express and conceal.

12 On satire and law, see Goodrich, 'Satirical Legal Studies', 103 *Michigan Law Review* 297 (2004).

The essays in this collection focus primarily and critically upon the emblem tradition as, at heart, a legal invention and project, an aspect of the humanistic study and transmission of a tradition that has always exceeded and turned back upon the singularly scriptural focus of the juridical. The historical themes and genealogical threads that the essays evoke and analyze range from the art historical to the properly rhetorical, from early emblem books to the *emblemata* in film, from the emblematic cube to the dark cube, from the gallery device to the courtroom scene. To help locate and introduce these themes and the disinterring of these simultaneously esoteric and emblematic, antique and continuing traditions, questions of terminology and specifically certain tropes and tricks of the visual, the tendrils and byways of the juristic history of the symbolic will be briefly annotated and explained.

Questions of terminology

The founder of the emblem tradition, the lawyer Andrea Alciato, stumbled in a sense by chance or accident upon the form of the triplex emblem, combining adage, *exemplum* or maxim, with an image and explanatory verse. The precise definition of *emblema* was not his immediate concern and so it has been the later legal exponents of *emblemata* and *pegmata*, the translators, annotators, followers, epigones and latterly contemporary historians who have worked to define and standardize or at least to circumscribe the roots and meanings of the term. The question of whether Alciato in fact had a concept of 'emblem' as opposed to other symbolic forms or categories is still an open one, not least because the actual form of the *Emblematum Liber* was in the first instance the invention of his printer. In all probability, whether he did or did not come to conceptualize and define the emblem is of less concern than the question of the process of emblematization, of making symbols which emerged from his foundational text and its initially somewhat rudimentary woodcut depictions. For present purposes, rather than seeking definitions or delimitations, it will prove more useful to argue that the contemporary wave or taxonomic storm of unsatisfactory definitions of '*emblemata*', the new consensus, has missed something of the power, inventiveness and subtlety of Alciato's thought. We can here, more profitably, reflect on Alciato's theory of language and endeavour to reclaim some of the territory ceded over *Belles Lettres* by Emblem studies.

The first corrective to make is that it is a mistake to reconstruct Alciato's emblems according to the principles of literary criticism for the simple reason that this will always end up being a one-way street, an aesthetic that follows an invariant trajectory from text to image. On the contrary, it is more important to note that, while emblematic icons are accompanied by texts, they are much better apprehended, more properly appreciated and their significance most fully explicated and expounded as gestures or, in Quintilian's vocabulary, as *lex gestus*, which is to say as elements in the art of delivery, the crucial dimension of rhetorical *actio*. The visual rhetoric of the *pictura* is thus always to be approached as an allusion to a frame, the context of the forensic arena or the symbolic threshold to the Sacred Temple of Justice. If these iconotexts are set aside from their legal contexts, the anthropology of judicial ritual, the symbolic dimension of solemnization and ceremony, of honor and obeisance is wholly missed. In this respect, it needs to be recollected that Alciato's philological method cannot be separated from his forensic practice. Alciato's writing is never simply referable to the 'ornament of eloquence'. His anti-systematic approach to mimesis and tradition is the very substance of his engagement with the practice of law and the politics of law application. What appears to be a basic, indeed trivial or flippant book of epigrams thus turns out to be a sophisticated verbal and visual 'montage' concerned with the construction of proof.

Prior to the 1980s, emblem scholars failed to arrive at a consensus around the definition of *emblemata*. The starting point of their analyses was almost invariably an important philological article by Hessel Miedema, and most scholars relied on his recourse to classical Latin: *emblema* is a technical term for *objets d'arts* and is used to describe inlaid work, meaning insertions into tile, pottery or metal objects.[13] Miedema explains its application as twofold: there is a general usage, qualified by adjectives such as *vermiculatum*, which refers to mosaïc work. A second sense refers to ornamentation and, specifically, to the insertion of metal (particularly gold and silver), in which ornamental pieces were of greater value than the tableware or vessels on to which they were soldered. They were removable pieces, precious stones or jewels, that were often used for other purposes elsewhere. The French jurist Jean Brèche comments on this technical sense when he explains the legal definition of *exception* in a *casus*.[14] This legal commentary helps us to understand what was at stake when Cicero sued Verres for the return of the

13 Hessel Miedema, 'The Term Emblema in Alciati', *Journal of the Warburg and Courtauld Institutes*, 31 (1968), 234–50.

14 Jean Brèche, *Ad Titulum Pandectarum. De verborum et rerum significatione commentarii* (Lyon, Jean Temporal, 1556), p. 33. '*RES ABESSE. Si quis adversum te ad exhibendum actione experiri conatur, exceptione summovere poteris, quod scilicet, ea res quam exhiberi a te petit, tibi abest. (...) Qua ratione, et si vas elegantis artificis celatum manu et emblematum circumtectum, tandem constatum sit, et forma massa mutata, ac veluti in aliud corpore translata, abesse videbitur*;' and for a longer discussion of this *casus*, see *Mens emblematica ...*, pp. 164–5.

emblemata he had stripped from other people's tableware, leaving his hosts with only the *argentum purum*, the unadorned silver. Not only had Verres plundered the whole island of Sicily but he had, according to Cicero's highly effective prosecution speeches, broken the sacred bonds of hospitality. Cicero's tactic was meant to short-circuit the plans of the defence, changing the format of the trial so as to allow him to bring evidence and eye-witnesses much sooner than expected. Among the numerous seizures of art from private individuals and sacred temples, Verres had stolen the golden candelabrum of a Syrian prince and had coveted the Mercury statue of Tyndaris. In the face of local opposition, he even stripped the magistrate Sopater: he made his opponent sit naked, strapped on a bronze equestrian statue in the middle of the public square (the forum), subverting the then usual procedure of *effigies infamans* and *damnatio memoriæ*.[15] These seizures of valuable public and private property were but an instance of the dozens of crimes Verres allegedly committed, according to Cicero's *Verrine Orations*.[16] This forensic context is well known to the ciceronians, and for the orators and lawyers of the sixteenth century, these texts were exemplary and were frequently used as patterns to imitate.

The term *emblema* is also used by rhetoricians in a figurative sense. As Miedema reports, Lucilius uses it in an ironic sense, to refer to a speech which is composed of interwoven points. This sense is taken up by Quintilian who speaks disapprovingly, in a much quoted passage, of speakers who learn *loci classici* by heart in order to adorn their pleadings *velut emblematis*.[17] This irony is central to Alciato's way of thinking. Far from being a slavish imitator of *loci classici*, his pieces are powerful pleas for critical scholarship, for skeptical analyses and for secular reason. His *mens emblematica* is overtly anti-systematic: aside from his *prælectiones*, where he develops his own teaching method, poetry is for him a serious form of play. Humanism, in his eyes, is not an institutionalized curriculum subject, it is a posture, a philosophical ideal, a mode of life. In this sense, Alciato is an aggressive 'champion' of an '*érudition de combat*', of an idiosyncratic and

15 In his review of Gherardo Ortalli, 'Pingatur in Palatio … 'la pittura infamante nei secoli XIII–XVI', *Annales, Économies, Sociétés, Civilisations*, 1981, vol. 36, no. 2, 231–2, Jean-Claude Schmitt points out the political and ideological implications of this phenomenon. Oral slanders, offensive rituals such as '*charivari*' or '*scampanata*' should perhaps be analyzed more in depth.

16 Cicero, *Verrine Orations*. Available online at www.thelatinlibrary.com/cicero/ver.shtml (accessed 7 January 2015).

17 Quintilian, Inst. Orat. II, 4, 27: '*Quidam neque ignobiles in officiis civilibus scriptos eos memoriæque diligentissime mandatos in promptu habuerint, ut, quotiens esset occasio, extemporales eorum dictiones his velut emblematis exornarentur*'.

sparring, critical epistemic elaborated by means of a sophisticated philology, and always carried out on the margins of the 'severe' and often melancholy discipline of civil law.

Alciato's critical erudition, his political and practical commitment to elaborating a complicated and expansive philology of legal concepts was rooted in his trans-historical and interdisciplinary conception of juridical study. This, in turn, had its ultimate roots in a classicist sense of the symbolic and in a profound appreciation of the mythographic roots of the literary and poetic sources of legal knowledge and judgment. At a time when humanism is debunked and devalued, the study and revival of interest in legal emblems is not simply a scholastic exercise or mere trope of a recondite and removed critical legal methodology. To the contrary, it is an attempt to re-enter the symbolic and to shore up the imaginary bases of knowledge, thereby acknowledging the crucial role played by images in the invention of thought and the elaboration of judgment, including the literally and figuratively emblematic promulgations of law.

Symbolic forms and structures

While Andrea Alciato's several references to Renaissance hieroglyphs have repeatedly been studied with an eye to making sense of the use of the Greek word 'emblema' as a *species* of the *genus* 'symbolon', other visual strategies or representations have not been dealt with in a particularly coherent manner. The key to understanding the significance of emblematic structures is perhaps to be found in a wider apprehension of the early modern reception of symbolic forms.

Historical attention has been focused on, and has tended to isolate the emblem as one particular form of expression, understood as a genre or a bi-medial structure. This focus has, in turn, tended to ignore the interrelated nexus of other and related symbolic forms. According to Anthony Grafton and Lisa Jardine, the 'direct impact of humanism' lay in 'producing growing numbers of people fluent in the ancient languages, rather than in any perceptible results of the 'moral training' or 'preparation for life', supposedly provided by humanism'.[18] This analysis can work in reverse in relation to early modern lawyers. Humanistic emblems were not merely rhetorical devices, cut and pasted by logorrheic and cupidinous lawyers, into diverse legal texts and contexts. The ailing Judge Bridlegoose, the comically ambivalent character invented by François Rabelais, may represent one facet of the

18 Anthony Grafton and Lisa Jardine, *From Humanism to the Humanities* (London: Duckworth, 1986), 122.

mens emblematica as a simpleminded expression of the role of chance, of *alea judiciorum*, in the practices of the tradition, but one should also recollect the critical and satirical import, the powerful humour and persuasive significance of the esoteric and sometimes obscene references of these complex depictions.[19] Aside from the outrageous legal comedy of Rabelais, legal emblems are no less erudite for being, at times, *obscene*. As Hugh Roberts has shown,

> Obscenity is one of the key fault-lines along which the reception of representations potentially becomes a subject for the control and sanction of the law. Hence emblem books, with their twin legal and hermeneutic concerns, become a privileged site for explorations of the notion of obscenity and indeed a pre-history of obscenity laws.[20]

The *pegma In ἀστόμους poëtarum prurientium, Ex Polycleto* (*On the silence of lascivious poets, After Polycletus*) was translated by Lanteaume de Romieu as *Sur le dire de Polycletus paintre*, or more properly traduced, the obscene content of the classically orientated work.[21] Coustau's emblem, *Contre les livres obscènes* is followed by a philosophical *narratio* that presents a powerful plea for strong censorship of obscene writings. It is important for the Judges, says Coustau, to avoid wrath or anger and remain *æqui certe et placati* (completely calm and equable). Alciato by contrast chooses an overtly obscene theme (a man defecating into a 'chœnix') for his notorious *Adversus naturam peccantes* (*Against those who sin against nature*) which first appeared in 1546, published by Aldus Manutius, in Venice. Coustau avoids any such obviously irreverent icon. His *Pegma* could be understood as a reaction (a retaliation) against Alciato's deliberately obscene emblem. Coustau would then have lumped Alciato together with the poets, whether antique or modern, in an attempt to reinstate the condemnation of poets from book 10 of Plato's *Republic*.

Legal emblems cannot be understood as a coherent discourse: they can be obscene or normative. Variable in content and purpose, ranging from the extreme to the clichéd, they remain in essence ambivalent, highly personal and often idiosyncratic to their author. The example of Pierre Coustau's *pegmata* is central here. Alciato's creations were hybristic by nature and in practice over ambitious. The obscene image used in his emblem *Adversus*

19 See, in particular, François Rabelais, *Le Tiers Livre*, ch. 39–44.

20 Hugh Roberts, Guillaume Peureux et Lise Wajeman, eds, *Obscénités renaissantes*, préface de Michel Jeanneret, Travaux d'Humanisme et Renaissance, no. 473, (Geneva: Droz, 2011), 93; for a discussion of 'obscene emblems' see ibid., 93–100.

21 Pierre Coustau, *Pegma*, Lyons : 1555 at 257.

naturam was expunged from subsequent editions. Coustau's perspective is quite different: knowing that titillating poetry, accompanied by obscene images, will always arouse more than judges would allow, he does not ban the image, but only the obscenity of certain figures. Instead of choosing to use an obscene picture, his *pictura* shows an ancient *locus*, the indictment of Polycletus, in which the lascivious poets are damned for the obscenity of their acts, conduct which 'fouls your fingernails'. The potential suggestion of visual obscenity is removed from the stage. Readers and viewers are left with a perfectly decorous image of a laborer filling a gaping hole in the wall of a building. Ruins surround the toiling figure.[22]

A second example, drawn from a quotation in the preface of the *Digest*, shows that Coustau does not repeat Alciato. Far from being transgressive, Coustau offers a very original emblem book, where morality is an end and not a means. Instead of following in the lengthy and well-established exegetical tradition of interpretation of Homer's Glaucus' and Diomedes' unequal exchange (*Iliad*, VI, 232–5), Χρύσεα χαλκείων ἑκατόμβοια ἐννεαβοίων '*Aureis aereis, centena novenariis*', Coustau explains in his *pegma* '*Pax auro redempto*' and in the subsequent *narratio philosophica* argues that this unequal exchange is a good one: instead of following Martial or Erasmus who interpret this *potlach* as a fool's bargain (*marché de dupes*), Coustau praises true wisdom, which is, according to the insertion of this *locus* in the opening of the *Digest*, a way of preferring peace over gold. Peace has been bought by Gold, says the *motto*. This gesture is exactly the opposite of bribery: both fighters are ready to duel, the fighting has already started. But instead of fighting for the sake of fighting, a compromise is preferred: '*De bon accord fut par eux moyenné*' says French translator Lanteaume de Romieu.[23] This emblem hints at contemporary attempts, made by Chancelier Michel de l'Hospital and his circle, to find a peaceful resolution to imminent religious conflicts. This moral choice will lead the wise to immortality, a glory born of their trustworthy service to the state and the laws.[24] By exchanging his golden armour for bronze, Glaucus has not lost his power of judgment; he has earned, says Coustau, a token of everlasting armistice.

The example of Coustau's *pegmata* can be used to expand and diversify the rather linear and narrow sense of emblems that we inherit from too great

22 See www.emblems.arts.gla.ac.uk/french/emblem.php?id=FCPa063 (accessed 26 February 2015).

23 Pierre Coustau, *Pegme* (Lyons: Molin, 1560): 'You should buy peace with gold, settle a duel by payment, for peacemaking adds to the wealth of your fatherland', French Emblems at Glasgow. Available online at www.emblems.arts.gla.ac.uk/french/emblem.php?id=FCPa050 (accessed 7 January 2015).

24 See a full discussion in *Mens emblematica*… op cit, pp. 220 *et seq*.

a degree of attention being expended exclusively upon Alciato. The *pegmata* are pageants, multivalent scaffoldings and frames for new perceptions: instead of slavishly repeating a common interpretation of an enigmatic fragment, Coustau offers his reader a reflective and vigorous plea to finally put an end to sterile duelling. Coustau uses the verb *redimere* in a double sense here: Glaucus literally buys back peace by giving his gold armour to his opponent but, in doing so, he frees himself from the necessity of fighting, he obtains in turn a much more precious gift, a peace treaty which preserves his *patria* from war. In a beautiful book, Nathalie Zemon Davis has explored the way in which gifts are tokens of bestowal and of power: her interpretation of Coustau's *pegmata* shows the extent and significance of the spirit of gifts in sixteenth-century France.[25]

Justice's blindfold: ambivalent attributes

As a final and much elaborated example, we can use the well-known representation of Justice blindfolded. According to Robert Jacob, the question of why Justice is represented blindfolded and, specifically, the reason for the adoption of such a negative attribute is still an open question. Dominant discourses and normative commentaries have tended to interpret it as a mark of blindness and, in this regard, the blindfold has consistently encouraged a wide spectrum of misinterpretations. These, in turn, make this attribute into the most ambivalent ally that Justice could have ever invented. As O. R. Kissel, for instance, relays the 1907 Prussian censorship of blindfolded images of Justice, the concept of this blindness limiting and indeed deforming the primary juridical virtue led here to a prohibition on all such images in courthouse building projects.[26] A magnificent but, we would argue, unnecessary misinterpretation.

A lexical study of the etymology involved can lead to another hypothesis and a potentially important emendation. The invention of the blindfold may in fact be based on a pun in Isidore of Seville, a root that would do much to explain the inappropriateness of the prevalent interpretations of this attribute. Instead of assuming that medieval and Renaissance words have a constant form and meaning, Isidore's etymologies imply that words are better conceived as meaningful crossroads of significations. Start with Jean Wirth's reconstruction of the implications of images of breasts. He recounts how, around 1160, the Siegburg Madonna (Köln, Schnütgen-Museum) is

25 Nathalie Zemon Davis, *The Gift in Sixteenth-century France* (Oxford University Press, 2000), 18–21, n. 2 and 4, p. 227.

26 *Die Justitia*, 92–4.

depicted offering her son a little round object, placed exactly in front of her right breast. Wirth explains how this stands for the iconic representation of an isidorian etymology, which understands *mamilla* (breast) as a diminutive of *mala* (apple).[27]

Isidore of Seville's etymologies bring to the fore a wide array of inventive associations. Puns and formal analogies serve as mnemonic devices and as reflective aphorisms:

> A *fideicommissum* (that is, a request to an heir) is so called, as it specifies what 'may be done' (*fiat*) as commissioned (*committere, commissum*) by the deceased – and indicates that faith (*fides*) is so called because 'it may be done' (*fiat*); it is, however 'requested not in obligatory language, but as a wish'.
>
> (V. xxiv.17)

> *Mancipatio* is so called because the property is 'taken from the hand' (*manu … capitur*).

> Switches (*virga*) are the tips of branches and trees, so called because they are green (*viridis*), or because they possess the power of persuading (*vis arguendi*); if it is smooth, it is a switch, but if it is knotty and has points, it is correctly called by the term *scorpio* ('scorpion'), because it is driven into the body leaving a curved wound.
>
> (V. xxvi.18)

> Tortures (*tormentum*) are so called because they discover the intention (*mens*, gen. *mentis*) by twisting (*torquere*).
>
> Ibid.

As the *Trésor de la Langue Française* establishes,[28] confirmed by the FEW,[29]

27 Isidore of Seville, *Etymologiæ*, XI, 75: *Mamillæ vocatæ, quia rotundæ sunt, quasi malæ, per diminutionem scilicet.*

28 The Trésor de la Langue Française Informatisé is accessible publicly online at http://atilf.atilf.fr (accessed 20 January 2015). The dictionary *Trésor de la langue française, dictionnaire de la langue du xixe et du xxe siècle* (TLF), (CNRS, 1976–1994), is the widest and most complete dictionary of the French language. It was published in 16 volumes of more than 1500 pages each. The first was completed in 1971, the last in 1994. It has been digitized in a searchable format by ATILF, CNRS.

29 *Französisches Etymologisches Wörterbuch. Eine Darstellung des galloromanischen Sprachschatzes*, ed. by Walther von Wartburg et al., (Bonn: Klopp/Zbinden, from 1928 onwards), see 3, 425b '*FASCIS [Bundel] et FASCIA [Binde, Band] stehen einander formell und auch semantisch sehr nahe*'.

the blindfold is derived from a masculine form of the word, derived from FASCIA, Æ (Ancient French. *faisse*: ('head-band, strip') and is most probably itself derived from a conflation with the Latin FASCIS, IS, m (a bundle of rods, symbol of the *imperium*).[30] If this hypothesis is right, the connundrum of Justice's blindfold could be understood as an iconic concatenation of both significations: Justice has a double sense, she wears a *fascis*, which is a *fascia*. When, at the end of the fifteenth century (that is, at the time when the iconic motive of the band appears in Sebastian Brandt's *Ship of Fools*) this double sense was already present in literary criticism. Jean de Rovroy, translator of the *Stratagèmes* of Frontin comments on the Latin *fascis* which he associates with *fascia*:

> A proper definition of the word *fasces* requires an understanding of how these imperial signs called *fasces* were ribbons of purple or gold which Roman Princes wore tied around their heads. The Consul or Judge was thus recognizable by virtue of these ribbons tied around their head, and by the axe that they bore in front of them, in the same way that today the Prince carries a sword in front of him as a sign of office.[31]

Jean de Rovroy thus describes a kind of purple and gold bandage worn around the head by Roman emperors. A second hypothesis could well be that a mistake has been made but this error has generated a stimulating and long-lasting dialectical symbolism, which does not necessarily imply that the bandage is to be understood initially as a blindfold. It would not, in this case, represent any impossibility of communicating, nor should it then be interpreted as the visible token of an irremediable blindness on the part of the judges. On the contrary, this type of etymological *vis arguendi* is well adapted to the art of law. The *verbis nostræ artis*, as early modern lawyers put it, are not defined as normative tools. Their definition is always dangerous (*omnes definitio juris periculosa est*) and their multiple and changing meanings are constant resources for the development of law.

30 TLF informatisé: http://atilf.atilf.fr (accessed 20 January 2015).

31 '*Pour declaration de ce mot fasces est assavoir que ses signes imperiaulx appelez fasces c'estoient bandes de pourpres et dorees que les princes romains portoient entour leur chief. Et a ce cognoissoit on les consulz ou le dictateur, pour ce qu'ilz avoient ces manieres de bandes liees entour leur chief, et portoit la hache devant eulx, comme on porte au jour d'huy l'espee devant les princes.*' Strat. II, IV, 35, A, fol. 46, quoted by Robet Bossuat, who sees this phenomenon as a regrettable confusion, '*Jean de Rovroy traducteur des Stratagèmes de Frontin (fin)*', *Bibliothèque d'humanisme et renaissance*, 22/ 3 (1960), 469–89.

CHAPTER 1

The Gordian knot of *emblemata*: from the *Labyrinthus absconditus* to the affirmation of the *Prisca Jurisprudentia*

Valérie Hayaert

Throughout the sixteenth century, legal studies were frequently satirized or even vilified: their status (is it an art or a science?), their place in the curriculum (propaedeutic or belonging to a 'higher faculty'?) and their institutional substance were constantly debated and disputed. Aside, however, from excessive vituperation, such as Lorenzo Valla's attacks against the illiterate 'leguleos', Renaissance jurists were then commonly known as the new '*Prudentes*', their method and pattern of thinking being inspired by the ancient belief that jurisprudence, as a part of practical philosophy, was grounded in *phronesis*.[1] Aside from the parallel tradition of *encomion*, every jurisconsult was in this vein considered to be a more or less accomplished example of the *vir eloquentissimus* so praised by Cicero. What remains to be explained, however, is the fact that Roman laws were at the same time paid lip service but were generally forgotten and actively ignored more than ever. In his *Éloge de Michel de l'Hôpital*, Doigny du Ponceau claims in 1777 that all these 'clameurs du palais' had only given birth to mice:

> What is the result of all this? It is that their science and their glory is almost entirely forgotten in our time, that the laws of Rome are more obscure and are more ignored than ever, and that the study of Jurisprudence is almost everywhere reduced to texts merely put on display in the Schools. What then is this science that the enlightened obscure in the very act of relaying, and which becomes impenetrable at the precise moment of its transport to perfection?[2]

1 *De officiis*, i.43.153.

2 Doigny du Ponceau, *Éloge de Michel de l'Hôpital*, epigraph on the title page: '*Grand Législateur, dans un temps où il n'y avoit point de loix, et Philosophe intrépide, dans un temps d'enthousiasme et de fureurs*', taken from Voltaire's novel, *Essai sur l'esprit et les mœurs des Nations* (Paris: Demonville, 1777), 74.

Always positioned between obscurity and *illuminatio*, legal emblems are coined by *jurisconsulti* as a body of moral principles which are used as performative tools to arouse persuasive opinions inside the *respublica jurisconsultorum*. The Lesbian rule (taken from the *Nicomachean Ethics*, vol. 10, 1137b, 11–33) is one of these powerful images that helps to grasp the very notion of *épiékëïa/æquitas*: this practical rule, used in Ancient times by Lesbian builders, was a flexible rule, that could adapt and be shaped to each and every stone (Figure 1.1).[3]

Choosing a moral *otium* (the leisure of inventing emblems) was not a vain entreprise: during the early modern period, it was thought to be a noble and moral activity, that used the metaphorical register of duelling to explain

In normam Lesbiam.

Bonus iudex.

Aſpice vt in partes ſemper tornatilis omnes,
Se ſubiectam operi Lesbia norma facit.
Intus ſæpe latet ſcriptæ ſententia legis,
Quæ ſolet in tota iudicis eſſe manu.
Hanc ille in varijs rerum variare figuris
Debet, non vnum ſemper, idémque ſequi.

Figure 1.1 Pierre Coustau, *Pegma cum narrationibus philosophicis*, '*Bonus Judex. In norman Lesbiam*', engraving by Pierre Eskrich, Lyon, Macé Bonhomme, 1555 (reproduced by permission of Glasgow University Library, Special Collections)

3 Pierre Coustau, *In norman Lesbiam*, Bonus judex; available online at www.emblems.arts.gla.ac.uk/french/picturae.php?id=FCPb022 (accessed 7 January 2015).

the process of resolving the agonistics of law. Specifically, the novel method devised was that of duelling with *nodos juris* (knots of Law), *aenigmata juris*, the Sybilline leaves of law, (*les feuillets de la sybille* coined by Philibert Bugnyon) and *emblemata Triboniani*, coined, among others, by François Hotman, that would uncover the pristine truths that time and use had covered over. Ancient Laws, the treasure inherited by the *Prudentes*, were then transformed into the mythical origin of Law, the very source of Civil Law (*Fontes Juris*).

The legend (*legenda est!*[4]) of the three Minos

The title page of the Senneton edition shown here (Figure 1.2) offers a genealogy of Ancient legislators; that is, a new legitimation of the history of transmission of divine and civil laws. Four effigies of the Law are linked by the *cathena Homeri*, the symbol of the *prisca theologia* here applied to a new discipline: the *prisca jurisprudentia*. Moses – the hebraïc motto reads, [Moses] seek justice – receives the Divine tables directly from Jupiter (Figure 1.3), opposite him stands Solon (the motto reads *Nomos Theodoros*) (Figure 1.4). Under them, two other niches oppose *Draco aimatonomos* (Figure 1.5) symbolizing the extreme rigor of Law, as according to Plutarch, Draco would only punish by one penalty, all crimes were subject to a death sentence and *Ceres Thesmophora* (Figure 1.6) holding a cornucopia, instigator of the Thesmophoria, the Greek cult of marriage bonds and civil *amicitia*. Each emblematization of the Law receives a dynamic pose, and the role of legislators is represented by means of the dialectical bond of the chain of eloquence. An inferior register (Figure 1.7) is assigned to the representation of the Judges. According to one version of the myth, well known to Renaissance mythographers, 'Knossos was where Minos reigned, and every nine years he had a conference with Zeus himself' (Odyssey, 19, 178–80),[5] meaning that Minos was thought to have received laws for Crete directly from Zeus. Minos was held to be the author of the older Cretan constitution.[6] It is for this reason, according to Homer, that Minos is judge in Hades (Odyssey: 11, 568–71). In a later legend (Plato, Gorgias: 523–7), Minos and his brothers, Rhadamanthus and Eacus, serve as judges of the dead in the

4 In Latin, *legenda est* (worth reading) has the force of an imperative rule.

5 Homer, *The Odyssey*, trans. Samuel Butler, based on public domain edn, Timothy Power and Gregory Nagy, eds. Available online at www.perseus.tufts.edu/hopper/text?doc=Hom.%20Od.%2019&lang=original (accessed 7 January 2015).

6 See *Classical Myths and Legends in the Middle Ages and Renaissance: A Dictionary of Allegorical Meanings*, H. David Brumble, art. 'Minos' (London: Fitzroy Dearborn, 1998).

Figure 1.2 *Sennetoniana*, frontispiece engraved by Pierre Eskrich, *Digestus* volume, Lyon, 1549 (reproduced by permission of Bibliothèque de la Cour de Cassation, Paris)

Figure 1.3 Moses receives divine laws from Zeus, בקשת צדק bqšt ṣdq (seek justice), our thanks to Rabbi David Bleich for advising us on the translation, by Pierre Eskrich, detail from fig. 2 (reproduced by permission of Bibliothèque de la Cour de Cassation, Paris)

Underworld (Æneid, 6.432–4). This title page is a graphic concatenation of several paraphrases of Homer, Plato and Virgil, transmitted by their commentators (Servius *et alii*). The transmission of ancient myths of the origin of Law is authorised by several commentators; one of them, Lynche, paraphrased Plato, and quoted by H. David Brumble, deserves special attention, as it probably derives from the same interpretative tradition and glosses

Figure 1.4 *Solon Nomos Theodoros*, by Pierre Eskrich, particular of fig. 2 (reproduced by permission of Bibliothèque de la Cour de Cassation, Paris)

many of the details contained in the lower part of the engraving:[7]

7 For an earlier comment on this image, see V. Hayaert, Mens Emblematica *et humanisme juridique* (Geneva: Droz, 2008), p. 195–9.

Figure 1.5 *Draco Aimatonomos*, by Pierre Eskrich, particular of fig. 2 (reproduced by permission of Bibliothèque de la Cour de Cassation, Paris)

Figure 1.6 *Ceres Thesmophora,* by Pierre Eskrich, particular of fig. 2 (reproduced by permission of Bibliothèque de la Cour de Cassation, Paris)

Figure 1.7 Minos (quæsitor), Rhadamanthus and Eacus, by Pierre Eskrich, particular of fig. 2 (reproduced by permission of Bibliothèque de la Cour de Cassation, Paris)

[Jupiter said] my pleasure is, that my three sonnes, two of them borne in Asia, being Minos and Rhadamanthus, and another in Europe, which is Eacus, standing in a certain green meade, out of which do part and are divided several waies, the one into Hell, and the other into Elisium (for so we may call them) shall bee appointed there as Judges of the soules of mortals, Rhadamanthus judging those of Asia, and Eacus those of Europe. And that, if it fortune that

> any doubt or undecided scruple, shall arise between them, that then the same bee referred presently unto Minos … This (sayeth Plato) was the order and decree of Jupiter … First upon the examination of their sins, Rhadamanthus and Eacus sate together in two yron chaires, holding in either of their hands a white rod. And Minos (divided from them both) was seated all alone, holding in his hand a golden scepter, who seemed to meditate and ponder with a musing & sad countenance upon the punishments, torments or pleasures, to be denounced & due to the offenders.
>
> (*Fountain of Ancient Fiction*, i–ii)

This title page attempts a graphic interpretation of an interrelated stemma of ancient texts: the insistence on the dialogue between Zeus and Minos derives from three main interpretations[8] of the figure of Minos the legislator, derived from two verses from Homer (*Odyssey*, 19, 178–9), which resist any plain or simple interpretation. In the Greek tradition, three interpretations were rooted in texts composed between the fourth and the third century BCE. In the tradition derived from Plato's *Laws* (624b–5a; 630d; 632d), Minos would visit Zeus's cave (Mount Dikté) every nine years so as to receive Cretan legislation from him,[9] while Lycurgus would receive Spartan Laws from Apollo in Delphi. In the dialogue, *Minos*, attributed to Plato but of an uncertain origin, the King of Crete is described as a disciple of Zeus, and Zeus acts with him as a Sophist. Lastly, in Ephorus's fragments transmitted by Strabo, the scene is rationalized and Minos and Lycurgus are described as imposters who have attributed their own Laws to a divine origin so as to have them accepted.

When the inventor of this title page inscribes a graphic presentation of a genealogy of legislators, the *stemma* (family tree) of *emblemata* enables him to leave the enigma as it is. No rational discourse intrudes to reduce the oral and global nature of the myth. *Emblemata* are not meant here to serve as pedagogical iconotexts: they offer rather a new way of rehearsing the allusive genealogy of a myth. The origins of divine and civil laws are visually linked

8 See in *Le rivage des mythes: une géocritique méditerranéenne, le lieu et son mythe*, ed. Bertrand Wesphal, *Espaces Humains* no. 2 (Limoges: Presses universitaires, 2001), the article by Charles Delattre 'Identités et contradictions dans la définition d'un espace mythique: l'exemple de la Crète dans l'imaginaire grec antique', p. 73–4.

9 Horace expresses it as follows: 'Et Jovis arcanis Minos admissus' (*Odes*, 10, I, 1). See an apologetical interpretation of the same myth in *La Mythologie et les Fables expliquées par l'histoire*, by the Abbé Banier, Paris, tome VIII, 1740 ed. openlibrary.org, p. 142–6: '*Minos allait donc tous les neuf ans … dans l'antre de Jupiter pour y apprendre de nouvelles choses, ou pour réformer, suivant l'exigence des cas, ce qu'il avoit appris dans la précédente neuvième année. L'antre où ce sage Prince se retiroit, fut appellé dans la suite, l'Antre de Jupiter.*'

to their results in terms of eschatology and symbolic geography. According to Plato, Minos was the *Quæsitor* (president of the infernal court). His brother Eacus would judge the Europeans and his other brother Rhadamanthus would judge Asians and Africans. Minos acted as a mediator when judgments conflicted. His superiority over his brothers is evidenced by his role as agitator of the urn where all the fates of mortals are contained (*Quæsitor Minos Urnam movet, Æneid,* VI, 432–3) according to the motto.[10] Rhadamanthus and Eacus are subaltern judges, whose role is that of making the witnessses testifiy, conducting the trial and obtaining confessions of guilt (by persuasion or torture). Their brother Minos pronounces the sentence and has it executed. Pierre Eskrich's version of the myth offers a powerful plea for a symbolic reading of what could serve as a model for the establishement of legislation. Legal emblems do not promulgate laws in the same way as our contemporary discourses would suggest: the syncretic bond instituted between Minos and Moses legitimates a new publication of the byzantine *Corpus Juris Civilis,* and the two figures serve together as symbolic warrants of a new conception of legal history.

The opening *stemma* of *emblemata* is built as a mosaïc, in the same way that the exegetical gloss acts as a frame for the text. But images are always left to a hazardous plurivalence (their only unity is an optical one) whereas texts are arranged into academic forms such as *quæstio, casus, repetitio* or *disputatio.* The internal ordering of the gloss itself (verbal analysis, *antinomiæ, æquiparatio, notabilia, memoralia*) will never reduce the potential disruptiveness of illustrations. Contemporary readers should bear two points in mind: expensive in-folio volumes establish a reference library for legal practictioners but they are also a visible sign of status. Sustained reading of these monumental texts is clearly not a current practice, the manuscript *marginalia* contained in the example just used show that these prestigious intruments have scarcely served any practical use. Secondly, their indexes are to be studied carefully since they are used as important tools of forensic *inventio.* That is why emblems will always defy the *usus modernus Pandectarum,* which is in its turn also cluttered with enigmatic abbreviations. This voluminous edition reproduces the characteristic features of the manuscript tradition of law books (Vivianus Tuscus'[11] *casus,* Accursius' gloss, humanist *lectiones* of Greek words, by Catelliano Cotta, Andrea Alciato, Angelo Poliziano *et alii*).

10 For another interpretation of this endlessly suggestive title page, see Valérie Hayaert, *Mens emblematica…*, p. 195–9.

11 The series is described as a *Corpus Juris Civilis cum Glossis Accursii,* 5 vol. in fol. 1549, 1550, but it contains a wider stemma of glosses: the *casus longi* added to the ensemble are the work of Vivianus Tuscus, son of Oseppus Tuscus, according to F. K. von Savigny. He became famous during the uprisings of 1228 in Bologna, as the chief of the *Popularii.*

This new publication of the *Corpus Juris Civilis*, under the auspices of the golden chain of Homer, states that only a cult dedicated to these figures of legislation will be sufficiently legitimate to institute a new genealogy of transmitted knowledge of Laws. This title page adorns each volume of the Senneton ensemble (*Digestus vetus, Infortiatum, Digestus novus, Codex, Authentica*). As the *Institutes* volume is essentially a pedagogical tool, catering for law students, it does not bear the architectonic title page of the *sanctissimum templum justitiæ*. Jurists are the acknowledged guardians of the sacred language of law, they should not *cornicum oculos configere* (go about deceiving God, nor blinding those who are most wise). This proverb is used, among others, by Cicero (*Pro Murena*, XI, 25) and explained by Erasmus (*Adagia*, I, iii, 75). Emblematic structures, when applied to Law, not only offer a new iconology for forensic practice, these iconotexts build a new *divisio* and, as I will suggest here, this new model is to be understood as a heuristic distinction between various meanings of words. Instead of giving axiomatic definitions, these tools, along with the discourses of the *casus*, but not by the same means, also build a graphic interpretation of the indefinite nature of particular legal situations.

Early modern jurists use the method of collecting topical *loci classici* to collocate them into their pleas. This method derives from Aristotle and Cicero, and is well known as a tool of persuasive argumentation: *emblemata* are inserted into legal discourses as *sedes argumentorum*, their power of persuasiveness is all the more visible when they are accompanied by an image. These tools are rooted in the desire to achieve the *enkyklos paideia*, understood as the circle and sum (*enkyklos*) of all knowledges. The ideal of the accomplished orator is to master every knowledge which will help him to decipher the meaning of Roman laws and will thus legitimate the rectitude of interpretation. The *orator perfectus* (*per-fectus* meaning perfect and accomplished)[12] should follow the ideal expressed once by Cicero, *jus civile in artem redigere*. In several passages, Cicero evokes the possibility of dividing civil law according to *species* and *genus*, to build an *ars* of civil law.[13] When Roman Law reference texts are rediscovered by interpreters fluent in Greek as well as in Latin, a great number of perplexities are approached. Witty and inventive spirits tackle the bulk of enigmas contained in the *Corpus Juris Civilis*, issues of meaning and interpretation arise particularly when a Greek verse or a

12 See Donald Kelley, 'Jurisconsultus Perfectus: The Lawyer as Renaissance Man', *Journal of the Warburg and Courtauld Institutes*, 51 (1988), 84–102; Michael L. Monheit, 'Guillaume Budé, Andrea Alciato, Pierre de L'Estoile: Renaissance Interpreters of Roman Law' *Journal of the History of Ideas*, 58/1 (1997), 21–40.

13 *Cicero, De off.* 1, 6, 19; *Top.* 31, *De orat.* 1, 42, 190.

literary fragment has been pasted into the text of the Roman laws. Given that Justinian's prohibition of all commentary has been an embarrassment for jurists from the beginning of the reception, one of the reactions to the prohibition was to use legal topics ingeniously.[14] I argue here that legal emblems are a *genus* of the *specie* of legal topics: relying on the efficacy of the *species immediata contraria*, emblems provide lawyers with *sedes argumentorum*, they trigger new lines of argumentation. Emblematic structures are tools that enable law to be considered in its generality as well as being applicable to individual cases. The dialectical structure of legal emblems, mediated by an iconotextual 'montage' is a vivid form and it never fits into any rigid taxonomy. Grounded in the Aristotelian distinction between equity and justice, these *loci* are fecund sources of new inventions. Instead of being preoccupied by intent and normative laws or statutes, these *loci* seek to retrieve the oracles of divine laws to offer new prescriptions or legal advice. In the same way that Ramist dichotomies seek to represent a new schema of interpretative modes (*divisio, partitio*), *emblemata* and *arbores juris* offer a wide range of visible *similitudines* leading to innovative ways of representing *nodos juris*. Anti-systematic by nature, these *loci* are meant to stimulate wits, prevent '*verbositas*' and avoid further '*discordia*'.

Emblematum liber/libellus* and the *Sennetoniana: libri da mano, libri da banco

If emblem books are used as leisure pocket books (*libri da mano*), easy to carry and to take along during extended travels, the volumes of the *Corpus Juris Civilis*, on the contrary, are heavy *libri da banco*. The complete series held today in the fonds ancien de la Bibliothèque de la Cour de Cassation (former Bibliothèque de l'Ordre des Avocats) weighs a little more than 5 kg: it would certainly justify the acquisition of a *ruota grande*, '*artificiosa machina molto utile a ciascuna persona che si diletta dello studio*' (Figure 1.8).[15] This rare example of an edition adorned with *hieroglyphica, figura* and *emblemata* sheds new insights on the theory and practice of interpretation. In this context, the Senneton emblems belong, I will argue, to a different configuration and novel organization of interpretation.

The manuscript which is lent by the College of Avignon, known today as the *Ottobonianus latinus* 3132, and held at the Vatican Library, enabled a

14 See Ian Maclean, *Interpretation and meaning in the Renaissance: The Case of Law* (Cambridge: Cambridge University Press, 1992), 56–7.

15 Agostino Ramelli, *Dell'Artificiose Machine*, (Paris, Léonard Gaultier, 1588), cap. 188, p. 316, digitized by CNUM. Available online at http://cnum.cnam.fr/CGI/redir.cgi?fDY3 (accessed 7 January 2015).

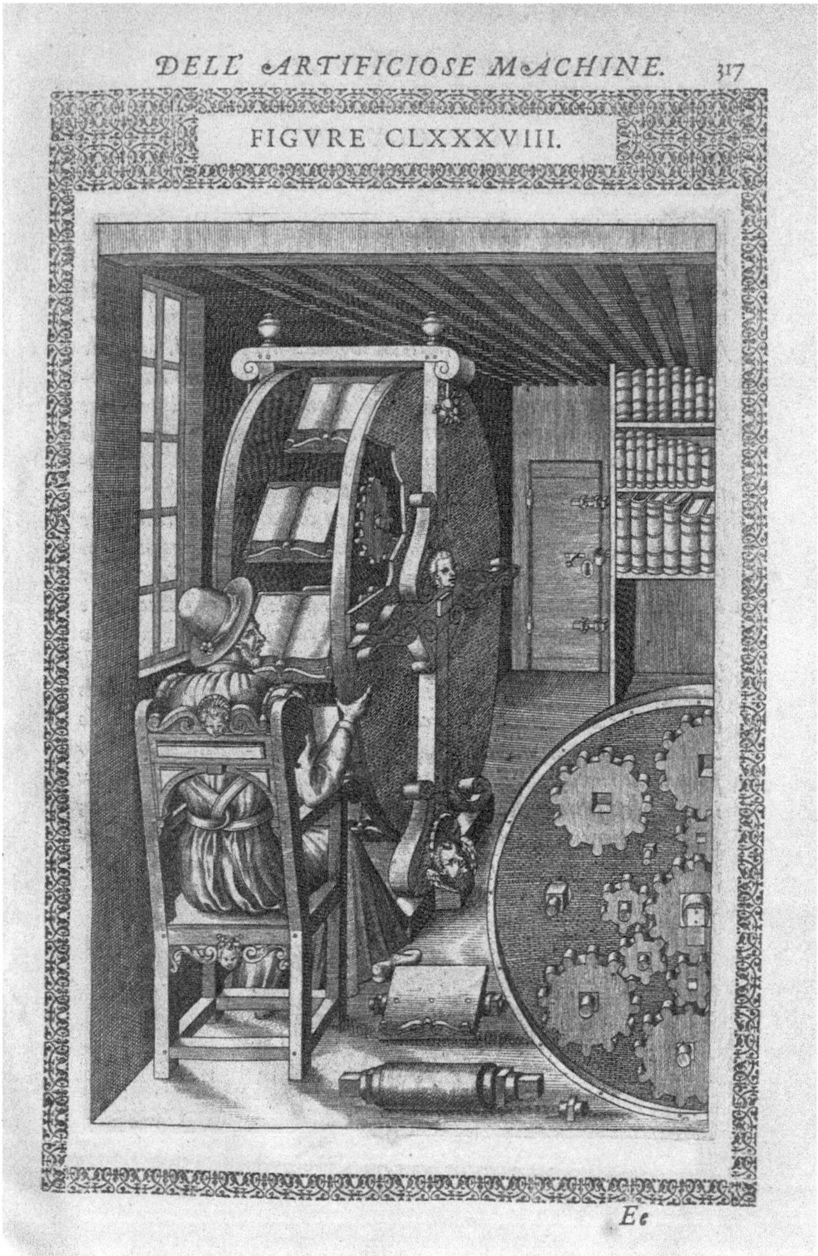

Figure 1.8 '*Ruota grande*' in Agostino Ramelli, *Dell'Artificiose Machine*, Léonard Gauthier, Paris, 1588, cap. CLXXXVIII, p. 316 (reproduced by permission of Conservatoire numérique des Arts & Métiers, Paris)

group of learned jurists to devise a new edition of Justinian's reference books, helped by the erudite printer Macé Bonhomme and financed by exceptional patrons of the arts, the brothers Senneton, aldermen of the town of Lyons. In this case, typical of the ambition of revitalizing legal pedagogy and interpretation in the manner of the *mos gallicus*, we are witness to a rare conjunction of several collaborators: Macé Bonhomme, attached himself to the Avignon Collège de Docteurs, and opened a '*succursale*' of his printing workshop with his brother in law Barthélemy Molin, to sell all types of editions of legal commentaries and treatises, catering for several audiences. The *Sennetoniana* is slightly different: it is meant to be a highly prestigious edition, especially designed for a small community of jurists, under the auspices of the King. Pierre Eskrich (Vase) produces two impressive cuts and many of the *emblemata* inserted into the six volumes of the printed ensemble.

The editorial strategy seems well considered, even if this expensive edition was not intended to generate any profit. Offered to Avignonese jurists and to King Henri II (the series preserved in the private Château de Terrebasse, Ain, France, has been bound with the arms and cipher of Henri II), the full-page cut representing the *Arbor Servitutum*,[16] shows that Pierre Vase (Eskrich) has completely assimilated the aesthetic style of Fontainebleau artists such as Rosso. My purpose here is to offer a new context for these trees, showing that only an expansive approach, drawn from the history of the book, the reception of Roman law and emblem studies can grasp the specificity of these sophisticated images. Luckily enough, for each *figura*, we have a *declaratio* that guides the topical reading of these images. In the same way that Flemish Lawyer Joost de Damhoudere produced an interpretative itinerary for his famous effigy of *Justitiæ Bifrons*, the inventors of these exceptional woodcuts have produced images where most of the details have been scrupulously thought through.

To build an interpretative method attentive to each detail and nexus of interrelated meanings, readers and viewers should first abandon most of our current reading habits. *Emblemata* and *figura* need an active reading, building meanings which are not given *a priori* but whose sense becomes clear only when one 'leafs rhough the ancient texts with a quotidian hand' (*feuillette, de main journelle, les exemplaires anciens*, as detailed by Du Bellay, *Defence et Illustration de la Langue Française*). All the actors

16 For a 'zoomable', high-definition image, see: Vanessa Selbach, '*Artisan ou artiste? La carrière de Pierre Eskrich, brodeur, peintre et graveur, dans les milieux humanistes de Lyon et Genève* (ca 1550–1580)', *Chrétiens et Sociétés* special issue 1 (2011), 23. Available online at http://chretienssocietes.revues.org/2726 (accessed 7 January 2015).

involved, the engraver, glossators, editors, proofwriters (prélecteurs d'imprimerie), '*facteurs*' and distributors, are conscious that their work is not the work of a single and isolated author. The analysis of three cases of illustration offered here (*Arbor Servitutum*, *Arbor Jurisdictionis* and botanical *emblemata*) are conceived as a heuristic typology rather than a firm taxonomy.

As Pierre Legendre, Anton Schütz, Marc Smith, Yan Thomas and Mayo[17] have discussed, the *arbor juris*, as most legal anthropologists know, is an inherited image ('*histoire de longue durée*', see Robert Jacob).[18] The choice of a tree (whether a simple diagrammatic one or a more elaborated image) is grounded in the Romanist tradition of measurement. The figure of the tree is a genealogically conscious visual strategy that helps to figure and teach the institutional order of patrilinear transmission. The '*calcul du comput*' is represented by a tree, whose roots and '*cime*' depend on a cosmographical order which legitimates the hierarchy of lineages and the power of kinships.

Emblemata juris are still integrated to trees but these are not rooted in the same *dispositio*. I argue here that these new arborescences revive some of the Roman principles of staging the images of ancestors (*stemmata*) and this is probably the main originality of the new emblematic grammar we find in the Sennetoniana. As Yves-Marie Brissaud surveyed, the genre of illustrated editions of Roman Law texts is born dead: '*mort-né*'.[19] Such editions as the Sennetoniana have survived as exceptional testimonies of an era that might seem very odd to contemporary lawyers or law professors. The *peritiæ linguæ* (Latin and Greek but also Hebrew) has certainly now become a remote survival of an obsolete ideal. Learned jurists have worshipped a humanist model that is now under serious threat. I think here of institutional threats and of short-term perspectives, which singularly succeed in ignoring the painstaking bliss of *Philologia*. Let us present this paper as a vibrant plea for

17 Pierre Legendre, *Leçons IV, suite. Le dossier occidental de la parenté*. Textes juridiques indésirables sur la généalogie, traduits et présentés par Anton Schütz, Marc Smith, Yan Thomas, précédés d'un avant-propos et d'un éloge de Mayo par Pierre Legendre (Paris: Fayard, 1988).

18 Robert Jacob, *Images de la Justice, Essai sur l'iconographie judiciaire du Moyen Âge à l'âge classique* (Paris: Le Léopard d'Or, 1994), 11.

19 Yves-Bernard Brissaud, 'Pistes pour une histoire de l'édition juridique française sous l'Ancien Régime', in Frédéric Barbier, *Histoire et civilisation du livre* (Geneva: Droz, 2005), vol. 1, 85–187.

philology, as an homage to Budé's mistress (he confessed that he had spent more time labouring with his muse (*Philologia*) than in bed with his wife.[20]

Hybrid of the *Emblematum libellus* bestseller

Macé Bonhomme is well known for his beautiful editions of Alciato's emblems.[21] The current digitization of most emblematic collections (Wolfenbuttel, Glasgow, Studiolum, etc.) has contributed to an enormous extent in making many corpuses that were only available through controversial dictionaries (Henkel and Schöne) generally accessible.

By drafting a new vexillological grammar, embodied in a wide array of devices: coat of arms, shirtails, *stemmata, emblemata, pegmata*, most authors of early modern emblems (namely Alciato, Coustau, Lebey de Batilly or Barthélemy Aneau) were influenced by three main iconological traditions: the sacred scripture of *hieroglyphica*, the symbolic efficacity of flags and heraldic devices and the various applications of civil symbolic creations: *emblemata, pegmata* or any of the iconotexts and objects invented to embody a symbolic gesture. *Emblema*, modelled on *problema*, is first and foremost a Greek root, that originally means any inserted or grafted part, from the insole of a shoe to a botanical 'graft' (*insita emblemata*). The meaning is asserted by Antiquarian Cælius Rhodiginus,[22] in his principal work, the

20 Guillaume Budé, *Philologie, De philologia*, ed. and trans. Marie-Madeleine de La Garanderie (Paris: Les Belles Lettres, 2001), 58. Pierre Bayle has emphasized this detail in his *Dictionnaire historique et critique*, vol. 1 (Rotterdam: Michel Bohm, 1720), 692, Remarque L: '*J'ai lu une Lettre de Budé, où il se contente de dire que les caresses de sa femme n'avaient pas été capables de le détacher de ses Livres ... Il se représente comme marié à deux femmes: l'une était celle qui lui donna fils et filles, l'autre était la Philologie, qui lui produisait des Livres ... il espérait qu'enfin il ferait plus de Livres que d'enfants.*' Guillaume Budé, *De Philologia*, ed. and trans. Marie-Madeleine de La Garanderie (Paris: les Belles Lettres, 2001). See, especially, Michel Magnien, '*Portrait de Budé en intellectuel*', p. 35: '*En outre, lorsqu'ils considèreront son mode de vie, sa complexion, ses mœurs, sa dignité, sa constance, sa prééminence et sa sagesse, les gens aussi comprendront – chose que de nos jours je trouve particulièrement salutaire et féconde – qu'avec les Lettres, ce n'est pas l'étalage du savoir que l'on recherche, mais bien plutôt la pureté des mœurs*'. Available online at http://jps.library.utoronto.ca/index.php/renref/article/viewFile/8660/5627 (accessed 7 January 2015).

21 Andrea Alciato's *Emblemes* (Lyons, Macé Bonhomme for Guillaume Rouille, 1549). Available online at www.emblems.arts.gla.ac.uk/french/books.php?id=FALb&o= (accessed 7 January 2015).

22 Ludovicus Cælius (or Cœlius) Rhodiginus (Lodovico Ricchieri) born in the town of Rovigo, Venitian Republic, in 1469 and died *ibidem* in 1525. Philologist and Classical erudite, he was in Milan between 1511 and 1516 and taught *humaniores litteræ* to young aristocrats as well as to law students. We assume that Alciato and Coustau knew his works very well.

encyclopaedic collection known as the *Lectionum Antiquarum* (ed. princeps, Alde Manuce, Venice, 1516). As I have been able to demonstrate elsewhere, the section '*Arbores*' of Alciato's book of emblems is inspired by an understanding of taxonomy which derives from classical poetry. In adding a further graft to his *Emblematum libellus* (the tree emblems were added in the Aldine edition of 1546 and included from then onwards), Alciato showed that he was well aware that the word *emblema* was not only an expression of the first figurative sense that is most commonly quoted: '"*emblema*" as an inlaid work'.[23]

Index juxta locos: tool for *inventio* or fixed authoritative classification?

Rhodiginus' *miscellanea* (more than 800 pages in folio, superbly typeset by Aldus Manutius), contains useful index tables that help the reader to find easily and rapidly the main *loci*, *adagia*, *mirabilia* restored by his care and *studium*. On the same pattern that the *Index juxta locos* added by Erasmus in his edition of his *Adagia*, Rhodiginus' indexes evidence the nature of such collections (*emblemata, adagia, pegmata...*): these 'gems' are meant to be inserted in all sorts of discourses; they are polysemic, ambivalent and at times plurivalent. They are important features of practical reasoning. In a letter dating from 7 October 1519,[24] Budé had reproached Erasmus for having devised his *Adagia* in the form of a fixed collection, the continuing progress of the *collectanea* (earlier collections of proverbs accumulated through a plethoric taste for *copia*) had been rearranged in a new volume, according to an *index justa locos*. Budé had wished this collection to remain common to all, open to a sort of dynamic and polyphonic syntax which would open up an infinity of possible combinations. The image used by Erasmus (a flowering garden, where *adagia*, *emblemata*, pearls and flowers were picked up randomly) in his *Quid sit parœmium?* has been transformed into an authoritative sum, a sort of enormous aggregate of lexica. The question of the integrity of the 'Œuvre' is debated in parallel ways by Alciato reorganizing his *Emblemata* driven from material adduced in his *Collectanea*, or by the way in which a new publication of the *Corpus Juris Civilis* is *de facto* restricted, because the material added is always very derivative. One way of seeing the problem differently is to look at the 'living metaphors'

23 Valérie Hayaert, '*Botanique et poésie dans les* Emblèmes *d'Alciat, emblèmes greffes et entregetz*' in *Le livre demeure, mélanges offerts à Alison Saunders*, ed. Philip Ford and Alison Rawles (Genève: Droz, 2011).

24 See CWE, ep. 915, Allen, vol. III.

(Paul Ricœur) used to think the notion of the integrity of an 'Œuvre'. Does an *œuvre* become a *chef d'œuvre* when it achieves some sort of integrity? The botanical principle, the metaphor of a garden which needs to be cultivated, might act as a more accurate metaphor to describe the process at stake here. *Emblemata* are not only moveable affixed ornaments, they are grafts, planted into earth and as such, they give way to a generative principle which is similar to Darwin's corals analysed by Horst Bredekamp.[25] An emblem can be a graft, and as such, the trees it generates or the branches it adorns have an important significance in understanding how legal emblems function.

Cælius Rhodiginus' Book VII, dedicated to the analysis of ancient sacred sacrifices, includes a whole section about the *Lucus veneratio* (cult of bushes) and the reasons why these sacred spaces were designed for the worship of special trees, understood as apotropaïc tools and places of worship. These sacred open spaces would welcome the *probatio victimarum*, around a sacred altar. Rhodiginus (VII, c. I) explains first why these sacrifices were used for healing (*sacrificia esse velut medicamenta*) and how the *adorantes* should be placed and what they were able to see (*quam partem spectare adorantes debeant*), then (VII, c. II), he dwells on the affects produced by such 'mises en scène' and seeks to grasp the reason for tears (*Lachrymarum ratio*) and the vices of seeing (*Oculis vitia*, XII, c. 4). In such a meaningful context, Rhodiginus then comes to the meaning of the *fasces* (symbolic gestures of coercion, VII, c. 4) and he insists upon saying that the rite of submission, '*submittere fasces quid*' has to be done *extra urbem*; that is, outside of the *limen* (frontier) of Rome.[26] Before analyzing his interpretation of the word '*emblemata*', one needs to bear in mind that these pieces are structurally similar to *parerga*, which means they have to be outside the frame (see Schopenhauer's *Parerga* and *Paralipomena*), and since the frame is here Rome (*Urbs*), these *emblemata* are civil devices, tools for the avoidance of conflicts, staged *pegmata* for litigating couples that have to be situated *obiter*, their performativity is exterior to their stage setting.

Rhodiginus then explains the three conditions for the edification of an *ara pacis*. It first needs to be secured by *fascibus junctis securibus* (VII c. 6 *faisceaux* – symbols of irrefragable *unitas* – and axes – right of life and death

25 Horst Bredekamp, for an excerpt of this most stimulating book, *Darwins Korallen. Die frühen Evolutions diagramme und die Tradition der Naturgeschichte* (Berlin: Wagenbach, 2005). See more at Cultural Histories of the Material World: www.culturalhistoriesofthematerialworld.com/books/ways-of-making-and-knowing-the-material-culture-of-empirical-knowledge/excerpt/#sthash.tqpPv2G6.dpuf (accessed 7 January 2015).

26 For a breathtaking analysis of this notion of frontier, see Florence Dupont, *Rome, la ville sans origine* (Paris: Gallimard, 2011), quoting Yan Thomas's penetrating studies of *origo*.

over citizens). It then needs to be instituted by a specific timing (VII, 8 *Duodecim hora ædificare, quid*, symbolized by several emblems – *Heliotropia, Gnomon, vel Umbilicus, Diopi, Diopteres, Astrolabii inventio*). The norms of time during the process of conflict resolution under the trees are called *apotelesmata*. And finally, the setting of a symbolic tree, bearing *emblemata*, understood here as iconotexts written in 'cartouches' (see *emblema* Figure 1.9, Title *De hæreditatis*), coat of arms (*servitutum scuti*, the blasons of Acteon, Figure 1.10) or embodied by symbolic animals or objects; see the *emblema* used to adorn the title Dig. XXXVI & XXXVII *(Infortiatum)* (Figure 1.11), the iconic choices are drawn from a curious syntax: a *dextrarum junctio* is handled by an arrow which departs from a trunk. The *emblema* (*pictura* only) added here is quite literally a graft, but of a curious kind, since it appears as an odd mechanical system bursting out from a stump. Trees in this edition are not necessarily realistic trees: they bear a diagrammatic resemblance with *arbores*, but their scheme is meant to appear as bizzarre as possible. Grafted olive-trees are enhanced in Cœlius' Rhodiginus' description: '*Olearum species aliquot emblemata quid. Judicio in Æropago primum tollit ex Plinium obscuritas … Trophæa prima ex olea Aggripeum quid*' (VII, c. 18).

As most humanists well understand, *emblema* is a *notio multiplex*. It is only by grasping the meaningful chain of polysemy that these iconotexts become eminently readable. The impressive work of Rhodiginus served as a basis for Alciato's *emblemata* and Coustau's *pegmata*. The purpose behind the borrowing of Greek words and Greek antiquarian objects, when made explicit, shows that philology, far from being the tedious mania of scholars of ancient times is, on the contrary, a vivid tool for inventing, drafting and reflecting on origins. Whether these fictions are true or false is not the issue: Alciato always repeats that fables and ancient myths were intended *allegorice* (that is, in an allegorical sense). The manner in which the allegory is constructed is more important, in his eyes, than the result achieved. *Emblemata* include sacred *effigies* (*imagines ancestris*) and shameful *stigmatas* (for the *Servitus* par excellence, Actéon), *pegmata* offer the display of a space of judgment outside institutional courts; *pegmata* are thought to be placed *beyond* the parisian '*table de marbre*', which served as the *limen* of Paris' Palace of Justice; and *stemmata* are horizontal garlands preserving the lineages and bonds in an orientation that is not necessarily hegemonical.

This paper has two objectives: it first intends to show that one of the figurative senses pinpointed by Quintilian in his *Institutio Oratoria* (*velut emblematis exornarentur*) is part of a wider philological picture. It is undeniable that the figurative sense of *emblemata* ('ornamental inlaid works' used by lawyers to adorn their pleas) has been, in the case of humanist lawyers, at

Figure 1.9 *Sennetoniana, Digestus vetus* volume, XXX, 1,1 XXXI, 1,1 and XXXII, 1,1; the same emblematic woodcut is reused for books I, II, III (*De Legatis primo, secundo et tertio*) (reproduced by permission of Bibliothèque de la Cour de Cassation, Paris)

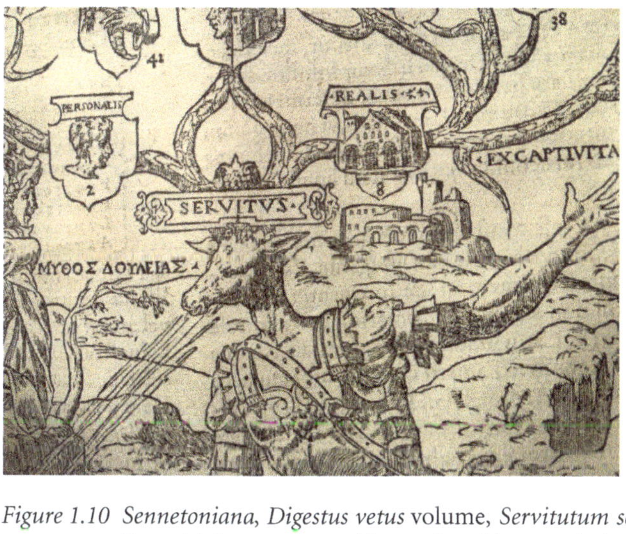

Figure 1.10 *Sennetoniana, Digestus vetus* volume, *Servitutum scuti*, detail from the figure '*Arbor servitutum*' (reproduced by permission of Bibliothèque de la Cour de Cassation, Paris)

Figure 1.11 *Sennetoniana*, *Infortiatum* volume, XXXVI, 1,1 *Ad senatus-consultum Trebellianum* (reproduced by permission of Bibliothèque de la Cour de Cassation, Paris)

the very heart of the redefinition of their rhetorical method and *ethos*. Building a new 'rhétorique des citations' (Marc Fumaroli), Alciato, Coustau or Hotman have shown that their way of dealing with the fragmentary texture of the *Corpus Juris Civilis* needed to be grounded in a new ideal of *ratio juris* and in a renewed approach to the art of interpretation.

In the wake of two precedent case studies on the *Sennetoniana*,[27] an edition of the CJC (five in-folio volumes, plus a manual of the *Institutes*, printed by the same trio and adorned with *emblemata* as well, but with a different title page) printed in Lyon by brothers Jacques, Jean and Claude Senneton between 1548 and 1550, this paper considers the genealogy of two

27 Valérie Hayaert '*Mens emblematica* et humanisme juridique: l'insertion d'*emblemata* dans l'édition Senneton du *Corpus Juris Civilis* (1548–1550)', *Journal de la Renaissance*, 5 (2007), 301–22; 'Du manuscrit juridique à l'édition ornée d'emblèmes et de 'hiéroglyphes': le cas de l'*Archion Avenionense* (ca 1475) et de la *Sennetoniana* (Lyon, 1548–1550)', in *Les détours de l'illustration*, ed. Olivier Leplatre, Cahiers du Gadges (Geneva: Droz, 2015).

exceptional *arbores juris*, invented by engraver and embroiderer Pierre Eskrich (alias Vase, Cruche) in the years 1548–1550.

I argue that the meaning of *emblemata* has different valences, potential meanings that are asleep, but at times revived for various purposes. Erudite lawyers practice philology as an art of interpretation; their tools are not only internal (cross references between legal palingenesia and reasonings derived from a boethian approach to categories) but also external to the usual flow of legal studies. Alciato often repeated that he knew that the conjunction of *studio juris* and *studiæ humanitatis* would attract wasps (*irritare crabrones*) and he also knew that by drafting a particularly fierce epigram against the landscape of the law professors of his time (embl. *Agnomina Doctorum*), he would add a few more wasps from the busy nest of the '*professionnels de la profession*' (Jean-Luc Godard). Picus a Monte Pico was nicknamed *Labyrinthus*, because, says Alciato, his way of teaching law was as obcure as the labyrinth's maze and that no Ariadne's string would ever let anyone escape from it. Alciato and his followers were duelling with many adversaries. In the crucial period of the Early Modern reception of Roman Law (ca. 1475–ca. 1580), lawyers invent a meaningful use of emblematic structures in order to assert, as Peter Goodrich has beautifully demonstrated, a visiocracy.

Tree schemes in the Sennetoniana

The exceptional richness of the Sennetoniana, especially when compared to the Vatican manuscript, cannot be fully grasped in a single article. To show the power of the insertion of the iconic parts of emblematic creations into the body of Roman law texts, we thus concentrate on the tree diagrams and the pattern of engrafting. The path going from portative emblem books (*libellus*, in quarto or in octavo) to the five in-folio of 300–1000 pages of the complete monumental edition of the CJC is interesting in itself. The traditional trees and diagrams (*arbor juridictionis*, *arbor servitutis*) are an important milestone of this survey.

The word '*emblema*' occurs in the prefatory epistle of the *Digestus Vetus* volume, the phrase '*per imagines decoratus et mythicis emblematum picturis illustratum*' (decorated with images and adorned with emblematic pictures of myths) refers only to the figurative part of emblems. This sounds more like a salesman's argument, given the enormous success of the genre at that time. This quotation does not necessarily imply that these engravings were conceived as emblems as such. In other words, importing the figurative aspect of emblems into a new edition of the body of Roman law texts certainly adds value and serves to embellish a new and prestigious edition but the use of those iconic supplements does not seem to be sufficient to constitute 'emblems' in the complete and autonomous sense of the term. They lack the epigrammatic part and the dynamic relationship between text and image which characterizes the genre invented by Andrea Alciato. Their emblematic nature is more linked with the original meaning of the term '*emblema*' meaning any mounted or inserted part, an inlaid work referring to mosaic work.[28] The legal emblems inserted in this edition are ornamental pieces, considered of greater value than the structure itself.

While examining the relationship between texts and images, the 'emblematic process' will be called into question. Legal emblems, enigmas and hieroglyphs are used as means of signalling as well as mnemonic tools. They interpret a body of written laws figuratively. The variegated use of epigraphic and archaeological material shows that the *emblemata* of the Senneton edition build a genuinely original iconography, one which goes beyond the uses of images in manuscript miniatures.

The Ottobonianus Latinus manuscript 3132

First, we look at the Ottobonianus Latinus manuscript 3132, which was used to establish the Senneton edition (Figure 1.12). Thanks to a groundbreaking article by Robert Feenstra, who, however, only analyzes its text, the link between the *Archion Avenionense* and the *editio Sennetoniana* of 1548–1550 has been firmly established.[29] This is one of the few mediaeval manuscripts containing all parts of the *Corpus juris civilis* along with the Accursian gloss; it also contains the *editio princeps* of the *Brachylogus* (or *Corpus Legum*) and an edition of the *Epitome* of Gaïus under the title *Caii Institutionum libri duo.* The Senneton brothers, with the help of the bookseller Macé Bonhomme, wished to offer a printed edition of a particularly precious manuscript: the *Archion Avenionense*, quoted in the title of the *Digestum Vetus* volume. It had been given to the University of Avignon by the Cardinal of Saluces in 1419. In 1746, it was proffered to Pope Benedetto XIV, as a mark of thanks for the privileges he had given to the University of Avignon. We know that it was frequently used in the sixteenth century by the lawyers Emilio Ferreti and Antonio Govea. It contains miniatures, which are close illustrations of the legal text. All the scenes depicted are narrative. Colours and gestures are particularly significant.

28 Hessel Miedema, 'The Term Emblema in Alciati', *Journal of the Warburg and Courtauld Institutes*, 31 (1968), 234–50.

29 Robert Feenstra 'Un manuscrit et une édition peu connues du Corpus Juris Civilis: l'Archion Avenionense et l'editio Sennetoniana', *Tijdschrift voor Rechtsgeschiedenis, Revue d'Histoire du Droit, Legal History Review*, 61/2 (1993), 277–95.

Figure 1.12 Mss *Ottobonianus Latinus* 3132, Vatican, sec. XIV, fol 2r. *Digestus Vetus*, I, 1,1 particular; Justinian receives from Tribonian the codex of the *Corpus Juris Civilis* (reproduced by permission of Biblioteca Apostolica Vaticana, Vatican)

Narrative emblems

First example, the illustration of the title *De interdictis*, Code, 8.1.1.1, shows that the Senneton woodcut integrates a textual fragment of the imperial rescript (Figures 1.13 and 1.14). The legal text (C. 8.1.1) involves a Roman veteran named Aper, who complained that roots from the yard of his neighbour, named Agathangelus, were threatening the foundations of his house:

Figure 1.13 Mss *Ottobonianus Latinus* 3132, fol. 516r. *Codex Justininanus*, VIII, 1, 1 (reproduced by permission of Biblioteca Apostolica Vaticana, Vatican)

8.1.1. Emperor Alexander to Aper, a veteran.
Since you say that the roots of trees situated and growing in the neighbouring yard of Agathangelus threaten the foundations of your house, the president will settle the matter according to equity in consonnance with the interdicts, which the praetor has written on his tablets, relating to a tree hanging over another's house, or to a tree hanging over another's field, and which show that a neighbour should not be injured even by trees. Promulgated March 26 (224).

Figure 1.14 *Sennetoniana*, *Codex Just.* volume, *De interdictis*, VIII, 1, 1. (reproduced by permission of Bibliothèque de la Cour de Cassation, Paris)

The miniature depicts the plaintiff (in red) pointing his index finger towards a tree growing too close to his house. He engages the Emperor, seated on his throne, to react. In the woodcut, the engraver has added a sign, which reads '*Si arbor*': this stands for the *incipit* of the imperial rescript: '*Si arbor in alienas ædes impendit*'. The written nature of this interdict is shown in the engraving, by a visible sign. The legal text indicates that the prætor had written the interdict on his tablets. This detail reveals a strong desire to insist on the writing of ancient Roman formulas.

Ancestors trees, grounded in sacred tombs

The woodcut illustrating *De Hæreditatis* (see Figure 1.9), is used three times. It represents a sacred tree, emerging from a tomb, with the *motto* D. M. (*In dies manibus*). The tree is here a meaningful setting: the exercise of justice needs a tree to be performed. The tree is a marker of the sacred space of patrilinear transmission in this case, but it can also serve as a significant setting for the staging of an *ara conjugalis* (Plutarch) repeated in Barthélemy

Aneau and Pierre Coustau's pieces about resolving conflicts between husbands and wives. Coustau devotes a *pegma* to the goddess *Viriplaca* (Figure 1.15) (She who calms down husbands), *In deæ Viriplacæ*. Barthélemy Aneau invents an arborescent composition *Figure de mariage* (Figure 1.16), which settles an ambivalent hermaphrodite ('*à double face et à double nature*') by showing that the fusion of two bodies is a mutual contract and is ambivalent by nature.[30] Whether fighting or loving each other, they need to unite when facing adversity for they both need to face the voluntary and salutary bond of marriage. The branches of this curious tree welcome four different types of emblematic birds: the pelican ('Le Pellican est labeur et l'effort pour les petitz travaillant – *i.e. torturing* for "travail" derives from "tripalium" – jusqu'à mort') for he who was believed to injure himself to feed his children; the *turtur*, sheltering and protecting his nestlings; a couple of turtledoves, symbolizing mutual love and finally a couple of crows, meant to signify the exchange of services between husbands and wives. In the Sennetoniana, prolific trees are vivid symbols for prolific alliances. The woodcut for the title *De ritu nuptiarum* (Figure 1.17) shows an exchange of rings in front of a flourishing garden of medicinal plants. The bride-to-be holds quinces, it alludes to Plutarch, *Coniugalia præcepta, Moralia, 138 D*: the 'Cotonea' locus is also developed in Alciato's emblem about the quince: 'Solon of old is said to have ordained that quinces be given to newly-weds, since these are pleasant both to mouth and stomach. As a result their breath is sweet, and winning grace drops from their lips'.[31]

The manuscript miniatures are a fine example of a close illustration (in the strong sense of the word, *illustrare* meaning shedding light on, *elucidare*) of the legal text. But the woodcuts of the Senneton edition aim to bring more details relating to the specifics of Roman legal procedures. Woodcuts often integrate legal texts and notions, they also show a will to describe antique objects, rites or settings. If the manuscript miniatures are all built on a narrative structure, the woodcuts of the Senneton edition bring into play a wide range of emblematic objects. Some features of the manuscript 'lettrines' are typical of medieval habits of representation; these will disappear from the Senneton edition: for example, the fact of putting a leg on the other was a typical gesture indicating the judging posture of the sovereign.

30 Barthélemy Aneau, *Imagination poétique* (1552), 19. Available online at www.emblems.arts.gla.ac.uk/french/emblem.php?id=FANb007 (accessed 7 January 2015).

31 Alciato, *Emblemata*, 279. Available online at www.emblems.arts.gla.ac.uk/alciato/emblem.php?id=FALc203 (accessed 7 January 2015).

Figure 1.15 Pierre Coustau, *Pegma cum narrationibus philosophicis*, 1555, Macé Bonhomme, Lyon, 'In statuam viriplacæ' (reproduced by permission of Glasgow University Library, Special Collections)

Figure 1.16 Barthélemy Aneau, *Picta Poesis*, Lyon, 1552, '*Typus Matrimonii/Figure de Mariage*'. (reproduced by permission of Glasgow University Library, Special Collections)

Figure 1.17 *Sennetoniana*, *Infortiatum* volume, XXIII, 1, 1, *De donationum inter virum et uxorem*, Lyon, 1549 (reproduced by permission of Bibliothèque de la Cour de Cassation, Paris)

Arbor servitutum

The *Arbor Servitutum* (Figure 1.18) is a full-page and quite exceptional woodcut, showing a tree, used here as a mnemonic diagram, where the different categories of servitudes are distributed in shields borne by Actæon's antlers. Legal texts of the time hardly ever contain woodcuts of this size and quality. It can be attributed with certainty to Pierre Eskrich (or Pierre Vase or Cruche): his monogram (P.V.) and an ideogrammatic signature under the form of an antique vase are pictured on the bottom left corner. Born around 1520 in Paris, he died in 1590; his career as a book illustrator and embroiderer had led him to Lyons and Geneva. He is famous for his acute depictions of archeological details and liturgical objects (for instance, in his Geneva Bible of 1560). He also collaborates actively on the illustration of several emblem books (Andrea Alciato, Pierre Coustau, Barthélemy Aneau).

Figure 1.18 *Sennetoniana, Digestus Vetus* volume, Lyon, 1549, *Arbor Servitutum*, col. 770–1 (reproduced by permission of Bibliothèque de la Cour de Caſsation, Pariſ)

Pierre Vase has depicted the encounter of the young hunter with chaste Diana. Actæon stumbles upon the scene of Diana, escorted by several nymphs, bathing. The woodcut depicts the moment when Diana, in a fit of embarrassed fury, splashes water upon Actæon. The Greek myth is used here to illustrate the legal concept of servitude. To explain the figure of the stag properly, its textual source should not be overlooked. Next to Actæon's head, the motto *muthos douleias* ('the myth of servitude') has been written in capital Greek letters. But this iconographical choice also relates to Petrus Crinitus' writings.

The *Declaratio divisionis Servitutis* follows the woodcut and aims to legitimate the use of Actæon myth:

> Since the definition of servitudes is not universal amongst jurists, it is useful to divide them in order to give proper definitions. Choosing to illustrate the law of servitudes by using the myth of Actæon is legitimate, since, according to Petrus Crinitus,[32] who understood it and wrote about it, the stag was meant by the ancients to represent slaves. This is the reason why the figure shows the image of a stag: in his antlers, each type of servitude has been distributed in a little hieroglyph.[33]

Each little shield contains a hieroglyph, divided into an image and a *motto*. This combination of emblematic images with *mottos* is particularly interesting as it drafts an iconographic syntax of signifying objects. Each shield bears a number which refers to a single servitude, fully developed by the text of the *declaratio divisionis*. Since the Glossators, the first division falls into three main categories. Every servitude is either personal, real or mixed. The category of personal servitudes, such as *usus* or *usufructus*, is represented by a head profile, 'real servitudes', such as the one linked to houses or lands are represented by a large house. The third category (mixed servitudes) is figured by a shield cut in two halves, combining both icons.

Some servitudes belong to the *jus gentium*, others to the *jus divinum* and others to the *jus civile*. The symbol chosen to depict the notion of *jus civile*

32 Petrus Crinitus, *De Honesta Disciplina*, XIX, 8 (first ed. 1504, ed. cited Lyon: Gryphe, 1543, 295). In a chapter entitled '*Cervos pro servis & fugitivis accipi apud veteres, ac Martialis poetæ carmen expositum contra aliorum sententiam*', Crinitus demonstrates that for the Ancients (Martial, Terence, Ælius Donatus) the word '*cervus*' (stag) meant '*servus*' (slave).

33 '*Cuius singulas species in ceratinos ramos, cum parmulis hieroglyphicis distributas, exhibet imago Cervi, hominem Actæona tegentis, non prorsus inepta. Cervum etenim pro servo antiquos, & scripsisse, & intellexisse tradit Crinitus*'. *Declaratio Arbor Servitutum*, p. 771, in *Digestus Vetus* (Lyon: Senneton brothers, 1550).

is the bicephalous eagle of the Germanic Holy Roman Empire. The *Jus divinum* is represented by Moses and the Tablets of the Law. This last category falls into two subdivisions '*Honesta*' and '*Turpis*'. The *Declaratio* is silent on these two categories. The treatise on servitudes by Bartholomeus de Cæpolla gives an explanation of these two types of sacred servitudes.[34] The '*Turpis servitus*' is adopted by those who devoted themselves to false gods and idols, under the influence of the Devil. Cæpolla quotes examples from the Bible (Judges, 2, 11–19: 'They provoked the Lord to Anger because they served Ball and the Ashtoreths'). He also quotes Saint Paul who calls *avaritia* the servitude to idols.[35] The icon of the devil for the shield '*Turpis*' is thus quite appropriate.

At times, the icons chosen are relatively transparent, they are only called 'hieroglyphs' according to the early modern sense of the term (a verbal concept figured by a visual form, deriving from the tradition of Orus Apollo). For instance, shield 32, *Jus Pascendi* (one has the right to pasture on the land of another) is represented by a grazing cow but the heterogeneous accumulation of these small icons, all inserted in a bi-medial shield, tends to arouse a sense of oddity, which helps the viewer to memorize each item by means of a significant gesture.

Shield 12 '*Itineris seu aditus*' depicts the servitude (or common law easement) which enables a person to cross another's estate or field to access his own house. The woodcut shows a man, following a path, heading up to a house. The servitude called *oneris ferendi* occurs when a neighbouring house is charged with the service of supporting on its wall, vault or pillars, some portion of the neighbouring house. Shield 13 carefully includes all the elements needed to recall the rule: a house is charged with supporting on a column a ladder and a stone belonging to the neighbouring house.

The servitude *non altius tollendi* (21), was a constraint upon the natural law which allows a man to erect a building to an infinite height on his own land. Because the building of a house to an indefinite height not only affected the light and view of another but it also intercepted the free circulation of air.

34 Bartholomæus Cæpolla, *Tractatus de servitutibus, tam urbanorum quam rusticorum prædiorum*, (first edition, 1465) Pachel, 1503, p. 14, '*Honesta servitus est, qua quis volens se totum Deo mancipare, totum se illi devovet, ac præceptis illius sponte obsequitur*' [The honest servitude occurs when someone wants to devote himself entirely to God and to observe strictly his laws].

35 '*Turpis servitus est, qua quis per peccatum in mancipatum diaboli venit, qui & ipse peccati auctor est, & mendacii pater. De hac servitute mentio sit passim in sacris Litteris, tum in veteri, tum in novo Testamento: Feceruntque filii Israel malum in conspectu Domini, & servierunt Baalim, & dimiserunt Dominum Deum patrum suorum … Et Divus Paulus, avaritiam vocat idolorum servitutem*', *ibid.*

Shield 21 shows two buildings (a house and a castle) which have been built to the same height. Woodcut 19, depicting the *jus altius tollendi*, depicts, on the contrary, a castle of a greater height than the two neighbouring houses. The *jus altius tollendi* (19) arises when a man promises to allow his neighbour to build his house higher than the laws permit. The servitude called *tigni immittendi* (14) was the liability to suffer that a tile, a beam, a stone or a piece of iron (under the word *tignum*, all these building materials are included) should be placed in the wall for the benefit of the neighbour.

Shield 22 '*ne luminibus officiatur*' depicts the servitude restraining the owner of a house from making erections causing obstruction to the light of an adjoining house. One is prohibited from making a construction which will block light to his neighbour. The woodcut represents two opposite symbols, the sun and the moon, instead of depicting details of the scene. This topic is the point of departure of Alciato's emblem '*Bonis a divitibus nihil timendum*' (The Good shouldn't have anything to fear from the Rich),[36] where Alciato playfully complained of having his light obstructed by this neighbours. He had staged, in an allegorical and witty emblem, his case for the right to light which a neighbour should always respect.

Shield 33 bears the motto '*pecoris appulsus*', which stands for '*pecoris ad aquam appulsus*', which is the right of watering one's cattle on the land of the neighbour. The woodcut depicts a cow, drinking from a small river. '*Aquæ haustus*' is the name of a servitude which consists in the right to draw water from a fountain, spring or well situated on the property of another. Shield 34 depicts a man drawing water from a well. The servitude called *jus arenæ fodiendi* was the right to dig sand on another's land. Shield 36 represents a sand quarry, protected by a roof. Another straightforward woodcut in shield 35, the *Jus calcis coquendae*, depicts the right to dig and burn lime. The woodcut represents a lime oven in full activity.

Most of these 'hieroglyphs' are precise illustrations of each servitude. They are not meant to be deliberately obscure. Some items are metonymic (the sun and the moon are associative signs related to the servitude *ne luminibus officiatur*) but most of them aim at depicting narrative scenes. Their role is above all mnemonic. They help readers to memorize a long and complex list of servitudes. The combination of texts and images always leads to a convergence. The topic of servitudes has always been a privileged one for mnemonic images but the example of this tree reveals a new interest in

36 Alciato, *Emblemata*, 1531, F2ro; 1577, no 32, p. 162–5; 1621, no 32, p. 179–82. Drysdall has shown that this translation is much preferable. Most translations, including contemporary ones, indicate that Alciato has not been understood. See Denis Drysdall, '"The Good have Nothing to Fear from the Rich." Did Alciato Really Believe that?', *Emblematica*, 19 (2012), 115–31.

mythological structures and emblematic inventions. Aside from *emblemata* or *pegmata*, we have an example of a type of device used as a symbolic form (*impresa*) where a *scutum* is adorned with a picture and a motto only. This unusual mythical tree links the tradition of *arbores juris* to a myth understood *allegorice*. Iconic elements belong to an inventive vexillological syntax, made especially for this edition. Moreover, this curious and fictitious tree is a tool of and for metamorphosis. Its significance for the history of legal thought may have been overlooked or completely unknown but Eskrich's interests show that this piece questions much more than its own mythical origin: it is used to show the essence of metamorphosis inside legal thinking. This tree is not a usual tree of life, that would assign to each order (biological and social) a patrilinear transmission. It mixes animal and human species, it shows that reigns are not isolated in their own configuration. This curious tree assures *convenientia*, understood as a dynamic link between sympathy and antipathy, between trees and the living.

Arbor Juridictionum

In *Arbor Juridictionum* (Figure 1.19), Justinian is represented as a pedagogue, with his *ferule*. Pierre Vase has chosen a miraculous tree where some branches revive because of new grafts. Thus, viewers are inclined to understand that Justinian himself, showing the new branches of a sound interpretation, rejects the dead branches used previously by the glossators and their wrong method of *divisio*. The new graft (an *emblema*) brings a new, authoritative, interpretation of the controversial issue of the *Imperium*. This new figure of a tree is supported by a long *declaratio*, which gives to the image a paramount importance. The tree represented, and taught, a new *doxa* of *Imperium* while also evincing novel particularities. It does not proceed upside down, from genus to species, on the pattern of the model tree of the Neoplatonist Porphyry (233–304). Pierre Eskrich's tree contains dead branches as well as emerging and burgeoning limbs, it has the anarchic pattern of growing on one side only ('*port en drapeau*'). As such, and even if it thought to be used as a pedagogical tool, it appears to be more of a symbolic gesture, designed to legitimate new ways of approaching the power of *Imperium*.

Trees of legal thought are superior to any mechanical and typographical force, such as the technology of print. If we think that Pierre Eskrich was born in Geneva, but baptized some of his children in the Catholic faith in Lyons,[37] abstract models as well as academic concerns conceived to

37 Thierry Wanegffelen, *Ni Rome ni Genève: Des fidèles entre deux chaires en France au XVIè siècle* (Paris: Honoré Champion, 1997).

Figure 1.19 *Sennetoniana, Digestus Vetus* volume, *Arbor Jurisdictionum*, Lyon, 1549, col. 101–2 (reproduced by permission of Bibliothèque de la Cour de Cassation, Paris)

understand symbolic thought seem to forget the essential: 'everyone, says Darwin, must be struck with astonishment, when he first beholds one of these vast rings of coral-rock'.[38] Back in New York, November 2013, the discovery of old and new growths on the Ground Zero 'survivor tree' at the US National September 11 Memorial, led me to change the initial scope of this paper. Fossilized survival, this remembrance tree, also symbolizes at a glance the separation between the dead and new corals of life.

As a final word, let me be brief and leave to the reader the pleasure of perusing and interpreting these pieces both literally and plurally, of seeing with the soles of the feet, *kata podas*.

38 Charles Darwin, 'The Structure and Distribution of Coral Reefs' in *The Works of Charles Darwin*, ed. Paul H. Barrett and R. B. Freeman, vol. 7 (London: Pickering, 1986), 3. Quoted by Horst Bredekamp; see more at: www.culturalhistoriesofthematerialworld.com/books/ways-of-making-and-knowing-the-material-culture-of-empirical-knowledge/excerpt/#sthash.tqpPv2G6.dpuf (accessed 7 January 2015).

CHAPTER 2

The evidence of things not seen

Peter Goodrich

omnia sunt posita ante oculos

The study of images of justice has tended, for understandable reasons, to focus primarily upon the blindfold or band that covers the eyes of Justice. The image of an unseeing *Justitia* is variously interpreted as marking the removal of judgment from venal corruption (because the blind cannot be bribed), oblivion to the persons appearing before the judge (and so impartial decision) and as an indication of the spiritual, as opposed to the material content of justice (because the blind perforce look inward to an invisible law). In a more theoretical vein, the blinding of justice raises the paradox of law's relation to vision and specifically the irony of the juridical mandate to appear before a law that cannot see. The paradox or enigma of a blind justice is properly speaking hieroglyphic in origin and arcane in practice, and it will be argued here that it both dissimulates and invents by occluding the vision of law. The blindfolding of justice, whether accidentally or intentionally, hides the eye of the judge and in doing so both separates justice from legality and represents law ironically by means of an image of what it is not.

The emblematic depictions of blindfolds capture the cunning of justice through the refusal to represent the dependence of judgment upon the sources and procedures, the power and awe of legal imposition. The image of justice is that of a *plus ultra* of legality, the indefinable something more and something other that screens the mundane procedures of rule application and so attaches the subject to judgment. The best interpretation of this paradoxical depiction, I argue, lies in addressing not the blindfold, the liminal sign of the hierarchy and separation of the various distinct orders of governance, but rather what is absent, the place and significance of the eyes of this emblematic figure that are not depicted in the standard emblems of *Justitia*. The hidden dimension of the image, the *arcanum* that the blindfold, the 'skarf', band, *fascis* or *fascia*, represents and conceals, is the representation of the practice of law and the power of judgment, which in emblems is termed the doctrine of the two swords. The key to law's relation to vision lies not only in the veiling of the eyes but equally in the unveiling of the organ and faculty that is obscured and, in whole or in part, is removed from these representations. The signal feature of the invisibility of the eyes of justice and, by extension, of the portrayal of law lies as much in what is not shown, in the hidden character of legal structures, as it does in the symbols that are represented. What, in sum, is the significance of the eye that is not portrayed, of the vision that lurks secreted behind the veiling that the blindfold performs?

The trajectory of images

First, I make a few remarks on the context and trajectory of the images of law and justice in the early modern period. There are certain non-obvious features that I approach first by way of a reference to an essay by Ernst Kantorowicz on 'Apolline Ethics'.[1] There, he touches upon the opening sentence of Justinian's *Institutes* where, departing for obvious reasons from Gaius, we read: 'Imperial Majesty should not only be decorated with arms, but also armed with laws'.[2] Arms, meaning war, on the right, and laws on the left, war the greater cause and more heroic symbol in the early emblems that portray the sovereign in the role of commander[3] (Figure 2.1). The source of this opening, however, intriguingly lies in a reference to earlier Greek representations of Apollo as the model for the emperor. Apollo carries a bow in his right hand and a lyre in his left or, as Themistius puts it, 'the emperor needs the missiles for his enemies, and for his subjects he needs the lyre'. It is a Pythagorean principle of the harmony of music being the appropriate mode of calming disputes and settling social conflict.

The link between lyre and law, can be seen in images of the order of knowledge, such as that of Chasseneuz from 1572 (Figure 2.2), where *scientia legalis*, top left, is linked directly in the schema of symbolic interpretation, to *musica* at bottom right.[4] *Ideologia*, meaning doctrine, dexter chief in the heraldic argot, is by the same token linked to astronomy at the bottom left. A similar schema is discernible in Pierre Coustau's image of justice from 1555 (Figure 2.3), with war on the right breast and 'loving justice', a nursing

1 Ernst Kantorowicz, *Selected Studies* (New York: Augustin, 1965) 399 ('On transformations in Apolline Ethics').
2 Justinian, *Institutes*, 'In Nomine Domini Nostri'.
3 Gabriel Rollenhagen, *Nucleus emblematum selectissimorum* (Cologne: Passei, 1613) *Centuria secunda*, 29.
4 Barthelemy Chasseneuz, *Catalogus gloriæ mundi* (Venice: Valgrissi, 1576), 183.

Figure 2.1 Gabriel Rollenhagen, *Nucleus emblematum selectissimorum* (Cologne: Passei, 1613) *Centuria secunda* at 29 (reproduced by permission of P. Goodrich)

Figure 2.2 Barthélemy Chasseneuz, *Catalogus gloriæ mundi* (Venice: Valgrissi, 1576) at 183 (reproduced by permission of P. Goodrich)

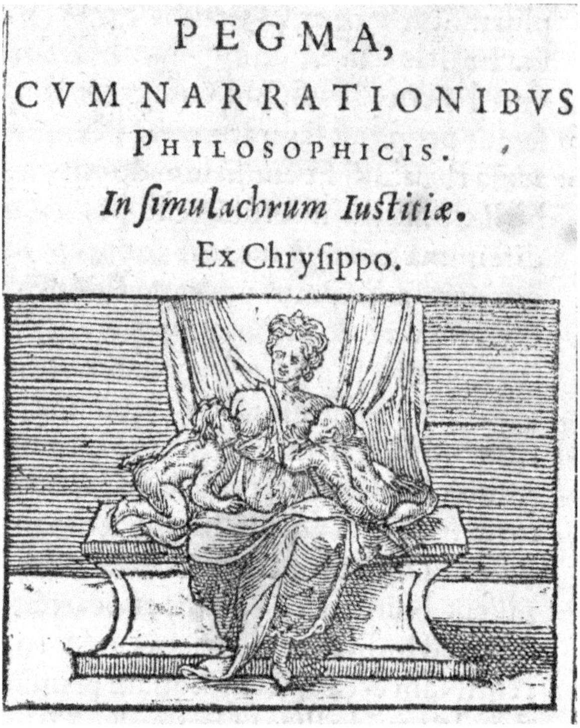
PEGMA,
CVM NARRATIONIBVS
PHILOSOPHICIS.
In ſimulachrum Iuſtitiæ.
Ex Chryſippo.

Figure 2.3 Pierre Coustau, *Pegma cum narrationibus philosophicis* (Lyons: Bonhomme, 1555) at 2 (reproduced courtesy of the Rare Books Division, Lillian Goldman Law Library, Yale Law School)

mother, again a principle of harmony, but a more abstract one, on the left.[5] The more usual representations, however, in the early emblem tradition, show arms dominating law rather than the lyre, with a book replacing the earlier representations of Muses or music. The humanist emblematists, however, soon came to change this order. As early as 1583, the heraldic scholar and divine Claude Paradin represents the sovereign under the motto *ex utroque Caesar*. The emperor is shown dominating a globe with sword and book, respectively, in right and left hands (Figure 2.4).[6] Note that the emperor is turned away from the sword, towards the book, which is held higher and forward, toward the viewer and into the wind. Here, the

5 Pierre Coustau, *Pegma cum narrationibus philosophicis* (Lyons: Bonhomme, 1555), 2.
6 Claude Paradin, *Symbola heroica* (Antwerp: Plantin, 1583), 284.

284 SYMBOLA

En vtroque Cæſar.

Hoc Apophthegmate: *Ex vtroque Cæſar*, ſignificatur, his duobus, armis ſcilicet & literis, Iulium Cæſarem recto corporis ſtatu ſemper rebus gerendis ſtrenuè inuigilantem, factum totius orbis dominatorem.

Sele-

Figure 2.4 Claude Paradin, *Symbola heroica* (Antwerp: Plantin, 1583) at 284 (reproduced courtesy of Duke University Library)

subscription indicates that it is '*armis scilicet et literis*', to wit, arms and letters or, literally, 'signs marking sounds' to which the emperor should be attentive. The 1591 edition suggests, with even more force than the original, that the emperor must always have 'a watchfull eye to the execution of justice' and places the emphasis upon 'good letters', the harmony of equity taking precedence over the blunt thrust of war.

By the seventeenth century, as Kantorowicz shows, the initially dominant position of the sword and the accompanying doctrine of the two swords, those of war and justice, arms and inquisition has been superseded by the emblematists' attention to *studium* and the arts. The glossatorial doctrine of the two swords treated arms as primary, in that law was to be imposed by force, the sword accompanying and dominating the books. The humanist emblematists, however, reversed the dominant role of the sword and visually as well as verbally elevated arts and letters, in short, *ars iuris*, above the bludgeon and the scythe. Some select examples can illustrate the trajectory from force to letters and from text to emblem. Covarrubias, in his *Emblemas Morales* of 1610, shows the sword captured and immobilized by the book (Figure 2.5).[7] The motto reads '*tu vince loquendo*': words ought to conquer or, literally, you, conquer by speaking. Words trump force and just laws

CENTVRIA. II. 122

TV VINCE LOQVENDO

EMBLEMA 22.

A donde la razon, y la juſticia
Tienen lugar, y viuen reſpetadas,
No pueden, o la fuerça, o la malicia
Turbar ſus leyes firmes, y aſſentadas:
Mas ſi ſe da lugar a la milicia,
Y que juzguen los pleytos las eſpadas,
No es marauilla, la juſticia tuerça
Donde la ſinrazon, le haze fuerça.

Pre

Figure 2.5 Sebastián de Covarrubias, *Emblemas morales* (Madrid: Sanchez, 1610), at 2: 22 (reproduced courtesy of the Rare Book and Manuscript Library, University of Illinois at Urbana-Champaign)

7 Sebastián de Covarrubias, *Emblemas morales* (Madrid: Sanchez, 1610), 2:22.

belong to the arts, to justice and, in Coustau's metaphor, to love, the *lex amatoria*, rather than simple imposition. Jacob Bruck, a few years later, in a work titled *Emblemata Politica* of 1618, represents arms and laws in an even more explicit subjection of force to letters (Figure 2.6). The sword is capped, its tip rendered harmless, by a book. A divine hand holds the sword and also a quill and a laurel branch. A crown rests on the table and the accompanying text announces that it is by inscription of the truth, through letters that glory is manifested. In the accompanying essay, a proper administration (*rectè*

POLITICA. 29

AD ILLUSTRISSIMUM PRINCIPEM ET DOMINUM, DN. MAURITIUM, Landgravium Hassiæ, Comitem in Catzenelenbogen, Dietz, Zigenhain & Nidda &c.

EMBLEMA VIII.

UTRUMQUE TUETUR.

Cuspide cur gladij Liber hæret fixus acutâ?
Cur calamum & laurum comprimit,(arma) manus.
Vera stilo & pilo Ducibus quòd gloria constet.
Alterum & alterius quòd benè vincat ope.
Laus est magna Ducis, qui gnavus utrumq; tuetur,
His quoniam victor certa tropæa locat.
Præ reliquis Rhetor, Prætor, Consulq; cluebat,
Dux tandem CÆSAR, *Martis & Artis ope.*

E 3 Qui

Figure 2.6 Jacob Bruck, *Emblemata politica* (Cologne: Hogenberg, 1618), at 29 (reproduced courtesy of the Rare Book and Manuscript Library, University of Illinois at Urbana-Champaign)

administrandà) operates by virtue of the assistance, foresight and moderation of letters. Bruck provides an intriguing hierarchy of disciplines, which begins with the Prince moving to expansive interpretation (*latas interpretari*) and then to the analysis of legal controversies, law suits and the prescriptions of justice.[8] It is only where instruction, knowledge of letters, fails that law has to be followed and enforced by military force. The text goes on to praise the virtues of the literary, which, we are told, cultivates the best in the soul and is the source and augmenter of all things – *quae omnia sunt ex fontibus hauriuntur literarum*.[9] The Prince, who brings a fertile wit cultivated by study (*studium*) of the literary monuments of the past, is the best and most admirable of rulers. The general principle gains its most extensive confirmation and exposition in Chasseneuz who begins his 'Fifty Two considerations on the pre-eminence of learning' with the statement that 'learning belongs to the order of honorable goods, and scholars (*literati*) who have knowledge are to be greatly praised (*multum laudandi*) ... there is no good where knowledge is lacking'.[10]

In the spirit of the arts and learning, Bruck's emblem places significantly less importance upon the sword than the book and letters, the *flores quae faciunt coronam*, in the common lawyer's maxim. It is to this end that the troops are figured in the background, in the distance, arranged in a panegyric figure of triumph and in support of the evidently divine moving hand that writes upon the table of the laws. The figure six in the background is interesting, being in the hieroglyphic symbolism of the time the mark of the merely human, the mortal and corporeal as distinct from the spiritual and divine. The troops so figured, albeit triumphantly, are the lesser players, the subjects of providence and of the book. Another example, contemporary with Bruck but this time from a theologian with a strikingly anachronic and arguably somewhat morbid sense of the proper relation between arms and letters, law and literature. The much commented image of death and of the eternal life that it can unleash, *ingenio vivitur*, ably captures the essence of the *mens emblematica* and the paradox of visual depictions of law. Under the rubric of wit living on, Schoonhovius in his *Emblemata* of 1618, again depicts the sovereign but with a radical twist (Figure 2.7).[11] *Maiestas* and, specifically, the arms and force of corporeal subjection and worldly authority, has here turned to bare bones, a skeletal frame from whose right hand a crown drops to earth and sceptres and coronets, discarded, lie upon

8 Jacob Bruck, *Emblemata politica* (Cologne: Hogenberg, 1618), 30.
9 Bruck, *Emblemata*, 31.
10 Chasseneuz, *Catologus gloriæ mundi*, 183 col.1–2.
11 Florentius Schoonhovius, *Emblemata partim Moralia partim etiam Civilia* (Gouda: Burier, 1618), 89.

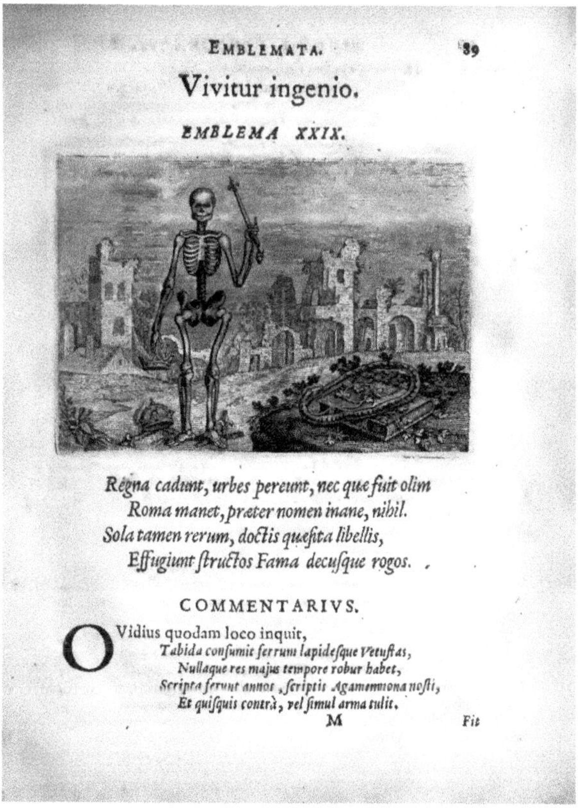
EMBLEMATA. 89

Vivitur ingenio.

EMBLEMA XXIX.

Regna cadunt, urbes pereunt, nec quæ fuit olim
Roma manet, præter nomen inane, nihil.
Sola tamen rerum, doctis quæſita libellis,
Effugiunt ſtructos Fama decuſque rogos.

COMMENTARIVS.

OVidius quodam loco inquit,
Tabida conſumit ferrum lapideſque Vetuſtas,
Nullaque res majus tempore robur habet,
Scripta ferunt annos, ſcriptis Agamemnona noſti,
Et quiſquis contrà, vel ſimul arma tulit.

M Fit

Figure 2.7 Florentius Schoonhovius, *Emblemata partim Moralia partim etiam Civilia* (Gouda: Burier, 1618), at 89 (reproduced courtesy of the Rare Book and Manuscript Library, University of Illinois at Urbana-Champaign)

the ground. In the skeleton's left hand a sceptre is ironically raised on high above a large closed tome, itself covered by a snake biting its tail and so forming a ring, *annulum*, the sign of eternity. Laurels, also the sign of immortality, here through the victory of letters, lie on the book. It should be noted as well that the snake is also a symbol of affect and desire, meaning that in letters true desire is expressed and triumphs eternally. The motto is to this effect, and reads literally 'as nature survives' but usually means that genius, wit, letters and arts live on while the mortal body dies. *Litera non moritur*, to coin a phrase, but I want to take the image a little further.

Schoonhovius, in his essay on the emblem, begins by pointing out, obviously enough, that worldly glories, high titles, feats of arms, crowns and sceptres, even the mortar and stone of cities, crumble and turn in time to dust. It is only the taught learning, the doctrine deposited in books – *doctis quaesita libellis* – that lives eternally. In the later discussion, Schoonhovius invokes the great books of antiquity, the erudition that has come down from the ancients to the moderns. The poets are the immortals and books are the form of their living on; their tombs are their tomes. That, however, is far from all. The message of the eternity of the poetic and inscribed takes the peculiar form of an image of desire. The book sits upon a leafy pedestal, covered by a snake, a symbol of lust and eternity, desire and immortality. The circle made by the serpent biting its tail, in fact suggests a controlled desire for eternity, a lawful lust, while the laurel leaves placed on the book indicate a further rhetorical power, being figures of the sovereignty of nature and the inexorability of time. Erudition does not live in the tomb but in the tome. More than that, it lives on in images, in the visibility of the poetic, in words and laws viewed as signs. These take precedence over temporality, and it is, as Schoonhovius endeavours to explain in his commentary, the image as marker of memory, as visible monument, as immemorial sign that we inherit from the great libraries and authors of the past – *auctoritas, non veritas facit legem* takes on a very different meaning because it is the image, the visibility of the non-present that screens and guards the authority that subtends and legitimates rule.

The book, finally, is closed, its metal clasps firmly shut. It is here figured as pure *potential*; it is all possibility and portent of the afterlife that even the skeletal sovereign evidently inhabits once the kingdom has fallen, the city is ruined and relics, books and the abstract scripture of the *corpus juris* are all that remain. The image, which fills in for what is no longer there, the image, which is shadow and has no substance or being in itself, stands in for the book in two senses. First, this scripture, this monumental book is itself an image. It is an emblem in a collection of emblems, an image of a book in a book of images. The book is in this sense the *mise en abyme* of books, meaning that it represents the longevity and significance of books in terms of their endless duplication, their insertion as images in the scopic domain of images. They belong to the visiocratic regime of governance and effectuate the visual disposition of subjects, the ordering and placement of *œconomic* roles and rules. Secondly, and precisely as an insertion, as an emblem which grafts an image into a vase, a garment, a text, the depiction is the medium through which the book inscribes itself into the eternal. The book, in short, is the book of emblems, the book of images that insert themselves into the eternal and so mark the transition between the temporal and the infinite, the existential and the evanescent. The image, in the end, will lead the subject, the soul, into the kingdom of souls, the angelological dominion of the spirit whose only manifestation is in images. Here, the image is markedly more powerful than the word and, indeed, it is only when the word becomes figure and image that it takes on its true transformational and transitory role as conveyance of the spirit toward things unseen.

A final example, an optical crescendo from the Dutch legal emblematist Rollenhagen, is in the form of the depiction of the sovereign astride the globe as governor and reformer of the entire world.[12] And here, originally published in 1611, the book is now in his right hand and the sceptre in his left (Figure 2.8). I use an English version of this image as most pertinent to

Figure 2.8 George Wither, *A Collection of Emblemes Ancient and Moderne* (London: Allot, 1635), at 31 (reproduced courtesy of Peter Goodrich)

12 George Wither, *A Collection of Emblemes Ancient and Moderne* (London: Allot, 1635), 31

my theme, *scilicet*, the emblematic representations of justice at common law. The motto reads as 'wisdom dominates the stars'. For the purposes of interpreting emblems of justice and law, of eyes and blindfolds, the above legal humanist trajectory towards the emblematic, towards the *ars iuris* and the depiction of norm and governance in pictorial and vanishing form, emphasizes an increasingly scopic conception of rule and specifically of law. In the image of wisdom dominating the stars, the sagacity of the sovereign gains direct expression in the book held open, in the right hand of the sovereign, immediately under the heavens. The celestial light rains down upon it and the book of wisdom, which as sovereign speech is the highest law, fills up with knowledge divine and human, the very definition of law according to the opening of Justinian's *Institutes*. Illumination comes directly to the sovereign who, in anticipation of Leviathan, is here presented as standing *super terram*, as the greatest body and visibly the supreme power. Note also the varied sources, the triune expressions of illumination in the image. There are the heavenly bodies, stars and moon, which shower light upon the sovereign and more distantly, just out of their reach, upon the sages. If we recollect Chasseneuz's earlier depiction of the disciplines, the direct expression of wisdom, figured in the top right-hand corner, dexter chief, of the image, is *ideologia* or what we would term doctrine, dogma itself. Far below, bottom left in the hierarchy of disciplines, is *astronomia*, the figure of the astronomer as secondary and remote interpreter of the stars, lacking in wisdom and tending to the impious and occult. Then, finally, there is the sun, the heliotropic source of all light, the figure of the divinity itself, as *lux lucis*, light in our darkness, the dispeller of shadows, the illuminator of the lucifugous path of humanity.

Next, and this is the third and last source of light in the image, there is the eye in the chest of the sovereign, the figure of the *illuminatus*, the knower, the seer, *oculata fides* or more literally *pectus oculata*. The sovereign is vividly and visibly among the stars, part of the firmament. At the same time, however, the most striking feature of the image is the final source of emanation of light, the movement of the eye from the heavens to the human, from the divine to the sovereign. The eye of law, as the historian Michael Stolleis has so admirably detailed, experiences a somewhat similar trajectory to the emblem of arms and laws, which is to say a shift from limitation to expansion, from particular to universal. Where the emblem of arms and laws places the universality of the image and the angelological path of knowledge that it opens up inside the symbolic depiction of the book, the eye too places the image at the heart of law and in the now omnivoyant spiritual surveillance of the sovereign: 'the eye of God migrated to the prince as the secular governor of God. His 'omniscience', as fictitious as it may be, became the crucial basis of legitimation of the just content of laws'.[13] The surveillant, all-seeing prince alone could take account of the *universalia* or simple immensity, the expanse and diversity of things, and so rule justly. As the Roman lawyers put it: *Omnia sunt posita ante oculos*, judgment requires that everything be put before the eyes of the judge.[14] Later commentators make the same point in relation to this emblem by reference to 'the best kings are those who neglect nothing by virtue of seeing and attending to all things'.[15] In the place of the sword, finally, we encounter the open pages of the book – *semper apertus*, as the motto goes.

Dissimulations of the visual

The prominence of the eye is first a further indication of the importance of the visual, of the *ius imaginum*, the symbolic law of precedence and persons.[16] This imagistic law connotes a vision of a genealogical kind, in which the images are depictions of virtues, markers of an inherited and so distant nobility, the power of the ancestors and of lineage as expressed in the dignity of the contemporary bearer of the name in its variable depictions. The eye placed in the figure of the sovereign's breast thus marks the lineage of sovereignty and the spectral source of their authority. Where it is a question of *maiestas*, of the mystery of government, the progenitor and parent of the sovereign is directly the divinity. The pectoral eye seems at one level, as Stolleis suggests, to place God, depicted as vision, in the heart of the prince and so not only is the divinity visible but also incorporated and made manifest in the temporal bearer, the vicarious living law or, to borrow from Bruck again, the sovereign is and is called the living law – *qui aliàs lex viva est et appellatur.*[17] This embodiment of the divine, *in imitatio imperii*, as the vicarious of the divine father, is more than anything else a lucent and illuminating apotheosis of the visible, of omnivoyance and most particularly, implicit in such a concept, the ability and faculty of seeing what is not there.

13 Michael Stolleis, *The Eye of the Law* (Abingdon: Birkbeck Law, 2004), 36.

14 Edward Whitehouse, Fortescutus Illustratus, *or a Commentary on that Nervous Treatise De Laudibus Legum Angliae* (London: Dicus, 1663); Nicolas Causin, *De symbolica Aegyptiorum* (Cologne: Kinckium, 1623).

15 Julius Wilhelm Zincgref, *Emblematum ethico politicorum centuria* (Heidelburg 1665), 87.

16 Pierre Legendre indeed suggests that *ius personarum*, the first classification of the juridical triunity of persons, things and actions, could properly be translated as law of masks or of images: 'In all institutional systems, the politics of the subject passes through masks. My translation contributes thus to rehabilitating, at the heart of the legal order, the problematic of the image' (*Le Désir politique de Dieu*, Paris: Fayard, 1988), 225–6.

17 Bruck, *Emblemata*, 30.

There is a scopic imperative to knowledge and law but, and this is the second crucial feature of the emblem, the eye has moved from exterior to interior, from the firmament to the body, from the heavens to the breast of the sovereign. It is a shift from outside to inside, from exterior and merely physical eye to *oculi animi*, the spiritual eyes of the soul, and it correlatively also suggests a subtle shift in the jurisdiction and power of vision. The prior and exterior eye surveyed and ruled a vast but visible external world, the realm of nature seen and in principle extant and real. The interior eye, however, also views the inner realm and so the placement of the eye in the chest of the sovereign also indicates a second realm and inner vision rather than, as in other emblems, where eyes proliferate on the garments of the sovereign, on rods of office, in triangular specters, and simply depict additional lenses upon the administration of the polity. The pectoral eye signals a new 'pretended' (meaning precedent) jurisdiction, the power of the invisible upon which the extant depends and of which only the sovereign has knowledge and view. The referent, emblematically, is to the Aegyptian, to the dark contexture of the hieroglyphic depiction that we find most authoritatively in the early emblem book of hieroglyphs, translating Horapollo into French and into images (Figure 2.9).

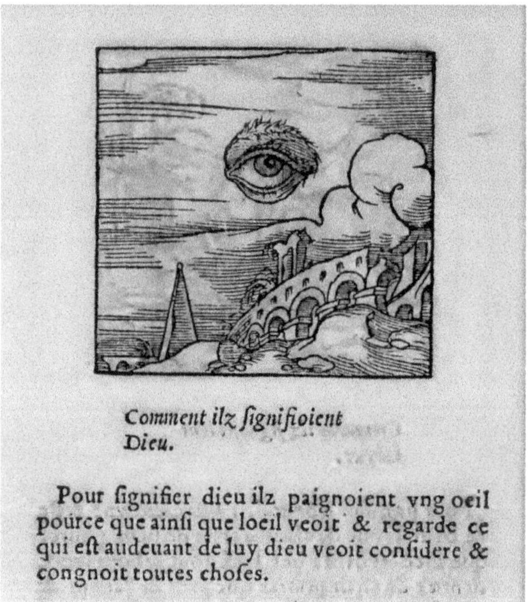

Comment ilz ſignifioient Dieu.

Pour ſignifier dieu ilz paignoient vng oeil pource que ainſi que loeil veoit & regarde ce qui eſt audeuant de luy dieu veoit conſidere & congnoit toutes choſes.

Figure 2.9 Orus Apollo de Ægypte, *De la signification des notes hieroglyphiques des Ægyptiens* (Paris: Kerver, 1543) (reproduced courtesy of Getty Images)

Orus Apollo (Horapollo) depicts the divinity as a solitary eye, a strangely hirsute, almost feathered, floating speculator, an ocular image of a divinity looking down from above, from the heavens, from beyond death, upon his pastoral realm of merely mortal things. The obelisk, bridges, arches, columns and dome signify the monuments of human endeavour, subject as they are to time and erasure. Such things do not pass through the clouds to eternity. At the same time, the explanatory text notes that the mortal eye simply sees what is in front of it, but the divinity sees and knows all things because, to borrow another emblematic motto, the eye of justice sees all things – *oculus Justitiæ qui Omnia videt.* Obvious though it may on reflection seem, the pectoral eye cannot be taken at face value; it not only sees more than can be shown but it also marks what cannot be seen, the realm of the invisible that can only be known through faith or through divine apprehension of the umbrageous and invisible. The lawyer Aneau in *Picta poesis* of 1552, nine years later, takes up this theme again in a more juristic mode (Figure 2.10).[18]

POESIS. 81

PRINCEPS IVSTITIAE ADVIGILANS.

SCEPTRVM *oculo ſuperimpoſito geſtabat Oſiris*
Rex Pharius: quo non iuſtior alter erat.
Sceptrum iuſtitiæ eſt index, oculus nota ſacra
Mentis, quæ nunquam non agit, & vigilat.
REGIBVS *exemplū præbens (quod munus eorū eſt)*
Iuſtitiam vt vigili diſtribuant animo.

F

Figure 2.10 Barthélemy Aneau, *Picta poesis* (Lyons: Bonhomme, 1552), at 81 (reproduced courtesy of University of Glasgow Special Collections)

18 Barthélemy Aneau, *Picta poesis* (Lyons: Bonhomme, 1552), 81.

The image here is again expressly stated to be Egyptian in origin, deriving from Osiris, and the motto, *princeps iustitiæ advigilans*, urges the prince to be vigilant of justice. The sceptre is the sign of justice, the mark of the royal office of supreme judge, while the eye signifies a spirit that sees and surveys all. The eye in this context is a sacred sign – *oculus nota sacra* – and indicates that justice is a spiritual enterprise, a work of the soul, a vicarious exercise of a divine vision.

What is evident from the emblems of the eye is that everything is at stake in these more esoteric marks of rule. The floating eye, the omnivoyant scopic signal of divinity and law marks the visible as that which the eye of the divinity can be see through and beyond, all the way to its essence, its non-being. As an aside, returning to Orus Apollo, it is interesting to note a further image of eyes, but this time of false gods.[19] The infernal deities are depicted as a mask without eyes, a blind injustice, a deceptive appearance, while the divine or supernatural character of deities of the underworld is signaled by the eyes that hover above them. The eyeless mask deserves attention. The underworld, the realm of the dead, is without light. In the tenebrous space of the nether world, reigning over darkness, the eyeless face marks the impossibility of seeing through the impenetrable opacity of the shadow world. The face is a mask because the face cannot be encountered and can neither see nor be seen. Torches, lights, the sun are, as another emblematic motto puts it, useless to the blind. Everything is dark to those who cannot see – *res omnes caecis sunt tenebrae.*[20]

In contradistinction to the eyeless mask, the false face of the infernal, the divinity is monocular and resident far above. A political woodcut from 1641 can make the point (Figure 2.11). In some variants, the image bears the motto *video rideo*, I see and I laugh, and its referent is the attack upon the Houses of Parliament in 1605 by the Catholic Guy Fawkes. The gargantuan eye of the divinity stares down from the clouds, its line of sight a spear of light that penetrates the darkness and displays the kegs of gunpowder and fagots that are piled up at the front steps of the building. Most intriguingly, Fawkes is portrayed as a shadow figure, a dark satanic form with the head of a wolf, the mark of the outlaw, of the friendless, and replete with a tail and claws. The devil, as a shadowy form, is slipping along the wall of the building like a hologram, passing unnoticed but for the incursion of light that throws the shadowy form into relief upon the wall and so renders it visible, *in*

19 Orus Apollo de Ægypte, *De la signification des notes hieroglyphiques des Ægyptiens* (Paris: Kerver, 1543).

20 Georgette de Montenay, *Emblematum Christianorum centuria* (Zurich: Froschover, 1584), f36r.

Figure 2.11 Francis Herring, *Mischeefes Mysterie: Or, Treasons Master-Peece, the Powder-Plot* (London: Hartford, 1641) (reproduced courtesy of the British Library)

flagrante delicto and equally *in flagrante depicto*. It is the scopic regime of divine power that is imitated in the detection of the culprit as also in the omnivoyant floating eye in the clouds.

The reverse of this aggrandizement and privileging of vision is the anathema of blindness, of darkness, of shadows and their folds. The inability to see renders everything indistinct and corruptible. Thus, to belabour the obvious yet less often acknowledged, the light upon which knowledge, power, signs and laws all depend is the medium of vision and of dogma alike. This, as the triangulation of the divine eye, policing light and satanic shadow indicate, is not a simple opposition. The evident and immediate message can be iterated through further emblems of blindness as error and as enigma (Figures 2.12 and 2.13). The figure of error, blindfold, is from Ripa and

Figure 2.12 Cesar Ripa, *Iconologie* (Paris: Jacques de Bie, 1643) (reproduced courtesy of Peter Goodrich)

Figure 2.13 Cristóbal Pérez, *Proverbios morales y consejos cristianos* (Madrid: del Hierro, [1618] 1773) (courtesy of the Online Internet Archive)

shows a pilgrim tapping his path with a stick, unable to see but nonetheless attempting to follow the path to salvation. The blindfold signifies falling into error by virtue of the lures of sight and the distractions of worldly things and the diverse and immediate pleasures of the flesh. Unable to see, protected against the errors of sight, it is the spirit, the sign of things invisible, faith that must mark the path to righteousness, truth and law. The figure of enigma, blindfold and feet chained is a similar, humanistic emblem of the paradoxical disability of blindness that, through time, patience, wit and perseverance, leads beyond the physical and visible to the unseen and superior truth. The blindfold, we can hazard, has an immediate signification of blindness, debility and absence of both sight and law for its human bearers but that is simply its liminal mark, its portrayal of a boundary in the hierarchy of knowing. The human may be blind and sinful but the band also signifies the obverse, the figure of *Justitia* herself, manifest in the heavens, as an all-seeing depiction of a divinity whose gaze penetrates all, including the blindfold. At the same time then, as the figure of *ingenio*, of wit, pursuing the blindfolded figure of enigma suggests, there is more to the blindfold than simple lack of sight. The figure of faith in a somewhat later emblem of Iglesia's indeed suggests this principle in the insistence that fidelity, like love and justice, be blindfold and unseeing. The emblem depicts a disabled female figure of faith who is led by the miraculous right hand of God emergent from the clouds, towards the beyond, which is to say initiated into the realm invisible, the afterlife of Christian mythology.

Seeing law

In each of the last three emblems, it is apparent that the blindfold symbolizes much more than blindness and, be it error, enigma or things unseen, the bandage, the missing eyes are markers of potential passage and transition. The blindfold signals a boundary, a border on the path to a greater knowledge and truth resident beyond the realm of things corporeal, merely visible and simply extant. A reformist image of justice from 1569, from a work by Stephen Bateman, can identify the crux of the issue. Here, justice is seated in the center of the emblem, on her pedestal and throne, sword and scales in her hands. To her right is a lawyer with a flayed human skin and skull falling from his lectern while the parties approach from the front (Figure 2.14). The most striking feature of the image, however, is that while *Justitia*'s two eye sockets are empty, she has a third eye in the centre of her forehead. The sighted forehead is only apparently paradoxical in indicating the vision of the blind, a sightedness in the face of one who, according to the Theban convention, should not see. The apparent blindness of the judge

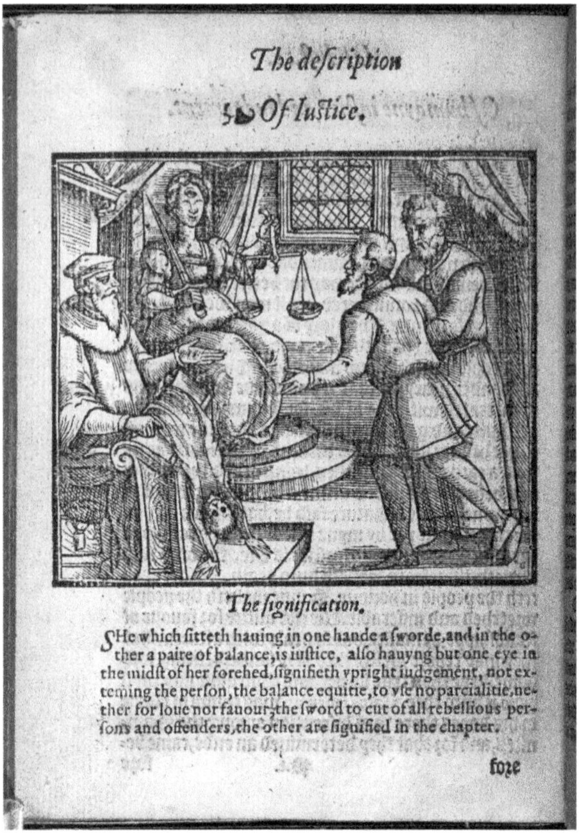
The deſcription
Of Iuſtice.

The ſignification.

SHe which ſitteth hauing in one hande a ſworde, and in the other a paire of balance, is iuſtice, alſo hauyng but one eye in the midſt of her forehed, ſignifieth vpright iudgement, not exteming the perſon, the balance equitie, to vſe no parcialitie, nether for loue nor fauour, the ſword to cut of all rebellious perſons and offenders, the other are ſignified in the chapter.

fore

Figure 2.14 Stephen Bateman, *A Christall Glasse of the Christian Reformation* (London: John Day, 1569) (courtesy of the British Library)

here indeed signals a refusal to account for the status or personage of those that 'appear' before her. But it already signals rather more: what is visible is not what matters. The material and actual rapidly fade, and in the finely evocative words of Bateman, the judge should know no faces in judgment for 'what is your lyfe, it is even a vapour that appeareth for a little tyme, and then vanisheth away'.[21]

The 'third' eye in the forehead, which is in this depiction the only eye, is clearly the marker of a greater vision, and in this regard symbolizes a divine law, a higher norm and surveillance that was earlier depicted in terms of all

21 Bateman, *A Christall Glasse of Christian Reformation* (London: John Day, 1569), p4r.

seeing sovereignty and in the jurisprudence of the time the interior jurisdiction of the monarch as nursing father, and common law as a nursing mother.[22] The *oculi animi* looked upon the *specula pastoralis*, the souls of the subjects, their ethical being, their place on the map of salvation. The band marks separation and is, in effect, here the visible representation of the avoidance of images, the prohibition of idols and suchlike Reformist dogma. The blindness signified by the blindfold thus has to be apprehended in terms of the lure and danger of eyes and, more specifically, the eye that is missing, which marks the propriety of faith in the observant but not observing. Here, the depiction initially shows the prohibition on vision and the displacement of the scopic regime into an alternate world. The two human eyes are missing, blinded, obscured but justice also has a face with an eye which the woodcut places in the centre of the forehead as a figure of another order and alternate scopic regime. Two images of the surveillant eye from the gallery of the frontispiece emblems of legal texts can make the point (Figures 2.15 and 2.16).

Figure 2.15 Don Juan de Borja, *Empresas morales* (Brusselas: Foppens, 1680) (courtesy of the Rare Book and Manuscript Library of the University of Illinois at Urbana-Champaign)

22 Roger Coke, *Justice Vindicated from the False Fucus put upon it by Thomas White Gent, Mr Thomas Hobbes and Hugo Grotius* (London: Newcomb, 1660); the source is, of course, the Psalms.

Figure 2.16 Pagenstecher, *Aphorismi juris* (Harderovici: Brinkink, 1648) (reproduced courtesy of Peter Goodrich)

Bateman's image of *Justitia*'s solitary third eye, the *frons oculata*, suggests a complicated political theology of blindness and insight, of error and enigma, as also of governance and faith. The question that jurists and theologians contemporary with Bateman were asking was precisely that of the relation between the visible and the more than visible, the unseen that exceeds and subtends the terrestrial view and mortal eyes. For the Anglican theologian Perkins, whose views were central to the Reformation debates in England, the visible was to be at all times distrusted. Images were admissible for limited political ceremonies and observances but the great architecture of faith and the promise of salvation belonged to a spiritual sphere that defied perception and depended rather upon the blindfolded vision of faith. His definition of the primary substrate of belief is educational: '*faith*, is a perswasion, whereby we beleeve things that are not'.[23] The definition is a common one and is interesting for its inversion of the relation between the extant and the non-existence whereby ontology properly belongs to that which is not. The temporal is, as James Calfhill, another Anglican divine of the era puts it, the 'spectacle of things invisible', again an inversion of the relation between the extant and visible world of custom, use and law, and the metaphysical realm of the providential and determinatively unseen.[24]

The jurisprudence of the period picks up on this theme and, from Fortescue onward, we find a strong subordination of the merely extant and visible to the unseen sources, the antique roots of common law dogma. Custom and use evaporate, like life itself in this view, into their divine and unseen sources. Where Fortescue writes in his dialogue of the mysteries that underlie the maxims and other rules of common law, the most ancient of all laws, it is his commentator Whitehouse who picks up the theme and predicates common law explicitly upon the *ultra quod non*, the point beyond which mortals can neither see nor go: 'Let then Principles remain Mysteries, not to be dived into, but adored, because of their coparceny with Divinity … And as no man can define light, as it is in its principle, because it is like God indescribable, being a Ray of his essential glory: so can no wise man properly and wisely determine principles by any common notion, or rational apprehension of them'.[25] Governance, the administration of things, what Agamben recuperates as the theology of *œconomy* is one thing, a practical matter, a question of things being done, and it is quite distinct from the crescendo of optical metaphors, the figuration of sovereignty and rule in terms of a blinding light, the sight of what cannot be seen.[26] Thus, just to round out the jurisprudential trajectory, Whitehouse goes on to define knowledge as the 'Image of God', and faith the means to knowing him and his laws: 'As it is the evidence of things not seen, and the substance of things hoped for'. He continues to define the theology that structures law in the following term: 'Then we know and understand what faith is, when we live not by sense, not by the impulses of putid reason, but as seeing him that is invisible … who calls us in our desires and delights from this world …'.[27]

23 William Perkins, *A Discourse of Conscience* (Cambridge: Legate, 1608), 6.

24 Jacques De Ville, 'Mythology and the Images of Justice' 23 *Law and Literature* 324 (2011).

25 Whitehouse, *Fortescutus illustratus*, 122.

26 Giorgio Agamben, *The Kingdom and the Glory. For a Theological Genealogy of Economy and Government* (Palo Alto, CA: Stanford University Press).

27 Whitehouse, *Fortescutus*, 126

The political theology of legal sources, of evidence of origin of maxim and rule is distinctively paradoxical and strikingly eschatological. It is not immediately apparent that it is a plausible explanation of tellurian legal judgment, especially granted that invisible causes, by definition, cannot and should not be apprehended by the uninitiated. The dogmas of the law are a vanishing point that cannot operate as anything other than a legitimizing substrate of mundane municipal administration and regulation. Law has to be able to see, it needs to be sovereign, omnivoyant and determinedly present in signs, texts and institutions. Law is *officium*, and its spectacular office is precisely one of surveillance and oversight, as well indicated in the frontispiece image of Borja's 1680 *Empresas Morales*.[28] The symbol of legal office rests on the antique (and somewhat worn) tables of the law and overlooks the ruins that the female justices are seated either lazily or precariously upon. The two approaching figures from the right of the frontispiece bear a bridle – an equine 'bit' – precisely to restrain desire and so to indicate that law, Christian morality, must supercede and oversee the machinations of a ruined and potentially ruinous justice, the non-positive rule of desire.

Law cannot hide and it cannot be blind, whereas it is *Justitia* who is lucifugous, a matter of being bound ineluctably to illation and not vision, blind in the strongest sense, that of opening her eyes to faith. Law sees and surveys, the eye of the sovereign legislator looks down from the tables of the law in Borja's depiction and from the chest of Justinian in Pagenstecher's splendidly bibliophilic and baroque frontispiece to *Aphorismi juris*. Take it apart. The eye of the law is in the breast of the clearly sighted sovereign. He holds an orb in his right hand upon which an angel dances, raising a halo towards Justinian's head, the circular mark of eternity and of the angelological governance of the world. In the angels left hand, a quill, the mark of what is writ, and being writ, as the Psalmist has it, 'nor all your piety nor wit / shall lure it back to cancel half a Line, / Nor all your Tears wash out a Word of it'. The image of the emperor floats at the top of the tableau in the form of a medallion appearing as a theatrical emblem, a *pegma*, replete with proscenium arch and stage curtain. The emperor, the holy father, the source of all law, makes the various images that appear below, possible. And below is a heavily scriptural scene of law, a juridical theology acted out in pictorial form. Dogma is mirrored here in image, with the sovereign father of law, all powerful, all knowing, all seeing, embodying in idealized Christian form the myth of the roman tradition of the founding of laws. The dogma of the origin of law gains plastic expression and the imaginary takes form for all to see. As the emblematists fondly put it, pictures 'make words deeds' and, in the

28 Don Juan de Borja, *Empresas morales* (Brussels: Foppens, 1680).

formulation of P. Tempest, the translator and editor of the 1709 edition of *Iconologia*, these 'Images are the Representations of our Notions; they properly belong to Painters, who by Colours and Shadowing, have invented the admirable Secret to give Body to our Thoughts, thereby to render them visible'.[29]

Below the angelic father floating in his circular medallion, eternal, unbroken, married to God and to the infinite, is the feminine principle of *Justitia* and of the mother Church. The pectoral eye is joined to the image of a blind *Justitia,* seated on a throne, the image of the Ten Commandments, writ in stone, and possibly also connotative of the *leges duodecim tabularum*, the Twelve Tables, behind her, and then in the background, visible through the arch, is a monumental bookcase of massive tomes of the law. *Justitia* herself has her eyes closed, a scale and sceptre in her left hand, a sword in her right. *Justitia* sits below low, she is feminine and blind, sedentary and below in comparison to the masculinity, eternity, vision and floating superiority of law. She is visibly secondary, less, and, while she is not blindfolded, note that the right portion of her lower body is in fact obscured from view by a partial screen made from a portion of the theatrical curtain that she holds in her right hand. The theatrical screen is a common emblematic sign of demarcation between finite and infinite, tellurian and celestial, the figured and the veiled. Here the partial veiling of *Justitia*, as also her correlative blindness – no eyes are visible – establishes her intermediary position as relay and transmitter, the hermeneut and messenger of a divine law that is only knowable through faith. She does not see because she is not the law but rather she is the faith through which law, slowly, enigmatically, through writ, becomes manifest and rendered in judgment.

Justitia's right index finger points toward the legal scribe seated in front of her. She, too, in other words, gives, which is to say passes on the law through the screen, across the divide between human and divine, unwritten and written. For where the divinity writes, it writes in images and such law is apprehensible only in emblems. What is inscribed in texts, as doctrine, is later and less, a shadow of the source, a relic of the law, *litera mortua*, a tomb, a tome, which only the sovereign and its delegates, only *maiestas* itself or through its delegates can bring to life. In either event, the image, the pictorial depiction is the most immediate presence of the juridical in its sovereign and most secretive moment. It is the front and the frontispiece, the face of a justice without face, a justice that is a medium and mediator between law

29 Respectively, Thomas Combe, *Theatre of Fine Devices* (London: Field, 1614 edn): 'To the Reader'; and Caesar Ripa, *Iconologia or Moral Emblems* (London: Motte, 1709): 'To the Reader'.

and application, between and inscription. There are several features of the role as mediator that deserve emphasis in terms both of the juridical theology of law and in terms of the historical shift from the early emblems of Theban *Justitia*, enigmatically and hieroglyphically blind, to the later more civilian and domesticated *Justitia* in the latter portions of the seventeenth century.

First, the domestication of *Justitia* and the Romanization of the blindfolded figure. She cannot see, and this is perhaps most evident in Bateman's depiction because another and greater force sees for her and in her stead. *Justitia* has therefore no vision of her own but, rather, like *fortuna* and like Wither's sovereign, she embodies and transfers the dogmas of another and greater power. She is dwarfed by the heavenly eye and blinding light of a superordinate law. Secondly, and relatedly, *Justitia* is grounded, subordinate and subservient to the greater cause and law. She is not winged, she is not sighted, she is not even ambulant. Rather, her marginalization in relation to law, to the greater symbol of celestial glory the sovereignty that founds juridical theology is ever more marked. Justice comes to play the role of the merely *œconomic* and administrative and, if I dare so hypothesize, there is a certain satirical irony to this. Justice, sightless and in the world, is increasingly the figure of the distance that separates the sovereign from its subjects, *super terram* from tellurian, law from the gubernative process. In this sense, *Justitia* becomes more a symbol of injustice, a figure of administrative practices, a frame and ornamentation that screens and so legitimates a governance that exists and reproduces itself without reason, pretext or consideration beyond that of the choral benediction of a sovereignty and law that the subject cannot see.

Returning to the earlier image from Schoonhovius, *vivitur ingenio*, symbolizing the Christianization of the hieroglyphic, the image of death defeated by the humanistic genius of the book of the laws is mirrored in the transition to a disabled justice directly in thrall to a higher law. The message is not simply that law comes from above, sovereign, supreme, unquestionable and irrefragable but, equally, that we can only know them indirectly, through the mediation of a blind justice, through faith. The consequence is that visible governance, administrative practice, tellurian laws and the *ius terrae*, do not matter. The visible does not matter. The law and the truth are elsewhere in the persuasion of what is not, in the evidence of things unseen, in the image of the Emperor, in the closed book of *vivitur ingenio* and in the sorry non-substance of things merely hoped for.

CHAPTER 3

Metamorphosis, mythography and the nature of English law

Paul Raffield

Introduction

I begin with a tale of transformation. It is a story of violent death and magical rebirth. I begin with the creation of Pegasus. Not the tale of the flying horse's emergence from the blood of the slain Gorgon Medusa, as adapted by Ovid and related in Book IV of *Metamorphoses* but a lesser-known, though equally fantastical, tale of a different Pegasus, as told by the Master of His Majesty's Revels, Sir George Buck, in a work entitled *The Third Universitie of England*. In his brief treatise on the numerous academic institutions housed in London in the early seventeenth century, Buck narrated the story of the transformation of the original seal of the Knights Templar (two knights of that Order, sitting astride the same warhorse) into the heraldic device adopted in the sixteenth century by the Honourable Society of the Inner Temple. That device was the mythical flying horse, Pegasus (Figure 3.1). Common to the stories told by Ovid and Buck is the theme of distinction between self, or subject, and image, or object. In the version told by Ovid, it is the image of Medusa reflected in the bronze of Perseus' shield (rather than her actual self), that the son of Zeus saw, prior to decapitating the Gorgon. In the version told by Buck, the crucial distinction is between the actual origins of the Inner Temple in a religious order of medieval knights and the image of its provenance in the immemorial and heroic mythography of the ancient world.

In the first line of the Prologue to his epic poem *Metamorphoses*, Ovid explained that his purpose was: 'to tell of bodies which have been transformed into shapes of a different kind';[1] and through these astonishing tales of transformation, the reader witnesses the intellect acting upon the natural world to create an image of nature itself. In similar fashion, but in a juridical as well as a literary context, the lawyers of early modern England perceived

1 Ovid, *Metamorphoses*, trans. Mary M. Innes (Harmondsworth: Penguin, 1955), 29 Bk.1.1.

Figure 3.1 Pegasus, emblem of the Honourable Society of the Inner Temple (courtesy of Paul Raffield)

themselves to be applying their intellects and their technical knowledge to natural law, that they might create in the common law an image of nature itself. Hence, Sir Edward Coke would declare that 'causes which concern the life, or inheritance, or goods, or fortunes of his [the King's] subjects, are not to be decided by natural reason, but by the artificial reason and judgment of law'.[2] My purpose in this essay is to explore the capacity of a particular artefact – the heraldic, legal emblem of the Elizabethan and Jacobean eras – to signify the transformation of the subjective human form into the objective subject of English law, thereby illustrating the indivisible relationship between citizen and legal institution. Throughout, I make especial reference both to the derivation of the emblem from the narratives of classical mythography and to its idiosyncratic fusion with the imagery of Judaeo-Christian theology. I investigate the correlation between the imagined natural world (*ordo naturae* or the order of nature) and a jurisprudence

2 *Prohibitions del Roy* in Part 12 (1658) of *The Reports of Sir Edward Coke, Knt In English*, ed. George Wilson, 7 vols. (London: Rivington, 1777), 7: 64a, 65a.

whose apologists asserted the primacy of *lex naturae*, *lex terrae*, and *leges non scriptae* or unwritten law, and the superiority of these to all forms of statute and royal proclamation. In the words of the poet, jurist, and eminent lawyer Sir John Davies: 'the *lawe of nature*, which the schoolmen call *Ius commune*, and which is also *Ius non Scriptum*, being written only in the hart, is better than all the written lawes in the worlde'.[3]

I The emblazonment of common law

Written in 1612, and published in 1615 as an appendix to a new edition of *The Annales, or Generall Chronicle of England* by John Stow (first published in 1592), *The Third Universitie of England* does not refer exclusively to the four Inns of Court. Rather, as the alternative title of Buck's short book explains, it is *A Treatise of the Foundations of All the Colledges, Auncient Schooles of Priviledge, and of Houses of Learning, and Liberall Arts, Within and About the Most Famous Cittie of London*. Apart from the various academies of the common law (the four Inns of Court, eight Inns of Chancery,[4] two Inns of Sergeants-at-Law and two Inns for the officers of the Court of Chancery, known as 'the sixe Clearks Inne, or Kedermisters Inne' and 'Bacons Inne, or Corsiters [Coristers] Inne'), the Third University counted among its conglomerate: numerous Schools of Theology; the College of Physicians; 'the Colledge of Civilians, called Doctors Commons' (home to 'The Professors of the civill, or imperiall lawes');[5] and other, smaller educational establishments at which a diverse range of disciplines might be studied (including 'Cosmographie'; 'Calligraphie'; 'the art of Horsemanship'; 'the Art gladiatorie'; and 'the Art of Dancing'). The identity of the dedicatee of *The Third Universitie* is, however, indicative of the privileged position that Buck accords the colleges and hostels of the common law over the other educational establishments cited in the treatise.[6] The book is dedicated to

3 Sir John Davies, *Le primer report des cases & matters en ley resolves and adiudges en les courts del Roy en Ireland* (Dublin: Iohn Franckton, 1615), sig. *2r.

4 On the Inns of Chancery of this period, see Paul Raffield, *Shakespeare's Imaginary Constitution: Late Elizabethan Politics and the Theatre of Law* (Oxford: Hart Publishing, 2010), 166–8. More generally, on the early modern Inns of Court, see Paul Raffield, *Images and Cultures of Law in Early Modern England. Justice and Political Power, 1558–1660* (Cambridge: Cambridge University Press, 2004).

5 Sir George Buck, *The Third Universitie of England* in John Stow, *The Annales. Or Generall Chronicle of England* (London: Thomas Adams, 1615), 958–88, 978.

6 Buck explains that 'Hostels' is the name given to 'the houses of the French Noblemenne in Paris … which commeth from the Lattin worde *Hospitium* (and is the same, which Inne is in English)', *ibid.*, 968.

Sir Edward Coke, who (at the time Buck wrote the dedication, in August 1612) was Chief Justice of the Common Pleas. Buck admits to Coke that 'the greatest part of this Booke is bestowed in the description of the Colledges, and collegiate houses founded in this Cittie, for the professors of the Municipall, or common Law'.[7] The dedication to Coke is understandable, given the great judge's iconic status as principal apologist for the juridical supremacy of common law, but in 1612 it would have been contentious in certain circles.

Following his appointment in 1606 as Chief Justice of the Common Pleas, Coke committed himself to defending the constitutional hegemony of the courts of common law from threats posed to their superior juridical status by the rival jurisdiction of civil law, which manifested itself in the prerogative courts of the king.[8] The most notable of these at this particular time was arguably the Ecclesiastical Court of High Commission.[9] During the first decade of Jacobean rule, High Commission increasingly asserted its power (contested by the courts of common law) to arrest, indict, convict, imprison and otherwise punish alleged offenders, thereby arrogating to itself the legitimate authority of the common law.[10] On numerous occasions after the accession of James I, the judges of Common Pleas convened to discuss the lawful capacity of High Commission to arrest and imprison individuals (Part Twelve of Coke's *Reports* alone records no fewer than five such instances between 1607 and 1611). Consistently, their decision was that Commissioners 'could not in any case have punished any delinquent by fine or imprisonment unless they had authority so to do by act of Parliament'.[11]

In the summer of 1611, only a year before Buck wrote his dedication to Coke in *The Third Universitie*, James I ceded to pressure from Coke and his fellow Justices and agreed to 'reform the high commission in divers points,

7 *Ibid.*, 961.

8 See Brian P. Levack, *The Civil Lawyers in England, 1603–1641: A Political Study* (Oxford: Clarendon, 1973); also, Daniel R. Coquillette, 'Legal Ideology and Incorporations I: the English Civilian Writers, 1523–1607', 61 (1981) *Boston University Law Review*, 1–89. Specifically on civil law and early Stuart absolutism, see Glenn Burgess, *Absolute Monarchy and the Stuart Constitution* (New Haven: Yale University Press, 1996), 63–90.

9 Upon the accession of Elizabeth I, the appointment of ecclesiastical commissions was validated by the Act of Supremacy, 1559 [*1 Eliz. cap. 1*].

10 On the juridical procedure of High Commission, see Roland G. Usher, *The Rise and Fall of the High Commission* (Oxford: Clarendon, 1913), 106–20. On *ex officio mero* prosecutions and the constitutional implications of *Caudrey's Case* (1591), see John Guy, 'The Elizabethan Establishment and the Ecclesiastical Polity' in John Guy, ed., *The Reign of Elizabeth I: Court and Culture in the Last Decade* (Cambridge: Cambridge University Press, 1995), 126–49, 131–2.

11 Coke, *If High Commissioners have Power to imprison*, 12 *Reports*, 7: 19.

and reduce it to certain spiritual causes'.[12] Coke's vociferous resistance to the unconstitutional excesses of prerogative rule was the primary factor in the decision by the king to translate him from the Court of Common Pleas ('the lock and key of the Common law')[13] to the Court of King's Bench.[14] Sir Francis Bacon suggested that the punitive action would 'be thought abroad a kind of discipline to him for opposing himself in the king's causes',[15] a belief which turned out to be spectacularly misplaced. Coke continued his outspoken attacks upon the ranks of civil lawyers, writing in 1614:

> It is a desperate and dangerous matter for civilians and canonists (I speak what I know, and not without just cause) to write either of the common laws of England which they profess not, or against them which they know not.[16]

In 1616, Coke was dismissed as Chief Justice of the King's Bench, never to hold judicial office again.[17]

I include the above sketch of Coke's judicial career, and of the clash between the rival jurisdictions of common law and civil law, because it locates *The Third Universitie* in a particular juridical moment, in which the apologists of common law were impelled to present the ancient credentials of their indigenous jurisprudence to an audience increasingly subjected to the peculiarities of civil law, as manifested by the imperatives of Jacobean prerogative rule. Apart from the reference to 'The Professors of the civill, or imperiall lawes' and the ensuing description of their college, 'Doctors Commons', Buck is ostensibly reticent on the subject of civil law. It may be argued that this is entirely understandable, given his thesis that the site of the Third University is the city of London: the institutional home of common

12 Coke, *High Commission*, 12 *Reports*, 7: 85, 85–6.

13 Sir Edward Coke, *The Fourth Part of the Institutes of the Laws of England: Concerning the Jurisdiction of Courts* (London: M. Flesher, 1644), 99.

14 On the rivalry between Common Pleas and King's Bench, see Raffield, *Shakespeare's Imaginary Constitution*, 55–8; also, J. H. Baker, *An Introduction to English Legal History* (London: Butterworths, 2002), 37–52.

15 *The Works of Francis Bacon*, ed. James Spedding, Robert L. Ellis, Douglas D. Heath, 14 vols. (London: Longmans, 1857–74), 4: 381.

16 Coke, 10 *Reports* (1614), 5: xviia.

17 Thomas Garden Barnes accurately notes 'that Coke has never found a decent biographer', Thomas Garden Barnes, 'Sir Edward Coke' in Thomas Garden Barnes, *Shaping the Common Law: From Glanvill to Hale, 1188–1688*, ed. Allen D. Boyer (Stanford: Stanford University Press, 2008), 114–35, 130. For a recent study of Coke in the reign of Elizabeth I, see Allen D. Boyer, *Sir Edward Coke and the Elizabethan Age* (Stanford: Stanford University Press, 2003).

law, in the form of the Inns of Court and Chancery, and the courts of law at Westminster. Insofar as civil law had a similar *locus amœnus* in England at this time, then it was to be found in the more refined academic environment of the University of Cambridge, in which institution John Cowell had presided as Regius Professor of Civil Law. The publication in 1607 of Cowell's *The Interpreter* aroused the hostility of Parliament, for the comparison made by Cowell between the powers of the English king and those of his continental counterparts. Parliament accused Cowell of betraying the liberties of the people and the personal intervention of James I was required to save him from imprisonment.[18] In a speech made in March 1610 to both Houses of Parliament, James I distanced himself from Cowell, claiming that 'as a King, I have least cause of any man to dislike the Common Law'.[19] But given the claim made in *The Interpreter* that the royal prerogative bestowed 'all that absolute height of power that the Civillians call (*maiestam, vel potestam, vel iu simperii,*) subject only to god',[20] it is not surprising that Parliament and common lawyers remained suspicious of the motives both of Cowell and of their king. If, as D. H. Willson claimed, one of the principal objectives of *The Interpreter* was 'to reconcile the civilian and the common lawyer',[21] then its author singularly failed in his design. It will come as no surprise to learn that Coke despised Cowell, whom he is alleged to have given the derogatory title of 'Doctor Cowheel'.[22]

Whilst Buck does not engage directly with the topical, political debate surrounding the relative authority of civil law and common law, he makes two references to the relationship between the rival jurisdictions, the second of which places the heraldic emblem at the symbolic heart of the controversy.

18 E. R. Foster, ed., *Proceedings in Parliament, 1610*, 2 vols. (New Haven, CT: Yale University Press, 1966), 1: 18.

19 Johann P. Sommerville, ed., *King James VI and I: Political Writings* (Cambridge: Cambridge University Press, 1994), 184.

20 John Cowell, *The Interpreter: or Booke containing the signification of words wherein is set foorth the true meaning of all, or the most part of such words and termes, as are mentioned in the law writers* (Cambridge, Iohn Legate, 1607), sig. Ddd3.*v*. For the argument that Cowell 'was simply careless in discussing politically sensitive matters', rather than an absolutist, see Burgess, *Absolute Monarchy*, 78 n. 74; also, Glenn Burgess, *The Politics of the Ancient Constitution: an Introduction to English Political Thought, 1600–1642* (Basingstoke: Macmillan, 1992), 149–55.

21 D. H. Willson, *King James VI and I* (London: Jonathan Cape, 1959), 261.

22 'It is said by some writers that when Lord Coke spoke of this learned person, he would call him Dr. Cowheel; this certainly is not in unison with the Judge's usual gravity; but, if it be true that he uttered such an expression, it was indeed a low jest': H. W. Woolrych, *The Life of the Right Honourable Sir Edward Coke, Knt., Lord Chief Justice of the King's Bench, &c.* (London: J. & W.T. Clarke, 1826), 205.

In his encomium to London (described in the Latin verse, which immediately precedes the dedication to Coke, as '*cornu-copia abundans*'), Buck argues that were the city to contain no colleges other than the Inns of Court, 'yet might London (as Justice Fortescue well observed, and holdeth) bee as worthily stiled an university as either Angiers, or Orleans…wherein the study of the civill law, is only professed'.[23] The observation made by Sir John Fortescue, to which Buck refers, was contained in *De Laudibus Legum Angliae*, written during the last years of the Lancastrian Chief Justice's exile in France, *circa* 1470, and published in English in 1567 as *A Learned Commendation of the Politique Lawes of England*, translated by Robert Mulcaster. In 1513, John Rastell had referred in passing to Fortescue's book as '*de laudibus legum Anglie*' but it received that enduring, published title only when John Selden produced a new edition of the work in 1616.[24] Fortescue compared the universities of Orleans and Angiers unfavourably with the Inns of Court, on the basis that neither of the French universities had 'so many Students, who have past their Minority, as in Our *Inns of Court*, where the Natives only are admitted'.[25] It is perhaps a truism to state of a work the title of which loosely translates as 'In Praise of English Law' that its pervading tone is nationalistic, if not xenophobic. But it is a statement that must be made, because for Fortescue the unique sense of immemorial nationhood and the antique customs of its indigenous race defined England and distinguished its laws from those of other nations (especially those of France). Fortescue was emphatic that civilian compliance with the maxim of the emperor Justinian, *quod principi placuit legis habet vigorem* ('the will of the prince has the force of law')[26] was consonant with injustice and oppression of the French populace. Consequently, he claimed that 'the [French] *Peasants* live in great Hardship and Misery'. In England, by contrast, 'the Inhabitants are Rich in Gold, Silver, and in all the Necessaries and Conveniencies of Life'.[27] In Chapter 17 of *De Laudibus*, entitled '*The Customs*

23 Buck, *Third Universitie*, 966.

24 Barnes, 'John Fortescue' in Barnes, *Shaping the Common Law*, 46–60, 243 n. 2.

25 Sir John Fortescue, *De Laudibus Legum Angliae*, ed. John Selden (London: R. Gosling, 1737), 112. Selden notes of Orleans that it is 'an University, erected by King *Philip le Bel*. An. 1312. tho', to speak properly, it be an Hall only for the reading the *Civil Laws*, the only learning there professed, and for that considerable', ibid., n. (i).

26 Justinian, *The Institutes*, Bk I, Title II, '*De Iure Naturali, Gentium et Civili*'. The quotation continues: '*cum lege regia, quae de imperio eius lata est, populus ei et in eum omne suum imperium et potestatem concessit*' ('for by the royal law which is passed to confer authority on him, the people yield up to him all its authority and power'); see Ewart Lewis, 'King Above Law? "Quod Principi Placuit" in Bracton', 39 (1964) *Speculum* 240–69.

27 Fortescue, *De Laudibus*, 80, 83.

of England *are of great Antiquity*', Fortescue claimed that neither the civil laws of the Romans, nor the laws of the Venetians, were 'so venerable for their Antiquity' as those of the English. He concluded this particular chapter with the following resounding exaltation: 'So that there's no Pretence to say, or insinuate to the contrary, but that the Laws and Customs of *England* are not only *Good*, but the *very Best*'.[28] For Fortescue and his judicial successors, antiquity conferred not mere legitimacy but actual jurisdictional supremacy. To quote Peter Goodrich in support of the thesis that the emblem of origin inhabits an indefinite and imaginary historical period, Fortescue 'refers to a past which was never present ... an archetypal time whose function is iconic and not representative'.[29]

The second reference by Buck to the increasingly fractious relationship in England between civil law and common law is more explicit than the first. He explains the structure of his book in logical, hierarchical terms. First, he lists and describes the functions of the schools of divinity, because the study of the law of God 'hath by due right the first place'. Next to the schools of divinity, he places the colleges of municipal or common law, emphasizing to the reader as he does so the coextensive and indivisible bond between divine law and municipal law. It is paradoxical, given the stated ambivalence of James I to the common law (and in particular his injunction to the judiciary that they 'Incroach not upon the Prerogative of the Crowne'),[30] that Buck should justify placing what he terms 'the law of this Lande before the Lawe of the Empire, or Civill Lawe' on the singular ground that he 'preferre my Soveraigne Lorde, and Kinge, before all other Kings and Keysars, and my native Countrey before any countrey in the world'.[31] The close proximity of Buck, as Master of the Revels, to the king and the royal court would have made it impolitic for him to engage in public debate over the relative authority of either jurisdiction. But he articulates the perceived sense of rivalry between the common law and the civil law when he describes a 'matter of controversie, which is betweene the professors of the municipall, and civill Lawes about precedence'. Rather than becoming further embroiled in the 'controversie', he bows out of

28 Fortescue, *De Laudibus*, 33–4.

29 Peter Goodrich, 'Poor Illiterate Reason: History, Nationalism and Common Law' 1 (1992) *Social and Legal Studies* 7–28, at 11.

30 Sommerville (ed.), *King James VI and I*, 212; in the same speech, made in Star Chamber in June 1616, James I described the Danish constitution as 'governed onely by a written Law ... and there is an end, for the very Law-booke itself is their onely Iudge. Happy were all kingdoms if they could be so: But here, curious wits, various conceits, different actions, and varietie of examples breed questions in Law', ibid. On the exercise of prerogative powers by James I, see Raffield, *Shakespeare's Imaginary Constitution*, 182–217.

31 Buck, *Third Universitie*, 966.

the fray, conceding that 'I will not meddle with it'. But neither does he ignore the controversy. Instead, he leaves 'the determination thereof to the learned Heralds and to their most noble Surintendents the high Constable and high Marshals of England, to whome of right it belongeth'.[32]

II Heraldry and the encoded signs of legitimacy

Suddenly, and without warning or expectation, the reader is plunged by Buck into the realm of the symbolic and the imagistic, in which the sign takes precedence over the written word: the determination of precedence between common law and civil law is left by Buck 'to the learned Heralds'. It is the word 'precedence' (used by Buck himself) which links heraldry to common law, both of which disciplines sought to identify the original fount of lawful authority, thereby providing historical evidence of authenticity. The lawyers found exemplars of reason in the past, sometimes recent but more often of immemorial origin. Coke recommended the readers of his *Reports* to 'cast thine eye upon the sages of the law, that have been before thee'. He was referring there to the patriarchs of the common law, the judiciary. The provenance of these judicial archetypes was celestial. They had (according to Coke) 'sucked from that divine knowledge, honesty, gravity, and integrity, and by the goodness of God hath obtained a greater blessing and ornament than any other profession to their family and posterity'.[33] Through his systematic (if opinionated) reporting of contemporary cases, and his emphasis on the antiquity of common law and the legitimacy that its immemorial origins conferred on judicial decision making, Coke elevated the binding power of precedent or *stare decisis* to hitherto unknown levels.[34] In similar fashion, but in relation to an order of signs, predicated on an idealized and pictorial version of a medieval past, heralds (under the supervision of the Marshal of England)[35] conferred legitimacy on those who claimed

32 Ibid., 966.

33 Coke, 2 *Reports* (1602), 1: x–xi. Kevin Sharpe makes the important observation that the synthesis between past and present gave to history an exalted status in the governance of early modern English society: Kevin Sharpe, *Politics and Ideas in Early Stuart England* (London: Pinter Publishing, 1989), 174–81. On patterns and precedent in early modern law and drama, see Paul Raffield, 'The Dramatic Imagination and the Dream of Law' in Marco Wan, ed., *Reading the Legal Case: Cross Currents between Law and the Humanities* (Abingdon: Routledge, 2012), 175–89.

34 *Stare decisis et non quieta movere* ['Stand by that which has been decided and do not disturb that which has been settled'].

35 On the judicial roles of the High Constable and the Marshal in the Court of Chivalry, see M. J. Russell, 'Trial by Battle in the Court of Chivalry', 29 (2008) *Journal of Legal History* 335–57.

gentility through antiquity. In part, the revival of interest in heraldry in the Elizabethan era, or more especially in books whose authors sought to explain the arcane symbolism of heraldic devices, was an inevitable consequence of the English Reformation: an assertion of power, identity, and (most of all) legitimacy in the face of the threat posed to the sovereign, English nation-state by Rome and her Catholic allies in continental Europe.[36] The Papal Bull, published by Pope Pius V in April 1570, not only excommunicated Elizabeth I from the Roman Catholic Church on the grounds of heresy but also declared 'her to be deprived of her pretended title to the aforesaid crown and of all lordship, dignity and privilege whatsoever'. Heraldry provided a visual medium through which legitimacy of title might be reclaimed and proven: a possible reason why in 1572 John Bossewell should have dedicated his book on heraldic devices, entitled *Workes of Armorie*, to Elizabeth's Lord High Treasurer, Sir William Cecil.

The heraldic device was of especial significance also to the professors of municipal law, who sought to provide form and shape to a body of law that was unwritten: *lex terrae*, rather than *leges scriptae*. As the seventeenth-century historian William Dugdale expounded: 'And that their [the laws of England] being not written doth no whit extenuate the authority and esteem justly due to them';[37] but, still, it was expedient, to say the least, that signs of their 'authority and esteem' be manifest: especially in the face of opposition from a jurisdiction, the civil law, the authority of which was founded in the written word. The image not only lent form and shape to unwritten law, the order of signs also performed the crucial function of capturing the imagination of the subject of law: an argument that has been advanced by numerous legal theorists and semioticians. Goodrich has written extensively on the capacity of the image to 'hold the invisible body, the emotional body, the affective subject or soul of those subject to law'.[38] Goodrich acknowledges the influence of the legal historian and psychoanalyst Pierre Legendre, whose work has engaged throughout with the idea that the image is 'the trace of an absent presence'.[39] Representing something that is present but

36 Goodrich argues that 'The fictional unity of the English nation was thus the assertion of an identity against foreign influence and against the power of Rome and of Roman law', Goodrich, 'Poor Illiterate Reason', 10.

37 Sir William Dugdale, *Origines Juridiciales or Historical Memorials of the English Laws* (London, F & T Warren, 1666), 3.

38 Peter Goodrich, *Languages of Law: From Logics of Memory to Nomadic Masks* (London: Weidenfeld and Nicolson, 1990), 262.

39 Pierre Legendre, *Law and the Unconscious: a Legendre Reader*, (trans.) Peter Goodrich, with Alain Pottage and Anton Schütz, Peter Goodrich (ed.), Basingstoke: Macmillan, 1997), 214. On the tale of Narcissus (in Book III of *Metamorphoses*) and an introduction to the theory of the image, see *ibid.*, 211-254.

simultaneously is not; the image is the structure of authority and it is the particular form of this structure that enables capture of the subject of law.

It may be considered a serious understatement to assert that the meaning of the sign was an obvious point of contention in Reformation Europe but the assertion serves as a starting point for understanding the role of the arts in early modern England, which was didactic as well as decorative. Sir Philip Sidney, writing of the poetic art *circa* 1580, implied that poetry had much in common with figurative art. For Sidney, poetry was a form of mimesis (a definition which he derived from *The Poetics* of Aristotle). It was 'a speaking picture: with this end, to teach and delight'.[40] In a work from the same genre, by Sidney's near contemporary George Puttenham, entitled *The Arte of English Poesie*, the author locates the origins of western law in the mythography of ancient Greece; implying that law was originally recorded neither as imperial edict nor as statute but rather as an aesthetic form. Puttenham related the myth of Orpheus, who tamed wild beasts through the harmonious music of his lyre. Thus was recorded through metaphor the civilizing moment when law was introduced into society.[41] Just as Fortescue described judges as *Sacerdotes* or priests, giving or teaching 'Holy Things',[42] so Puttenham depicted the ancient poets as 'the first Priests and ministers of the holy misteries'. It was their 'holiness of life' (in addition to their sagacity and worldly experience), which enabled poets to become:

> The first lawmakers to the people, and the first polititiens, devising all expedient meanes for th'establishment of Common wealth, to hold and containe the people in order and duety by force and vertue of good and wholesome laws, made for the preservation of the publique peace and tranquillitie.[43]

40 Sir Philip Sidney, *The Defence of Poesie* (London: W. Ponsonby, 1595), sig. C2v. In the opening few lines of *The Poetics*, Aristotle states that epic poetry, tragedy, comedy, dithyrambic poetry, and music "are all (taken together) imitations," Aristotle, *The Poetics*, (trans.) Malcolm Heath (London: Penguin, 1996), 3, Chapter 1.1 47a.

41 See Horace, *Ars Poetica*, on the myths of Orpheus and Amphion: "Poets the first Instructers of Mankind, / Brought all things to their proper, native Use; / Some they appropriated to the Gods, / And some to publick, some to private ends: Promiscuous love by marriage was restrain'd / Cities were built, and usefull Laws were made," *Horace's Art of Poetry made English by the Right Honourable the Earl of Roscommon* (London: H. Herringman, 1680), 23.

42 Fortescue, *De Laudibus*, 4-5.

43 George Puttenham, *The arte of English poesie* (London: R. Field, 1589), 4, 5. On the 'poet-judge' as the embodiment of equitable justice, see Martha Nussbaum, *Poetic Justice: the Literary Imagination and Public Life* (Boston, Mass: Beacon Press, 1995), 80.

Graeco-Roman mythography was a resource to which common lawyers of the early modern period made frequent reference, as they sought to establish the legitimate foundations of English law in an antique and imaginary past. In his report of *Postnati: Calvin's Case*, concerning the naturalisation of a Scottish subject in the Jacobean English state, Coke went so far as to incorporate the legend of the Trojan Horse (from Book II of Virgil's *Aeneid*), with which to depict the threat posed by aliens to the security of the realm.[44] The imagery employed by Coke in *The Reports* was often drawn from the philosophical, literary and political texts of the ancient world. The mythical Trojan king, Brutus (grandson of Aeneas), became for Coke the prototypical author of the ancient constitution, describing him as 'Brutus the first King of this land'.[45] According to Geoffrey of Monmouth, writing in the twelfth century: Brutus, after fleeing Italy and landing eventually at the unlikely destination of Totnes in Devon, travelled east, to found a new city, Troynovant (London), on the banks of the Thames.[46] For Fortescue, Coke, and other jurists of the early modern period, Brutus was the father of the Britons, the archetype and icon of English nationhood and English law.[47] Fortescue credits Brutus with the foundation of *dominium politicum et regale*: 'So the Kingdom of *England* had its Original from *Brute* and the *Trojans*, who attended him from *Italy* and *Greece*, and became a mixt Kind of Government, compounded of the *Regal* and *Political*'.[48] It matters not to the story of common law and its origins that, as John Selden perspicaciously noted, the myth of Brutus was 'patched up out of Bards Songs and Poetick Fictions taken upon trust, like *Talmudical* Traditions, on purpose to raise the *British* name out of the *Trojan* ashes'.[49] The importance of Brutus lay rather in his iconic status, as an archetypal patriarch of English law.

44 'then strangers might fortify themselves in the heart of the realm, and be ready to set fire on the commonwealth, as was excellently shadowed by the Trojan horse in Virgil's Second Book of his Æneid': Coke, *Postnati. Calvin's Case*, 7 *Reports* (1608), 4: 1a, 18b.

45 Coke, 3 *Reports* (1602), 4: viiia.

46 Geoffrey of Monmouth, *The History of the Kings of Britain*, trans. Lewis Thorpe, (London: Penguin, 1966), 53–74.

47 'as soon as he had settled himself in his kingdom, for the safe and peaceable government of his people, [Brutus] wrote a book in the Greek tongue, calling it the Laws of the Britons, and he collected the same out of the laws of the Trojans': Coke, 3 *Reports*, 4: viiia.

48 Fortescue, *De Laudibus*, 23–4.

49 John Selden, *The Reverse or Back-Face of the English Janus*, trans. Redman Westcot (London: Thomas Basset & Richard Chiswell, 1682), 8. It is noteworthy in this context that the Latin word with which to describe members of the Order of Serjeants-at-Law (the early modern equivalent of Queen's Counsel) was *narratores*: Dugdale, *Origines Juridiciales*, 110; Latin *narratores* translates not only as 'storytellers', but also as 'historians'.

Brutus of Troy returns us to the issue of precedence and, by implication, of genealogy. He returns us also to Buck and to the insistence that 'no man can be made a Gentleman but by his father'. According to Buck, a king has the power to make esquires, knights, baronets, barons, viscounts, earls, marquises, and dukes (recalling the imperial maxim: *quod principi placuit legis habet vigorem*), but he cannot 'make a Gentleman, for Gentilitie is a matter of race, and of blood, and of discent, from gentile and noble parents, and auncestors, which no Kings can give to any'.[50] According to Buck, the honourable members of the Inns of Court are all 'Registred by the stile and name of Gentlemen', the status of which Buck affirms by reference to the eminent Elizabethan scholar and herald, Gerard Legh, author of *The Accedens of Armory*. Legh's book, which contains over 300 heraldic emblems, each of which is accompanied by detailed interpretation and exposition of the meaning of the hieroglyphs and their component parts, is perhaps best-known for the description near the end of the book, of Legh's visit to the Inner Temple in December 1561, at which he met Sir Robert Dudley, playing the role of Palaphilos (High Constable to Pallas Athene) in the Candlemas revels.[51] Legh, a member of the Inner Temple himself, emphasised that within the idyllic enclave of the Inner Temple is contained 'the store of Gentilmen of the whole Realme'.[52] His description of the membership has much in common with the description by John Ferne (a fellow Inner Templar) in a similar work, entitled *The Blazon of Gentrie* (published twenty-four years after *The Accedens*, in 1586). In Ferne's opinion, the members of the Inns of Court were gentlemen 'of bloud and coate-armour, so perfect and auncient'.[53]

The account given by Ferne in *The Blazon of Gentrie* of the noble genealogy of members of the Inns is qualified by the author's own admission

50 Buck, *Third Universitie*, 969.

51 *The Accedens* and the visit by Legh to the Inner Temple in December 1561 are discussed in Peter Goodrich, 'Eating Law: Commons, Common Land, Common Law' 12 (1991) *Journal of Legal History* 246–67; see also, Raffield, *Images and Cultures*, 99–106.

52 Gerard Legh, *The Accedens of Armory* (London, Rychard Tottel, 1576), fo. 119v.

53 John Ferne, *The Blazon of Gentrie* (London: Toby Cooke, 1586), 92. On the depiction by Ferne of nobility at the Elizabethan Inns of Court, see Raffield, *Images and Cultures*, 35–36, 79–82. Interest in heraldry remained strong throughout the Jacobean era, as instanced by *The Third Universitie*, and in 1618 by the publication of Sir Henry Goodyere's compendium of heraldic emblems and accompanying verses, entitled *The Mirrour of Maiestie: or, the Badges of Honour Conceitedly Emblazoned: with Emblems Annexed, Poetically Unfolded* (London: W. Jones, 1618). For analysis of *The Mirrour of Maiestie*, see Raffield, *Images and Cultures*, 61–71.

that the hegemony of the landed gentry within those institutions was increasingly threatened by the incursion of:

> yeomanrye and Merchauntes, [who] set their broode, to the studye of common lawes: that faculty is so pestered, yea many worthy offices, and places of high regarde, in that vocation, (in olde time, left to the support of gentle linage) are now preoccupated, and usurped by ungentle, and base stocke.[54]

It is worth mentioning here that although Ferne was a member of the Inner Temple, his own genealogy failed to meet the requirement of 'a gentleman of bloud and coate-armour'. His grandfather was a yeoman (from Uttoxeter, Staffordshire), and his father acquired the family's land in Lincolnshire only in the 1570s. The same might be said of Legh, who was the son of a draper in Fleet Street and who had been apprenticed to his father and joined the Drapers' Company.[55] According to Ferne's definition of those members of society who were forbidden honour, dignity or pre-eminence, described by him as 'the estate unnoble … that which is called *Plebeian*, that is to saye, the vulgare and common sort of the people', Legh's father would have been in the category either of merchant (*Mercatores*) or burgher (*Burgenses*);[56] either of which would have made Legh ineligible to bear arms. By his insistence that the late Elizabethan Inns 'have much ado, to conserve the estate of their former honor',[57] Ferne was harking back nostalgically to a literary portrait of the Inns, painted in the late fifteenth century by Fortescue in *De Laudibus*, according to which: 'Knights, Barons and the Greatest Nobility of the Kingdom, often Place their Children in those Inns of Court'.[58] Even in the late fifteenth century, when *De Laudibus* was written, Fortescue's claim that the gentlemen of the Inns of Court were all descended from the English nobility was exaggerated, and has been dismissed by Wilfrid R. Prest as 'an extravagant boast'.[59] Exaggeration notwithstanding, the myth was perpetuated by lawyers and historians, well into the seventeenth century. The reasons for this near obsession with genealogy, and of being identified with the estate

54 Ferne, *Blazon of Gentrie*, 93.

55 S. Healy, 'Ferne, Sir John (*c.*1560–1609)', and J. F. R. Day, 'Legh, Gerard (d. 1563)', *Oxford Dictionary of National Biography* (Oxford: Oxford University Press, 2004).

56 Ferne, *Blazon of Gentrie*, 92–3.

57 Ibid., 92.

58 Fortescue, *De Laudibus*, 111–12.

59 Wilfrid R. Prest, *The Rise of the Barristers: A Social History of the English Bar 1590–1640* (Oxford: Clarendon, 1991), 94.

which Ferne describes as *nobilitas Polytica*,[60] are twofold. The first is entirely to do with increased social mobility: the need for existing members of the nobility and gentry to assert their ancient status and for the *soi-disant* elite, the *arrivistes* of the burgeoning middle classes, to establish theirs.[61] Of greater interest to the current analysis, the second reason for the obsessive concern with genealogy (and hence, with the Elizabethan revival of interest in heraldry, the craft of which served to represent in graphic form the genealogy of its subjects) at the Inns of Court is to do with the identification of a symbolic, originary father: the imaginary source of common law. Both Legh and Ferne include dedications at the start of their respective books: 'To the honorable assembly of gentlemen in the Innes of Court';[62] so it is reasonable to assume that each writer had in mind the English legal institution, rather than its individual members, when expostulating on the subject of 'gentlemen of bloud and coate-armour, so perfect and auncient'.

III Pegasus and other hieroglyphs of English law

In the first line of the first chapter of *Origines Juridiciales*, entitled 'Of Government the Original', Dugdale states unequivocally with reference to the chapter's title: 'That this, at first, was in the Father of the Household'. He is referring to the classical idea that government and the father are inextri cable. Thus is the symbolic father imprinted indelibly on the reader's conscience as the founder of law. A couple of pages later, Dugdale asserts that the common law 'is, out of question, no less ancient than the beginning

60 Ferne, *Blazon of Gentrie*, 6.

61 On the social composition of the Bar between 1590 and 1640, see Prest, *Rise of the Barristers*, 83–126. Prest concludes (somewhat cautiously) that the survey provided evidence of 'the broadening of the bar's social composition over the early modern period as a whole', ibid., 95. The growing threat posed to extant social hierarchy in the early seventeenth century was represented by the abolition in 1604 of sumptuary legislation (*1 Jac. I cap. 25*). Regulation of the sartorial image had provided the lawful means through which hierarchy and social distinction were enforced and represented throughout the sixteenth century. See Alan Hunt, *Governance of the Consuming Passions: A History of Sumptuary Law* (Basingstoke: Macmillan, 1996); Hunt perceives sumptuary law in terms of Foucault's thesis that power takes two distinct forms: 'disciplines' acting on 'bodies', and 'regulation' acting on 'populations', 11. See also, Susan Vincent, *Dressing the Elite: Clothes in Early Modern England* (Oxford: Berg, 2003), 117–52; Peter Goodrich, 'Signs Taken for Wonders: Community, Identity, and "A History of Sumptuary Law"' 23 (1998) *Law and Social Inquiry* 707–28; Raffield, *Images and Cultures*, 157–76; Wilfrid Hooper, 'The Tudor Sumptuary Laws' 30/119 (1915) *English Historical Review* 433–49.

62 Legh, *The Accedens*, sig. A.ii.r; Ferne's dedication is 'To the honorable assemblyes of the Innes of Court', Ferne, *Blazon of Gentrie*, sig. A.iiii.r

of differences betwixt man and man, after the first peopling of this land'.[63] The indigenous law of England is, according to its apologists, of primeval origin; it is as old as the world itself. In strict, Roman legal terminology, the image or *imago* was the social representation of the father, in symbolic terms the ultimate lawgiver. As *paterfamilias*, the Roman father had power that mirrored that of the emperor.[64] His authority was absolute; he was *lex loquens* – the living, speaking law. In strict classical terms therefore, the heraldic emblem was the iconic image of the originary: a graphic symbol that guides the viewer to understanding and perception of the intangible and the invisible.[65] Striking also about the imagery of heraldic devices is their derivation from the natural world. Animals are taken from their natural environment, transplanted into a symbolic realm of hieroglyphs and transformed into images of antiquity, honour and legitimacy. I refer above to the transformation of natural law into municipal or common law, enabled by the application of the 'artificial reason' of man, to which Coke alluded in his report of *Prohibitions del Roy*.[66] In one of several acrimonious encounters between Coke and James I, this particular one taking place in Michaelmas Term 1607, the King argued that as the law was 'founded upon reason', then as he James was endowed with reason, he should have the right, 'as well as the Judges', to sit in judgment in the King's courts. Coke rejected this argument on the grounds that cases were decided by artificial, rather than natural, reason, and by the judgment of law: 'which law is an act which requires long study and experience'.[67] In *De Laudibus*, Fortescue described a similar transformation, of nature and customs into '*Constitutions* or

63 Dugdale, *Origines Juridiciales*, 1, 3.

64 On the paternal source of law and the Roman origins of the Western legal tradition, see Legendre, *Law and the Unconscious*, Introduction, 8–12. On the classical law of images, see Pierre Legendre, *Le Désir politique de dieu: Etude sur les montages de l'état et du droit* (Paris: Fayard, 1989); the title of Legendre's work derives from an essay by Lacan, in which he discusses the iconic image and its capacity to 'arouse the desire of God', Jacques Lacan, *The Four Fundamental Concepts of Psycho-analysis*, (ed.) Jacques-Alain Miller, (trans.) Alan Sheridan (Harmondsworth: Penguin, 1979), 113.

65 Of the 'other-worldly character' of Legh's account of his visit to the Inner Temple, Goodrich convincingly argues that 'The originary is invariably hieroglyphic, it exists only in the trace or vestige, the ruin of a present form': Goodrich, 'Eating Law', 247.

66 See text to n. 2, above.

67 Coke, *Prohibitions del Roy*, 12 *Reports*, 7: 65a. Coke is referring here to the prolonged period of training at the Inns of Court and apprenticeship in the courts at Westminster, a process which Sir John Doderidge described as 'the worke of many yeares, the attaining whereof will waste the greatest part of the verdour and vigour of our youth': Sir John Doderidge, *The English Lawyer: Describing a Method for the managing of the Lawes of this Land* (London: I. More, 1631), 29.

Statutes', which 'oblige the Subject to the Observance of them'.[68] This is not to say that the law of nature was not central to the foundation of common law and its practice in the king's courts: Fortescue was emphatic that 'the power of the king took its beginning under and from the law of nature'.[69]

Famously, Fortescue was to state that English law was 'deduced from the *Law of Nature*',[70] while Coke would later argue not only 'that the law of nature is part of the law of England' but that it was of greater antiquity than 'any judicial or municipal law'.[71] On the title page to Part One of *The Reports*, Coke quotes the Ciceronian maxim: *Lex est certa ratio e mente divina manans, quæ suadet, prohibetque contraria* ('Law is certain reason flowing from the mind of God, which commands right and prohibits the contrary'), thereby acknowledging the line of descent of natural law theory from the ancient world to the present day. For Coke, as for Cicero, 'True law is right reason in agreement with nature; it is of universal application, unchanging and everlasting'.[72] But Coke and other early modern jurists looked beyond Cicero, to Aristotle, for authority of the claim that English law derived from the law of nature. Coke noted the influence of Aristotle over the founding fathers of early modern English law, recording in his report of *Postnati. Calvin's Case* that Henry de Bracton, Sir John Fortescue and Christopher St. German all agreed with the Aristotelian proposition that 'God and nature is one to all, and therefore the law of God and nature is one to all'.[73] It is not surprising that Coke should refer approvingly to Aristotle as 'nature's secretary'.[74] The coextensive bond between reason and nature is fundamental to the Aristotelian and Ciceronian definitions of law but, within these philosophical frameworks, the juridical application of law is an aesthetic exercise in which 'artificial reason' dominates and determines both process and outcome. In the classical imagery employed by Nietzsche in *The Birth of*

68 Fortescue, *De Laudibus*, 28.

69 Sir John Fortescue, 'On the Nature of the Law of Nature' in Shelley Lockwood (ed.), *On the Laws and Governance of England* (Cambridge: Cambridge University Press, 1997), 127–36, at 131. On Fortescue's *De Natura Legis Naturae* and the subjection of *ius regis* to the law of nature, see E.F. Jacobs, *Sir John Fortescue and the Law of Nature* (Manchester: Manchester University Press, 1934), 12–13.

70 Fortescue, *De Laudibus*, 29; on the universal authority of the law of nature, see Aristotle, *The Nicomachean Ethics*, trans. J. A. K. Thomson (London: Penguin, 2004), 130, Bk V.VII.1134b18–20.

71 Coke, *Postnati. Calvin's Case*, 7 *Reports*, 4: 12b.

72 '*Est quidem vera lex recta ratio naturae congruens, diffusa in omnes, constans, sempiterna*' Cicero, *The Republic* in *On the Republic; On the Laws* (trans.) C. W. Keyes, (Cambridge, MA: Harvard University Press, 1928), 211, Bk III.XXII.

73 Coke, *Postnati. Calvin's Case*, 7 *Reports*, 4: 12b–13a.

74 Ibid., 12b.

Tragedy, art (which for the purpose of the present analysis I take to include law in its juridical context) 'derives its continuous development from the duality of the *Apolline* and *Dionysiac*'.[75] In the aesthetic scheme imagined and related by Nietzsche, these two opposing artistic powers 'spring from nature itself'.[76] The Apolline represents the ordered dreamland of artistic illusion, creating aesthetic artefacts that are based on observation of natural phenomena. It is into this aesthetic framework that the present analysis places the heraldic device.

The influence of Aristotle and Cicero over the development of the western legal tradition (and more generally, the influence of ancient eastern thought over modern western thought)[77] is evidence of what might be termed the transfer of rule from east to west: the *translatio imperii*, progressing on a westerly course.[78] From the east came not only light but also law: *ex oriente lex*. Revolutionary printing technology facilitated the publication of seminal texts in unprecedented numbers. As F. W. Maitland noted of the Renaissance of English law in the sixteenth century: 'medieval books poured from the press'.[79] He was referring to juridical texts of late-medieval and early modern origin that had hitherto been current mainly in manuscript: works such as Littleton's *Tenures*, Statham's *Abridgement*, and St. German's *Doctor and Student*. But the new technology also exposed the ancient classical writers to a hitherto undiscovered audience, especially when these works were popularised by translation into English. This applied as much to poetic works as it did to those of philosophy or law. One such work was Ovid's *Metamorphoses*, the first four books of which were published in 1565 (the full version was published in 1567), in a translation by Arthur Golding. Golding's translation was so popular that Shakespeare parodied (while not replicating) the verse style (rhyming couplets of iambic heptameter, commonly known

75 Friedrich Nietzsche, *The Birth of Tragedy*, trans. Shaun Whiteside, ed. Michael Tanner (London: Penguin, 2003), 14.

76 Ibid., 18.

77 See Arthur Schopenhauer, *The World as Will and Idea*, trans. R. B. Haldane and John Kemp, 3 vols. (London: Kegan Paul, Trench, Trübner, 1906); also, Donald R. Kelley, 'Vera Philosophia: The Philosophical Significance of Renaissance Jurisprudence' 14 (1976) *Journal of the History of Philosophy* 267–79.

78 On the medieval, Christian formulation of *translatio imperii*, see Wayne Cristaudo, Paul Caringella, Glenn Hughes, 'History, theology and the relevance of the translatio imperii' 116 (2013) *Thesis Eleven*, 5–18.

79 Frederic W. Maitland, *English Law and the Renaissance* (Cambridge: Cambridge University Press, 1901), 29; see Elizabeth L. Eisenstein, *The Printing Press as an Agent of Change: Communications and Cultural Transformations in Early-Modern Europe*, 2 vols. (Cambridge: Cambridge University Press, 1979).

as 'The Fourteener') in the play of 'Pyramus and Thisbe', which the mechanicals perform before Theseus and Hippolyta in the last Act of *A Midsummer Night's Dream.*[80] In *Shakespeare and Ovid*, Jonathan Bate describes the antique literary texts from which Shakespeare and his contemporaries derived the themes (and sometimes the entire plots) of their plays and poems as '*precedents*, not *sources* ... a conceptual exemplar, not a reservoir of raw material'.[81] Shakespeare's contemporary, George Puttenham, made a similar observation, concerning '*Paradigma*, or a resemblance by example', whereby the past is compared with the present, 'gathering probabilitie of like successe to come in the things wee have presently in hand'. Whether Puttenham had the juridical process in mind when he wrote in the same sentence that 'judgements precedent' were 'authorized by antiquitie' is unclear;[82] but it is a useful image with which to draw together some literary and juridical threads on the theme of precedents and paradigms.

Golding's translation of Books One to Four of Ovid's *Metamorphoses* was published in 1565. He dedicated the work to Sir Robert Dudley, Earl of Leicester. It is probable that the work was circulated in manuscript form for several years before its publication, as was the fashion (Sidney's *Defence of Poesie*, for example, was written *circa* 1580, but remained unpublished until 1595).[83] In which case, it is likely that Dudley (and indeed, Gerard Legh) would have read the translation prior to participating in the Inner Temple Candlemas revels of 1561, at which Dudley played the role of Palaphilos. The story of the birth of Pegasus, in Book IV of *Metamorphoses*, was anyway one with which Legh would have been familiar from childhood, as the work formed part of the curriculum at grammar schools. Carol Chillington Rutter has noted that, in some schools, *Metamorphoses* was 'memorized, word for word, at the rate of a book a year'.[84] Legh is attributed with the adoption of

80 Anthony Brian Taylor, 'Golding's Ovid, Shakespeare's "Small Latin", and the Real Object of Mockery in "Pyramus and Thisbe"' 42 (1990) *Shakespeare Survey* 53–64.

81 Jonathan Bate, *Shakespeare and Ovid* (Oxford: Clarendon, 1993), 84.

82 Puttenham, *Arte of English Poesie*, 205.

83 On the Elizabethan proverb 'Manuscript is a virgin, the printing press a whore' ['*Est virgo haec penna, meretrix est stampificata*], see Douglas A. Brooks, ed., *Printing and Parenting in Early Modern England* (Aldershot: Ashgate, 2005), Introduction, 4; also, Laurie Maguire and Emma Smith, 'Shakespeare Was Not Interested in Having his Plays Printed' in *Great Myths About Shakespeare* (Chichester: Wiley-Blackwell, 2013), 26–33.

84 Carol Chillington Rutter, 'Shakespeare and School' in Paul Edmondson and Stanley Wells, eds., *Shakespeare Beyond Doubt: Evidence, Argument, Controversy* (Cambridge: Cambridge University Press, 2013), 133–44, at 138; also, Caroline Jameson, 'Ovid in the Sixteenth Century' in J. W. Binns, ed., *Ovid* (London: Routledge and Kegan Paul, 1973), 210–42; more generally, see J. W. Binns, *Intellectual Culture in Elizabethan and Jacobean England: the Latin Writings of the Age* (Leeds: Francis Cairns, 1990).

Pegasus as the heraldic device of the Inner Temple, and it was inaugurated as such at the 1561 revels.[85] The original seal of the Knights Templar (two Knights, sitting astride the same warhorse) was, as Buck explained, 'a symbole of piety … an Emblem of Love, and Charitie, and a true Ierogliffe of ingenious kindenesse, and Noble courtesie of Souldiers' (Figure 3.2).[86] Unfortunately, the emblem was liable to misinterpretation. Buck expressed his outrage that 'they which loved to deprave, and make scandalous, and ridiculous, interpretations of every thinge … would have it supposed that it was taken, and devised to shew and expresse the poore, and needy

Figure 3.2 Original seal of the Knights Templar (courtesy of Paul Raffield)

85 See Robert A. Pearce, *A Guide to the Inns of Court and Chancery* (London: Butterworths, 1855), 219–20; also, Paul Raffield, 'The Elizabethan Rhetoric of Signs: Representations of *Res Publica* at the Early Modern Inns of Court' 7 (2011) *Law, Culture and the Humanities*, 244–63.

86 On the history of the Knights Templar, see Edith Simon, *The Piebald Standard* (London: Cassell, 1959); specifically on military campaigns in the Holy Land in which they fought, see Sir Hamilton Gibb, *The Life of Saladin: From the Works of 'Imad Ad-Din and Baha' Ad-Din* (Oxford: Clarendon Press, 1973).

beginnings' of the Order of Templars.[87] That is to say, the emblem falsely implied that the Order could afford only one horse between two knights. The Knights Templar therefore exchanged their emblem for an explicitly religious one: 'a Shield argent, Charged with a Crosse Gules, and upon the Nombrill thereof, a holy Lambe' (Figure 3.3).[88] The likelihood in Elizabethan England that the Inner Temple would choose the Paschal lamb as its emblem was nil. Indeed, in 1570, the graphic portrayal of *Agnus Dei*, the Lamb of

Figure 3.3 Seal of the Knights Templar of the Languedoc (courtesy of Paul Raffield)

87 Buck, *Third Universitie*, 972. Buck presumably refers to the claim of Joseph Holland that 'These Templers were at the first so poor as they had but one house to serve two of them, in token whereof they gave in their seal two men riding on one horse': Joseph Holland, 'The Question is, Of the Antiquity use and privilege of places for Students and Professors of the common law' [1601], in Thomas Hearne, ed., *A Collection of Curious Discourses, Written by Eminent Antiquaries Upon Several Heads in our English Antiquities* (Oxford: Thomas Hearne, 1720), 128. The original device exists in monumental form opposite Temple Church, where two knights sit astride a bronze horse, atop a stone plinth. The monument was erected in 2000, to celebrate the start of the new millennium. It is situated on the site of the former cloister courtyard of the Knights Templar.

88 Buck, *Third Universitie*, 971.

God, was prohibited by a statute that described all such religious emblems as 'vain and superstitious things' (*13 Eliz. C. 2*). In 1612, the year in which Buck wrote *The Third Universitie*, the Middle Temple had yet to choose the device of the Lamb and Flag as its emblem (Figure 3.4). In 1561, the Inner Temple reverted to the original emblem of two knights on the same mount. Retaining the body of the horse, the two knights were transformed into wings. Thus was Pegasus the Flying Horse born: not from the blood of Medusa, but from the original seal of the Knights Templar. Legh describes the new device thus: 'He beareth Azure, a Pegasus Argent, called the horse of honour': a silver, winged horse on a blue background.[89] Of course, the sign is never innocent, and in the encoded visual grammar of heraldry, Azure 'is Royal, & a colour of heavenly hew'. When combined with Argent (silver), it denotes 'vigilan[ce] in service'.[90] Through the creation of a new emblem, the Inner Temple has undergone a symbolic rebirth; its imaginary genealogy

Figure 3.4 The Paschal Lamb and Flag, emblem of the Honourable Society of the Middle Temple (courtesy of Paul Raffield)

89 Legh, *The Accedens*, fo. 118r.
90 Ibid., ff. 6v, 7r.

tracing its origin to the mythographies of ancient Greece, and the re-telling of these stories in Ovid's *Metamorphoses.*

IV Conclusion

Returning briefly to the theme of *translatio imperii* and its westerly progress, the origins of heraldry itself are to be found in the east: in the hieroglyphs of the ancient Egyptians and in the pages of the Bible. 'Every man of the children of Israel shall pitch by his own standard, with the ensign of their father's house': thus, God spoke to Moses and Aaron, as reported in the *Book of Numbers.*[91] The source of *translatio imperii* itself is Biblical; its foundations lie in Nebuchadnezzar's dream, as interpreted by Daniel. Most notable about the Old Testament text of *The Book of Daniel* is the centrality of the image to the narrative. In his dream, Nebuchadnezzar saw 'a great image, whose brightness *was* excellent'. The image, we are told, was of a human body: the head of gold, the breast and arms of silver, the belly and thighs of brass, the legs of iron, the feet of iron and clay. The image is destroyed by a stone, 'which smote the image', and the broken pieces 'became like the chaff of the summer threshing floors'. Daniel interprets the dream as an allegory of the transience of earthly empire: Nebuchadnezzar's golden empire would be followed by empires of silver, brass, iron and finally, a divided empire of iron and clay. All would perish: only the kingdom of God 'shall stand for ever'.[92] There are obvious thematic parallels between the Biblical depiction of *translatio imperii* and the story of the four ages of the earth – gold, silver, bronze, and iron – narrated by Ovid in Book I of *Metamorphoses.* Central to this narrative is the transference of power, from Saturn (the golden age) to Jove (the age of silver), before the descent into warfare (the age of bronze) and wickedness (the age of iron).

In the story told by Gerard Legh of his visit to the Inner Temple, the sense is conveyed of empire originating in the east and of progressing westward, until its arrival in the symbolic heart of the English legal institution, the Temple. The appearance of Sir Robert Dudley, disguised as Palaphilos, High Constable to Pallas Athene, the goddess of law and justice, compounds the impression that the empire of laws has been transplanted in the west. In a dedication 'To the reader' at the start of *The Accedens of Armory*, Richard Argall (a member of the Inner Temple) outlines the imperial theme, stating

91 Numbers, 2.2 (Authorised King James Version). On the ancient, eastern origins of heraldry, see Arthur Charles Fox-Davies, *A Complete Guide to Heraldry* (London: Studio Editions, 1993), 1–18.

92 Daniel, 2.31–44.

that 'All knowledge and artes rising first in the east, emonges the children of God'. He subsequently traces the history and the journey of empire from Egypt, to Greece and then Rome, before intimating strongly that the next site of empire is England: 'this our countrey, may compare with those, who therein thynke themselves most victorious'.[93] When Legh begins his narrative, he informs the reader that he has 'traveiled through the Easte partes of thunknowen world'.[94] He casts himself in the role of a traveller, returning home with strange tales of his adventures in the east. He narrates the myth of Pegasus, striking with his hooves 'the highest toppe of Mount Helicon, from whence immediatelye, rose the fountaine (Hypocrene)'.[95] The waters of the Hippocrene imparted poetic inspiration and the Inns of Court were perhaps best known during the early modern period for presenting a poetics (or aesthetics) of law through their arcane rites;[96] of which the Inner Temple Candlemas revels of 1561 are exemplary. In less specific terms, the use by Legh of the Hippocrene metaphor reflects the extent to which learning in general (and in the context of the Inner Temple, the study of law in particular) had been affected by the influx of humanism.[97] Indicative of the new learning was the adoption by the Inns of Court of Christopher St. German's *Doctor and Student* as a set text.[98] This seminal work placed unprecedented emphasis on the correlation between English law and conscience. Divine law, natural law and common law were represented as coexistent; while Aristotelian *epieikeia* or natural equity was acknowledged as a guiding principle of the common law.[99] The waters of the inspirational Hippocrene have, according to Legh:

93 Richarde Argall, 'To the reader' in Legh, *The Accedens*, unpaginated.

94 Ibid., fo. 119r.

95 Ibid., fo. 118v.

96 See Jayne Elisabeth Archer, Elizabeth Goldring, Sarah Knight, eds., *The Intellectual and Cultural World of the Early Modern Inns of Court* (Manchester: Manchester University Press, 2011).

97 The fountain or stream was widely used as a metaphor for the origin of law. See for example, Cicero: 'Well, then, shall we seek the origin of Justice itself at its fountain-head?' ['*Visne ergo ipsius iuris ortum a fonte repetamus*'], *The Laws*, trans. Keyes, 319, Bk I.XX; also, 'Law is certain reason flowing from the mind of God' ['*Lex est certa ratio e mente divina manans*'], Coke, 1 *Reports* (1600), Title-page; see text to n. 72.

98 John Guy, 'Tudor Monarchy and its Critiques', in John Guy, ed., *The Tudor Monarchy* (London: Arnold, 1997), 78–104, at 88.

99 See John Guy, 'Thomas More and Christopher St. German: The Battle of the Books', in Alistair Fox and John Guy, eds., *Reassessing the Henrician Age: Humanism, Politics and Reform, 1500–1550* (Oxford: Blackwell, 1986), 95–120, at 102; also, John Guy, *Christopher St. German On Chancery And Statute* (London: Selden Society, 1985), 19.

> watered the growinge plantes of the pleasaunt countries adjoining. And latelye, so wythe cleare streames hath abounded, as exceeding tholde lymittes, burste foorthe the bankes, reaching themselfe, to countries, farther distant, sweetlye moystinge the soiles thereof. And emongst other, pleasauntlye washte over tholde forworen Temples.[100]

Legh's work is a celebration of the Renaissance and its pervasive influence over the development of the English legal institution. Whilst the Inner Temple is described by Legh as an 'Iland';[101] it is an island washed by the waters of the Hippocrene. Legh heralds the nativity of a new empire of laws in the west; a sovereign state, independent from Rome and Roman law, but one that embraces rather than denies its classical forebears. In Legh's fantastical narrative, the Inner Temple is a microcosm of the ideal constitution, simultaneously embodying the classical model provided in Plato's *The Republic* and the Christian model of St. Augustine's *De Civitate Dei*.[102] As Michel Foucault wrote of the ill-fated Actaeon, whose tragic story is told in Book III of Ovid's *Metamorphoses*: 'in the complicity of the divine with sacrilege, some of the Greek light flashed through the depths of the Christian night'.[103]

100 Legh, *The Accedens*, fo. 118v.

101 Ibid., fo. 119v.

102 'that heavenly city which has Truth for its King, Love for its Law, and Eternity for its Measure': St. Augustine, *The City of God*, trans. John Healey (London: Dent, 1931), Introduction, xii. On the theme of *translatio imperii*, it is noteworthy that St. Augustine wrote *De Civitate Dei* when the Roman empire was on the verge of collapse. On the architecture of the early modern Inns as the representational synthesis of Augustinian and Platonic ideals, see Paul Raffield, 'Bodies of Law: The Divine Architect, Common Law and the Ancient Constitution', 13 (2000) *International Journal for the Semiotics of Law*, 333–56

103 Michel Foucault, *Aesthetics, Method, and Epistemology: Essential Works of Foucault, 1954–1984*, ed. James D. Faubion, 3 vols. (London: Penguin, 2000), 2: 125.

CHAPTER 4

Confessio infirmitatis, or, a productive digression: iconic difference taken apart and put to good use in legal affairs

Anselm Haverkamp

For a century or two, emblems were the rage and were forgotten only a little later. Both the rage and the forgetting evidence that a threshold had been crossed. A divide fearfully approached and experienced with enthusiasm, but lost after the effect had settled in, was taken for granted and had sunk under the surface of being perceived: a lesson had been learned and the time before seems to have become embarrassing. The threshold, I submit, was of an epistemological nature and the divide overcome implied a rupture that was painful, even though it had felt glorious at first. In this, it may have been similar to the media revolution that we have experienced and almost left behind, while the prize to be paid is still up in the clouds and of little interest except for future historians. But of what history? This question, too, is up in the air and to historicize epistemology seems to offer little more than a frame for histories of the sciences and scholarship. What is at stake on the threshold marked by the rising and waning of the art of emblems is a difference of apprehension that has to be traced below the terminological determination of scientific conceptual frameworks; it lies in a preconceptual sphere of coming to know and to conceive of. In this respect, it is close to legal affairs where laws are pronounced after a considerable period of legal uncertainty or, even less predictable, in revelation of some unregistered latent necessity.

In brief, and still tentatively, I investigate the rise and fall of emblems as a series of significant steps in a history of conceiving, of coming to know and coming to terms with multiple and, at the time, urgent questions of what there is to know and conceive of as knowledge. Or, to put it in the tentative terms of a historical epistemology that has yet to be developed, I try to work out the paradigmatic place and value of the emergence of emblems as an achievement in the *Advancement of Learning* – in the sense of Francis Bacon's adaptation of Quintilian's *Institutio oratoria* as an institution of learning – a most remarkable accomplishment that had its day and disappeared as suddenly as it emerged (and shall, maybe, re-emerge) on the same grounds and for the same reasons. In this respect, the emergence of emblematic presentation and representation may belong to the larger complex of the *Principle of Reason*, whose surfacing from a period of latency of more than a thousand years may be regarded as close to being an emblematic feature in the emergence of the modern world-picture, the world *as* picture.[1] Emblematically, the world had turned into a world successfully *pictured*, fit to be *viewed as* picture: to be *conceived of* in pictures.

I. The law of insertion (Quintilian)

Let me begin historically, from scratch, if only to show that the concept of history, as we use it and have become used to it, was created in that historical process and is part of the story to be told. Quintilian, an author to begin with in all cases of advanced learning, would have treated emblems (that is, discourses that provide insertions like emblems) as an admission of a great weakness, rather, than a strong argument:

> *Nam locos quidem* [he resumes], *quales sunt: de testibus 'semperne his credendum' et: de argumentis 'an habenda etiam parvis fides', adeo manifestum est ad forensic actiones pertinere, ut quidam neque ignobiles in officiis civilibus scriptos eos memoriaeque diligentissime mandatos in promptu habuerint, ut quotiens esset occasio extemporales eorum dictiones his velut* emblematis *exornarentur* (2.4.27).[2]

There, the word occurs, pops up, and quite innocently, at that, without meaning as yet what we encounter much later as emblems. The 'general topic' is commonplaces, *loci quidem, quales sunt*, and in this case, Quintilian exemplifies, it is witnesses or arguments, *de testibus et de argumentis*; so far, so

1 I am referring here to Martin Heidegger's model case *Der Satz vom Grund* (Pfullingen: Neske, 1957), also published as *The Principle of Reason* (Bloomington, IA: Indiana University Press, 1991); as well as the pilot study 'Die Zeit des Weltbildes' [1938], in *Holzwege* (3rd augm. edn, Frankfurt am Main: Klostermann, 1957), 69–104; 'The Age of the World Picture', in *Off the Beaten Track* (Cambridge: Cambridge University Press 2002), 57–85.

2 I use the new *Loeb Classical Library* edition of Quintilian, *The Orator's Education*, ed. and trans. Donald A. Russell, 5 vols. (Cambridge MA: Harvard University Press, 2002), vol. II: 292–3.

good: a commonplace of legal affairs. Here, and as a general rule enforced by Quintilian throughout, the term introduced and exemplified – *locus* – is not defined but, instead, is illustrated and itemized. Rhetoric does not proceed and is not learned by philosophical definitions but by *met-hodos*, by the way, in a step-by-step exposition of the features to be used and to be learned by using them. In this case, since here it is *loci* in general, the commonplace of commonplaces is exemplified according to the two legal respects of witnesses and of arguments – 'should we believe them' and 'should we rely on them' in Russell's apt and illustrative translation. The commonplaces applicable according to occasion, *occasio*, have to be 'ready at hand,' as Russell puts it, and that means that, above all, they have to be 'carefully committed to memory', *memoriae mandatos*, in writing first, in order to learn them by heart and to use them *extempore*. To repeat:

> General topics, such as on witnesses ('should we always believe them?'), or on rational arguments ('should we rely on them, however trivial?'), so obviously relate to forensic pleadings that some people, by no means undistinguished in public life, have been known to write these topics out, carefully commit them to memory, and have them ready at hand so as to embellish their extempore speeches with these insertions when necessary. I used to think – I cannot bear to hold my opinion back – that this amounted to an admission of great weakness.
>
> [Russell's translation 293/95]

As 'insertions' which 'embellish', if the occasion arises, *quotiens esset occasio,* Russell renders the Greek derivative *emblema* quite literally, as something like, *velut*, 'thrown in' and, that is, it turns out, as a dubious ornament that betrays, in Quintilian's view, a predicament of sorts. In an afterthought added by Quintilian – 'I cannot bear to hold my opinion back' is Russell's slightly exaggerated translation – he comes to the conclusion 'that this amounted to an admission of great weakness'. These thrown-in pieces of prefabricated everyday wisdom seem to betray, if not to confess, some *infirmitatem de se confiteri.* There seems more than one reason for this harsh judgment; Quintilian illustrates his reservations in a long digression of his own, which does precisely what it exposes; namely, too much. The modes of the too much-ness all run down to the same self-ironic insight: 'The things are attractive and useful if, and only if' – Russell quite aptly mimes analytic philosophy in his translation – 'they arise' *ex causa* – Russell exaggerates: '*naturally* out of the Cause'. There is no 'nature' in Quintilian 'but', he clarifies, 'the most beautiful verbal expression, *pulchra elocutio,* unless it helps us to win (the case), is always unnecessary, *supervacua* (means entirely empty) and sometimes actually damaging, *contraria*. Quintilian's insight does not lack self-irony in the face of his digression: I have wandered far enough, *satis*, from the point' (II: 294/95).

The unobvious point in Quintilian's use of the word *emblema* — not yet meant to signify the later art of emblems – is the barely marked mnemotechnical implication of the use of 'insertions', which amounts to an implicit *confessio infirmitatis* on the part of its user. Memory has to compensate for a certain and most common shortcoming in the necessary alertness or presence of mind in court. Mnemo-technique offered help not just in terms of rote learning by heart but these terms were also conceived of as quasi-visual; *memoria*, rhetoric proclaimed, was to be imagined as a hall of images and thus the commonplaces to be memorized were conceived of as emblematic *avant la lettre*.[3] They had a visual format that was duly literalized in the art of emblems. The metaphorical use of mnemo-technical imagery, whose linguistic, metaphorological nature was taken for granted by Quintilian, was exploited in Renaissance emblems. They were no longer mere discursive insertions but literal illustrations and, thus, they were able to support the verbal evidence to be achieved by an additional evidence whose pictorial nature was no longer of help in learning, remembering and applying an argument but organized the arguments' presentation in a new way, as the *re*-presentation of what everybody was ready to agree as a given contained in common knowledge. This supplement was not only dubious in its rhetorical value, not just dangerous in its quasi-aesthetic appeal, it was also attractive, as well as overwhelmingly successful, because of its public efficacy. Like Shakespeare's theatre, it changed the law's part and role in and for the public as a sphere. The circumstantial, historical reasons are evident; the theoretical ones enigmatic. They do not meet the eye anymore, since they changed the eye. Quintilian's digression on the genuine rhetorical weakness of the insertion of emblems gives us a first clue. According to his reasoning, it modifies the illocutionary potential of the speech act itself, and to no avail, he fears. As confessions of weakness, they are latently self-destructive. Saint Augustine's *Confessions* drew salvation from this potentially self-destructive act turned into salvific deconstruction. In Quintilian's case, which is primarily the case of legal procedures, this act asks for grace, indeed, even though this might not be on the agenda of rhetoric, and this may be the reason that

3 This was the starting point of the rather recent, modern reception after Frances Yates, *The Art of Memory* (Chicago IL: Chicago University Press, 1966), where the birth of modern imagination is imagined to draw on images like those, if not the same as those used in rhetoric's art of memory.

Quintilian does not feel at ease in this point. The force of law, he seems to feel, is forced to have an unpredictable outcome, one against the grain, and even more so against the shelter, of secure, well-contested legal reasoning: *nulla [argumenta] esse firmiora quam quae ex dubiis facta sunt certa* (5.12.3), 'there are no firmer propositions than those which were doubtful and have now become certain' is the common experience (II: 456/57) and not the more dangerous alternative by which what seems certain in common sense transpires to be dubious in legal terms.

II. Hyper-reflection cut apart (Merleau-Ponty)

Quintilian does not exactly anticipate the emergence of the emblem book in a much later age. He not only situates it in a strictly forensic scene, in which one could not very well foresee the technological advances made by print, he also marks the systematic place – and, that is, as we shall see, already a quasi-transcendental place – where emblems will occur, in print. Print culture not only added a greater visibility to argumentation but, more decisively, as a cognitive achievement, it added hyper-reflection to perception and representation. What does this mean, theoretically, with respect to the new literary form of the emblem in emblem books? And what does it mean, in the practice of theory, regarding the use of emblems and emblem collections, for its legal use by lawyers and judges, and for a law-conscientious public sphere?

In short, without enough reference to Merleau-Ponty's intricate fine-tuning of the word, the hyper-reflection of word and image is cut apart in the emblem, as it arises as a new technique of presenting the state of rhetoric in a new age: the Renaissance. Merleau's apt example for what happens in 'hyper-reflection' is an impressive emblem of rhetoric.[4] It is the un-decidability of which of two hands touching each other feels the other – not to speak of that epoch-making instance of washing one's hands in innocence, that Pilate tried to get away with.[5] The two hands discover or, rather, the second one discovers as the first hand's other, the image that is rhetoric's other. Metaphorologically embedded in the mnemo-technical use of

4 Maurice Merleau-Ponty, *Le visible et l'invisible*, ed. Claude Lefort (Paris: Gallimard, 1964), 61; *The Visible and the Invisible* (Evanston IL: Northwestern University Press, 1968), 38.

5 See here and in the following, Peter Goodrich's groundbreaking study, *Legal Emblems and the Art of Law:* Obiter depicta *as the Vision of Governance* (Cambridge: Cambridge University Press, 2013), a book to be consulted throughout; on the motif at hand see chapter 6: 'The Missing Hand of the Law'.

6 See Anselm Haverkamp, *Figura cryptica: Theorie der literarischen Latenz* (Frankfurt: Suhrkamp, 2002), chapters 7–9 on 'The Memory of Rhetoric'.

memory images, the emblematic image surfaces from the oratorical underpinnings of every competent speech, part five of rhetoric.[6] The new use as a method of learning, enabled by the new means of print, takes apart what was mentally a unitary endeavor: remembering words with the help of word-pictures. In emblems, the reference is mutually doubled: the memorized rule or wisdom illustrates and, in turn, is illustrated by a memorable image. The mode of mutual reference, undecidable like hands touching each other, makes use of, and with the same stroke brings out another discovery, which precedes print technically and enables its format conceptually: the art of panel painting.

The crucial feature developed in this art and inherited by printing is the iconic difference inscribed on to the flat panel in the spacing of represented things; perspective is the best-known mode in which iconic difference is technically absorbed and pictorial rhetoric is accomplished. In the printed emblem, this difference, which had been successfully hidden in painting to illustrate scripture, the writing to be represented, is unfolded: the book of nature as well as the bible, the book of liturgy as well as the performance of legal acts. In emblems, thus, a *modus operandi* comes to the fore – the *forum* as public scenery – congenial to the act of legal judgment, whose hidden pre-supposition (to be worked out in each case) is likewise to reconcile and put together the interlacing of appearance and adequate verbal statement of the case at hand.[7] Whereby – in the process of equation – visual illustration serves as the metaphor of the obvious: common sense – while the subscription presents itself most deceivingly as the identity of the word with itself. In that respect, structurally, not just ideologically, the emblem – although perhaps not the emblem as such but the historical format, whose seminal success we have to explain – remains subjected to the exemplary rule of the word, *sola scriptura*, to be enacted on the world's manifold stages, the altar, the court, the law and, last but not least, the theatre and the book. The scenery of these enactments is topic and subject matter of emblem books – in short, is emblematic of the world pictured. As such, the book of emblems – Alciatus – offered itself to, and triggered promptly extensive further philosophical elaboration in Coustau's commentary (1555).[8]

A most striking illustration of the structural transition brought about by the art of panel painting, I owe to Valérie Hayaert's juxtaposition of the

7 See Erwin Panofsky, *Architecture gothique et pensée scolastique* (1951), ed. Pierre Bourdieu (Paris: Minuit, 1967), postface 135–67: 159 ff. on 'l'*habitus comme modus operandi*'.

8 See Valérie Hayaert, Mens emblematica *et humanisme juridique: Le cas du Pegma cum narrationibus philosophicis de Pierre Coustau* (Geneva: Droz, 2008), esp. the impressive example in chapter III: 106 ff.

Senneton edition of the *Corpus Juris Civilis* (printed in Lyon between 1548 and 1550) and its model, the Ms *Ottobonianus Latinus* 3132 (Bibliotheca Vaticana) (Figure 4.1a,b).

Under the same heading, *De Justitia et Jure*, the difference could not be more significant and the features of representation, brought about by the advanced techniques of painting, could not be more pointed. Although far more artful, the illumination of the *Ottobonianus* seems almost primitive, while the modern print reproduction seems to be more detailed and elaborate. The crucial conceptual difference is one of pictorial space. What appears to be more primitive in the older *illustratio* seems to be more realistic in the modern print version, through the coherent application of perspective. Perspective, however, is far from absent in the manuscript but, there, it belongs to the things and persons and is no unifying feature of spatial continuity.[9] In this case, the *re-presentatio* of law and justice, perspectival space is proper to or, more precisely, an extension of the law itself, producing justice: speaking *ex cathedra*, justice shows three-dimensional space as the very dimension of its rule; the *cathedra*'s compact three-dimensional shape is the symbolic property of legal authority. The seat of Justice establishes a space within a timeless non-space surrounding it in blue flatness, on whose golden framework, like on a threshold, the involved parties take their respective spaces, according to their roles. The royal judge, wielding the sword, does this on the three-dimensional ground of his legal seat. In the emblem version, on the other hand, perspective rules the representation of legal details in the civil confines of a thoroughly public space. City and country, architecture and landscape, are offered as fully complementary perspectival constructs, the landscape as a backdrop of streets, pillars and arches, where the refinement of diversified and specified instruments of legal affairs are in place. The mythical figures and tools: books, scales, and sword, are provided *more geometrico*, in short: law's perspectival quality is unfolded and rules the common world.

The law, common law in particular, lends itself gladly to such picturing but this is not the law's special point and place in this success story of iconic difference, exploited and brought to public acclaim by the medium of print – circumstantial historical evidence not yet included in the account. Quintilian's qualms about the non-technical, if ever so commonsensical means that insertions and other mere ornamentation were grounded in circumstances, legal as well as public, of a bygone republican era, whose disappearance was notoriously mourned by his disciple Tacitus. The

9 See, for example, August Nitschke, *Kunst und Verhalten: Analoge Konfigurationen* (Stuttgart: Fromann-Holzboog, 1975), 17 ff. 83 ff., for a trans-historical view on perspective and the continuity of representation.

Figure 4.1a *De Justitia et Jure*, mss *Ottobonianus latinus* 3132, f. 3r, Biblioteca Apostolica Vaticana (reproduced by permission of Biblioteca Apostolica Vaticana, Vatican)

Figure 4.1b *De Justitia et jure*, *Digestus Vetus*, 1, 1, 1, *Sennetoniana*, Lyon, 1549 (reproduced by permission of Bibliothèque de la Cour de Cassation, Paris)

emergence of a public sphere – not yet necessarily one of bourgeois consent and civil institutions – thrived on the epiphany of a genuinely opaque, esoteric – theologically pre-approved – iconic politics, disclosed and opened up, to be read in the open difference between words and things presented, *verba et res*, whose intricate relationship was recognized and highlighted by Erasmus, as the very substance of rhetoric, now newly fashioned. What was the law's pay off beside the justification of the public spectacle? Which is more, one has to admit, than just illustration. Here, the 'new learning' comes in and Bacon's obsession with metaphors of legal investigation, when it came to scientific research and, if necessary, to metaphorically – emblematically, in fact – 'torture' nature, is more than mere professional bias.[10]

III: A chapter from the history of learning

The epistemological threshold crossed implied a rupture deeper and more decisive than the symptoms betray, a divide in learning, which can plausibly be described in terms of an emerging public sphere and which, in the process, changed the attitudes and horizons of expectation towards the law and its institutions: The law no longer represented some sovereign power but re-presented itself in the re-iteration of its acts; it acquired, step by step, a history of its own. This self-translation of a former *translatio imperii* into the self-maintenance of a legal constitution is the most general topic of legal emblems in the shared context of the common wisdom of life and the grounding norms of custom. Common law became common that way – a lady of common grace, rather than of sovereign upbringing. The plausibility of this story is not complete, however, since it does not include the epistemological change that brought it about as a cognitive step in history. The metaphorological development leads us from ancient rhetoric's memory-imagery to the literal emblematic display of images in an explicitly illustrative relation to the shared contexts of legal concerns and rhetorical common places. The law – and, that is, from now on, Justice herself in her emblematic function – governs and takes its new found legitimacy from a freshly established mental habit, or *modus operandi*, the illustrative force of printed images, roughly cut pictures, making explicit the common ground of law's empire. It is all too easy to take the cognitive advancement of learning for granted, which has gone into the cognitive habitualization of this operation, an operation that does not, in turn, imply a confession of weakness but gives way to a new sense of the political as a sphere of its own.

10 Hans Blumenberg, *Paradigmen zu einer Metaphorologie* (1960), Kommentar von Anselm Haverkamp (Berlin: Suhrkamp, 2013), 331 ad. 38 ff.; *Paradigms for a Metaphorology* (Ithaca NY: Cornell University Press, 2010), 21 ff.

Let me insert here an emblematic example (Figure 4.2), which I ran into in a law firm in the centre of Munich, Bavaria. On the wall of this office hangs the sign, *signum*, of one of the forefathers of the firm, a *Norariatus Apostolici et Caesarii Jos. Anton Ellenrieder* of 1715.[11] The *pictura* comes under the

Figure 4.2 *Omne patet, nihil latet* (photograph by Anselm Haverkamp, collection of Dr. Peter Baltzer, Munich)

11 Collection of Dr. Peter Baltzer, Munich, which includes many, although mostly less striking, examples with variations of the same stock items, book, table, etc. in careful perspectival setting, provided by architectural means, as in the frontispiece of the imperial legislation on the profession by Maximilian I from 1512, which remains relevant through the 19th century: *Kaiserliche Notariatsordnung von 1512*, ed. Herbert Grziwotz unter Verantwortung der Bundesnotarkammer Köln (Munich: Beck, 1995). Also August Meyer, *Die Notariatsordnungen von 1512 und 1871 als Beiträge zur Rechtssicherheit. Festschrift des Delegiertentages der österreichischen Notariatskammern* (Salzburg, 1971).

heading *Omne patet, nihil latet* as professional maxim, illustrated by the picture of an eye illuminating everything and highlighting the office, *officium*, in the form of a table with documents and charters sealed – no doubt a rather conventional but all the more telling emblem of legal office (the photograph, taken by my mobile phone, aptly duplicates the evidence). Evidently, the law's evidence, written down, sealed and kept by the notary's office, brings everything into the open – *omne patet* – and keeps it accessible, so that nothing remains obscure and threatening – *nihil latet,* in both senses of *latere,* nothing hidden, nothing threatening – in this city proud to be free of feudal obscurantism; a city, let me add in passing, in which young Mozart was a couple of years later to revolutionize the *Opera seria* of feudal representation under the name of *Idomeneo* (1781), ancient tyranny reformed. *Omne patet, nihil latet* defines the conditions of possibility of doing justice in the practice of the law and this definition comes in a transcendental form that Kant would have enjoyed. The emblematic use of a pregnant formula is illustrated and the sealed writing of the charter lies securely folded but accessible in the universal light of the self-illumined legal sphere.

The law's office, defined not first of all by justice to be done but by public transparency to be reached and secured, is no longer justly allegorized by the pre-emblematic figure of a blind *Iustitia* and her scales. This office, the law's *officium,* is not just the result of the more or less refined modes of interpretation reached by divine inspiration or else by old precedence – reached with the help of a good old god's good old laws – but is the result of a shared, new, political insight, based on the newly acquired cognitive competence to read the law and understand the law's office accordingly as the negotiation of public affairs, rather than the maintenance of a world order. However, the picture unfolding from the many emblems' manifold folds of writing did not only visualize what needed public recognition. In the variegated emergence in emblems, of one medium from another, of a *pictura* from the *scriptura,* the one illuminating the other, a differentiating momentum surfaces from the very mode of its im-plication. From the *plis* (which may be pleas) of writing, a new sense of the political arises, which asks for a new economy of recognition, where an older scene of speech and representational logic is displaced and replaced, and visibility conditions are changed.

So far, I have more or less underlined the socio-political aspect of this change, as it has been reconstructed in Habermas' *Structural Transformation of the Public Sphere.*[12] I do not question the plausibility of his 'blueprint' but

12 Jürgen Habermas, *Strukturwandel der Öffentlichkeit* (Neuwied: Luchterhand, 1962); *The Structural Transformation of the Public Sphere* Cambridge MA: MIT Press, 1989), ch. 4, 'The Basic Blueprint'.

its reach and depth. The cognitive economy responsible for this change cannot as easily be taken for granted as Habermas describes it. Jacques Rancière has made some effort in *Le partage du sensible* to describe the socio-political frame in terms of a new regime of the arts, emerging from this change. Rancière's intuition that art not only affects but, in fact, does politics long before (or even without) artists coming around to actually do politics and behave politically, proposes a supplementary support function of aesthetics for politics, which is more than the usually assumed compensatory function.[13] The new economy does more than just meet the eye in various aesthetic ideologies. Rancière's *Future of the Image* (the fate or destiny, to be precise, inscribed in images) gives us a first idea beyond the limited support economy of writing – in this case of the law itself in its communicative function – through pictures.

Primordially, the law was written, it came in writing and was handed down in writing, and this preponderance of writing gave support and special pathos even to the un-written laws as laws, which did not lack writing because they came to us from primordial times but they do not need writing, since they were always already implied in the writing down of laws. If anything, the law – as much as literature – came to ground itself in writing. Thus, to insert images into writing, under written headings and explained by sententious subscripts, is a significant change of regime, 'that gives visibility and signification to the [cultural] practices of arranging words' and 'displaying' pictorial features. Rancière picks a crucial instance of a truly exemplary '*partage du sensible*' in the aesthetic realm: 'The *ut pictura poesis/ ut poesis pictura* did not simply define the subordination of one art – painting – to another – poetry. It defined a relationship between the orders of making, seeing, and saying whereby these arts – and possibly others – were arts'.[14] In the emblem, to cut a lengthy story short, the relationship, which would develop into the *ut pictura poesis* doctrine, defined or, more precisely, re-defined the practices of making, seeing and saying in and as their mutually shared illocutionary potential. The law, indeed, is not only but also a most exemplary field affected by and – that is the question – subjected to this change of economy.

> Perspective [Rancière adds, and this is as apt a side-remark as Quintilian's digression] was not adopted in order to demonstrate a

13 Jacques Rancière, *Le partage du sensible: esthétique et politique* (Paris: La fabrique, 2000), 66 ff.

14 Jacques Rancière, *Le destin des images* (Paris: La fabrique, 2003), 90; *The Future of the Image* (London: Verso, 2007), 74 f.

> painter's ability to imitate the depth of space and the contours of bodies ... If perspective was linear and theatrical before becoming aerial and sculptural, it is because painting first of all had to demonstrate its capacity for poetry [i.e. the economy of writing in its strongest form].[15]

The emblem's shared, though very rigid, economy of writing and drawing originates on the well prepared groundwork of an iconic difference, which finds itself thematized and exploited in perspective; 'first of all,' Rancière says, 'it had to demonstrate'. What there was to be demonstrated is the economy and, that is, the ability to act effectively in that economy. After this newly acquired ability of making, seeing, saying has become an established practice, the extraordinary attraction of its display vanishes in the routine of trademarks and business slogans. Like the perspectival display, which was in Renaissance paintings the apex of meaningful representation and the witness of a new way of conceiving things, is today perceived only when it is missing or faulty. However, to what extent the emblematic display of words and things, of preconceived sentences and things pre-spaced by iconic difference, went into the media structure of a later age and into the design of a more advanced interlacing of visual and linguistic means, remains an open question.

The variety of psychoanalytical intimations triggered by an advancement less of learning than of modern media conditions – like intimations according to which emblems perform a positivization of the negative – mostly underestimate (or overlook, so to speak) the technological achievement of iconic difference that conditions the emblematic effect of a bringing out – no, not of some theologically grounded 'negative' but of the implication of the visual in writing and revealing it in or as 'picture'. The hybrid thus pro-duced and ex-posed (the pre-fix remains an essential feature in this production) is nothing 'un-sayable' or hinted at, it is rhetoric's self-proclamation. Emblems may be witty or (mostly) dull but they are never mystical. On the other hand, and not to be confused with this one, there is Peter Goodrich's fair adaptation of Pierre Legendre: There, 'The structural role of the emblem, the primacy of the legal image' is that of 'an unconscious form' to the extent that 'the image is the dogma'. And 'It is in this latter sense' ['of the visible form of an invisible grace'] that 'The emblem passes on a dogmatic truth ... but also shows, demonstrates, and pictures the rule and offers a vision of its proper meaning and interpretation as enacted for its

15 Ibid.

viewers'. In short, 'The emblem is nothing other than the point of intersection of sovereign rule and administrative practice, of law and governance'.[16] Emblem books may implicitly be confessions of weakness, insofar as they give the game of lawmakers away to the juridical practice: to the *mens emblematica* as a methodology *sine manu*. In the graphic format of starkly framed post-perspectival drawings, emblems explicitly deny what iconic difference in the heydays of Antonello da Messina and Giovanni Bellini was about: a theo-rhetoric that articulated its divine source in the refinement of perspectives: no re-presentation, in any event, but the 'presencing' of an act-potential.[17]

Emblems draw much of their secularized efficacy from a paradoxical denial of their sources, while the transcendentalized former transcendence proclaims immanence, the 'force of law' to begin with.[18]

16 Goodrich, *Legal Emblems*, 248–50 (my reductive collage of a text with farther reaching consequences). The Legendre reference is to *Dieu au miroir: Étude sur l'institution des images* (Paris: Fayard, 1994), 228.

17 See Anselm Haverkamp, '"To Conceive of" in Pictures. Antonello da Messina, August Sander' (2008). *Res: Aesthetics and Anthropology* 59–60 (2011), 266–82.

18 See, needless to say (inevitable in this context), Jacques Derrida, *Force de loi: Le 'Fondement mystique de l'autorité'* (Paris: Galilée, 1994); 'The Force of Law: The "Mystical Foundation of Authority"', *Cardozo Law Review* 11/5–6 (1990), 919–1045

CHAPTER 5

The heart and the law in the scales: allegorical discourse and modes of subjectivation in early modern religious emblematics

Agnès Guiderdoni

In the quest for both promoting and channelling new forms of individual piety, sixteenth-century religious emblematic literature made use of the methods elaborated in the wake of the fifteenth-century methods of meditation that developed across Europe from Spain to Germany and the Netherlands. The techniques were perfected by investing these practices with the complex philosophical and theological doctrines in which humanist symbolics were rooted. Meditation emblem books flourished in the second half of the sixteenth and the early seventeenth centuries, propelled by both Catholic and Protestant pastoral efforts aimed at spiritual reconquest and education. While emblematics were used by both camps, and the same emblems or even entire emblem books circulated rather freely from one confessional side to the other, various visual and allegorical strategies may be identified that delineate differing modes of moral subjectivation of the reader or beholder, looked at from the point of view of their goal of persuasion and conversion. These conversion strategies as modes of subjectivation could otherwise be called 'apparatuses (*dispositifs*) of the subject', because of their ambition of fashioning the subject and, from this perspective, meditational emblem books could be considered as 'technologies of the self', being the instruments used to achieve this subjective fashioning under the supervision of a legitimate church authority of some sort.[1] These 'technologies of the self' are procedures contained in

1 On the fashioning of the subject, see '*Dispositifs du sujet à la Renaissance*', *Rue Descartes* 27 (2000), entirely devoted to this question.

> texts written for the purpose of offering rules, opinions, and advice on how to behave as one should: 'practical' texts, which are themselves objects of a 'practice' in that they were designed to be read, learned, reflected upon, and tested out, and they were intended to constitute the eventual framework of everyday conduct. These texts thus served as functional devices that would enable individuals to question their own conduct, to watch over and give shape to it, and fashion themselves as ethical subjects; in short, their function was 'ethico-poetic'.[2]

Yves Michaud comments on this quotation:

> *En ce sens, elles sont des procédures de production de l'identité, des modes de subjectivation. En même temps, elles ont à voir avec le suivi de règles et comportent donc un élément éthique ou moral. Elles passent par des modes de discours qui sont autant de jeux de la vérité.* [In this sense, they are procedures for the production of identity, modes of subjectivation. At the same time, they are also modes of following rules and thus carry with them an element of the moral or ethical. They proceed by means of a discourse that is also a game of truth.][3]

Subjectivation, moral rules and truth in (and of) discourse are the three ingredients that we will see at work in the emblems selected for this study, which all represent divine judgement of the sinful soul. Representation of divine judgement and of how the guilty soul is treated is certainly one of the most pertinent places to study the use of an allegorical discourse at the service of subjectivation because, in the early modern period, the substance of man was identified with the substance of sin, which implied total submission to divine law and judgement.[4] Indeed, the late medieval and early humanist discussions on the vexed issue of sin and freewill acquired remarkable pre-eminence during the Reformation upheaval and led theologians and philosophers to try to find both orthodox and acceptable solutions to this question.[5] Central to these discussions was the degree of responsibility

2 Michel Foucault, *The History of Sexuality*. vol. 2, *The Use of Pleasure*, trans. Robert Hurley (Harmondsworth: Penguin, 1985), 12–13.

3 Yves Michaud, '*Des modes de subjectivation aux techniques de soi: Foucault et les identités de notre temps*', *Cités* 2 *Michel Foucault: de la guerre des races au biopouvoir*, (2000), 11–39, at 28.

4 '*L'identification du péché avec la substance de l'homme [impliquait] la soumission de l'homme à la loi divine*', Wolfgang Pross, '*Le péché et la constitution du sujet à la Renaissance*', in *Dispositifs du sujet à la Renaissance*, *Rue Descartes* 27 (2000), 79–116, at 108.

5 See Pross, '*Le péché et la constitution du sujet à la Renaissance*'.

assumed by man in his actions and therefore how the law of God should be implemented in human life. On this point, Catholics and Protestants opted for different answers but it seems that both pursued a common objective, which was to shift man's subjection from the supernatural to 'formal prescriptions and positive laws established by ecclesiastical authorities as much as the civil ones'. The Reformation chose to subject the entire human life to the strict implementation of faith and thus sacralized profane life, whereas Catholicism opted for the possibility of man choosing between good or evil, with the help of divine grace.[6]

In this chapter, I examine how different emblems of divine judgement develop specific discursive forms, rooted in a Christian allegorical context. This gives us a clue as to the conception of the law of God contained within it and also indicates the kind of subjectivation it transmits. I do this by comparing three emblems drawn from three religious emblem books, published between 1617 and 1629. Each of these emblems represents the weighing of the human heart against the law of God. I show that, although they use the same objects (the scales, the heart and the tables of the law), each emblem elaborates a different discourse about the subject that it means to represent and also to which it is addressed, and I pay particular attention to the treatment to which the human figure is submitted in these engravings as a vantage point from which to decipher these representations.

The first emblem (Figure 5.1) comes from *Emblemata sacra* by the Lutheran Daniel Cramer.[7] Each emblem, one after another, repeats the same layout: the engraving as a medallion, *impresa*-like, on the right-hand page, surrounded by a biblical pericope in Latin and translated into German, and a *subscriptio* in the form of a gloss distich, while the left-hand page contains a four-verse epigram in four different languages (Latin, German, French and Italian), with the matching translation of the Latin quotation. The second

6 '*l'objectif commun ... unissait les Églises rivales: briser la chaîne qui liait l'homme au surnaturel pour l'assujettir complètement aux prescriptions formelles et aux lois positives établies par les autorités aussi bien ecclésiastiques que civiles. Pour atteindre ce but, deux possibilités s'offraient: la première, saisie par la Réforme, consistait à plonger l'homme dans les ténèbres les plus épaisses face à Dieu et à lui imposer l'observance la plus stricte des exercices de la foi et de l'obéissance, toujours dans l'espérance vague d'attraper une lueur fugitive de la grâce divine. ... le catholicisme renonce à la systématicité dans la conduite de la vie en faveur d'un "occasionnalisme" de la grâce; à la sacralisation de la vie profane des réformateurs, il substitue, pour compenser, la possibilité de faire le mal et le bien sans contrainte divine. Cette solution optimiste n'est que le revers de la même médaille*', Pross, note 4, at 104–5.

7 Daniel Cramer, *Emblematum Sacrorum Prima Pars. Das ist: Fünfftzig Geistlicher in Kupfer gestochener Emblematum auss der H. Schrifft von dem süssen Name und Creutz Jesu Christi. Erster Theyl Inventirt und angegeben durch ... Daniel Cramer*, (Francfort: Lucae Jennisi, 1624; 1st edn, 1617).

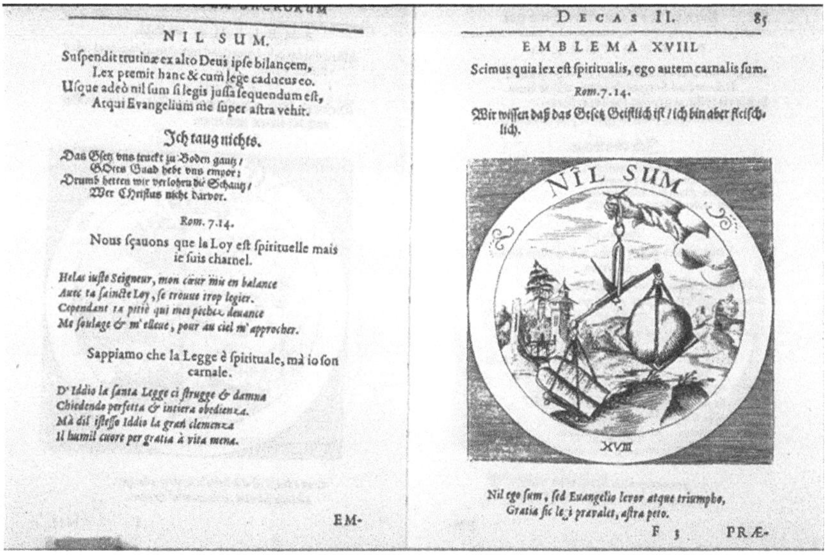
NIL SUM.

Suſpendit trutinæ ex alto Deus ipſe bilancem,
Lex premit hanc & cum lege caducus eo.
Uſque adeò nil ſum ſi legis juſſa ſequendum eſt,
Atqui Evangelium me ſuper aſtra vehit.

Ich taug nichts.

Das Gſetz uns truckt zu Boden gantz /
GOttes Gnad hebt uns empor:
Drumb hetten wir verlohren die Schantz /
Wer Christus nicht darvor.

Rom. 7.14.

Nous ſçauons que la Loy eſt ſpirituelle mais ie ſuis charnel.

Helas iuſte Seigneur, mon cœur mis en balance
Avec ta ſaincte Loy, ſe trouve trop legier.
Cependant ta pitiè qui mes pechez devance
Me ſoulage & m'elleue, pour au ciel m'approcher.

Sappiamo che la Legge è ſpirituale, mà io ſon carnale.

D'Iddio la ſanta Legge ci ſtrugge & damna
Chiedendo perfetta & intiera obedienza.
Mà dil iſteſſo Iddio la gran clemenza
Il humil cuore per gratia à vita mena.

EM-

DECAS II. 85

EMBLEMA XVIII.

Scimus quia lex eſt ſpiritualis, ego autem carnalis ſum.

Rom. 7.14.

Wir wiſſen daß das Geſetz Geiſtlich iſt / ich bin aber fleiſchlich.

NIL SUM

XVIII

Nil ego ſum, ſed Euangelio levor atque triumpho,
Gratia ſic legi prævalet, aſtra peto.

F 3 PRÆ-

Figure 5.1 Daniel Cramer, *Emblemata sacra,* 1624, embl. II:18, '*Nil sum*' (courtesy of the University of Glasgow Library, Special Collections)

emblem (Figure 5.2) is drawn from the *Schola cordis* by Benedictus Van Haeften, published in 1629 in Antwerp,[8] and devoted to the improvement and spiritual progress of the soul represented in the form of the heart. The layout is here quite different and less complex, playing with fewer elements: the engraving with the title, the biblical quotation and a commentary (a sentence only) occupies the left-hand page, opposite a *lectio*, with the same title, the quotation and the comment sentence. The use of the word *lectio* – a long prose development – should obviously draw our attention to the close relationships between spiritual emblematics and the *lectio divina*, practised as an exegetical meditation in monastery. This *lectio* is divided into several *considerationes*, four to five stages ascending from the most concrete interpretation of the biblical quotation, the most literal, to the most abstract remarks, and the most spiritual meaning, and thus following the traditional (patristic) exegetical scheme. This is not a trivial remark, as we discover how the understanding of each of these three emblems is related to a variation on

8 Benedictus Van Haeften, osb, *Schola cordis sive aversi a Deo Cordis ad eumdem reductio et instructio* (Anvers: Jérome Verdussen, 1629).

Figure 5.2 Benedictus Van Haeften, *Schola cordis*, 1629, embl. II: 17, '*Cordis ponderatio*' (courtesy of the University of Glasgow Library, Special collections)

the exegetical process. Finally, the third image (Figure 5.3) comes from the Jesuit Herman Hugo's *Pia desideria* (1624), an emblematic meditation book where the emblem is divided into three parts, corresponding to three moments of meditation: an untitled engraving, accompanied by a biblical quotation, opens a new stage on the way to perfection, followed by a long elegy and concluding with a lengthy compilation of quotations from sacred writers, which provide the *auctoritates*.[9]

9 Herman Hugo, sj, *Pia Desideria Emblematis Elegiis & affectibus S.S. Patrum illustrata* (Anvers: Henri Aertssen, 1624).

Figure 5.3 Herman Hugo, *Pia Desideria*, 1624, embl. I: 10 (courtesy of the University of Glasgow Library, Special Collections)

At first glance, the variations that occur from one image to the other with regard to their symbolic language and style are obvious and could be summarized roughly as a trajectory from hieroglyphic (Cramer) to narrative discourse (Hugo).[10] This is mainly discernible through the progressive introduction of the human figure, which seems to lead us towards an allegorical representation, in the understanding of the Jesuit Ménestrier, who hints at the constituent narrative quality of allegorical emblems, in his 1662 *Art des emblemes.*[11] Because of this specific variant among the three engravings, and because the human figure is progressively taking on board an emotional discourse about guilt, we need to explore the significance of the human figure and the body in the early modern allegorical system in order to understand how the same elements may be composed to convey three different conceptions of divine justice and therefore three different human interpretations of the law.

We could start with the simple observation that it is somehow paradoxical to use the human figure as a means of conveying an allegorical meaning. We are so used to seeing representations of (mainly) women incarnating moral virtues and abstract concepts or even reading their discourses (as in *prosopopeia*) that we tend to take that common and widespread practice for granted. When reconsidered in its Christian context, however, it does not go without saying but rather it demands at least some accommodation with the negative values that pertain to the flesh, assimilated to the letter – as opposed to the spirit.

According to the exegetical patristic tradition, the literal meaning of a text and, especially, the Holy Scriptures, is the 'body' of the meaning, while its spiritual sense is its soul. This body-and-soul metaphor comes originally from Origen and was abundantly exploited by the early sixteenth century humanists who undertook to renovate biblical exegesis. Erasmus, among the most prominent players of this major hermeneutical change, used this metaphor in the *Enchiridion militis christiani*, combined with the one of the Silenus, which he also developed in the *Adagia.*[12] Other sacred writers used other metaphors (the bark and the tree, the nutshell, the bone and the marrow, etc.), the common ground being the obvious and conspicuous, therefore visible, aspect of meaning assimilated to literal meaning in a

10 For a definition of the 'hieroglyphic mode of thought' in the emblem, see Peter M. Daly, *Emblem Theory; Recent German Contributions to the Characterization of the Emblem Genre* (Nendeln-Liechstenstein: KTO, 1979), 82.

11 Claude-François Ménestrier, *L'art des emblèmes* (Lyon: Benoist Coral, 1662), 56.

12 See André Godin, *Érasme, lecteur d'Origène*, Geneva: Droz, 1982), 60, 103, 252; Henri de Lubac, *Exégèse médiévale: les quatre sens de l'Écriture* (Paris: Aubier, 1959–1964), vol. 4, p. 439–42; Érasme, *Les Silènes d'Alcibiade*, trans. Jean-Claude Margolin (Paris: Les Belles Lettres, 1998); Manfred Hoffmann, *Theology and Rhetorics: The Hermeneutic of Erasmus* (Toronto: University of Toronto Press, 1994), 27–8.

metaphorical spatial view on the topic.[13] As such, no spiritual sense of any sort can be found in the literal sense: all the (rhetorical) figures are mere 'poetic fictions'.[14] When it comes to allegorical representation and symbolic literature (that is, humanist symbolics and emblematics), it seems all the more relevant to configure a complex system, a multilayer process to account for the status of that body and human figure when used as a meaningful device. Here, obviously, allegorical representation and biblical exegesis are closely related at a paradigmatic level. The body-and-soul relationship is the starting paradigm for both allegorical representation and biblical exegesis. I argue that, from biblical exegesis to allegorical representation, one goes from a paradigmatic to a syntagmatic use of the body-and-soul dichotomy or, in other words, one goes from a metaphor that 'speaks' about and represents the allegorical quality of the biblical text to the discursive deployment of the voices that were implicit in the body-and-soul metaphor. In this process, the body is no longer the symbol of a signifying level of discourse but becomes meaningful in itself and serves the organization of the signification process. It speaks for itself, which leads to a narrativisation of the image. To support my argument, I now study these three emblems of judgement by comparing them and trying to understand how one goes from the first to the last picture, how the human figure is gradually introduced and what status of the human body it reveals in the figurative signification process.

A renewal of Biblical exegesis took place in the sixteenth century, which recast the traditional patristic hierarchy of the senses and entailed a positive new status for the literal sense. In a complementary way, Erasmus and Jacques Lefèvre d'Etaples were prominent figures in this renewal, especially with regard to the visual quality of the hermeneutic process that they both initiated. While Erasmus advocated an allegorical interpretation of the Bible (following most preferably, he says, Origen, Ambrose, Jerome and Augustine), his method of approaching the true meaning, the spiritual sense of the Scriptures did not differ from his method of understanding poetic texts, such as those of Homer and Virgil; it is 'an undifferentiated universal *allegoresis*':[15]

> Viewing allegory as a technique and as a universal language, there was no need to establish any relation of dependence between its disparate fields of application. Rhetoric, and specifically allegory, its

13 For a more complete review on these metaphors, see Henri de Lubac, *Exégèse médiévale*, vol. 2, p. 480 sq.

14 This is the orthodox line stated by Aquinas, *Quodl.*, VII, q.6 a.3 ad. 2, and *Quodl.*, VII, q.6 a.3 co.

15 '*une allégorèse universelle indifférenciée*', André Godin, *Érasme*, 254.

> privileged mode of expression, applicable to profane texts and to the Holy Scriptures alike, are the integrating parts of this wholly coherent, more or less hierarchical system of Erasmian humanistic and Christian thought.[16]

In his opinion (*Enchiridion*), the reading and exercises of the Pythagoreans and the Platonists, with their ornamented style, best prepare future theologians and exegetes to interpret and understand biblical allegories. Erasmus also establishes, however, that the literal sense is important in itself as the irreducible basis for correct *allegoresis.*[17] Erasmus provides us here with the first step of our demonstration: the equation between the literal sense of the Scriptures and poetic discourse. In doing so, he paved the way for a more radical transformation, which shifted the delivery of divine Truth from theology to poetry.

Jacques Lefèvre d'Etaples gives us the second step, mainly through his definition of what he called a 'figurative literal' sense, elaborated in the preface of his *Quintuplex Psalterium*, (1509):

> Each time they [the monks] stopped on I don't know what literal sense, especially when they wanted to understand the holy Psalms, they would leave their reading completely sad, the soul depressed. Then I began to think about whether this literal sense was the true literal sense ... or whether it was mistaken for another sense. Therefore I immediately turned to our primary guides, I mean the Apostles, the Evangelists and the Prophets ... and then it seemed to me that I could see another sense, the one that is in the intention of the Prophet (*intentionis Prophetae*) and the Holy Spirit speaking through him.[18]

16 Ibid., 255. [*Envisageant l'allégorie comme une technique et un langage universels, il n'a pas à établir une quelconque relation de dépendance entre ses divers champs d'application. La rhétorique et son mode privilégié d'expression, l'allégorie (qu'elle s'applique à un texte profane ou à la sainte Écriture), sont partie intégrante de ce tout cohérent, peu ou pas hiérarchisé, qu'est la pensée humaniste et chrétienne d'Erasme.*]

17 Ibid., 260.

18 '*Et si qui eorum ex sacris litteris pastum quaererent, saepius interrogavi quid in illis dulcedinis experirentur, quid saperent? Responderunt plurimi quoties in nescio quem sensum litteralem incidissent et maxime cum divinorum psalmorum intelligentiam queritarent, se multum tristes et animo dejecto ex illa lectione abscedere solitos. Tum coepi mecum ipse cogitare ne forte ille non verus litteralis sit sensus sed ... sit res pro re, et sensus pro sensu inductus. Illico igitur me contuli ad primos duces nostros, apostolos dico, evangelistas et prophetas, qui primi animarum nostrarum sulcis divina mandarunt semina et litteralem sacrarum scripturarum aperuerunt januam. Et videor michi alium videre sensum qui scilicet est intentionis prophetae et spiritus sancti in eo loquentis*', Jacques Lefèvre d'Etaples, *Quincuplex Psalterium*. Facsimile of the 1513 edition (Geneva: Droz, 1979).

He goes on with his explanation, calling this other meaning 'literal', which he makes coincide with the spiritual sense:

> I am calling this sense 'literal' but also coincident with the spiritual sense. The letter does not offer any other sense, neither for the Prophet, nor for those who see (and I do not want to deny the other senses, allegorical, tropological and anagogical, especially where the topic calls for them). But for those who do not see and yet believe that they see, another literal sense emerges: the one that, according to the Apostle, kills and goes against the Spirit. ... This sense, they call it literal ... This is the reason why I believe that there is a double literal sense: one, improperly called, for those who have a troubled sight, who do not see and who understand divine things from a sensual and carnal point of view; the other, the true one, for those who see, who are enlightened.[19]

Obviously, for Lefèvre d'Etaples, the literal level of the biblical figure contains the spiritual sense; not the only such sense, but at least one level of spiritual meaning.

The 'contamination' of the theological figure by the rhetorical figure (Erasmus), together with the possibility opened by Lefèvre d'Etaples of 'seeing' some spiritual content in the literal level will finally lead, in the longer term, to the recognition of the poetic value of the figure and will allow for the attribution of a spiritual sense to it.[20] This means a paradoxical use of the body-and-soul metaphor, all the more so when it aims at representing, in a picture, the soul in the form of a human character as depicted in emblems books.

We can now turn to the comparative exercise and examine the passage, from Cramer's to Hugo's emblem, of the various statuses occupied by the

19 '*Et hunc litteralem appello sed qui cum spiritu coincidit: neque prophetis, neque videntibus alium littera praetendit (non quod alios sensus, allegoricum, tropologicum et anagogicum, praesertim ubi res exposcit, negare velim). Non videntibus autem qui se nichilominus videre arbitrantur, alia littera surgit quae (ut inquit apostolus) occidit, et qui spiritui adversatur ... Et hujusmodi sensum litteralem appellant ... Quapropter duplicem crediderim sensum litteralem, hunc improprium caecutientium et non videntium qui divina solum carnaliter passibiliterque intelligunt; illium vero proprium videntium et illuminatorum; hunc humano sensu fictum, illum divino spiritu infusum*', Jacques Lefèvre d'Etaples, *Quincuplex Psalterium*. Facsimile of the 1513 edition (Geneva: Droz, 1979).

20 See Agnès Guiderdoni, '*Figures de l'âme pèlerine: La méditation emblématique aux* XVIe *et* XVIIe *siècles*', *La Meditazione in età moderna, Rivista di Storia e Letteratura Religiosa*, 41 (2005), 695–723; Agnès Guiderdoni, *De la figure scripturaire à la figure emblématique. Emblématique et spiritualité, 1580–1740* (Paris: Garnier, 2014)

human figure and therefore by the literal level of the figure itself, as well as the different means through which these are gradually introduced.

We start with Cramer's emblem (Figure 5.1), in which two important things should be emphasized. First, the entire signification of the engraving is concentrated in three objects whose combination makes sense but where each one constitutes an element, like a segment, of a symbolic syntagm. Second, the continuous dialectics between literal representation and spiritual interpretation keeps running throughout all the elements of the emblem. Thus, by adding the scale with the uneven plates, symbolizing the judgement, the representation is already an interpretation of the biblical *pericope*: 'We know that the law is spiritual but I am made of flesh' (*Romans* 7: 14). This interpretation is developed in the epigram, which uses the concrete elements of the engraving (the heart, the scale, the tables of the law) in order to draw a moral teaching:

Suspendit trutinae ex alto Deus ipse bilancem,
Lex premit hanc et cum lege caducus eo.
Usque adeo nil sum si legis jussa sequendum est,
Atque Evangelium me super astras vehit.

The effect is to reverse the initial interpretation of the engraving, which literally shows that the law is heavier than the heart, but this is precisely the weight that allows for a possible raising of the heart. This is the sense of the Latin distich. In other words, apparent weight and lightness have relative values in the salvation economy. So, while the engraving seems to present already an interpretation of the quotation, this 'literal level' of the image (though already symbolic) must be overcome to attain its spiritual sense, and a Christological one, which in fact turns out to be the strict literal reading of the engraving: the heart is higher, and so closer to God, than the law and precisely the ancient law. Following a hermeneutics consistent with the Lutheran conception of exegesis, the literal sense (here the literal level of the figure) contains the true meaning.

The only human element here is the heart, used as a synecdoche for man or his soul, completely subject to the judgement of God, depicted through the hand holding the scale. Moreover, the relationship between the body/letter and the spirit is organised in such a way that the image cannot be fully understood without the text: it needs speech but an external one, which enunciates the rules defining the true discourse, the true meaning for the true (spiritual) Christian. The full meaning of the image is thus articulated, through the *amplificatio* of the biblical quotation, which I now compare with the other engravings.

If we move on to Van Haeften's emblem (Figure 5.2), the same elements are represented in the engraving: the heart, the tables of the law and the scale, in a true literal application of the biblical quotation, this time without any over-imposed interpretation: 'The Lord weighs the hearts' (*Proverbs* 21: 2); the notion of judgement is already contained in the quotation. A fundamental difference consists in the presence of two characters that Ménestrier defines as 'allegorical'.[21] The introduction of these human characters is key to understanding the merging of biblical allegory and poetic allegory and the gradual shift from the one to the other. Each element of the allegory is doubled within the image: the Lord is represented by the tables of the law and divine love; similarly, the soul is represented by the heart and the little female figure and judgement by the scales and the expression of the guilt of the soul. So, two scenarios are taking place here: one similar to Cramer's emblem (if we single out the three elements, we get back to the Cramer emblem), which is a literal translation of the biblical quotation, and a new one, acted by the human figures and achieving the spiritual meaning: indeed, what is divine love compared with the tables of the law, if not the redemption of Christ, and what is the Soul compared with a synecdoche of the heart, if not the soul, refigured (after the disfiguration of original sin) through divine love and, moreover, a soul capable of expressing feelings (remorse), capable of expressing *affectus*, as a restored human being? More precisely, it is the human body that conveys and even contains the spiritual meaning. The symbolic elements are partially deprived of their full status as symbols: they are instrumentalized and begin to regain their status as things over their status as signs but the transformation is not yet fully achieved. We are still in between. This induces a shift, on the part of the reader, from the interpretation of the symbolic objects to the agencies of discourse, the agents of a relationship (the dialogue between the soul and divine love): one that moves from the moral realm to the affective realm. The objects acquire then the value of mere attributes, losing their structuring, figuring function, in this interpretation. This interpretation is elaborated in the commentary, in the implicit dialogue about these objects, which takes place between the soul and divine love. However, this direction is only hinted at, because the textual part is entirely devoted to exegesis. To sum up at this point, from Cramer to Van Haeften, the symbolic motifs that previously functioned as isolated entities begin to be structured within a narrative sketch. The sharpness, the precision, the symbolic delimitation

21 Ménestrier, *L'art des emblèmes*.

of Cramer's figure begins to become diluted, if I may say, disseminating its symbolic signified into anthropomorphic forms. Some kind of narrative is here initiated but still remains at an abstract stage; there are no landscapes, no concrete situations and each emblem is loosely linked with the others. This leads us further away from theological and exegetical discourse proper (the body-and-soul paradigm) and draws us closer to a poetic use of the body and soul relationship. Moreover, it opens up the possibility of developing a sense of judgement and guilt as affects, as internalized feelings, manifested in the physical presence and attitude of a human body that represents the soul. From this point of view, the process of subjectivation is fashioned by the awareness *and* the expression of guilt and remorse.

Finally, the last engraving, drawn from Herman Hugo's emblem book (Figure 5.3), shows the process of figuration and subjectivation reaching its final stage. Here, the emblematic process reaches its most achieved poetic stage, wherein the symbolic part proper of the representation is somewhat diluted or diffused through the whole of the engraving and the text. The engraving again contains the tables of the law, which ornament the room in which the scene takes place. This judgement is therefore placed under their authority. These tables are placed above divine love, which acts as the 'judge', who notes the sins of the soul in a large accounting book. The soul itself shows clear signs of guilt and remorse in her bodily countenance. Finally, the scales have now become one of the attributes that help us identify the allegory of Justice, worthy of Ripa. The diffusion of the symbolic signified is complete here when the judgement is taken on board in its entirety in the narrative subtending the engraving. The picture is telling a little story, inserted in a very solid context. Iconology occupies a well-delimited portion of this traditional representation of Justice, placed like a deictic sign and providing the meditating reader with guidelines for reading. What structures the emblem is the narrative. The poetic level is then transparent to the allegorical level (in the sense of the Christian allegory): the image is staged and contains many realistic details; moreover, this image is at one with the accompanying text, the elegy, which is all affectivity. Doctrine, as such, has disappeared, partly rejected at the end of the chapter in the compilation of *auctoritates*. The elegy develops at length the theme of the impossible and useless defence, amplifying the biblical quotation: 'And enter not into judgment with thy servant: for in thy sight shall no man living be justified' (*Psalms* 143: 2). This elegy stages and brings to life the various actors of the trial, making them speak, react, and so on: the judge, the lawyer, the accused, divine love and the soul. The soul, however, is the only enunciator throughout. The biblical figure that alludes to the final judgement but which also stresses the absolute power of God, is integrated into the discourse of the soul: the chosen point of view is totally subjective. From Cramer's emblem to Hugo's, the focalisation has shifted from an external point of view to an internal one. As a consequence, the poetic level of discourse is the organizing authority of the scene: to make sense of it, what is developed is not the exegesis of the holy text but a fully poetic allegory that the soul draws from the quotation. The poetic figure has absorbed the biblical figure and has made the human, individual figure emerge as an emotionally guilty and repenting individual. We can also put it another way. The body of the image has totally absorbed its soul, which in return is totally subjected to that body. Justice is a matter of narrative and representation and, above all, of expression of guilt and remorse; the soul acknowledges her guilt, in a totally internalized moral attitude of self-judgement, conveyed by the visible constraint of her body. The representation of the soul as a self-aware body under surveillance,[22] in the scenery of a human tribunal controlled by law (situated above divine love) and justice (given in its iconological form as an eternal and somewhat institutionalized ideal) or, in short, the incarnation of divine judgement into a legal narrative apparatus, which finds its achievement in the confession of guilt on the part of the repenting accused, could well be the expression of subjectivation along the lines of modernity. Indeed, one of the consequences of Molina's doctrine of grace and freewill,[23] which pervades Jesuit morality, was to establish the 'apparatus of his autonomy, which constitutes also the

22 '*En réalité, ce qui fait qu'un corps, des gestes, des discours, des désirs sont identifiés et constitués comme individus, c'est précisément cela l'un des effets premiers du pouvoir*', Michaud, '*Des modes de subjectivation aux techniques de soi*', 13; and '*Foucault met donc en relation doctrine de la liberté politique et délégation aux individus de leur propre gouvernement: plus de liberté veut dire quadrillage plus serré des corps et des comportements et autorépression*', ibid., 24. The judgement has been 'delegated' to the soul who shows the signs of her guilt *and* remorse.

23 Luis de Molina published his *Concordia liberi arbitrii cum gratiae donis* in 1588. The book stirred up much argument within the Catholic world, mainly in Spain, in the Netherlands (even before its publication), in France and in Rome, where the Pope, in particular Clement VIII, tried to come to terms with the controversy by establishing the Congregation *De Auxiliis* but neither the Dominicans (supporting a strict Augustinian doctrine, which takes away from Man nearly all credit for any good works) nor the Jesuits (supporting a more co-operative doctrine, in which Man contributes actively to his salvation) involved in the dispute found a way out. The only solution recommended by the Holy See was to forbid any discussion on that matter or any publication on the issue of grace. This ban may also explain the fact that the dispute, and its consequences, found its way in an implicit discourse, at work in devotional literature, all the more powerful for being implicit.

basis of his subjection under positive laws, be they established by the Church or by the State'.[24]

As I recalled in the introduction of this paper, subjectivation, moral rules and truth in (and of) the discourse are the main ingredients of the technologies of the self. Their interplay determines different discursive configurations in which the individuals are taken. From Cramer's to Van Haeften's and then Hugo's emblem, the introduction of the human figure embodies – literally – the awareness of the notion of 'being a subject', 'being subjected to'. It is striking that the human figure is absent of all Cramer's emblems, the biblical quotation and its exegesis through the symbols and the text functioning as a voice over, disembodied. The moral rules are given from outside, directly drawn from the exegesis of the Bible, which provides the truth of the discourse. The contrast with Van Haeften and, above all, with Hugo's emblem is reinforced by the fact that the enunciation of both the image and the text is supported by the repenting soul, thus a subject judging and judged, which, almost exclusively in Hugo's emblem, enunciates emotions, feelings of guilt and repentance, providing the code of moral conduct. Moreover, divine love may also be understood as an internal agency of the soul,[25] which transforms further the picture into the internalization of the judging authority. As Foucault puts it: '*Les individus sont appelés à se constituer comme sujet de conduite morale*'.[26]

The comparison between Cramer's and Hugo's frontispieces (Figures 5.4 and 5.5) allow us to synthetize these configurations. The monumental frontispiece of the Lutheran emblem book shows a clear architectonic composition, decorated with the allegories of two cardinal and two theological virtues and the evangelical symbolic animals of the Evangelists. God is represented by the tetragramme and the garden of Eden, so that the world before the fall and the sin forms the basis of the monument. By contrast, the frontispiece of the Jesuit emblem book is all affect, a huge winged burning heart being surrounded by several biblical figures. Both are emblematic of

24 '*en péchant, [l'homme] affirme la contingence de son être dans un monde qui, de sa part, est devenu le royaume d'une nécessité absolue, qui n'est plus gouverné par Dieu mais par la causalité des lois naturelles. En Molina, l'homme moderne a trouvé le 'dispositif' de son autonomie qui représente en même temps la base de son assujettissement sous les lois positives, qu'elles soient érigées par l'Église ou par l'État*', Pross, '*Le péché et la constitution du sujet à la Renaissance*', 112.

25 See Agnès Guiderdoni, '*Les figures angéliques dans les recueils de méditation emblématiques des* XVI*e et* XVII*e siècles*', *La parte dell'angelo – Documents de travail et pré-publications*, D 370-372 (2008), Centro Internazionale di Semiotica e Linguistica, Urbino, 18–29.

26 *Histoire de la sexualité*, t. 2 : *L'usage des plaisirs* (Paris: Gallimard, 1984), 12–13 [my emphasis].

Figure 5.4 Daniel Cramer, *Emblemata sacra*, 1624, frontispiece (courtesy of the University of Glasgow Library, Special Collections)

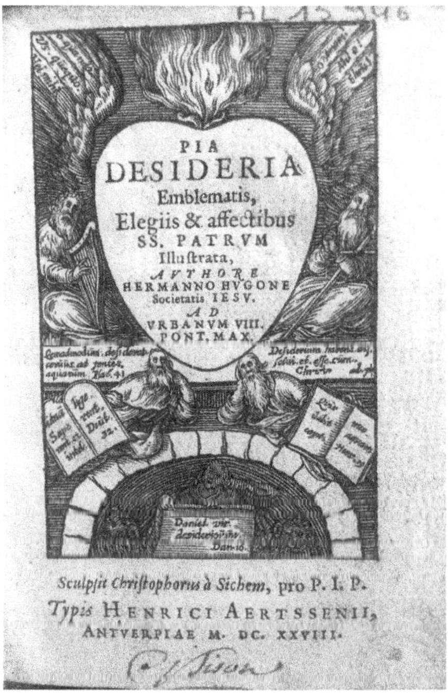

Figure 5.5 Herman Hugo, *Pia Desideria*, 1624, frontispiece (Université Catholique de Louvain, bibliothèque universitaire)

the figurative quality of the content of the books, which can be observed by the different statuses taken on by the human figure and therefore emblematic of the contrasted sketch of the subject that emerges out of their pages: from an intellectual voice reading and interpreting the external and literal law of God to an emotional body governed by the internal and spiritual law of his guilt and repentance.

CHAPTER 6

From pornography to moral didactism: how the French play with emblems

Christian Biet

Emblems are made to be interpreted, performed and betrayed. Provided that it is sufficiently well known to be recognized and identified as a message shared by enough readers, it has always been possible to play with an emblematic image. Some diversion is consubstantial with the experience created by emblems, through the interplay of the images and the commentary. A variety of interpretations is the proper modality of emblems, even if there is a code, at a certain time, saying that one meaning has to be chosen, is understood or efficient. Even if the content of emblem books is an infinite repetition of standard topics, even if the drawings and the symbolic and allegorical figures are systematically cut, pasted and recycled, it is sometimes striking to see how, from one period to another, the emblematic tools, mottoes, texts and images can be detached and can follow different paths. It is not really surprising, then, to see, at different periods, different interpretations, different games or different diversions devised from standard topics and emblems. It is not very surprising, either, to observe that emblems themselves can change according to the evolution of society itself. To follow these ideas, we take two such examples of emblematic evolution.

How to pervert an emblem with a riddle

The first example dates from sixteenth-century France, when Jacques de Fonteny transformed the meaning of classical emblems into a mostly gay pornographic, libertine and poetical miscellany. This example is not one of judicial emblems, it is just an example of the conduct and behaviour of the authors – anonymous or not, here anonymous and unpublished (we will see why) – when confronted with emblems. It is a code, just a code, with which one can play and, before actually analyzing the laws of emblems by means of a very serious example, I would like to show how far the play can lead during the early modern period.

Fonteny, a well-enough known author from the very end of the sixteenth century,[1] wrote some interesting poems in a manuscript, in the form of riddles that diverted the standard interpretation and engaged the readers in the pleasures or disturbance of transgression. The manuscript was recently discovered and edited online by Gerard Strasser and we are working together on editing it for *Classiques Garnier*. The album lately found in the Wolfenbuttel library is a manuscript album[2] written by Fonteny, who was also the playwright of the *Beau berger*, a gay pastoral of the same period performed in the Hôtel de Bourgogne (the official theatre of Paris) and published in several editions.

The manuscript seems to be an incomplete printer's copy to which the author himself might have made corrections and might have intended to add further sonnets. It was written around 1600 and consists of 45 letter-size sheets, of which 44 have a small square engraving printed on the upper part. Only 26 sonnets accompany the 44 engravings, leaving 18 pictures without text and open to the addition of a later commentary. They are written in what appears to be the Italian handwriting in vogue in France at the end of the sixteenth century.

For our common purpose, I first say a few words on the close similarity between enigmas (or riddles) and emblems at the time. Emblems, just as enigmas and riddles, require work by the reader and his knowledge of the usual interpretations of the images quoted or recycled in the latest proposition (which can be a published book or a manuscript). The Fonteny manuscript thus re-uses traditional and functional emblems (such as a bell,

1 In the early 1600s, Jacques de Fonteny was to become an important figure in the *Confrérie de la Passion*, the financial auditor at the Hôtel de Bourgogne, the owner of a theatre box that he could rent for his own profit, and the author of a tragedy, *Cléophon*, on the assassination of Henry III. In 1587, he published *L'Eumorphopémie*, or *Le Beau pasteur*, which would become *Le Beau berger* [The Fair Shepherd] in later editions. One can see that the dramatic pastoral, a genre developing in France at the time, was free to explore or bend rules that were only emerging and still malleable. The laws of the genre were always eminently plastic and relative. The genre originated in Italy. It was already practised in England and was progressively establishing itself in France. Nicolas de Montreux had already published pastoral dramas and other writers were following this burgeoning fashion, using the Italians as models, Tasso and Guarini in particular. Still, their freedom was boundless, since, even if there were some general conventions, no fixed rules seemed to have been set.

2 *Jacques de Fonteny's Livre d'Enigmes – Manuscript of an Early 17th-Century Para-Emblematic, Illustrated Sonnet Sequence*, edited by Gerhard F. Strasser, assisted by Eva Christina Glaser (Wolfenbüttel: Herzog August Bibliothek, 2012), available online at http://diglib.hab.de/wdb.php?dir=edoc/ed000166&distype=start&pvID=start (accessed 2 January 2015).

a reed, a mill, etc.) and other images (a writer inscribing a text on antique tablets, etc.) but commenting and redrawing them in sexual or allegorically pornographic poems. While it has not yet been possible to identify the engraver, and although there are certainly quite a few images that have emblematic roots, the question remains why some of the better illustrations that are very close to emblematic themes (such as the mirror in folio 31, the ship in folio 36, the rose in folio 41 or even the bellows in folio 39) do not sport accompanying sonnets. We will never be able to determine why Fonteny did not complete the entire sequence, especially since engravings such as those just listed should have invited accompanying poems. The year of the writing of the manuscript – 1600 – did, after all, find Fonteny at the height of his productivity.

On the first engraving (and poem), a man is seated at a table writing on a tablet. A wax pad with a stylus and two small objects (one of them is a cup) are on the table. A city is visible through the opened lower part of a sash-window and the sonnet is as follows:

Si je sers un marchant de cire, je suis vestûe
Pource qu'avecques luy il me convient trotter
Le courtisan me faict or & velours porter
Mais tous deux sont jaloux si quelqu'un m'a tenue
Au courtisan je suis plus qu'au marchant tenue
Dans les Palais des grandz il me faict frequenter
Le marchant ne m'espargne & ne me faict hanter
Que les mers et les ports d'une terre inconnue
L'un et l'autre voulant ma jouissance avoir
Vn long chose pointu sur moy ilz font mouvoir
Après qu'en quelque endroit ils m'ont mise et couchee
Ils me font et refont ce qu'ils veulent et puis
Afin que leur afaire à chacun soit cachee
En me lavant d'une eau, vierge presque je suis.[3]

3 Variants:
Si je sers un marchant de cuir (de cire ?) je suis vestûe
[B il + Je ne suis que de cuir (de cire ?) en [?] noir ou blanc vestue]
Pource qu'avecques luy il me convient trotter
[B il + Si je sers aux marchands de peur de trop couster]
Le courtisan me faict or & velours porter
[B il + L' homme de cour me faict or & velours porter]
Mais tous deux sont jaloux si quelqu'un m'a tenue
Au courtisant je suis plus qu'au marchant tenue
Dans les Palais des grandz il me faict frequenter

The idea of the sonnet is to present (and let the reader interpret) a wax tablet and the stylus which accompanies it. Behind the tablet and the stylus, the text allows readers to guess that it describes a body and the male sex in motion. The tablet can help the merchants to count and to take notes and the courtiers, who love luxury, can put the tablet and stylus inside a beautiful cover. The text assumes that, if you have taken the tablet (the body) or the stylus (the penis) in your hands, you do not want anybody else to touch them, even if 'everybody wants to enjoy it, and wants to move "something sharp" on it'. Then, 'the owners store the tablet and the stylus, and laying the tablet down, they do with them what they want. When it is done, they just wash it to restore its virginity'. As we can see, this is an allegorical riddle: under an evident description of the image (of the emblem), the reader can guess that there is a hidden sexual meaning but not so hidden as not to be understood, which gives the reader the impression of being clever and, at the same time, communing with a community of clever and open-minded readers. If the interpretation is left open, everybody knows that readers must search along the sexual track.

A second example could be the bell (image 6 in the manuscript). The image shows a bell hanging in a bell tower. The text inscribed on the bell (hard to read) could be … VS NA … [(IE)SVS NA(ZARETVS)]. The bell ringer's rope is hanging down to the left of the bell and the sonnet is:

Il faut ouvrir ma mere alors que je suis faicte[4]
De son ventre aultrement on ne peut m'arracher
Si tost que j'en suis hors on me faict attacher
Par l'oreille bien hault afin que je caquette
L'air grossier et malin je dissipe et rejette[5]
Le tonnerre de moy je ne laisse aprocher

Le marchant ne m'espargne & ne me faict hanter
Que les mers et les ports d'une terre inconnue
L'un et l'autre voulant ma jouissance avoir
[B il – Après m'avoir couché il fait sur moy ravy [?]
Vn long chose pointu sur moy ilz font mouvoir
Après qu'en quelque endroit ils m'ont mise et couchee
[A il + Après qu'en quelque endroit ils *m'ont à plat* couchée]
Ils me font et refont ce qu'ils veulent et puis
Afin que leur afaire à chacun soit cachee
En me lavant d'une eau, vierge presque je suis.

4 Bells were melted down into two clay moulds and, to extract the cooled metal shell, one had to break the mould.

5 Bells are against storm and hail.

Je fais les escoliers à la leçon marcher
[A Je fais les escoliers à leur debuoir marcher]
Et revenir disner alors qu'elle est parfaicte
On ne me voit mouvoir ni faire bruict beaucoup
Si l'on ne faict bransler un gros choze en mon trou
Des moynes par sur tous je suis le plus branlee[6]
Cinq ou six le matin me branlent tour à tour
Je le suis à midy et sur la fin du jour
Mais de nuict je ne suis qu'au besoin reveillée.

To make a bell, you have to free it from its matrix, then hang it to make some noise and tell the time: that is the first meaning of the emblem and the description of the image. But, says the sonnet, to get some sound, you have to move the bell and, especially, you must move '*un chose dans son trou*' [a thing in its hole]. And, by the way, the monks know that very well as they do it every morning together and one after the other, every noon, every evening, and sometimes at night.

My last example is the reed plant, number 9 in the manuscript. There is a reed in the middle of a pond, hills in the background, a farm on the right with trees behind it, and the poetic text is:

Le vent non plus qu'amour ne me faict trebucher
Je loge dans les eaux ayant quitté la terre.
Pour me sauver d'un dieu qui me faisoit la guerre
Cuidant sous son vouloir me faire en fin broncher[7]
Bien que diversement l'on me voie pancher[8]
Si demeuray je ferme et l'effort ne m'atterre
Quand j'ay trempé long temps corps et piedz on déterre
Et aux rays de Phœbus on me met pour seicher
Alors que je suis seiche et qu'on me pense morte
C'est lors que mieux je chante et que d'une voix forte[9]
Je reveille la feste à la ville et aux Champs
Où je suis la joye est, tristesse n'y peut estre
Mais je deviens muette et on n'oit poinct mes chants
Si je ne suis baizee et touchée de mon maistre.
[*B il-: Si je ne sens la bouche et les dois de mon maistre*]

6 Anti-monk topic: they have bad manners and they make noise.
7 Syrinx escaped the god Pan: Ovidus, *Métamorphosis*, I, 698 sq.
8 The oak and the reed.
9 Flutes.

The reed plant leans when it is windy, that is a fact. Then it can be dug out, dried and when it is dried, it makes music. But to make music it has to be wet and kissed ('*baisé*' meaning both kissed and fucked) and touched 'by its master'.

As we can see, this is a multiple pun between the writer and the reader. The writer chooses images, generally classical and well-known images which can figure in other enigmas or emblem books with poetic or moral mottoes or interpretations, and he diverts the interpretations of the 'normal' reader in a sonnet hiding a pornographic riddle. The Wolfenbüttel manuscript gives us an idea not only of the genre of the enigma but also of the humorous uses of it. We know that Fonteny has the habit of playing on riddles, even in his theatrical plays – in the *Beau Pasteur*, there is a riddle about the snail which in the *Livre d'Enigmes* manuscript is not complemented by a poem.

Returning to the Wolfenbüttel manuscript, we should assume that the 26 sonnets accompanying the small engravings do indeed contain such enigmas and that the reader is invited (explicitly or otherwise) to find one or several solutions (some are listed at the end in the table of contents/alphabetical index, although the pornographic solutions are, of course, not revealed or listed).

In the year 1600, the repeated interconnection of image and text on a page would certainly have been considered emblematic when we consider some of the sixteenth-century emblem collections. Even though Fonteny may follow such patterns as were well established by the time he wrote his sonnets, the underlying moral and didactic assumptions of much of sixteenth-century French emblem literature are missing and they are replaced by sexual solutions. This process of diversion, very often used by the 'libertines', the unbelievers of the period – and some, such as Fonteny, follow marginal homosexual patterns of behaviour – leads us to think that Fonteny knows what he is doing perfectly well. On a formal level, such a bipartite arrangement of each manuscript page, seen together with the relevant index entry, brings this collection somewhat closer to the field of emblematics proper. This is the emblematic apparatus but, at the same time, each image commented on in a sonnet generally leads the reader to pornographic interpretations. And where there is just an image without any poem, which is sometimes the case, the reader is free to imagine the type of sonnet that could be written under it. Even if the manuscript remains incomplete, its incomplete form requires it to be filled by the inventive complicity of the reader.

The *Iconologie*: a political and 'bourgeois' role for 350 moral emblems

The other example, which is clearly within the scope of this book, is much more serious (and bourgeois). It is a collection of 350 moral emblems that

Gravelot et Cochin published at the end of the eighteenth century, just before and during the first part of the French revolution, under the following title: *Iconologie ou traité des allégories, Emblèmes.* The ideology of the eighteenth century, then, modified the meaning of regular emblems but also changed the emblems themselves, recycling mythological ones and mixing them with new moral ones for the didactic sake of the readers. But, at the end of the eighteenth century, the discrepancy between appearance and meaning, between the figure and the idea, had become intolerable; *hyponoia* was replaced by the rational body. If the allegory thus lost some of its narrative subtlety, it gained in transparency. At the other end of the early modern period, then, before and during the French revolution, one can observe another way to play with traditional emblems: the appropriation of the canonical way in which artists generally represent their topics becomes moral and typical of late enlightenment mentality. Here also, the time is given to re-drawing and re-commenting but not to disturbing and transgressing. The album wants to help citizens to be good fathers, good husbands, good citizens with a stainless morality.

The book, in four volumes,[10] is sufficiently well known at the end of the eighteenth century to provide some emblematic sources for Goya and this reference in itself gives an idea of the importance of this publication. Gravelot (who died in 1774) was the artist who originated the project and, after his death, the idea was completed by Cochin, with the collaboration of Gaucher.[11] This *Iconologie* was published to convey accumulated knowledge that is supposedly useful for everybody: artists, young persons, 'amateurs', in one word, *citizens.*

10 Hubert-François Gravelot and Charles-Nicolas Cochin, *Iconologie par figures ou traité complet des allégories, emblêmes, etc. Ouvrage utile aux artistes, aux amateurs et pouvant servir à l'éducation des jeunes personnes* (Paris: Lattré, s.d. [1791] 4 volumes).

11 The illustration consists of two portraits engraved by Gaucher, one by Gravelot after Delatour, the other by Cochin after Monnet, four front titles engraved by Choffard, Ghendt and Legrand after Gravelot and 202 figures drawn by Gravelot and Cochin and engraved by Aliamet, Baquoy, Duclos, Gaucher, Ghendt, Ingouf, Legrand, Lemire, Masquelier, Née, Ponce, Saint Aubin and Simonet. Charles-Nicolas Cochin (1715–1790), keeper of the drawings of the king's chamber, is one of the most gifted draughtsman and engraver of the time. This intelligent and cultivated man wrote with a style that was at once witty and pliant, fertile and lively, which was the wonder of his contemporaries. This brilliant illustrator was solicited by the greatest editors of the time. Apart from two new plates, these figures had already been published before in a different order by the authors in the *Almanach iconologique* (1765–1781)

As new citizens of the new regime,[12] readers had to know the images and notions of the old world to build the new one, and all of that in a blink, at first reading and with a quick look. Looking at the emblems and images, then reading (or not) the texts should lead the new citizens to endorse the evolving system, the evolutions of the political and judicial systems and to accept them. To illustrate is to interpret. The power of allegory resides in its ability to link narrative and understanding, meaning and knowledge, interpretation and knowledge of the other former interpretations (the former code out of which the new allegories are built and commented). The allegory is a visual form which tells the story of power and the story of the ultimate notions that a society has to observe in its structure and reality. This reference code – a science reaching far back into the deepest antiquity – has, at the same time, the visual and textual legitimacy of history, reason, and a lot of accumulated knowledge.

Personifications and symbols

What these allegorical figures (a collective work from Gravelot to Cochin, with the help of others) offer to the researcher, then, is an historical object of the highest order, a vehicle used by artists and politicians at the end of the eighteenth century to express and understand themselves as a community overwhelmed by history: a political self-representation, as Antoine De Baecque called it in his article.[13] It is also a way to show there is a common and permanent ideology before and after the revolution, residing in the moral that the narrative text unfolds with the illustration next to it, at its side. History, old and new morality, eternal values and new ones are thus united in a code of 350 ideological steps. The reader can browse the pages or read and browse from cover to cover; the result will be the same: continuity and discontinuity will lead him to the ultimate goal which is the permanence of the nation and French civilisation (observed through the lenses of the eighteenth-century classically educated and morally brought-up citizen).

A few examples, chosen among judicial figures, illustrate these statements. Let us first remember that there are 350 images but an even greater number of definitions. For one image there can be several figures commented on by several mottoes, definitions or explanations. And we may suspect that, when

12 From July 1989 to September 1792 the politically divided French legislative assembly tried to give its chance to a constitutional monarchy. September 22 1792 : proclamation of the First Republic in France by the new Convention.

13 Antoine Debaecque, 'The Allegorical Image of France, 1750–1800: A Political Crisis of Representation', no. 47 (1994), *Representations*, Special Issue: National Cultures before Nationalism, 111–43.

the notion or allegory is very important, there is only one figure drawn but it is not an absolute rule. And as for the representation of justice, as we can see, it is obvious that the allegory has to stand alone with only one comment.

Vol III.
JUSTICE (Figure 6.1)
L'emblème généralement reçu pour désigner la Justice est la balance qui pèse les droits du citoyen et l'épée qui sert à venger ces mêmes droits offensés. Les devoirs que s'impose la Justice et qui distinguent cette vertu sont la pureté de conscience, exprimée par le soleil représenté sur son estomac et la connaissance des lois, ce qu'indiquent les livres du code et des instituts sur lesquels la Justice est appuyée. Le bandeau royal qui ceint sa tête, ainsi que le trône sur lequel elle est assise, désignent une des plus augustes fonctions du pouvoir souverain. Les attributs qui sont à ses pieds caractérisent la magistrature, à qui son administration est confiée. Tels sont à peu près les emblèmes sous lesquels Raphaël a représenté la Justice dans le Vatican.

Figure 6.1 'Justice', *Iconologie* by Gravelot et Cochin, Paris, Lattré, 1791, III, fig. 6, p. 29 (Hathi Trust Digital Library)

[The generally acknowledged emblem of Justice is the scales which weigh the rights of the citizen and the sword which serves to avenge the breach of such rights. The duties that Justice imposes and which distinguish this virtue are purity of conscience, represented by the sun on her stomach and knowledge of the law, hinted at by the books of the *Code* and the *Institutions* where *Justice* is administered.

> The royal crown which circles her head, as well as the throne on which she is seated, designate it as one of the most august functions of sovereign power. The attributes (figures) which are at her feet designate the magistracy to which her administration is entrusted. Such are the emblems with which Raphael represented *Justice* in the Vatican.][14]

So, *Justice*, as it is represented, is, as we read, 'more or less' the same allegory that Raphaël and the whole tradition have represented for a long time. The figure is, of course, a woman but also a sketch, a sort of '*grisé*' on which the artist puts emblems. And even if Justice is a woman, in fact, it is a neutral notion, the abstract essence of justice itself, the illustrated idea of its power; a power which does not show other signs than its emblems on a neutral support: it just shows its legitimacy, its history, its permanence, its strength through an abstraction (the conventional body of a woman) on which essential signs and symbols are placed. Balance and sword, the sun on the belly revealing purity of consciousness and all the objects added to the image are not new or even renewed. This 'virtue' has been left unchanged even if the definition of the '*pouvoir souverain*' is much different after 1791 from what it was in 1774 but, even if absolute monarchy changed into a constitutional monarchy soon to become a republic, the idea, the notion and the allegory of Justice have to remain the same to be valid. There must be no gap between the image and the text, no gap between a supposed former justice and the new one, no discrepancy of any sort when the ultimate power is in question. And that is why things have remained so unchanged. And at the same time, we are in front of a hyper-legitimisation of the notion through the history of allegory itself. This permanence leads us to say that the iconography, the book itself, purposely presents itself as a synthesis of knowledge, an aggregate of the main symbols known to the artists to sum up the quintessential knowledge of yore, as well as synthesize emblems the new political order considers as a legitimate discourse on justice.

But *Judgement* (an innate faculty of the soul to which is added the weight of experience) is different. The process of historical legitimation does not work then; the image of this other abstract notion (the judicial, philosophical or moral *judgement*) is new and created from various pieces as an aggregate of symbols.

14 I would like to thank Peter Goodrich for the translations.

Vol III.
JUGEMENT (Figure 6.2)
Faculté de l'âme fortifiée par l'expérience dont le symbole est ici la colonne sur laquelle s'appuie le Jugement. La maturité de l'âge est l'expression qui lui convient. Le Jugement pèse ses discours et mesure ses démarches, ce que désignent la balance et la règle qu'on lui fait tenir. Les creusets propres à éprouver les métaux signifient que le Jugement y met les opinions. Il est aussi la pierre de touche du vrai mérite, c'est ce qu'on a cherché à faire entendre par l'action de l'enfant qui est à ses pieds. La petite figure de Minerve qu'on aperçoit plus loin indique le rapport intime du Jugement et de la sagesse.

Figure 6.2 'Jugement', *Iconologie* by Gravelot et Cochin, Paris, Lattré, 1791, II, p. 22v (Hathi Trust Digital Library)

[JUDGEMENT
The faculty of a soul strengthened by experience for which the symbol is here the column on which *Judgement* leans. The maturity of age is its proper expression. *Judgement* weighs its words and measures its actions, which is why it is made to hold weighing scales and a ruler . The crucible used to test metals signifies that *Judgement* places its opinions to the test. It is also the touchstone of true merit, this is what we have striven to make explicit through the action of the child sitting at its feet. The small statue of Minerva visible in the distance signifies the intimate link between *Judgement* and wisdom.]

As for Justice, there is an accumulation of emblems but if the emblems are well known and part of the usual corpus, the aggregate had to be newly made, freshly minted. This patchwork is composed of a strong column, a mature man, the scales of justice and the ruler of the law, the scientific way of evaluating opinions (the crucible), the touchstone with which the putto is playing, and Minerva, the goddess of wisdom. This time, these figures together can be surprising for the reader, even difficult to get and needs to be commented on. After reading the comment, the reader will be able to assemble the pieces, to make with them a sort of sentence which can specify the notion of judgement and unify concerns around that term.

In the fourth volume, another representation simultaneously depicts one notion and its opposite: bias/*partiality and impartiality*. Through the two representations, we can see a simplification/modernization of the iconology.

Vol IV.
PARTIALITÉ (Figure 6.3)
Quoiqu'on fasse très rarement usage de cette figure, on n'a pas cru devoir l'omettre ; mais comme les emblèmes employés par les iconologistes sont la plupart inintelligibles, on a jugé à propos d'y substituer ceux-ci. La Partialité, sous les traits d'une femme laide, l'air sombre, le regard faux, portant un bandeau qui lui cache un œil ; de la main droite elle écarte un flambeau dont la lumière pourrait l'éclairer et de la gauche fait pencher une balance vide pour lui ôter son équilibre.

Figure 6.3 'Partialité', *Iconologie* by Gravelot et Cochin, Paris, Lattré, 1791, IV, fig. 8 p. 3 (Hathi Trust Digital Library)

[PARTIALITY
Even though one very rarely makes use of this figure, it did not seem proper to omit it; but as the emblems used by iconologists are in the main comprehensible, we thought it appropriate to substitute these. Partiality, in the form of an ugly woman, of sombre demeanor, with a dissembling air, wearing a blindfold that covers one of her eyes; with her right hand she pushes away a bright torch which would have given her light and with her left hand tips one of the empty scales to destroy its equilibrium.]

> *IMPARTIALITÉ*
> *On peut représenter l'Impartialité sous l'emblème d'une jeune femme dont le visage annonce la candeur et la sincérité ; d'une main elle tient en équilibre le fléau d'une balance, et de l'autre semble attester le ciel de l'intégrité de ses actions. L'Impartialité pose le pied sur une planche placée sur un cône afin de la maintenir en équilibre. Voyez l'article Equité, en observant cependant que ce mot ne doit point être pris dans la même acception.*
>
> [IMPARTIALITY
> One can represent *Impartiality* with the emblem of a young woman whose face displays candor and sincerity; in one hand she holds the poised arm of a scales, and with the other seems to invoke the heavens to attest to the integrity of her actions. *Impartiality* balances a plank placed on a cone with her foot. Refer to the article on Equity, while considering that that word should not be taken to hold the same meaning.]

The goal is clearly to help the reader decipher the collection of images and postures with ease, using a code which comes from the usual iconology code (without sophistication, as it is said) and from other codes, such as, for example, the pictorial and theatrical ones. And, for the notion of partiality, we can observe that the illustration is mainly pictorial and theatrical coming from postures adopted by actors of the time or depicted in paintings: *Partiality* is a woman who shows all the signs of betrayal commonly used on stage. She should, of course, be ugly, with a dark complexion, a false (one eyed!) look (since she is wearing a blindfold hiding one of her eyes…) and she acts symbolically: fleeing the light and making a balance tilt. And since the image is not perfect, even in the book (the reproduction is not great either) even if the elements chosen are not clear enough, the text is there to help the reader to identify the objects and the postures and to interpret both the image and the text without any ambiguity. Simultaneously, the text also gives the moral attitude to have in front of the illustration: aversion, admiration, etc. The reader, hence, has to choose the attitude of *Impartiality* and condemn that of *Partiality*. And, as this book is also a didactic one, there is, at the end of the definition of impartiality, a sentence observing the closeness between impartiality and equity, even in their representations, but also making clear that there is a difference between the two and referring to the equity drawing. This shows that the book is designed as a dictionary and as a textbook for students and citizens.

The final example is taken from the second volume and we see that one image can refer to four definitions.

Volume II.
ÉQUITÉ (Figure 6.4)
Vertu qui consiste à rendre à chacun ce qui lui appartient. On la représente par une femme d'un caractère grave, un diadème sur le front, tenant un fléau de balance mis en équilibre par deux poids égaux.

[EQUITY
Virtue which consists in rendering to each their due. It is represented by a woman of serious demeanour, a diadem on her forehead, holding a scale that is evenly balanced by two equal weights.]

Figure 6.4 'Equité', *Iconologie* by Gravelot et Cochin, Paris, Lattré, 1791, II, fig. 1. (Hathi Trust Digital Library)

INJUSTICE
Prévarication des lois, vice dangereux qu'on peint sous les traits d'une femme vêtue de noir, tenant d'une main le glaive de la Justice et de l'autre un crapaud, animal venimeux que les iconologistes donnent pour attribut à l'Injustice. Pour la caractériser davantage, on la représente brisant sous ses pieds les balances de Thémis et les tables de la loi.

[INJUSTICE
Corruption, a dangerous vice depicted by a woman dressed in black, holding in one hand the sword of Justice and in the other a toad, a venomous animal which the iconologists hold to be the attribute of Injustice. To characterise her further, one represents her trampling the broken scales of Themis and the tables of the law underfoot.]

CHICANE
Ainsi que dans la figure précédente, la Chicane peut être représentée par une femme qui foule aux pieds les lois et les balances de Thémis, mais on doit observer que la Chicane est peinte vieillie, maigre, hideuse, et qu'au lieu de lui faire tenir l'épée et le crapaud, elle dévore les sacs de procédure dont on la voit entourée.

[CAVIL
Here, as in the previous figure, Cavil can be represented by a woman treading on the laws and scales of Themis, but one should also note that Cavil is painted as old, skinny, hideous, and that instead of holding the sword and the toad, she is devouring the pouches of legal papers which can be seen everywhere around her.]

INIQUITÉ
On pourrait comprendre sous cette dénomination l'assemblage de tous les vices, mais l'Iniquité est représentée par les iconologistes sous la figure d'une femme laide, effrayante, vêtue de noir, la tête enveloppée de son manteau, fuyant à l'aspect de la lumière et entourée d'un serpent qui lui déchire les entrailles, emblème des remords vengeurs qui poursuivent le crime.

[INIQUITY
One could gather under this appellation a whole complex of vices, but *Iniquity* is represented by iconologists with the figure of a frighteningly ugly woman, dressed in black, her head wrapped in her cape, fleeing from the light with a serpent wrapped around her and tearing out her entrails, an emblem of the avenging remorse which pursues crime.]

Just as there are two opposite and obvious figurations of *equity* (in its French meaning, a general virtue) and injustice, the book also defines the notions of iniquity and '*chicane*' (judicial quibble). This is to say that iniquity and '*chicane*' are the consequence or the result of injustice and that all these three notions are the opposite of equity. So, the toad can be replaced by an ugly woman devouring the bags of procedure or by a snake tearing her entrails; the result is the same: these female figures coming from the traditions of classical sexism and witch hunting are here to give the reader an absolute disgust for vices. This is the first thing to understand.

The second is that the virtue of Equity is in front of these three vices and not the virtue of Justice, which is in the third volume, and alone. If Justice, as we have seen, is an aggregate of images, and emblems and has in common with *Equity* the balance ('The balance which weighs citizens' rights' that *Justice* holds in addition to the 'sword which serves to avenge the same offended rights'), *Justice* is not defined as a *virtue* or as a princess, or as a woman of grave character. *Justice* is an abstraction, a sketch wearing emblems, whereas *Equity* is a character and, more than that, a female character who returns to everyone what belongs to them. In other words, it could be interesting to see *Equity* as the new notion and the new virtue which can replace or help *Justice.* It is a modern notion, coming from the country of liberty, England, and revised or revisited by the French Revolution. Equity could be, then, the new goddess of the new regime because Equity *does* something, *she acts* and she is depicted as the woman who keeps the balance fair for everybody.

The sense of a pedagogical vocation, the need to refer to a common morality, the refusal to politicize images, the praise of the moral fable (*via* implicit references to the *Encyclopédie*), the reiteration of arguments in favour of the utility of allegory: all of this defined the *Iconologie* as a tool in the proper education of 'both sexes'. Above all, the project sought 'always to put morality into action'; that is, to associate the vices and virtues with particular figures. And if these figures and emblems very often come from the usual multi-secular iconological corpus, especially when the figuration of the emblems is well known and easily understandable, readable, the artists take the liberty of creating new figures, to help the reader to partake of their interpretation of the virtues. These illustrations, then, can come from paintings and from the postures of actors on contemporary stages. Traditional references, modern representations, everything is done to help the *Iconologie* to be THE precious repertoire that everyone must include in his library. And this book is also precious because it presents, categorizes and explains the 'good' and 'bad' figures according to their postures and gestures, age and sex, following a rigorous and respectable code of representation. It presents some 350 figures, detailing in each case the old and new corporal codes that allow the artist to identify 'virtues' and 'vices' with particular gestures and poses.

The significance of such a collection is considerable: the question of how to portray good and to designate evil using universally legible figures had haunted Enlightenment defenders of allegory even before the Revolution sought to direct the production of its 'regenerated' artists. The *Iconologie*, however, strictly codified allegorical representation: the authors announced their intention to give morality its true form (*son 'juste corps'*), according to a strict standard.[15] But in the gap between the norm and its corporal deviations, artists and politicians could insinuate themselves and try to build or to promote new modern virtues – such as equity. The artists of the Revolution inherited not only a rationalized definition of allegory but also a mode of embodiment to which it was possible to assign meanings. Ultimately, the Revolution sought to renew and politicize the rational definition of allegory by supporting antique topical representations and sustaining the emergence of new moral and political figures.

'Libertinage' or morals? Transgression or integration? Poetic game or didactics? Emblems have to be interpreted and so are, necessarily, betrayed.

15 Artists and engravers who faced the dictates of tradition, reason and morality, as well as of their specific subject, could refer to the corporeal code of allegory in a total of six instances; as appropriate, they could determine: 1) the gender of the figure ; 2) its age ; 3) its degree of nudity ; 4) its general movement ; 5) its posture ; and 6) the possibility of placing specific emblems on the body. *See* Debaecque, 'The Allegorical Image of France, 1750–1800', 138 *et seq.*

CHAPTER 7

The tongue and the eye: eloquence and office in renaissance emblems

Piyel Haldar[1]

Introduction: from dignity to eloquence

A symposium on legal emblematics, particularly in the context of renaissance humanism, provides an opportunity to examine the manner in which western institutions and their relevant offices are constituted. This is all the more pertinent since the very production and transmission of emblems performs what was essential to the renaissance re-evaluation of institutional life, namely the category of *decorum*. In rhetorical terms, decorum designated a platform best suited to achieving the goals of a public orator. This meant a concern for the physical and temporal localities within which public arguments, addresses or perorations took place. Decorum provided the conditions of service and ceremony within which dignitaries and their attendant cohorts of officials existed. It also determined the appropriate response from those who were granted audience. What applied in the courtroom, in the theatre or in the council chamber, also applied to the pages of *emblemata*. Each element of an emblem, like each functional aspect of the public institution, relied on a code of stylistic propriety. In this slightly extended sense, decorum might be regarded as providing an environment for the most appropriate style to bind both the composite relations between text and image into meaning, so as to cultivate the relationship between emblem and readership and to condition the appropriate method of viewing, reading and deciphering an emblem.

In short, decorum provided a space for a heavily regulated style of language considered by the humanists to be eloquent. It almost goes without saying that, for such humanists, the term 'eloquence' which, via Cicero,

1 With thanks to Peter Goodrich, Valérie Hayaert and Paul Raffield for comments and suggestions. I am heavily indebted to Shaun McVeigh, whose general theoretical framework for understanding the category of the modern office in relation to conduct provided a prompt and a point of reflection.

insinuated itself into the new methodological style of the *studia humanitatis,* carried more than the expressive qualities of speech. Certainly, eloquence signified the terms of address best suited to civic and public office but it combined a range of functions. Often, perhaps as a result of a heavy anti-Aristotelianism, the term linked forensic rhetoric with its ceremonial or epideictic counterpart. Persuasion and norm, argument and ceremony, past and present, mixed together without concerns for the niceties of taxonomy. What mattered more was that the term distinguished between licit and illicit forms of speech; it distinguished between formal speech and the everyday grammar of table talk.[2] It also entailed an appreciation of the topological and intellectual sites of enunciation. In other words, eloquence was a matter of what gave the institution its sense of propriety and its place within the public sphere and among the intellectual disciplines.

Part of the argument pursued here is that training in the art of eloquence bestowed upon those who took up institutional responsibility something more than the mere living atmosphere of the physical incumbent of office by performing a function similar to that of the notion of dignity. Indeed, eloquence, and the decorum of office, came to replace the function of dignity. The mediaeval *dignitas* was a term that referred to the sacral space of institutional office holders and carried the transcendental and immortal qualities of the *corpus mysticum.* According to one derivation, provided by Ernst Kantorowicz, the principle of dignity had been extrapolated from 'the profound seriousness, the worthiness, the aura of holiness' of the opening titles to Justinian's *Digest.*[3] In consequence, this juridical value provided the Christianised office (particularly that of the Emperor as *iuris religiosissimus*) with a potentiality that required the mortal *persona* of an office holder to activate it.[4] However, where dignity was justified by justice, by the very status of office and by its goals, eloquence required of the office holder a process of preparation. The renaissance re-evaluation of training meant that over a long period, eloquence would supplement and replace dignity as the characteristic of dignitaries and their office. One might have thought that categories concomitant to dignity, such as *honestum, illustris,* or *conscience* would be transposed on to the humanist scheme of things. However, we ought to note at the outset, that the values attached to the office had little to do with the humanist triumph of free will and of free speech. Of course, for

2 On the distinction between eloquence and table talk, see George Puttenham, *The Arte of English Poesie* [1589] (Kent, OH: Kent State University Press, 1971), 3.2, particularly 223.

3 Ernst Kantorowicz, *The King's Two Bodies, A Study in Medieval Political Theology* (Princeton, NJ: Princeton University Press, 1981), 138.

4 Kantorowicz, *The King's Two Bodies,* 437.

Dante, Machiavelli, Petrarch, Montaigne and others, the category of dignity remained essential to the matter of man. The term was applied, however, to the individual members of a more general idea of the human population. The dignity of man involved a philosophical and cultural expression of the emancipated individual somehow abstracted and set free from the description of institutional force-fields, although it ought to be noted that this general account of personhood was never far removed from the office of parson. As Peter Goodrich argues of the common law tradition, 'the person was originally a parson, a priest and so a representative of a parish'.[5] And, as Blackstone pointed out in his commentaries on the rights of persons, the dignity of the person rested on his parochial representation of the invisible body of the church.[6] Nevertheless, while the two terms share etymological links, the 'dignity' of man was distinguishable from the 'decorum' of the office. For some of the humanists examined here, to take up office meant an institutional existence removed from the glorious 'halo of perpetuity'.[7]

Once it is recognized that the function of eloquence replaces that of the medieval *dignitas*, a number of further points follow and need emphasising. First, to take up office meant existing within the order of eloquence itself. It meant being trained into a pre-existing theoretical vocabulary and style that could then be applied through practice. It was not so much that training for office enabled a mastery of eloquence but that eloquence, to varying degrees, possessed the neophyte, the student, and ultimately the officer. Those who inhabited office underwent a process of moral regeneration. In other words, the attempt was to constrain free will and to delimit the personhood of the office (beyond those limits already proscribed by nature and experience) through the very language of the institution. Second, this order of public existence meant being inserted, inlaid like ornamental *emblemata*, into a signifying regime in which what was spoken was not simply the empirical fact of a command but the truth of a legal order, its values and its techniques. A range of profound ethical values emphasized the ability of those who held institutional positions to persuade others to lead the good life. If eloquence determined office, it did so in order to transmit a range of values. So that, in a broader sense, eloquence was cardinal to the very functioning of civilized society and to the maintenance of social relations. What applied to questions of office applied to the matter of the emblem. In the terms set out by Cicero, eloquence was what enabled the emblem to teach, to delight and to

5 Peter Goodrich, 'The Theatre of Emblems: On the Optical Apparatus and Investiture of Persons' in 8 *Law, Culture and the Humanities* (2012), 47–61, at 47.

6 William Blackstone, *Commentaries on the Laws of England* (Chicago, IL: University of Chicago Press, 1979) 1.2.5, 372

7 Ernst Kantorowicz, *The King's Two Bodies*, 78–87.

move (*docere, delectare, movere*). The eloquence of an official and the eloquence of an emblem required an appreciation of normative values that attached to institutional life.

My concern here is to engage with the work of Shaunnagh Dorsett and Shaun McVeigh.[8] Briefly reduced, their overall task to rehabilitate a civil jurisprudence is pitched against the hegemony of a metaphysical corruption of what it means to hold office. Drawing on traditions that rival Kantian and post-Kantian philosophy, Dorsett and McVeigh seek to rehabilitate an account of civil jurisprudence by directing questions of the state office holders away from the theological/humanist notion of a *persona* endowed with conscience towards questions of conduct that do not fall into the trap of technical administrative positivity. For them, the conduct of office, becomes a matter of external manners and comportment far removed from any Christian, transcendental or Kantian internal court of morals. Such a project might be situated in terms of the northern European inheritance of civil jurisprudence bequeathed by those such as Pufendorf and Thomasius.[9] It identifies, within the very history and structure of western institutions themselves, points of almost forgotten alternatives.[10]

Any attempt to refresh jurisprudence and to revivify legal institutional existence, however, needs an account of eloquence as the fundamental shape of office. So that the third introductory point attends to what eloquence transmits and discloses in the name of civic ethics. This becomes more pertinent if it is considered that eloquence is as much about what cannot be said as what can be said. In this sense, the language of office hides as much as it reveals. Those aspects that breach decorum, whether illicit, profane or unspeakably sacred, take place off-stage. No democratically orientated requirement for transparency would be able to rid the modern office of such mystical obscenity or obscurity. Any account of eloquence as the language of office has to take into consideration the persistence of this obscure point of

8 Shaunnagh Dorsett and Shaun McVeigh, 'The *Persona* of the Jurist in Salmond's Jurisprudence: On the Exposition of 'What Law is…', *Victoria University of Wellington Law Review* 38 (2007), 771–96. See also David Saunders, 'The Judicial Persona in Historical Context: the Case of Matthew Hale', in Conal Condren, Stephen Gaukroger and Ian Hunter, eds, *The Philosopher in Early Modern Europe* (Cambridge: Cambridge University Press, 2006), 140–59.

9 On this point see Ian Hunter, *The Secularization of the Confessional State: The Political Thought of Christian Thomasius* (Cambridge: Cambridge University Press, 2007).

10 For an insight into how critical legal studies, both in the United States and in the UK, has failed to consider the internal alternatives within the history of the western state, see David Saunders 'The Critical Jurist and the Moment of Theory' in *Postcolonial Studies* 10/1 (2007), 77–92.

reference. In different terms, the problem may be posed as follows. Humanism sought to replace the divine as the organizing social principle. A study of eloquence, however, reveals that it replaces the divine cause with an equally, if not more, obscure source of civic illumination and civic organization. It is not that eloquence itself was necessarily obscure. In the most general terms, the style of renaissance humanists can be situated anywhere between the ornate and formal eloquence of Ciceronianism and the plain Attic style of the non-Ciceronians.[11] Even among the emblematists, as Denis Drysdall maintains, a contrast exists between Aristotelian and neo-Platonist influences.[12] According to the former, meaning was to be rooted in the natural quality of the thing being portrayed. In this sense, emblems were considered to be accessible to anyone willing to learn. For the latter, emblems were allegories often pre-figured by a divine intellect before existing in the real world. In spite of these differences in style, what remained obscure was the ultimate reference itself, the source of civic relations and organization. All emblematic depictions point to such obscure sources, hidden above clouds or behind veils. The *enargeia* or clearness of emblematic representation belies what the reader is compelled to do, namely to pierce these clouds of unknowing, to actively decipher what ought not to be made too obvious. In the words of one contemporary poet, 'Rich minerals are digged out of the bowels of the earth, not found in the superficies and dust of it'.[13] The obvious engenders complacency. Only by solving the riddle at the heart of the emblem can the *honestum* be made to see the obscure majesty of institution and what is required of him. Both senses and intellect have to be excited in the devotion to duty.

A further point therefore ought to be introduced. If, as Dorsett and McVeigh rightly claim, office is about conduct then such conduct had to be visually apparent, appreciable and regulated by codes of decorum. The language of office was a visual language. Vision here must be understood as being more than the empirical apprehension of a mere artefact. It involved a process by which those subject to the jurisdiction of any particular institution had to participate in the staging of office through a process of decoding and revealing the obscure source of civic organization. It is here

11 Marc Fumaroli, 'Rhetoric, Politics and Society: From Italian Ciceronianism to French Classicism' in James G. Murphy ed., *Renaissance Eloquence: The Theory and Practice of Renaissance Rhetoric* (Berkeley, CA: University of California Press, 1983) 253–71.

12 Denis L. Drysdall, *Hieroglyphs, Speaking Pictures and the Law: The Context of Alciato's Emblems* (Glasgow: *Glasgow Emblem Studies*, 2013), 55 *et seq.*

13 George Chapman, 'Ovid's Banquet of the Senses' in Eirian Wain ed., *Selected Poems* (Manchester: Carcanet, 1978), 21.

that the specific emblems I want to examine might be regarded as having revealed and, indeed, enacted, an emerging idea of institutional roles. Emblems enacted precisely what was required of the eloquent official. They staged a visual performance of the institutional function. They represented eloquence as that which had been divorced from the personality of the office holder. It is for this reason that eloquence was invariably depicted as an autonomous tongue, separated from the persona of a speaking subject. Emblems as 'transposable ornaments' or badges that could be placed on a variety of platforms and inserted into other devices, performed the automated activity of office.[14] They functioned according to the predetermined requirements of decorum. Moreover, these emblems were visible ciphers of an invisible source and, as such, they were intended to elicit an ethical reaction based on the complex process of active decryption and passive contemplation. Both emblems and officials 'spoke in pictures'. The required response was to comprehend what was latent with the mind's eye.

Eloquence and renaissance legal humanism

One way into a more thorough account of eloquence is to link it more forcefully to the range of legal offices that constituted the juristic and juridical sphere. The relationship between eloquence and law does not immediately raise concern about the hieratic nature of office. It does, however, situate the institution within the parameters of decorum and eloquence. If the trope of decorum provided a platform on which to stage the proper relationship between subjects and institution, a question arose among humanists, and particularly for Andrea Alciato, as to which institution was the more appropriate. For some, eloquence could only emerge from the decorum provided by lawyers.

The problem was compound. Unlike the concept of dignity, nothing about eloquence was specifically juridical. The term was used indiscriminately across the range of public offices. In the most general terms, Lorenzo Valla and Guillaume Budé pleaded for eloquence in all areas of learning and among all public officials, whether they were gentlemen scholars, philosophers, poets or miserable little pleaders such as lawyers. For the humanist civil lawyer, snatching the *corpus iuris civilis* out of the inventive and 'unwashed' hands of

14 Alciato explains that emblems could be used by artisans to fashion badges to be pinned to hats. They could also function as trademarks 'like Aldus's anchor, Froben's dove or Calvo's elephant', in Gian Luigi Barni, ed., *Le lettere di Andrea Alciato giureconsulto* (Florence: Le Monnier, 1953) no. 24, at 46, ii 28–35, cited in Denis Drysdall *Hieroglyphs, Speaking Pictures and the Law*, 2.

medieval scholars was more than a matter of 'method' (as we understand the term today).[15] It was a matter of style and the triumph of eloquence as the proper language of legal office and as the proper form of the *mos gallicus* (*iura docendi*). This idea of eloquence, however, necessitated a broader study of law than hitherto recommended by the medieval jurists. The humanization of law required the study of *all* the good arts of discourse.[16] Thus, the various exegetical techniques more peculiar to poetry, the various methods of reason more peculiar to philosophy and techniques of revelation more peculiar to the arts (conceived of as *belles lettres*) were hitched to the study of universal history and philology all subsumed under the French way. Similarly, and particularly for Guillaume Budé, understanding the *Corpus* entailed understanding both its juristic and non-juristic sources.[17] For common lawyers, too, the decorum of the office was founded in reason that was common not only throughout the island history, but across the sciences. To paraphrase Sir Henry Finch, it derived from the bowels of divinity, grammar, logic.[18] 'Ye Gods what monsters' was Gentili's response to the size of the legal appetite.[19]

Ironically, the application of eloquence to public offices that existed outside law was expressed largely by lawyers, albeit as part of a general 'defence of poetry'. Here, eloquence, more often than not, was illustrated with reference to legal examples (what Quintilian terms *emblemata*). Proper homage to any text, even for someone as antipathetic to lawyers as Lorenzo Valla, was exemplified by turning to the textual authority of the *corpus iuris civilis*. Eloquence meant a return to the very source itself, 'elegantly' dismissing the barabarism of Accursius's methodology of organizing the glosses and the further commentaries that had accreted on the *corpus*. Finch, just to prove that the point was not lost on the common lawyers, remarked that 'the sparkes of all Sciences in the World are raked up in the Ashes of the Law'.[20] Such a methodology, we might note, also established these other non-juristic disciplines and their relevant offices (those of the poet, the philosopher, the artist) in the image of law itself.

15 Andreas Alciato, 'No doubt the young person correctly trained in the art of eloquence would handle civil law with greater proficiency and not with "unwashed hands"', *Parergôn Iuris libri duodecim* in *Omnia opera* (Basle: Officina Isingriniana, 1558). 4:15, cited in Denis L. Drysdall, *Hieroglyphs, Speaking Pictures and the Law*, 232.

16 On this point, see Donald R. Kelley, 'Legal Humanism and the Sense of History' in *Studies in the Renaissance*, 13 (1966), 184–99.

17 Michael L. Monheit, 'Guillaume Budé, Andrea Alciato, Pierre de l'Estoile: Renaissance Interpreters of Roman Law', *Journal of the History of Ideas*, 58/1 (1997), 21–40.

18 Sir Henry Finch, *Law or a Discourse thereof*, [1627] (London: printed for Henry Lintot and sold by John Shuckburgh, 1759 edn), 41.

19 Cited in Donald R. Kelley, 'Legal Humanism and the Sense of History', 187.

20 Sir Henry Finch, *Law, or a Discourse Thereof*, 6.

This cross disciplinary application of eloquence may well be no more than something akin to the 'mental habit' that Erwin Panofsky alludes to in his account of Gothic architecture as a solid expression of scholastic principles.[21] It may well be no more than a concurrence of a way of thinking peculiar to all discourses (particularly those discourses whose subject matter interested the lawyers of the time). It may be no more than the transposition of a term across a shared habitus that might be termed humanism.[22] Nevertheless, the idea that eloquence formed some sort of mental habit shared by poets, lawyers, philologists, philosophers and monarchs, did not go uncontested. Eloquence depended on proper place. The idea that eloquence flowed freely across the full range of courses meant that it escaped the parameters of decorum. For Alciato, in particular, eloquence had to be appropriated by lawyers as a style proper only to the offices of jurists and magistrates since following Cicero's remarks in *De Officiis*, decorum was what controlled the law.[23] For Cicero, eloquence was what gave the individual jurist their character, their conscience and their abhorrence of moral turpitude. For Alciato, without the decorum of eloquence, law could only exercise itself with a harsh and strong arm amputated from the rest of the community. The general argument was illustrated in his disagreements with other humanist scholars such as Lorenzo Valla and Guillaume Budé. In 1439, Lorenzo Valla published his treatise questioning the authenticity of the transfer of Imperial authority from Constantine I to the papacy in the fourth century.[24] Valla's argument was that the original instrument gifting authority could not have been drafted at the time of purported donation. Based on philological methodology (focusing on the use and changing definition of terms found in the document), Valla claimed that the instrument itself could only have been drafted in the eighth century, some four centuries after the Papal claim. Alciato's criticism of Valla was entirely based on the question of style. What hinged on Valla's philological techniques amounted to no more than pure theoretical speculation, since nothing in Valla's work shed any light on the the contemporary legality of the Papacy. For the distinction between theory and practice to disappear, the matter had to be treated in a certain style and according to the standards and decorum of eloquence that were better suited

21 Erwin Panofsky, *Gothic Architecture and Scholasticism* (LaTrobe, PA: Archabbey, 2005).

22 The universal appeal of eloquence is emblematised by Andreas Alciato, *Emblemes* 182; eloquence is difficult, like the herb with strong black roots that Mercury pulls out, but its flowers attract everyone in *Emblemata* (Lyons; 1550 edn)

23 Cicero, *On Duties* (Cambridge: Cambridge University Press, 1991), I.4, 75.

24 Lorenzo Valla, *On the Donation of Constantine* (1440), trans. G. W. Bowersock (Cambridge, MA: Harvard University Press, 2008).

to lawyers than poets, philosophers and mere philologists. This was not to deny the value of those other disciplines. Rather it was the case, that for Alciato, the technique of eloquence properly belonged to the lawyers.[25] 'When Eloquence is not joined to justice' he claimed in the Avignon Oration 'it is the cause of disaster in the commonwealth'.[26] This is why jurists should be accorded the highest offices since they alone have the requisite eloquence combined with knowledge to fulfil the humanist task of eradicating the distinction between theory and practice. Again, in the Bologna Oration, Alciato argued that the practice of eloquence must be joined with legal studies since eloquence 'cannot in any way exist properly without them'.[27] Alciato was not alone, and similar points had been made by Zasius. For both, eloquence within law alone was what made law superior to moral philosophy.[28] The danger is not simply the fear of law being forced to renounce its position as arbiter of social questions and orchestrator of social bonds. Throughout his writings, lectures, notebooks and recorded orations, Alciato continually claimed that eloquence practised by non-jurists, by pure Ciceronians, was eloquence practised by elementary pedagogues, by *grammatici* and by those who mangled texts for the sake of glory. The danger of eloquence spilling over to non-juristic sources was a danger that eloquence and office would be corrupted by the very values that humanism sought to renounce. Such notions of intellectual glory and dignity would do nothing to stem an individual office holder from exercising their power of invention. The office holder, in other words, simply had to inhabit and obey the parameters of the new methodology. Are poets, as Percy Bysche Shelley suggested, really the unacknowledged legislators of the world? From the perspective of an Alciato, or Zasius, it is more the case that lawyers ought to be the true poets of the world.

Emblems of eloquence

Peter Goodrich's claim that emblems are *obiter depicta*, 'making visible [and] bringing the dead letters of the law to life ... as a form of legislation' is enough to render them a mode of eloquence specific to the concerns of

25 Andrea Alciato, 'Praetermissa' (1518), *Opera Omnia* (Basle, 1557 ed.) 4:1, 403.

26 Andrea Alciato, 'Avignon Oration' cited in Susan Longfield Karr, *Nature, Self and History in the Works of Guillaume Budé, Andreas Alciato and Zasius, A Study of the Role of Legal Humanism in Western Natural Law* (Chicago, IL: University of Chicago Press, 2008), 209.

27 Andrea Alciato, 'Bologna Oration' (1546) *Opera Omnia* (Basle, 1557 edn) 3:1, 155.

28 Ulrich Zasius's position on the place of law among the disciplines is given fuller treatment in Donald Kelley, *Foundations of Modern Historical Scholarship; Language, Law and History in the French Renaissance* (New York: Columbia University Press, 1970).

juristic and judicial office.[29] Aside from this, it is worth stressing that these emblems, particularly those depicting eloquence, *perform* the efficacy required of office. In so doing, emblems give further emphasis to Alciato's aim to dissolve the distinction between theory and practice. That is to say, emblems, as well as presenting a theoretical meaning, provided a space in which meaning is brought to light. Consider then Alciato's emblem of the Gallic Hercules as an image of the divine provenance and character of eloquence and as an image portraying models of virtue and regulation that determine the language of office (Figure 7.1).

In establishing eloquence as divine property the choice of Hercules, rather than Hermes or Mercury, might seem curious. Hercules, after all, was characterized in terms of his actions rather than his words. In this depiction, Alciato drew from Lucian's account of the Gallic God Ogmios. As far back as antiquity, Lucian had identified Ogmios (from a painting he had seen in Gaul) as

D'ALCIAT. SCIENCE. 119

Eloquence eſt plus excellente que force.

PROBLEME.

Maſſe en main dextre,en ſeneſtre arc cornu,
Et du Lyon la peau couurant corps nu,
C'eſt d' Hercules la forme,Mais tel art
Pas ne cõuient:qu'il ſoit chaulue,& vieillard.
La langue auſsi de chainetes perſée,
D'ond par l'oreille attraict gent,non forcée,
P 3

Figure 7.1 *Eloquence est plus excellente que force* [eloquence is better than force]; Andrea Alciato, *Toutes Les Emblemes* (Lyons, Guillaume Rouillé, 1558) (by permission of University of Glasgow Library, Special Collections)

29 Peter Goodrich, *Legal Emblems and the Art of Law; Obiter Depicta as the Vision of Governance* (Cambridge: Cambridge University Press, 2013), xviii.

the Gallic version of Hercules. According to Lucian, Hercules was not used by the Gauls as a symbol of force. To be sure, the figure shown in Alciato's emblem (and in all the other variations of this particular emblem published in other editions of his *emblemata*) shares similar features to a gnarled pagan warrior; he is old and grizzled, his clothes barely fit, he carries the club and wears a lionskin. Certainly, all these features are associated with Hercules. However, unlike any classical depiction, this particular figure of Hercules is depicted with light and graceful chains running from his tongue and attached to the ears of his followers. These links are nothing other than a metaphorical representation of persuasion. They represent the leading of a crowd through the sweetness of words. It is through persuasion alone that Ogmios leads these men away from Hades seen portrayed in the middle ground. In Lucian's words:

> That old Hercules of theirs drags after him a great crowd of men who are all tethered by the ears. His leashes are delicate chains fashioned of gold and amber, resembling the prettiest of necklaces. Yet, though led by bonds so weak, the men do not think of escaping as they easily could … in fact they follow cheerfully and joyously … Since the painter had no place to which he could attach the ends of the chains, he pierced the tip of his tongue and represented him drawing the men by that means.[30]

The basic point of the emblem is simply that eloquence has the power to mould the hardest of hearts (in the words of Alciato's *lemma*).[31] Ogmios asserts his power not through action or conduct but through eloquence. In Ciceronian terms, eloquence moves the soul and, in more Augustinian terms, it moves the soul to a state of holiness. Ogmios then is not simply a rhetor but a psychpomp guiding souls away from the underworld and from the collection of barbarous monsters (medieval scholastics, the free flow of imagination, the irrational crowd, etc.) that haunted the humanists. He guides his audience towards truth, towards an obscure point outside the frame and off the page. In so doing, he maintains their social bonds, fastening and uniting a disparate crowd of soldiers, priests, lawyers, perhaps even women.[32]

30 Lucian, 'On Heracles,' cited in Edgar Wind, 'Hercules' and Orpheus: Two Mock-Heroic Designs by Dürer', *Journal of the Warburg Institute* 2/3 (1939) 206–18, at 209.

31 I am aware that, while emblems are tripartite in structure, I have chosen in most instances to concentrate on the picture and the *lemma*. Where appropriate, the epigram will also be discussed.

32 Thanks to Peter Goodrich for pointing out the marked diversity of the crowd depicted in Alciato's emblem.

It is unsurprising that the Gallic Hercules was used as an emblem for those who wished to fashion themselves as civic minded heroes. Henry IV (of Navarre and France), for example, depicted himself in precisely these terms, as one who had descended to slay the monsters of war and restore imperial peace and justice in which civilization might flourish.[33] The point is repeatedly underscored by Guillaume Budé in the preface to his *Institute du Prince* and throughout his *Annotationes Pandectarum*.[34] For Budé, Ogmios was a Christ figure, a citizen of Corinth, a pre-cursor of the French monarchy of Francois I. It is equally unsurprising that the Gallic Hercules seems to have been adopted as a symbol by many of the humanists themselves. Erasmus uses the image to glorify the ideal of eloquence and philological reconstruction as well as the triumph of persuasion over the various monsters and enemies of the humanists.[35] While eloquence established social bonds as divine in provenance, the civilian reception of the image differs from the English. In Lucian's account, the movement towards divinity is a gentle, sweet motion and, while chained, the crowd of men following Hercules do so cheerfully and joyously (which conforms to one of the Ciceronian aims of poetry). In the English vernacular tradition, however, eloquence was not simply better than force. It *was* force. Thomas Wilson makes the point in his *Arte of Rhetoric*: 'Such force hath the tongue, and such is the power of eloquence and reason that most men are forced even to yield in what most standeth against their will'. On Hercules, Wilson adds 'His witte was so great, his tongue so eloquent, and his experience such, that no man was able to withstand his reason'.[36] In this apology, Wilson praises eloquence for the very features that the Lutherans would attack. What is exposed here is the

33 See Frances A. Yates, *Astrea* (London: Routledge, 1985), 210. On the more general features of Hercules as a propaganda image for the French monarchy, see Erwin Panofksy, *Hercules am Scheideweg und andere antike Bildstoffe in der Neueren Kunst*. ed. Dieter Wuttke (Berlin: Gebr. MannVerlag, 1997), particularly 218; Corrado Vivanti, 'Henry IV, The Gallic Hercules,' *Journal of the Warburg and Courtauld Institute* 30 (1967), 176–97; Theodor E. Mommsen, 'Petrarch and the Story of Hercules', *Journal of the Warburg and Courtauld Institute*, 16 (1953), 178–92.

34 Guillaume Budé, *Annotationes Pandectarum* [1508] (Lyon: Gryphium Lugduni, 1541 edn); Guillaume Budé *De l'Institution du Prince* (Paris, 1547).

35 See Desiderius Erasmus and St. Thomas More, *The Translations of Lucian* ed. Craig R. Thompson (Ithaca, NY: Cornell University Press, 1974).

36 Thomas Wilson, *The Arte of Rhetoric* [1560] G. H. Mair ed. (Oxford: Clarendon, 1909 edn). See also, Richard Sherry, *Treatise of the Figures of Grammar and Rhetoric Profitable for all that be Studious of Eloquence* [1560] ed. Peter Medine (University Park, PA: Penn State University, 1994). Angel day, *The English Secretary* [1599] (Scholars Facsimilies and Reprint, 1967) and Abraham Fraunce, *The Arcadian Rhetoric* [1588] (Kent, OH: Kent State University, 1971).

relationship between language and violence. In *The Arte of English Poesie*, George Puttenham notes that the Gallic Hercules (this 'lusty old man from Marseille' as he calls him) was often depicted as standing some distance from his audience who are drawn to him by the *force* of his persuasions.[37] Indeed, for Puttenham, the energy and *enargeia* (vividness) of eloquence cannot be taken lightly. It is a violent weapon that can only be handled with the wisdom of age, by 'those with hoary hairs than beardless boys'.[38] It is for this reason that Alciato purposefully presents Ogmios not as a nimble and graceful tempter of souls but as grizzled and aged. Further, illustrating that eloquence was a matter of high danger, Puttenham narrates the story of Hegesias, who spent so much energy inveighing against a transitory life and who so highly recommended death as a cure that 'a great number of hearers destroyed themselves'.[39] His advice was an attack on those 'common despisers of good utterance'.[40] In far stronger terms, Puttenham regarded puritan invectives against eloquence such as those by Richard Mulcaster, Roger Ascham (who associated eloquence with republicanism) and Agrippa von Nettesheim as resolutely anti-intellectual.[41] Knowledge, claimed Puttenham, has no enemy but the ignorant; *scientia non habet inimicum nisi ignorantem.*

Whether by force or by gentle persuasion, eloquence leads man to another place, towards a divine or, in more secular (and therefore more mysterious) terms, a more obscure province. The idea that eloquence was a measure of, and a contract with, God is clear in Alciato's emblem. In this sense, the chains depicted in Alciato's emblem are not simply to be regarded as functional, an illustrator's only device for showing the power of eloquence. They are, as the art historian Edgar Wind pointed out, a deliberate reference to the hermetic symbol of the golden mercurial chain.[42] They provided for the illustrator, the emblematist and the lawyer, a necessary mediation that enabled transmission from office to audience, from the one to the many, and so too, from the many to the one. Alciato's chain was a symbol borrowed from the mystical

37 'with a long chain tied by one end of his tongue, the other end at the peoples ears, who stood far off and seemed to be drawn to him by the force of that chain fastened to his tongue, as who would say, by the force of his persuasions.' George Puttenham, *The Arte of English Poesie*, 226.

38 George Puttenham, *The Arte of English Poesie*, 227.

39 George Puttenham, *The Arte of English Poesie* 226. Hegesias was eventually banished by Ptolemy.

40 George Puttenham, *The Arte of English Poesie*, 224.

41 Richard Mulcaster, *Positions for the Training of Children* [1581] (Toronto: University of Toronto, 1994 edn); Roger Ascham, *The Schoolmaster* (Menston: Scholar Press, 1967).

42 Wind, 'Heracles and Orpheus', 211.

deliberations of Marsilio Ficino.[43] More than simply illustrating the persuasive effects of eloquence, the chains also draw man and God, earth and heaven, together in closer proximity. Eloquence enabled man, the one who inhabits office, to be more like God. In the common law tradition, both Thomas Wilson and John Rastell stressed this proximity in near contractual terms.[44] Philip Sidney in his *Apology for Poesie* characterises eloquence as a contractual bond, a chain if you like, between between God and public orators.[45] Such public offices, he argues, mimic the divine function of David in his psalms, Solomon in the Song of Songs, Orpheus and a host of others who through eloquence attempt to imitate the 'excellencies' of God. A further point often made is that justice is only achieved by recuperating a lost language that carries the force of divine pronouncements (*eloquia*) and inhabiting that language. The argument is given fuller treatment by Thomas Wilson, Keeper of the State Papers Office, for whom eloquence is given to man by God and lost by man after the fall 'when all things waxed savage'. So that he 'who is among the reasonable of all most reasonable, and among the wittie of all most wittie, and among the eloquent of all most eloquent is not onely a singular man but rather to be coumpted for halfe a god'.[46]

This latter point by Wilson is interesting not simply because it illustrates the Christian flavour of eloquence but because it alludes to a more arcane, obscure and hermetically inspired provenance. That eloquence was a mystical pre-lapsarian language was a theme that runs through a number of contemporary tracts concerned with a *prisca theologia.* A return to eloquence was neither simply a return to the Latin sources nor to the language of the Christian and antinomain God. A return to eloquence meant a turning to Egypt and to the economy of pictorial hieroglyphics as containing the hidden secrets of Edenic language.[47] Only by syncretising the anti-nomianism of Christianity with the emblematic language of Horapollo (together with a whole range of other influences, such as chivalry, Latin

43 '*Non Esse ab uno ad infima sine mediis festinandum ... non esse ab infimis ad unum absque debitis mediis redeundum.*' Marsilio Ficino, *Opera* (1576) vol. II, 1236, cited in Wind, 'Heracles and Orpheus'.

44 Thomas Wilson, *Arte of Rhetoric*, 41; John Rastell, *An Exposition of Certaine Difficult and Obscure Words and Termes of the Laws of England* (London, 1566); see also John Cowell, *The Interpreter* (London, 1607).

45 Philip Sidney, *Apologie for Poesie* [1595] ed. G. Shepherd (Manchester: Manchester University Press, 1965), 101–2.

46 Thomas Wilson, *Arte of Rhetoric*, preface.

47 The key figure in Elizabethan England is Giodarno Bruno. For further articulation see Frances Yates, *Giodarno Bruno and the Hermetic Tradition* (University of Chicago Press, 1964) at pp181-186.

literature and Justinian himself) and only by setting this syncretic structure within the parameters of decorum could an ideal legal state be built.

The tongue

The mystical provenance of eloquence gives rise to a further characteristic. Eloquence had a spiritual agency independent of those mortals who were trained into its ways. This was most economically illustrated and performed through the use of the severed and autonomous figure of the tongue as a symbol of eloquence. That the tongue should be used by Alciato to represent the eloquence of Ogmios is of little surprise. The tongue and the mouth already had a long history of symbolic association with public speech and office. The papal investiture of cardinals began with the opening of the candidates' mouths (*apertio oris*) to renew and control speech required for public duty.[48] Most obviously, the tongue (*linga*) puns on the Latin for speech/language (*lingua*). The image was to be used time and again by later emblematists, such as Claude Paradin, Gabriel Rollenhagen, George Wither and Hadranius Junius. Cesare Ripa, too, depicts persuasion with a tongue wrapped around her head. To them, eloquence was to become a matter requiring governance and the surrender of individual will to the independent *voluntas* of the tongue.

It is unclear whether or not the pierced tongue depicted in Alciato's emblem of Ogmios influenced the use of the autonomous tongue by the later emblematists. It is more likely that such later references were to Petrarch's essay on the problem of the garrulous speaker and to the numerous references to the tongue in the *Adages* of Erasmus. Erasmus explicitly compares the tongue to the metaphor of a *governal d'un navire* (a ship's rudder) 'which though it make a small part of the vessel, yet upon its right or improper movement depends the safety and destruction of the whole'.[49] It is an image rendered emblematically by Jean Jacques Boissard ('the tongue is as a ships rudder').[50] In many ways richer and more

48 Peter Goodrich, *Law in the Courts of Love: Literature and other Minor Jurisprudences* (Routledge, 1996) at p84.

49 Desiderius Erasmus, '*Lingua Quo Vadis*' in Robert Bland (ed) *Proverbs chiefly taken from the Adagia of Erasmus*, (London; T. Egerton, 1814) at p257. The adage continues "... Confine your tongue or it will bring you confinement."

50 Jean Jacques Boissard, *Emblemes Latins* (Metz: Abraham Faber 1588), '*La Langue est à l'homme ce que le gouvernal est au navire*'; As a ship is safe with the control of a firm rudder when a storm has risen up and rages, with the sea lashed up; so any wise man who governs well the use of his tongue safely avoids the many dangers of life. n48 at p55.

provocative, however, is Gabrielle Rollenhagen's emblem, *Quo Tendis Lingua* (Figure 7.2). Here, a winged tongue takes off over a landscape composed of mountains, hills, pathways. In the middle distance, on our right a couple are arguing. In the distant background are two towns separated from each other by a valley. The two towns, one more splendid than the other, echo Erasmus's own gnomic citation of a Greek proverb: 'O tongue where are you going, are you about to destroy a city and raise it up again'.[51] Eloquence has its own energy and intention (*voluntas*). Without control, without training into its ways, the tongue has a tendency to fly of its own accord and commit whatever form of malediction it chooses, destroying cities, interrupting social bonds and civic peace.

Both the *lemma* and accompanying epigram support this immediate interpretation. The *lemma*, for instance, reads '*Garrula quo TENDIS? Quo te furor impia lingua Abripit? Ah presso, disce tacere, labro*'. It is often translated,

Figure 7.2 Gabriel Rollenhagen, 'Quo Tendis Lingua', 1611 edn, Utrecht, Arnheim, 1613. (reproduced by permission of GRI Digital Collections, Getty Research Institute)

51 Desiderius Erasmus, '*Lingua Quo Vadis*' op. cit. n 50.

more or less literally as 'Garrulity where are you going? Impious tongue where is madness carrying you away? Learn to be silent with closed lips'.[52] Training into eloquence is a matter of learning to distinguish between what can and cannot be said.

It might be objected that by the time of the renaissance in legal humanism, this self-regulation of speech was already firmly embedded within a literary and pictorial tradition. The emblematists were not depicting any transcendental qualities associated with eloquence but, rather, the potential aberrancy of free speech. However, in the medieval tradition, the tongue pointed to its subject matter of speech rather than to the question of its style and form. A divagation contrasting the renaissance tongue with this earlier medieval tradition allows us to address in more precise terms what is at stake in the emblematic depiction of the autonomous tongue. Take, as an example, the sins of blasphemy, envy, lying, obscenity (*turpiloquium*), back-biting or slander. These were sins that all involved the use of the tongue (*peccata linguæ*). In a range of traditions (artistic, pastoral and so on) extant during the late medieval period (thirteenth century), the sinner would inevitably be portrayed as possessing an uncanny serpent-like tongue. Such depictions as in the fresco of the Arena Chapel, Padua, by Giotto of *invidia* or in Alciato's own depiction of *invidia* were invariably influenced by Ovid. The *subscriptio* to Alciato's emblem reads: 'A hideous woman eating the flesh of vipers,/Her eyes torment her and she gnaws her heart,/ Leanness and pallor hold her in thrall. In her hand/A thorny staff: thus is envy depicted'.[53]

In another, more visceral, vein pastoral literature had its own visual protocols. The tale of the back-biting monk (by Robert Mannyng) even has the slandering monk eat the morsels of his own dismembered tongue. Dismembered tongues represented a body lacking in wholeness and therefore divinity. More than this, according to V. E. Langam, a tongue cut off from the body also represented man and his language cut off from the wholeness of God's word.[54] This aspect is not altogether unremoved from the

52 See, for example, Barbara C. Bowen, '*Lingua Quo Tendis*? Speech and Silence in French Renaissance Emblems' *French Forum*, 4/3 (1979), 249–60. Bowen translates the lemma as 'O garrulous tongue, where are you going? Whither, Oh Pious tongue, is madness carrying you away? Ah, learn to be silent, with compressed lips [or with a finger on your lips]', at 249.

53 Andrea Alciato, 'Invidia', *Emblemata* (Lyon, 1550), n. 71.

54 V. E. Langum, 'Sins of Tongues, Pain of Members; Speech and Sacrament in late Medieval Exempla' *Marginalia* 6 (2006–2007), 1–12.

concerns of some of the emblematists and is treated by Georgette de Montenay in her depiction of false worship (Figure 7.3).[55]

The dismembered tongue, that is to say the false and dissembling tongue, is torn apart not simply from the body but from the heart (seen trailing behind). The accompanying text reads as follows: 'with the mouth alone you will venerate god in vain. True religion is seated in the depths of the heart. Stop forming lies with a false heart but revere God with your mind'. These themes took on further emphasis after Lateran IV. The requirement of

Figure 7.3 Georgette de Montenay, *Emblèmes ou devises chrétiennes*, Lyons, 1571, embl. 25, '*Frustra me colunt*' (In vain they revere me)

55 Georgette de Montenay, *Emblematum Christianorum Centuria* (Zurich, 1584), 24. As the only woman, the theoretical and religious concerns of Georgette de Montenay might be differentiated from those of Alciato and others. Lady-in-waiting to Jeanne d'Albret (the mother of Henri IV of France), hers was a resolutely more Calvinist approach. It ought not to be taken as indicative of the more civic concerns of many of the male emblematists.

confession and the receipt of the Holy Eucharist were oral techniques that touched the moral ambiguity of the tongue; '*ex ipso/lingam ore procedit benedicto et maledicto*' [through the mouth/tongue man both praises God and curses men like Him].[56] A list of sins needed a special category, that of the *peccata linguae*, to distinguish evil from good.[57] This ethic is given almost legal footing by Bishop George Webbe (1581–1641) in his *Arraignment of the Unruly Tongue*.[58] To which, one might add, the particular place given by the mediaeval glossators to slander as that which was considered injurious to the reputation of the Emperor or *princeps*, as well as to the very jurisdiction of that to which the whole *Corpus* refers:

> The Imperial Majesty must needs be not only decorated with arms, but also armed with laws that it be able to govern rightly in either time, in war and in peace, and that the Roman Prince may come off as victor not only in hostile battles, but also by the paths of law may expel the iniquities of slanderers, and become the most religious observer of law as well as the one triumphant over conquered foes.[59]

The point is that what mattered, what was imprecated in the medieval context, was the content of speech rather than the style. The autonomous tongue in renaissance emblems, on the other hand (with the exception of Georgette de Montenay), was put to a different service. The tongue, by now far removed from any mortal body, carried its own energy far removed from any inherent energy or will. The practice of eloquence meant surrendering free will to a whole regime of spiritual self-management and regeneration not to avoid sin but to train for office. Paradoxically, what mattered for humanists such as Rollenhagen and Wither was the primacy of the tongue,

56 See article 21 of Lateran IV cited in V. E. Langum, 'Sins of Tongues, Pain of Members'.

57 The classic text, according to V. E. Langam, 'Sins of Tongues, Pain of Members', is Peyraut, *Summa de Vitiis*.

58 George Webbe, *The Arraignment of the Unruly Tongue* (1619). See also Jean de Marconville, *A Treatise on the Good and Evell Tongue*; William Perkins, *A Direction for the Government of the Tongue*. All three are collected in Nathalie Vienne-Guerrin, ed., *The Unruly Tongue in Early Modern England: Three Treatises* (Plymouth: Rowman, 2012). Also, Richard Allestree, *Government of the Tongue* (Oxford, 1674), John Bulwer, *Directions for Speech and Style* (London, 1600). Further bibliographical references can be found in Carlo Mazzio 'Sins of the Tongue in Early Modern England', *Modern Language Studies*, 28/3–4 (1998), 93–124. Mazzio's article itself is a rich examination of the somatic tensions of speech during the counter-reformation.

59 *Justinian's Institutes*, Prologue, trans. Peter Birks and Grant McLeod (London: Duckworth, 1994).

the sovereignty of eloquence, rather than the primacy or sovereignty of human will.

In this sense, the translation of Rollenhagen's *lemma* (as 'garrulity, where are you going?') is not so clear cut and further ambiguities arise. We ought to note that according to contemporary emblem theory, to which Rollenhagen would have subscribed, the picture would not have been so comprehensible without the rule.[60] The emblem of the tongue (or, for that matter, any emblem) portrays a mystical puzzle ingeniously and wittily charged with different layers of meaning. Similarly, the rule or sentiment that was expressed textually either in the *lemma* or in the verse would not have been self-explanatory. Image and text, *pictura* and verse were body and soul, respectively. The emblem's effect depended upon meditating upon the whole thing. The norms of these epigrammatical puzzles ought not to be so readily ignored and closer attention to the wit and ambivalence of the emblem reveals further layers than that which seems obvious. Thus, the word '*tendis*', which is normally translated as 'going' could also mean, without any force in the translation process, 'extension', 'stretching out' and 'erection'.[61] The tongue, our feathered shaft, in other words, signified a phallus. This is not as untoward as it might seem. Throughout renaissance literature, the tongue does not simply represent the tongue as biological matter. The author of an 'office' manual on chirography suggests that the tongue is both pen and penis.[62] Similarly ambiguous, in Rollenhagen's emblem *Quo Tendis*, is the use of the word *labro* in the *lemma*. The usual translation of the sentence in which it appears is 'learn to be silent with closed lips'. What is quite obvious, however, although surprisingly never commented on, is that *labro* means labia. The sentence '*Ah Presso, disce tacere, labro*' can mean 'discipline yourself to keep your labia closed'.

The relationship between eloquence and the sacrifice of passion was made again and again by emblematists.[63] Eloquence, in other words, subjects the

60 Tomasso Garzoni, *Piazza Universale* (1619), cited in Dietmar Peil, 'Emblem Types in Gabriel Rollenhagen's *Nucleus Emblematum*', *Emblematica* 6/2 (1992), 281.

61 Barbara Bowen, '*Lingua Quo Tendis?*'.

62 Martin Billingsey (*The Pen's Excellencie or the Secretaries Delight* (1618) ed. Heather Wolfe (Washington, DC: Washington University Press, 2002).

63 See for example, Hadrianus Junius, '*Linguam Conspectio*', *Emblemata* (Antwerp, 1565) Emblem 41. '*eoque symbolo innui, debere nos superare utrumque quidem et libidinem nimirem sen voluptatum seminarum et linguam petulanteiam. Sed hanc potissimum ... garrlum et effrenem ininitorum malorum esse causam.*' [Why are you holding your sluggish belly in your cupped hand, why your wet lips, Scythian, why your lustful genitals? Fight shy of a fondness for gratifying the senses and troublesome self indulgence. And above all put a check on your babbling tongue. We should hold our libido, the seedbed of our lusts and of the carelessness of our tongue. But most of all the latter…[since] a

office holder to a whole regime of self-governance. It takes over more than speech; it takes over life itself. Mortal passions surrender to codes of decorum. Only then can the office holder rise again, to float regenerated towards the clouds. The clouds, of course, refer to the task and honour of office which is to divine hidden knowledge from the formless mass that shadows the Earth. Sacrificing the body to eloquence and surrendering to the primacy of the tongue establishes the means to illuminate the Earth.

The visual decorum of eloquence

By virtue of sacrificing his passions to eloquence the official is steered towards a more general and appropriate comportment. It is here that the functions of office share with those of emblems since what matters is the visual apprehension and appreciation of comportment, elegance and style as ciphers of a hidden knowledge. In terms of textual eloquence, this meant that the page itself had to provide a suitable platform or *pegma* to stage the spectacle of the message. If Ernst Curtius regarded the physical book as a symbol in and of itself, it was because life relations were apprehended in their relationship to the book.[64] The Bible, the Book of Hours or the Book of Nature were not dead artefacts but manifestations of the living word that bequeathed to their readers an interior writing – a record. For the humanists, particularly in the wake of the print revolution, the same was true of the page itself. The page was considered more than a unit of paper, more than simply a matter of verso or recto. The word *pegma* referred to the manner in which ceremonial tilts and processions (the coronation processions Elizabeth I or James I, in particular) involved an intricate and sometimes mechanical system of support. The 'Arches of Triumph' by Stephen Harrison, for example, were temporary structures, wooden machines, which supported an allegorical (usually) or tableaux vivants.[65] The *pegma* and the page were not innocent structures that simply happened

talkative tongue and unrestrained tongue is the cause of endless evils.] The *subscriptio* (attributed to Anacharis), reads '*Linguae, ventri, pudendis impera*' [Govern you belly, your tongue, your genitals]. See also Guillaume la Perrière's depiction from the same source (Anacharis) in emblem 16: '*nempe magis vis est fraenanda loquelae, quàm Veneris, peius testibus ora nocent*' [It requires greater force to rein in speech since the mouth does more harm than the testicles]; Guillaume la Perrière, *Morosophie* (Lyon, 1553).

64 Ernst Curtius, *European Literature and the Latin Middle Ages*, Willard Trask (tr) (Princeton University Press, 1991) pp302 et seq.

65 Stephen Harrison, *The Arches of Triumph* (London 1604). http://luna.folger.edu/luna/servlet/detail/FOLGERCM1~6~6~293147~122207:The-arch%E2%80%99s-of-triumph-erected-in-ho.

to supporting a political or ideological motif. What was required was an understanding of these material and visual structures.[66] The visual eloquence of the page, in other words, was what gave meaning to the published emblem, as well as to legal documents, deeds of trust and so forth. Each page was turned into a unique visual medium through which the mysteries of antiquity were transmitted. Moreover, the page did not simply record what has been lost to memory but, in a fury of fastidiousness, curlicues and baroque detail, reminded that things have been forgotten. At stake was the eloquence and poetry of reception and re-birth at the heart of renaissance humanism. Although a late example, Scarlattini's *Eloquentia Verax* perfectly illustrates the visual economy at stake in both emblem and office. The baroque detail framing what lies latent within is not superfluous. The frame is itself an open orifice. It is the *labro* and labia that allow for meaning arrive into the world, re-born (Figure 7.4).

It is perhaps more difficult to argue that verbal eloquence surrenders to visual (rather than, as Walter Ong would have it, auditory) reception.[67] However, it needs reminding that the very word *emblemata* was one borrowed from Quintilian to mean speaking inlaid with examples, with emblems, common places, illustrations and pictures. The point was not lost on the common law tradition. For Sir Philip Sidney, eloquence was speaking in pictures.[68]

In this sense, the emblem by Scarlatini, *Eloquentia Verax*, provides an illustration of what is at stake in the visual apprehension of both textual and verbal eloquence. Eloquence needs to be seen so as to be trusted; it is the eye that allows us to see what is being spoken and to discern the soul of the matter. Horapollo's *Hieroglyphica* itself refers to the hieroglyphical use of the bloodshot eye as more than the empirical observation of eloquent speech.[69] Here, vision refers to a mystical phenomenon, to the ability to comprehend eloquence beyond mere expression. This mystical quality of apprehension is given neo-Platonic expression by Père Le Moine:

> I should say that there is in the Device something of those universal images given to the Higher Spirits which present in one moment and by means of a simple and detached notion what our minds can

66 A similar point is made in relation to letter writing by James Daybell, *The Material Letter in Early Modern England: Manuscript Letters and the Culture and Practice of Letter Writing 1512–1635* (Palgrave: Macmillan 2012).

67 Walter Ong, *Orality and Literacy: The Technologizing of the Word* (Routledge 2002)

68 Philip Sidney, *An apology for Poesie*, op. cit., n 46

69 Horapollo Nilous, *Hieroglyphica* (London, 1840 edn), 16.

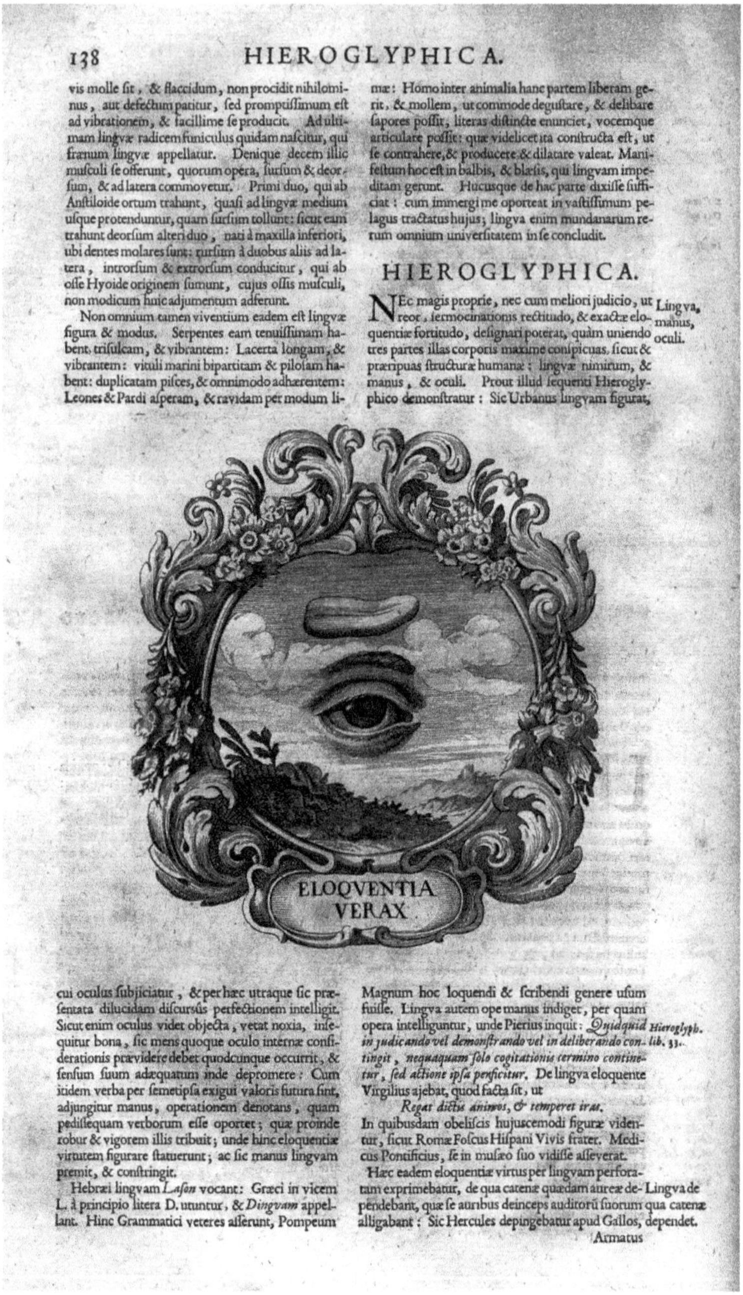

138 HIEROGLYPHICA.

vis molle ſit, & flaccidum, non procidit nihilominus, aut defectum patitur, ſed promptiſſimum eſt ad vibrationem, & facillime ſe producit. Ad ultimam lingvæ radicem funiculus quidam naſcitur, qui frænum lingvæ appellatur. Denique decem illic muſculi ſe offerunt, quorum opera, ſurſum & deorſum, & ad latera commovetur. Primi duo, qui ab Anſtiloide ortum trahunt, quaſi ad lingvæ medium uſque protenduntur, quam ſurſum tollunt: ſicut eam trahunt deorſum alteri duo, nati à maxilla inferiori, ubi dentes molares ſunt: ſurſum à duobus aliis ad latera, introrſum & extrorſum conducitur, qui ab oſſe Hyoide originem ſumunt, cujus oſſis muſculi, non modicum huic adjumentum adferunt.

Non omnium tamen viventium eadem eſt lingvæ figura & modus. Serpentes eam tenuiſſimam habent, triſulcam, & vibrantem: Lacerta longam, & vibrantem: vituli marini bipartitam & piloſam habent: duplicatam piſces, & omnimodo adhærentem: Leones & Pardi aſperam, & ravidam per modum limæ: Homo inter animalia hanc partem liberam gerit, & mollem, ut commode deguſtare, & delibare ſapores poſſit, literas diſtincte enunciet, vocemque articulare poſſit: quæ videlicet ita conſtructa eſt, ut ſe contrahere, & producere & dilatare valeat. Manifeſtum hoc eſt in balbis, & blæſis, qui lingvam impeditam gerunt. Hucusque de hac parte dixiſſe ſufficiat: cum immergi me oporteat in vaſtiſſimum pelagus tractatus hujus; lingva enim mundanarum rerum omnium univerſitatem in ſe concludit.

HIEROGLYPHICA.

NEc magis proprie, nec cum meliori judicio, ut reor, ſermocinationis rectitudo, & exactæ eloquentiæ fortitudo, deſignari poterat, quàm uniendo tres partes illas corporis maxime conſpicuas, ſicut & præcipuas ſtructuræ humanæ: lingvæ nimirum, & manus, & oculi. Prout illud ſequenti Hieroglyphico demonſtratur: Sic Urbanus lingvam figurat, Lingva, manus, oculi.

ELOQVENTIA VERAX.

cui oculus ſubjiciatur, & per hæc utraque ſic præſentata dilucidam diſcurſûs perfectionem intelligit. Sicut enim oculus videt objecta, vetat noxia, inſequitur bona, ſic mens quoque oculo internæ conſiderationis prævidere debet quodcunque occurrit, & ſenſum ſuum adæquatum inde depromere: Cum itidem verba per ſemetipſa exigui valoris futura ſint, adjungitur manus, operationem denotans, quam pediſſequam verborum eſſe oportet; quæ proinde robur & vigorem illis tribuit; unde hinc eloquentiæ virtutem figurare ſtatuerunt; ac ſic manus lingvam premit, & conſtringit.

Hebræi lingvam *Laſon* vocant: Græci in vicem L. à principio litera D. utuntur, & *Dingvam* appellant. Hinc Grammatici veteres aſſerunt, Pompeum Magnum hoc loquendi & ſcribendi genere uſum fuiſſe. Lingva autem ope manus indiget, per quam opera intelliguntur, unde Pierius inquit: *Quidquid in judicando vel demonſtrando vel in deliberando contingit, nequaquam ſolo cogitationis termino continetur, ſed actione ipſa perficitur.* De lingva eloquente Virgilius ajebat, quod facta ſit, ut *Hieroglyph. lib. 33.*

Regat dictis animos, & temperet iras.

In quibusdam obeliſcis hujuscemodi figuræ videntur, ſicut Romæ Foſcus Hiſpani Vivis frater. Medicus Pontificius, ſe in muſæo ſuo vidiſſe aſſeverat.

Hæc eadem eloquentiæ virtus per lingvam perforatam exprimebatur, de qua catenæ quædam aureæ dependebant, quæ ſe auribus deinceps auditorũ ſuorum alligabant: Sic Hercules depingebatur apud Gallos, Lingva de qua catenæ dependet.

Armatus

Figure 7.4 Ottavio Scarlattini, 'Eloquentia verax'; in *Homo et Eius Partes Figuratus & Symbolicus*… Augsburg, Dillingen, 1695

> only represent in succession and by means of a long sequence of expressions which form themselves one after the other and which more frequently get into each other's way rather than help each other by their multitude.[70]

Something like the hermetic trances recommended by Giodarno Bruno is involved in the visual apprehension of office and emblem. Vision, in other words, involved a form of contemplation in which intellect temporarily abandons the body. Man becomes more like an Egyptian god whose knowledge of things is not through thought but simply through the materiality of the thing itself.[71] The hermetic mysticism of Bruno and Ficino is not so far removed from the arguments expressed by Francis Bacon on emblems. For Bacon, the emblem is to be favoured over the rhetorical notions of invention, disposition, elocution and memory. Rhetoric involves the intellect. The preference for emblems on the other hand is that they are visual 'images (such as) of a sportsman hunting the hare, of an apothecary ranging his boxes, an orator making a speech, a boy repeating verses, or a player acting his part'. It is as images that they drive deeper by bypassing the linear manner of the easy interpretation.[72]

Conclusion

Returning to the question of office, the claim made here is that any current rearticulation of institutional structures cannot escape from what inheres in official language. Language carries with it an inheritance that ensures what is communicated is beyond simple message or rule. Emblems are emblematic insofar as they perform the very task of office. They do so within the non-ordinary parameters of decorum; they do so visually and they do so in order that the viewer engages in an active process, a personal odyssey of discovery. It was according to such a process that eloquence came to displace the mediaeval category of dignity as the cardinal characteristic of office. Moreover, while the style of eloquence might vary from Ciceronian to non-Ciceronian, what ought to be discovered remained obscured. Civic membership and duty did not come without effort and action. It is at this

70 Père Le Moine, *De l'Art des Devises*, (Paris, 1666), quoted in Mario Praz, *Studies in Seventeenth Century Imagery* (Rome: Storia et Letteratura, 1964) 53.

71 Marsilio Ficino, 'When Egyptians Priests wished to signify divine mysteries, they did not use the small characters of script, but the whole images of plants, trees or animals; for God has knowledge of things not by way of thought but like the pure and firm shape of the thing itself', cited in Ernst Gombrich, *Symbolic Images* (London: Phaidon, 1978), 158–9.

72 Francis Bacon, *De Augmentis Scientiarum*, (Whitefish, MT: Kessinger, 2002), 17

point that any attempt to refresh the institutional life of law from a strictly secular perspective becomes problematic, since any attempt to think about the institution and its role in social cohesion, interrelational bonds, subjectivity, peace or amity, necessarily refers us to some point that exists outside what is empirically posited. This transcendental space need not be Christian. Humanism was adulterated by broader non-Christian notions of the sacred and transcendent. This point might be more obvious in the more mystical emblems that borrowed from neo-Platonic philosophy which sought to redescribe eloquence as a cryptic and esoteric synthesis of pagan and Christian mysticism. The hieroglyph of the emblem, in other words, created a hieratic space of decorum through which a civic energy, in the spirit of an Egyptian ideal state of law, could be animated. This, however, is only one avatar of the mystical element that clouds the administrative apparatus. Even the more rational of the emblematists, such as Alciato, posited a transcendental and obscure source. Hidden beyond the clouds, outside the frame of emblematic representation, lay an obscure point of reference. Christian, mystical or secular, this point of reference was what determined the social order. It marked an absolute source of civic morals. It was that to which all things aspired. Moreover, borrowing from Christian theology, eloquence was the only means of accessing and expressing such principles.

The question of office can never rid itself of reference to a non-transparent organizing principle. Put differently, the bonding of social relations between subjects depends upon a religious inheritance; elements of a (syncretic) theology based on revelation and *mysterium* remain. No tradition of thinking about the law, either as an anti-lawyer or as a committed legist, can wholly free itself from the Christian/hermetic legacy of how the office is formed. The individual persona of a judge, a poet or a philosopher might hope to conduct herself in strict secular terms. She might hope to comport herself as an office based persona rather than as a metaphysical being. She might even hope to bracket her gender and conduct herself free of prejudice and with stern dis-interest. However, the problem of office is not the disavowal of private conscience and other such calibrations of transcendental humanity. The problem (for secular minded state legists) is that the concept of 'office' itself takes on the all the attributes of 'confessional man'. Conscience was never attached to the individual or to individual volition. It was only ever attached to dignity and to office. When the *persona* of the office holder inhabits eloquence, it is because eloquence has its own energy and volition independent of the mortal incumbent. Everything transfers to language. That is to say, it is the autonomous language of eloquence itself that governs the conduct of office and carries upon its tongue the conscience and volition of its relevant institution. In the emblems described, it is the tongue, as synecdoche of both eloquence and office, and not the mortal office holder that bears the capacity to speak in good or bad faith. It is the tongue that carries an arcane mandate. This idea of an institutional hieratism troubles all manner of offices but it mattered and continues to matter more to lawyers and, particularly, to common lawyers. It permeates at every level and confuses any attempt to fully provide for a secular institutional office in more recent times.

The language of office and the mystical structure with which it imbues the institution can be addressed in relation to what occurs within the legal academy and among legal scholars. In an articulate chastisement of critical legal theorists, David Saunders urges us not to forget the space carved out within the history of western statism for a normative ethics based on non or anti-Christian foundations.[73] Critical legal theorists, he suggests, have received and ingested social theory all too greedily. Such a reception of theory from outside the parameters of law and legal discourse blinds the legal academy to all that which might be considered beneficent within law. The history of law is replete with positive moments and allusions to the ideal structures best suited to the good governance of contemporary society. It provides an account for the ideal presentation of a well-ordered way of life. Furthermore, Saunders argues, critics of the law, particularly critical legal scholars, are anti-legists and, as such, are heirs to and partake of a specifically Christian inheritance (as the antinomian religion). As a corrective, Saunders turns his attention towards the question of the office, to the beneficence of its conduct and manners. The striking feature of the article, however, is exactly the feature that it shares with those critics and theorists of the law (whether anti-nomian or orthodox), namely that it cannot but avoid adopting a non secular and, in this case, specifically Christian, posture. First, the goals of state-centred law, its institutions and offices, are directed towards some salvific purpose. Whether it is the well-ordered state of civic life or peaceful relations within and among the international community, there is an *œconomia* of purpose, a household plan, a divined pattern that needs to be established for law to institute itself.

The second point revolves more specifically around the idea of eloquence. The very language used to account for a secular normative tradition is itself mystically imbued. The office of the legal scholar, both critic and apologist, involves a form of eloquence that is more than simply persuasive. It is an office filled by *magisters* and, whether they enjoy it or not, such *magisters* have their own attendant disciples who carry and care for the words and

73 David Saunders, 'The Critical Jurist and the Moment of Theory', *Postcolonial Studies*, 10/1 (2007), 77–92.

structure and ethos of the *magister*. There is no escape from the hieratic nature of the institution. What determines our office is that we transmit, some more magisterially than others, an esoteric and, at times, obscene form of knowledge. More than this, however, the eloquence of the legal scholar is such that she or he is able is able to open up a vista or a vision. It matters little whether this vision is a totalising theory or a partial glimpse. What is involved in all forms of argumentation is the act of spitting on the ground, making mud out of saliva, to open the eyes of the blind. By creating worlds from dust and by inextricably imitating Christ's own ministerial office, we are simply emblematic. And, in inhabiting a style of language that allows us to transmit and, it is hoped, to be received, we are no more than tongues. The task, critical or juridical, is to establish the terms of a public language that carries with it and reflects the ethical norms best suited to an active participation in civic life.

CHAPTER 8

Don't screw with the law: visual and spatial defenses against judicial and political corruption in communal Italy

Alick M. McLean

Appearances matter. The jurists and politicians in Italian city-states such as Siena, pictured among others in *The Effects of Good Government on the City* fresco by Ambrogio Lorenzetti (Figure 8.1) shared with the rest of their society a visual sophistication that rivals that of today's web addicts and YouTube junkies. The media were different but as omnipresent as cellular and wireless networks – the broadcasting system was the city itself. Not only building interiors but also their exterior elevations, their siting and the streets and public spaces they framed were and remain sites of display, posturing, observing and being observed – platforms, so to speak, for individual and institutional communications through words, images, clothing, gestures and actions. To paraphrase media commentator Marshall McLuhan,

Figure 8.1 Effects of Good Government on the City (photograph Wikimedia Commons, Google Cultural Institute)

these platforms were also the messages themselves.[1] Public interior and urban environments articulated institutional and private interests explicitly or subliminally. Such messages did not simply happen – governing bodies and powerful families invested considerable expense and energy in composing and crafting their media as messages.

It is within this dynamic visual and spatial context that I situate some emblems of justice in the Italian communal period. Images of justice and politics were more than visualizations that translated legal ideas, practices or institutions for a lay public. They provided a means for implicitly linking law and justice to less abstract, more immediate social institutions and practices connected to popular beliefs and daily life. As such, they humanized law, negotiating between law's basis in reason, its emphasis on uniform rights and the absence of favouritism on the one hand and, on the other hand, the lay public's difficulty in comprehending, let alone embracing, a form of authority that differed considerably from the faith and trust-based rules of extra-communal and rural institutions: the church and the nobility. To put it more simply, the move from rule by faith and man to rule by reason and law necessitated the law itself appearing credibly as both woman and man.

The imagination, energy and expense in humanizing communal justice through a variety of media derive from the fragility of Italian city-state justice and governance in general. Communes had to protect their judiciaries from competing claims by church jurisdiction, even by heretical cults, and to defend their autonomous rule from the superpowers of their day: the Emperor and the Pope, from myriad rival cities or from competing factions and powerful families within the cities themselves. The podestà of Milan Oldradus de Trexeno visualized his executive power with an equestrian statue on Milan's town hall, echoing the imperial statue of Marcus Aurelius, thought at the time to be of Constantine, originally beside the Lateran in Rome. The accompanying inscription copies yet cleverly distorts another, in this case literary source, transforming the praise of Abbot William of Hirsau's pedagogical skills to celebrate Oldradus's achievements in eradicating heretical factions from the city: 'he burnt Cathars as he ought to' (*catharos ut debuit uxit*) (Figure 8.2).[2]

1 Marshall McLuhan, 'The medium is the message', *Understanding Media: The Extensions of Man* (New York: McGraw-Hill, 1964), 7.

2 '*Qui solium struxit, catharos, ut debuit, uxit*', *Memorie della Città di Milano*. L.LI:469. Reported by Aubin Louis Milin (1817) and Jean-Charles Léonard Simonde de Sismondi (1809). The sequence '*struxit ... uxit*' puns morbidly on the '*Struxit et instruxit, quia recto tramite duxit, Collapsum dudum vitam reparans monachorum*' from Haimo of Hirsau's praise of the teaching skills of William Abbot of Hirsau. B. Wilhelmi Abb. Hirsaug. *Acta Sanctorum ordinis S. Benediciti in saeculorum classes distributa...* Luc d'Achéry, Thierry Ruinart and Jean Mabillon, 1738 edn, 739. My thanks to Valérie Hayaert for noting this play on words and its sources.

Figure 8.2 Oldoradus de Trexeno equestrian statue, Palazzo della Ragione, Milan (photograph Alick M McLean)

The worst threats to communal authority were noble families, whose tower houses bristled in the urban landscapes of Arezzo, Lucca, Florence, Siena and, still today, San Gimignano. The Genoese Annals describe, even visualize, families fighting by their tower houses and document the response of public authorities to families who rebelled against the state, the demolition of their house (Figures 8.3 and 8.4).[3] States were right to worry about unruly factions. Most communal regimes would eventually lose their sovereignty to tyrants arising within, such as the Della Scala family in Verona, who, in turn, sought visually to validate their positions by co-opting equestrian figures like that of Milan's Oldradus (Figure 8.5). Leonardo della Scala, generally known as Maestino, began as podestà in 1259, carefully negotiated

3 *Genoese Annals*. Paris, Bibliothèque Nationale, Ms. lat. 10136: f. 111v, 109v.

Figure 8.3 Fighting tower house families, *Genoese Annals*, Bibliothèque Nationale, Ms. lat. 10136: f. 111v. (Bibliothèque Nationale, Paris)

Figure 8.4 Destruction of tower house families, *Genoese Annals*, Bibliothèque Nationale, Ms. lat. 10136: f. 109v. (Bibliothèque Nationale, Paris)

Figure 8.5 Can Grande della Scala, Castelvecchio, Verona (photograph Alick M McLean)

his way to become in 1261 Podestà of the *Domus Mercatorum*, a role that he succeeded in passing on to his brother, in 1269, out of which the family transformed themselves into the lords of Verona, ruling there until 1387.[4] External conquests were themselves generally facilitated by internal betrayal; for example, internal factions in Verona supported Gian Galeazzo Visconti's expulsion of the della Scala.[5]

4 Lino Canepari, '*Un principio del medioevo europeo: Cangrande della Scala*,' in *Il Veneto nel Medioevo, Quaderni del Centro Studi Medievali Ponzio di Cluny*. n.s., I, 2009–2010. (Soanara (Pd): Casa editrice il Prato, 2010) 198.

5 A. Castagnetti e G. M. Varanini, *Il Veneto nel medioevo: Le signorie trecentesche* (Verona: Banca Popolare di Verona, 1995), 106.

The proliferation of equestrian figures in Milan, Verona and, later, Padua and Venice, suggests that communal officers or tyrants were well aware of the benefits of public visibility, using sculpture and other media, such as coats of arms (Figure 8.6) to plant their presence into the public imagination. Italian city states became visual and spatial battle grounds, indeed weapons themselves, in the war for power. The sustainability of any city state was not based on its capacity to eliminate such media war, as none was capable of attaining a monopoly of either media or actual violence. Italian city states

Figure 8.6 Della Scala coat of arms, fountain, Piazza Bra, Verona (photograph Alick M McLean)

that endured longer tended, not unlike Greek city states thousands of years before them, to accept both media and actual violence as givens and to focus rather on managing dissent through a mixture of intimidation, negotiation and, when necessary and possible, banishment. A typical example is the Duke of Athens in Florence, brought in by the oligarchy to manage both internal dissent and a severe economic crisis. He managed to get the *popolo* to elect him Signore for life and proceeded to plan to tear down surrounding structures to isolate the Palazzo Vecchio to function better militarily, like the Angevin castle in Naples.[6] On 26 July 1343, the city finally banished him, as shown here in a commemorative painting by the school of Orcagna, 'Saint Anne and the Expulsion of the Duke of Athens', commissioned and executed immediately afterwards (Figure 8.7). The painting's original location, in a tabernacle in the Stinche prison, rebuilt after being burnt down during the revolt against the Duke, shows the commune's own mastery of visual rhetoric.

Betrayal was to be expected and any member of the government working towards mitigating dissent was himself a potential dissenter or tyrant. The absence of any trustworthy party in the decision chambers and law courts of

Figure 8.7 Saint Anne and the Expulsion of the Duke of Athens (photograph Wikimedia Commons, Web Gallery of Art)

6 For the military aspirations and importance of the Duke of Athens in the development of the piazza, see Nicolai Rubinstein, 'The Piazza della Signoria', in *The Palazzo Vecchio, 1298–1532* (Oxford: Oxford University Press, 1995), 82–3; and Marvin Trachtenberg, *Dominion of the Eye* (Cambridge: Cambridge University Press, 1997), 90, 100, 105, 131.

Italian city states forced communal councils and jurists to collaborate in developing elaborate and creative institutional, visual and spatial means of protecting the state, essentially, against themselves. Although any counsellor or jurist was potentially aspiring to take over the state, all were in agreement that nobody else had the right to do so. One of the richest examples is the election process for Venetian Doges, a ten to thirteen-step ritual so effective at blocking corruption through generating at once random yet popular results that it has served as a model in a 2007 HP study on computer election protocols.[7] The election of the Nine Governors and Defenders of the Commune and People of Siena was nearly as complex and similarly resulted in limiting influence of individual families or special interests, while assuring qualified members and a certain institutional continuity.[8] Mowbray and Gollmann suggest that the degree of complexity of the Doge elections was so overengineered as to suggest a 'security theatre',[9] something likely also present in the election of Siena's Nine. Such staging of un-corruptibility may have been ways of distracting the public from the fundamentally oligarchic nature of both Venice and Siena's governments. It is also probable, however, that this was a means of projecting not only political but also economic credibility, which would have certainly been in the interests of the predominantly commercially active members of both oligarchies.[10]

The most prevalent deterrent, or apparent deterrent, to corruption was isolating not only election procedures from potential interference but also, afterwards, the governments themselves. When in session, Siena's Nine governors were kept separate from the public in the Palazzo Pubblico, so much so that a balcony had to be built for them to provide them fresh air.[11] The sequestering of juries is a contemporary instance of the same practice. Even

7 On counterbalancing and thereby neutralizing self-interest see Immanuel Kant, "Perpetual Peace," *On History* ed. and trans. Lewis White Beck (Indianapolis, Bobbs-Merrill, 1957): 112. On Venetian ducal elections, see Miranda Mowbray and Dieter Gollmann, 'Electing the Doge of Venice: Analysis of a 13th Century Protocol,' *20th IEEE Computer Security Foundations Symposium (Venice, Italy, July 6–8 2007)* (IEEE: 2008), 295–308. See also Jay S. Coggins, C. Federico Perali, '64% Majority Rule in Ducal Venice: Voting for the Doge', *Public Choice*, 97/4 (1998) 709–23, esp. appendix with transcription of protocol: 722–3.

8 William M. Bowsky, *A Medieval Italian Commune: Siena under the Nine, 1287–1355* (Berkeley, CA: University of California Press, 1981), 58–61.

9 Mowbray and Gollman, 'Electing the Doge of Venice', section 8.1.

10 Ibid. See also Yadira González de Lara, 'The Secret of Venetian Success: A Public-Order, Reputation-Based Institution', *European Review of Economic History*, 12/3 (2008), 247–85.

11 The Nine were secluded by law starting in August, 1296, residing first in rented quarters and then, after it was completed, in the Palazzo Pubblico. They were confined there day and night throughout their two-month terms, with their own cook, barber, messengers, even chapel for church services. See Bowsky, *A Medieval Italian Commune*, 58 and 62.

sequestering governing councils was deemed insufficient by most Italian communes and, by the time of the mid-thirteenth century, most had added a new official, distinct from major and minor assemblies, who was radically isolated institutionally: the podestà. Podestàs were generally of noble background, trained at once as knights and as jurists.[12] Cities hired them as essentially professional town administrators for six- to twelve-month terms in a mixed judicial and executive role, the balance of which varied over time and locality – the above-mentioned Oldradus de Trexeno enjoyed both during his term in Milan. Communes stipulated that podestàs have no significant familial or economic interests in the town, generally that they hailed from communities over a specified distance away, and that they take an oath to uphold the statutes and interests of the commune hiring them.[13] Some towns, like Siena, required them to put down a security upon taking office and, only upon syndication, the satisfactory balancing of state books and, implicitly, neutral execution of their offices, could they get this back.[14] Not unlike Ebay's buyer and seller rating system today, a mix of profit and honour provided incentives for podestàs to perform their jobs without corruption, as not only their current but also future salaries depended on both actual and perceived honesty and effectiveness.[15]

12 The first recorded podestà in mediaeval Italy was in Bologna, in 1151. Other cities followed across northern and central Italy, with some appointed by Frederick Barbarossa between 1159 and 1183. From the 1183 Peace of Constance onwards, they were generally elected. Siena elected its first podestà in 1199 and, after some recourse to the earlier consular governance, stabilized the position after 1209. For a brief but well-documented overview of the office, from Roman magistrates to the podestà's Fascist revival, with a focus on the communal period, see Lester K. Born, 'What Is the Podestà?' *American Political Science Review*, 21/4 (1927), 863–71. For Siena's podestà, see Ferdinand Schwill, 'The Podestà of Siena', *American Historical Review*, 9/2 (1904), 247–64; and Bowsky, *A Medieval Italian Commune*, 23–34.

13 For a contemporary description of the swearing in of a podestà in Pavia, see Born, 'What Is the Podestà?', 867–8.

14 Bowsky, *A Medieval Italian Commune*, 25.

15 For an analysis of the financial benefits of a parallel reputation-based system, that of medieval Venetian trade contracts, see Yadira Gonzàlez de Lara, 'The Secret of Venetian Success'. The noble background of the medieval Italian podestà by no means precluded them from seeking financial gain and, furthermore, for defending their financial rights if infringed by cities for whom they worked. One of the most interesting cases is that of the 1288 podestà of Siena, Tommaso de Anzola of Parma, who sued for the remainder of his salary after claiming to have been unjustly removed after serving only half of his term. What makes his case particularly important is that his home commune of Parma was willing to impose and in turn suffer financial reprisals vis-à-vis Siena. See Bowsky, *A Medieval Italian Commune*, 31–3. The seriousness with which individuals took their rights for compensation, and to which their home communes were willing to support them, helped to make the podestà institutionally credible.

I propose that the office of the podestà was not simply developed across communes, taking off and improved swiftly, owing to their short, itinerant terms. It was also designed, composed in each city institutionally, spatially, architecturally and visually based on variations of common practice. Local variations that were particularly successful quickly made their way to common practice, only to be varied further in a constant competition by sovereign communes to outdo one another.[16] The social origins of this institution help to explain aspects of its shared, albeit varied, visualization. One was the feudal lord and its mercenary variation, the condottiere, such as John Hawkwood. Florence's podestàs took over the quarters of the primo *popolo's* military and political leader, the Capitano del Popolo, at the Bargello, the tower of which was bought and visually co-opted from the tower-house family, the Vologona (Figure 8.8a and 8.8b). The feudal origins explain partial changes to the plan of the podestà's quarters added when he moved in – a separate residential structure with a chapel in the back of the site,

Figure 8.8 Bargello, Florence: a) view; b) plan (photograph/drawing Alick M McLean)

16 This is consistent with other studies analyzing Italian communes and some French counterpart as mosaics of distributed institutions. See Canepari, '*Un principio del medioevo europeo*'.

linked to the original building by two closed walls, which were later turned into an arcaded court with rooms added along the walls. Only when the structure switched to the *locus* of the Grand Council were grand doors and a stairway added, leading to an expanded upper-floor Grand Council room, circa 1340 (Figure 8.8b).[17] Until the doors and stairs changed the space, the podestà lived in a structure that was isolated like a closed castle court or a church cloister.

The cloister reference reflects the other institutional origin for the office of the podestà. Bishops, priests, abbots, canons and monks were frequently reassigned, as today, by the church. They had to be ready to be moved from one religious community to another, adapting and at the same time transferring and disseminating local practices into the larger ecclesiastical and monastic culture. While nobles were fixed to place, unless they opted to hire themselves out as condottiere or podestàs, churchmen or monks were purposefully not.

The cloister form's own history may help us in another way. Beat Brenk[18] has observed that after the purportedly standard-setting plan of St. Gall, dated in the early ninth century, other monasteries were slow to develop the regular, four-sided cloisters drafted for St. Gall. Only in the eleventh to twelfth centuries does the form take off, becoming diffused across Latin Europe, such as here at the canons' cloister of Santo Stefano, Prato (Figures 8.9a and 8.9b). I posit an explanation for this – the cloistering of the cloister, so to speak – coincided with the reform of cathedral chapters and monasteries. It also coincided roughly with the split between the eastern and western church and the growing emphasis by the latter on clerical celibacy. Monks, abbots, priests and canons were being separated within the emerging urban society spatially and also sexually. The motive for this was not primarily chastity in itself, as both Byzantine and later Protestant practices indicate that this is not intrinsic to Christian faith. Rather, while the first sons of nobility inherited family properties, second and later sons often took on the cloth. By the time of the early eleventh century, many benefices were becoming passed on across generations, even granted by one feudal family

17 Walter Paatz, 'Zur Baugeschichte des Palazzo del Podestà (Bargello) in Florenz', *Mitteilungen des Kunsthistorischen Institutes in Florenz*, 3/ 6 (1931), 287–321.

18 Beat Brenk, 'Der Klosterplan von St. Gallen und die Regula S. Benedicti,' in *Benediktinische Kunst: Kultur und Geschichte eines europäischen Erbes*, ed. Roberto Cassanelli and Eduardo López-Tello Garcia (Regensburg: Schnell and Steiner, 2007), 73–80, especially pages 74, 80; see also Beat Brenk, 'Zum Problem der Vierflugelanlage (claustrum) in frühchristlichen und frühmittelalterlichen Klöstern,' in *Studien zum St. Galler Klosterplan II*, ed. Peter Ochsenbein and Karl Schmuki (St. Gallen: Historischer Verein des Kantons St. Gallen, 2002), 185–215.

Figure 8.9 Cloister, Santo Stefano, Prato: a) view; b) plan (photograph/drawing Alick M McLean)

to another. Priests were hired to say masses in place of the actual 'owners' of the benefices, a practice condemned as simony.[19] Church property and authority was becoming thereby alienated and the radical but effective solution was enforcing the absolute poverty of canons and monks – all property was only held in common[20] – and sealing them off visually and sexually to assure no offspring through whom clerical or monastic nobles could attempt to bequeath church property.

Back to our Siena podestà: Siena's Palazzo Pubblico houses on its left side the quarters of the podestà (Figures 8.10a and 8.10b). The Torre della Mangia certainly recalls the castle and tower house type, emphasizing the noble background the podestà shared with his adversaries. The plan again could be castle court or cloister: the greater architectural regularity brings it closer to the latter. The place where the podestà took on his judicial and executive role, at the far end of the grand council room, reinforces his position: his chair was directly below the *Maestà* (Figure 8.11), with his back to his own cloistered, isolated court, accessible through the hidden door on the left. The *Maestà* herself amplified the podestà's general political status, as the protector of the city, and a trait they shared. Both were undefiled, he by political corruption, she by sexual corruption – Mary is frequently described

19 Lester K. Little, *Religious Poverty and the Profit Economy in Medieval Europe* (Ithaca, NY: Cornell University Press, 1978) 31.
20 For church reform, see Little, *Religious Poverty and the Profit Economy in Medieval Europe*, 99–112.

Figure 8.10 Palazzo Pubblico, Siena: a) view; b) plan (photograph/drawing Alick M McLean)

and depicted in her 'hortus conclusus'.[21] The virginity of the Virgin served to emphasize and encourage the perception of the podestà as pure – even Extra Virgin.

Another female figure of purity appears multiple times in the next room over, the Sala dei Nove: Justice (Figure 8.12). She, too, appears as chaste, isolated to the left, albeit part of the Commune's retinue of virtues on the right side of the painting. She is present, but not subservient to the town, upholding wisdom alone as her source of decisions. Only in the government of injustice (Figure 8.13) is she subservient – actually bound, perhaps even

21 '*Hortus conclusus, quasi duplici clausura corporalis et spiritualis virginitas*', Richard de St. Laurent, *De laudibus B. Mariae Virginis*, ed. A. Borgnet, in Aberti Magni, *Opera omnia*, vol. 36 (Paris: Ludovicum Viven Bibliopolam, 1898) Liber XII. For an electronic version: *Opus insigne de laudibus beate marie virginis. alias Mariale appellatu[m]*, Richardus de Sancto Laurentio (Argentine: Simus, 1493), available online at http://diglib.hab.de/inkunabeln/448-1-theol-2f-4/start.htm (accessed 5 January 2015); cited from Jill Ross, *Figuring the Feminine, The Rhetoric of Female Embodiment in Medieval Hispanic Literature* (Toronto: University of Toronto Press, 2008), 111.

Figure 8.11 Maestà, Palazzo Pubblico, Siena (photograph Wikimedia Commons, Google Cultural Institute)

Figure 8.12 Allegory of Good Government, Sala dei Nove, Palazzo Pubblico, Siena (photograph Wikimedia Commons, Google Cultural Institute)

Figure 8.13 Allegory of Bad Government, Sala dei Nove, Palazzo Pubblico, Siena (photograph Wikimedia Commons, Google Cultural Institute)

violated by the tyrant. Corruption is violation, lack of sexual purity. Incorruptibility is the Virgin, a virginal Justice – even the podestà.

In the town hall of another commune, San Gimignano, the quarters of the podestà reinforce this reading (Figure 8.14). The tower of the podestà adjoins the Palazzo Comunale, at once separated and connected. There is yet again a courtyard or cloistered space, reflecting its architectural origins, the canons cloister on the other side of the tower, separated by a narrow alley. The imagery inside the major council room is as close as one could get to the Sienese model, executed even by the pupil and son-in-law of Simone Martini, Lippo Memmi (Figure 8.15). There is a significant element in the fresco absent in Siena: not only are there saints on either side of the Madonna and child. Beside Saint Nicholas stands also a podestà, Nello Tolomei, presented by the saint directly to the Virgin and Child, recognizable by his coat of arms generously decorating the canopy and by two inscriptions.

While this strong connection to the Virgin seems a further way of emphasizing the incorruptibility of Tolomei and his role as podestà, apparently not all San Gimignanese were in agreement. C. Jean Campbell, to whose visual and textual sources I am indebted in the following analysis, noted that, within two decades, the local chronicler Fra Matteo Ciaccheri criticized Nello's placement of himself and his coat of arms on the *Maestà*, in the

Figure 8.14 Palazzo Comunale, San Gimignano: a) view; b) plan (photograph/drawing Alick M McLean)

Figure 8.15 Maestà, Lippo Memmi, Palazzo Comunale, San Gimignano (Musei Civici, Comune di San Gimignano; photograph Alick M McLean)

context of a general '*disfaciamento di San Gimignano*' – note the visual term 'defacing' – for which Nello was responsible.[22] According to Ciaccheri, Nello's biggest error was 'to curry favor with the people, which is always villainous' (*fece il popolo, ch' è sempre villano*). Nello followed the model of the della Scala in Verona and anticipated the Duke of Athens in Florence. In 1318, Nello secured the *popolo's* election of himself as Capitano del Popolo, reviving the role for the occasion.[23] According to Fra Ciacchieri, powerful San Gimignanese even staged a revolt due to Tolomei's insertion of himself in the *Maestà*.

Details of paintings were sufficiently important to spark revolts, from which we can infer that their meaning was carefully crafted to express, even achieve political attitudes, alliances and aspirations. The overall character of the room of the *Maestà* vaunts the power not only of Tolomei but also of an earlier podestà, figured generically in the 1290–91 frescoes showing Charles of Anjou (Figure 8.16) but identifiable as the Florentine Bengo dei Buondelmonti through his coat of arms, prominently placed directly over

Figure 8.16 Charles of Anjou, Palazzo Comunale, San Gimignano, (Musei Civici Comune di San Gimignano; photograph Alick M McLean)

22 C. Jean Campbell, *The Game of Courting and the Art of the Commune of San Gimignano, 1290–1320* (Princeton, NJ: Princeton University Press, 1997), 94.

23 Ibid.

Charles. In fact, it may be that Tolomei was doing more than vaunt himself in the *Maestà* – he may have been acting in the interest of his home commune, countering Florence's involvement in San Gimignano with a clear reference to Siena's *Maestà* and the government housing it.[24]

The excessively personal and even regional partisan politics covering the walls of the council hall of San Gimignano had a foil in another painted space in the Palace, where those responsible for decorating the private chambers for any podestà may have sought to counteract the apparently natural tendency of podestàs to overstep their bounds. To see these images, we need to pass from the great hall into the tower of the podestà, arriving at a space that served actually or symbolically as his bedroom (Figure 8.17). The first set of scenes, framing the window looking out towards the Collegiata, seems to confirm my earlier reading of the chastity of the podestà. Sex is simply getting our painted characters into trouble. Aristotle is at first seduced by a young woman, according to some contemporary written versions, Phyllis.[25] Something happens in between, in the void of the window brilliantly left by the painter for our own imaginations to fill, and we discover Aristotle on the left-hand side of the painting, as we move our eye from our point of entry in the room across the fenestrated wall from right to left, ridden by the same courtesan and, as if that were not enough, whipped gleefully. Even the quasi-patron saint of jurists, podestàs and philosophers can step out of role, get entrapped and suffer a fate not unlike the Duke of Athens: mockery. Just to rub it in, one of Aristotle's star students, Alexander the Great, whom Aristotle had previously warned of the dangers of seductive women, is looking on in enjoyment with his own courtesan; like Alcibiades at the end of Plato's *Symposium*, perhaps sex fits his role better than that of the philosopher.[26]

Above Aristotle appears yet another scene where a would-be mature individual is allowing himself to be led not by wisdom (here in the later depiction in Lorenzetti's *Justitia*) but by lust. In what some argue to be a rendition of the prodigal son legend, a young man from a family of means is receiving a sack of gold as his inheritance.[27] Naturally, he makes his way directly to the first brothel and finds himself in the arms, or rather arm, of yet another courtesan. I say arm, singular, as the other arm is reaching not for his crotch, however that may seem to be the case, but rather for the money-bag. Things get quickly worse – roles are changed. The courtesan's hand apparently never wanders from the bag of cash and picks up, yet again,

24 Ibid.
25 Ibid, 124–6.
26 Ibid. For Alcibiades's attempted seduction of Socrates, see Plato's *Symposium*.
27 Campbell, *The Game of* Courting, 130–4.

Figure 8.17 Aristotle; Prodigal Son scenes, Camera del Podestà, Palazzo Comunale, San Gimignano (Musei Civici, Comune di San Gimignano; photograph Alick M McLean)

a whip with the other hand, banishing our highly frustrated and now broke prodigal son before the contracted business is fulfilled. Breaking roles can lead anywhere and those that break should not be surprised that others do likewise. By inversion, this wall of images fully supports the message of chastity as incorruptibility and corruption as both licentiousness and shameful failure. The viewers, like the protagonists, are themselves lured by the eroticism of the image, rendering the moral lesson all the more powerful.

The next set of scenes seems to follow the same logic (Figure 8.18). Two young men meet two apparently noble women. One of the noble men returns, to be led by one of the two women into a bath house, essentially a hot tub, where he encounters the blonde who had earlier caught his fancy. It is not clear whether this is a tryst or a medieval massage parlour, as in the next scene – now reading left to right, mirroring the earlier wall – our male and female protagonists are in bed, naked, together, with no great humiliation falling upon the young man. Is extramarital sex in some instances acceptable for the podestà? According to the later recorded legend of 'Salabetto and Iancofiore' novel 10 in day 8 of Bocaccio's *Decameron*, the answer is less moral than pragmatic: it is highly risky and can be quite costly.[28] In the executive summary, the Palermitan Iancofiore ends up fleecing the rich young Florentine merchant after wooing him. However, there may be another source, in an epic legend popular at the time, Benoît de Sainte-Maure's *Roman de Troie*, here an illustrated Bolognese manuscript from the second half of the fourteenth century.[29] The author relates a version of the story of Jason and Medea. Medea entices Jason to marry her but feigns ignorance of any such plan, lying apparently sleeping and unaware that this

Figure 8.18 Tub and Bedroom scenes, Camera del Podestà, Palazzo Comunale, San Gimignano (Musei Civici, Comune di San Gimignano; photograph Alick M McLean)

28 Ibid, 132, 147–56.
29 Ibid, 156–69.

heroic hunk was about to join her naked in bed. The stories even share hot tub scenes, revealing that Medea really was not at all averse to Jason – rather that the bed represented a step literally beyond just a tryst – the consummation of marriage.[30]

One oddity in the image is the fact that not only is our supposed Jason approaching the bed with his hat on but also our would-be Medea is wearing a similar hat, indeed the hat generally associated not with magical princesses of the Medes but rather with jurists and podestàs. The hat may tip the scale that this scene, as happily as it appears to end, may instead be trouble and therefore – sorry – yet another support for the praise of political chastity and the send-up of the promiscuous. Richard Trexler unearthed a ritual in fifteenth-century Florence, of women stealing the hats of men, either to display their power over them or, more commonly, to assure payment for services provided.[31] The threatened effects were role reversal and, again, mockery. At least our protagonist is spared a whipping, but it looks otherwise like yet another frustrated, unconsummated sex scene. Not only is chastity the only way for the podestà to go but, again, promiscuousness is not even the fun it is supposed to be.

This entire room of romping yet unfulfilled sex does seem, in the end, to support, through negative example, the identity of chastity and political incorruptibility. The amount of bare flesh, the high count of courtesans and the multiplicity of ostensible, albeit frustrated, erotic scenes introduce, however, a dissonant element. As glorious as the *Maestà* is in the next room, the podestà's quarters are much more fun – not unlike Hell and Purgatory in Dante. The podestà is being mocked in his own bedroom, seemingly emasculated, and certainly provided a lesson in the woes of promiscuity and abandoning the true love of chastity. At the same time, he is being entertained. The cycle destabilizes the podestà's absolute authority, at least in his own eyes, in the privacy of his own chamber, warning him that although he

30 Ibid, 163–4.

31 Richard Trexler, *The Women of Renaissance Florence*, Power and Dependence in Renaissance Florence vol. 2 (Binghamton: Medieval and Renaissance Texts and Studies, 1993) 50–1, 53. My thanks to Sarah Matthews-Grieco for calling the hat theft and associated reference to my attention. What makes this all the more powerful a visual game in San Gimignano is the fact that podestàs were sometimes provided with 'caps of sincerity' to wear when innaugurated, such as with Bologna's first podestà: 'with great ceremony there was given to him by all the people authority over the city and the district; they presented to him the baton, which signifies power, the sword justice, and the cap sincerity, meaning that in the affairs of the city he should confer with the consuls, and arrange everything with them so that things should succeed in good order and peace', Born, 'What Is the Podestà?', 865.

has been hired to play the role of town executive and judge and has literally and figuratively the town's biggest tower, he is human and subject to error too. A slip in his role could easily precipitate others to do likewise, risking that the entire house of cards of public life might collapse. Or, he might be banished by the figure really in charge of the city, whether the Virgin or, in the case of the Duke of Athens, the other great female saint to give birth without sex, the Virgin's virginal mother, St. Anne.

The many media of space, architecture, painting and ritual in Italy's communes fused into one dominant medium that was indeed the message itself: theatre. The fact that political theatre appears to have been accepted as such by both politicians and citizens may have given what otherwise might seem a deceit its strength. This communicative system constantly reminded all that in public their behaviour was guided by roles, some customary, some determined by legislation. In the case of the podestà, this role was even contracted, with risk of forfeiting a considerable caution.[32] The imagery of chastity visualizing this contract focused rulers on the fact that, while in office, even their bodies served state, not personal interest.[33] Populating the role with family across generations – the essence of feudal lineage and power – was certainly not to be considered, whether in the church or in communal politics derived from church administrative models. Negative and positive reminders of sexual purity helped each podestà to detach, or at least to appear to detach, his private self from the mask of his public persona, even when lured by offers of signore for life or when tempted by a supposed princess of the Medes stealing his cap of sincerity. So long as apparent and actual detachment persisted, the podestà could sustain his itinerant work and the inter-communal network that reciprocally sustained it.

32 See page xxx and note 11 above regarding syndication.

33 For a study of the double nature of the body for medieval rulers, see Ernst H. Kantorowicz, *The King's Two Bodies: A Study in Mediaeval Political Theology* (Princeton, NJ: Princeton University Press, 1985).

CHAPTER 9

Epistemological doubt and visual puzzles of sight, knowledge and judgment: reflections on clear-sighted and blindfolded Justices

Judith Resnik and Dennis Curtis[1]

What can images of Justice teach us about the norms of judging, the bases of authority to judge and the role of courts over centuries? By looking at the iconography associated with justice and the development of purpose-built structures (today's courthouses), one can see the radical disjuncture between contemporary theories for legitimating the violence intrinsic in law's imposition of judgment and their historical antecedents.

Simply put, in ancient times, judges were loyal servants of the state; audience members were passive spectators watching rituals of power, and only certain persons were eligible to participate as disputants, witnesses or decision makers. In contrast, today, judges in democratic polities are independent actors in complex and critical relationships with the government and the public. Moreover, everyone – women and men of all colours – is entitled to be in every seat in the courtroom, including the bench.

The project of mapping the centuries, images and ideologies producing those changes is the purpose of our book, *Representing Justice: Invention, Controversy and Rights in City-States and Democratic Courtrooms*. In this

1 March, 2015. Thanks are due to Peter Goodrich, for creating this volume and for his ongoing commitments to the relevance of imagery to insights about law; to Valérie Hayaert for her thoughtful engagement with our work; to the other participants in the conference from which this essay emerges; to the Yale Law Library and the leadership of Fred Shapiro and Michael Widener; to Allison Tait, who joined us in much of this research; to Reva Siegel for many discussions of constitutional theory; to Ruth Weisberg for insights into iconography, and to Jason Bertoldi, Devon Porter, Benjamin Woodring, and Marianna Mao able research assistance. This chapter is related to our book, and we draw from several of the images provided there. See Judith Resnik and Dennis Curtis, *Representing Justice: Invention, Controversy and Rights in City-States and Democratic Courtrooms* (New Haven, CT: Yale University Press, 2011).

essay, we reflect on one facet – personifications of the Renaissance Virtue Justice, as clear-sighted or blindfolded – to explore how shifting approaches to Justice's sight illuminate the revolutions in the relationship of judges to the polities that deploy them.

As Figure 9.1 illustrates, blindfolds are today affixed to Justice in celebration of adjudication's virtues. But for thousands of years, sight was valorized and the failure to see derided. Powerful gods/monarchs were depicted as all-seeing and, from their imperial view, all-knowing. In contrast, blindness and blindfolds denoted the impairments of the wicked and misguided. Through the Mediaeval period in Europe, obscured vision was a marker of various vices.

Figure 9.1 *Lady of Justice*, William Eicholz, 2002, Victoria County Court, Melbourne, Australia (photographer, Ken Irwin; reproduced with the permission of the sculptor and the Liberty Group, owner and manager of the Victoria County Court Facility)

But with the rise of epistemological doubt about the singularity of religious and monarchical authority, coupled with the proliferation of needs for dispute resolution and the challenges of controlling the quality of local judges, sight was no longer unproblematic. Various new technologies – the camera obscura,[2] the telescope, the microscope, and then surgeries to remove cataracts – underscored that what one could see was not preordained and fixed. Eyes could play tricks, and optical instruments could enhance sight.

As theorists from various disciplines became quizzical about the nature of knowledge, authority, God, and truth, the valence of open eyes denoting an uncomplicated receipt of knowledge shifted. During the sixteenth century, the blindfold came to be reconceived, on occasion, as a useful addition to Justice's attributes. By the eighteenth century, the blindfold on Justice had shed many of its negative connections and was read, instead, as a symbol of law's commitment to rationality.[3]

Obscured vision came to represent sought-after qualities, as blindfolds were variously explained to represent incorruptibility, even-handedness and

2 The camera obscura came into wide use by 1550; debate exists about how much earlier comparable devices existed, which artists had access to them, and their import. See Michael John Gorman, 'Art, Optics and History: New Light on the Hockney Thesis', 36/4 *Leonardo* (2003), 295–301 at 296.

3 Many commentators have reflected on a blindfolded justice; see, for example, Peter Goodrich, *Legal Emblems and the Art of Law:* Obiter Depicta *as the Vision of Governance* (Cambridge: Cambridge University Press, 2013); I. Bennett Capers, 'Blind Justice', *Yale Journal of Law and the Humanities*, 24/1 (2012), 179–90; Jacques de Ville, 'Mythology and the Images of Justice', *Law and Literature*, 23/3 (2011), 324–64; I. Bennett Capers, 'On Justitia, Race, Gender, and Blindness', *Michigan Journal of Race and Law* 12 (2006), 203–27; Christian-Nils Robert, *La Justice dans ses Décors (XVe–XVIe siècles) [Justice in its Settings during the Fifteenth and Sixteenth Centuries]* (Geneva: Droz, 2006), 97–101; Mario Sbriccoli, '*La tirade, le bandeau, le genou: Droit et procès pénal dans les allégories de Justice du Moyen Âge à l'âge moderne*', *Crime, History, and Society* 9 (2005), 33–78; Martin Loughlin, *Swords and Scales: An Examination of the Relationship Between Law and Politics* (Oxford: Hart, 2000), 55–65; Martin Jay, 'Must Justice Be Blind? The Challenge of Images to the Law', in *Law and the Image: The Authority of Art and the Aesthetics of Law*, eds Costas Douzinas and Lynda Nead (Chicago: University of Chicago Press, 1999), 19–35 at 19–21; Robert Jacob, *Images de la Justice: Essai sur l'iconographie judiciaire du Moyen Âge à L'âge Classique* (Paris: Le Léopard d'Or, 1994), 233–7; Christian-Nils Robert, *Une allégorie parfaite: La Justice, vertu, courtisane et bourreau* (Geneva: Georg, 1993); Robert M. Cover, Owen M. Fiss and Judith Resnik, *Procedure* (New York: Foundation, 1988), 1231; Otto Kissel, *Die Justitia: Reflexionen über ein Symbol und seine Darstellung in der Bildenden Kunst* (München: Beck, 1984), 82–92; Robert Jacob, '*Le jugement de Dieu et la formation de la fonction de juger dans l'histoire européenne*', in *Archives de Philosophie du Droit*, VOL. 39 Le Procès (Paris: Sirey, 1995), 87–104; Desmond Manderson, 'Blindness Visible: Law, Time, and Bruegel's Justice', forthcoming. See, generally, *Law, Culture and Visual Studies*, eds Anne Wagner and Richard K. Sherwin (Dordrecht: Springer, 2013).

constrained reasoning. With the rise thereafter of the ideology of judicial independence and separation of powers, additional explanations were put forth for the presence of a blindfold, read to indicate both the detachment from and the political insulation of judges from the very governments that empowered them.

Over the past two centuries in the United States, the trope of blindness has been central to debates about the federal constitution's obligations to remediate the effects of slavery and other sources of inequality. Yet, in the twenty-first century, to focus attention on what the law can see, whether Justice can see and be seen, and what she looks at or like deflects attention from the radical transformations in the functions and obligations of courts in democracies. We argue not only that eyes have had 'legs' (a remarkably long run as a central marker in Justice iconography and as a rhetorical trope in legal debates) but also that reliance on personifications of Justice, with or without obscured vision, is anachronistic.

Twentieth-century modernism fractured the singularity of Renaissance perspective. Post-modern critical theory insists on a multiplicity of legitimate points of view and on the interdependencies of viewer and viewed. Democratic adjudication locates the public as entitled and participatory – authorized to know and to critique the bases for judgment. Social and political movements have demonstrated the capacity to reinscribe meanings to constitutional texts. Blindfolds draped on women may serve to identify buildings as places of law but no longer serve to reference the relationship of the public to law in democratic orders or the complexities of how law needs to do its work.

Impartiality – or obstinance, ignorance and caprice

In contemporary discussions of Justice iconography, the female personification of Justice is often assumed to have always been depicted with a blindfold; the blindfold, in turn, is assumed to mark the stance appropriate for wise and constrained judgment. Thus, as illustrated by Figure 9.1, designers of courthouses regularly rely on blindfolded justices. This example comes from a 2002 courthouse in Melbourne, Australia, where a six-metre aluminium windswept female form serves as the court's shingle on a busy street corner. The degree to which the blindfold is easily read is demonstrated by *Lady Justice Lucy* (Figure 9.2), a whimsical statue placed in front of a Minnesota law school as a tribute to the comic series 'Peanuts' and its creator, Charles Schultz.

These two images enable us to make two points. First, the Renaissance Virtue, Justice, has had a remarkable run as political propaganda. Unlike

Figure 9.2 *Lady Justice Lucy*, Jim and Judy Brooks, 2002, William Mitchell College of Law, St. Paul, Minnesota (courtesy of the William Mitchell College of Law and reproduced with its permission)

Prudence, Fortitude, and Temperance, which once joined Justice as a set of four Cardinal Virtues, the personification of Justice remains legible to a wide array of people in diverse – albeit not all – cultures. Second, today's Justices are often marked by blindfolds, which, together with scales and swords, function to celebrate facets of adjudication.

But, and third, the blindfold is a relatively late addition to Justice iconography, and its valence has changed over time. Clear-sighted authority was once the norm, as ancient cultures praised the sun for illuminating the world. The theme of sight as knowledge and power can be traced from descriptions of the 'eye' of Egyptian gods[4] to Christianity's embrace of '*sol Iustitiæ*' – that Christ, the God of Light, will 'appear ablaze when he will judge mankind'.[5] Albrecht Dürer's rendition (Figure 9.3), circa 1499, makes the point by portraying a wide-eyed and haloed Christ-Justice, with scales and sword, perched on a lion.

Figure 9.3 *Sol Iustitiæ*, Albrecht Dürer, 1499–1500 (reproduced with the permission of the Fritz Achelis Memorial Collection, Yale University Art Gallery; gift of Frederic George Achelis, B.A. 1907, No. 1925.23)

4 See, for example, Geraldine Pinch, *Egyptian Mythology: A Guide to the Gods, Goddesses, and Traditions of Ancient Egypt* (Oxford: Oxford University Press, 2002), 19, 68–9; Erik Hornung, *Idea into Image: Essays on Ancient Egyptian Thought*, trans. Elizabeth Bredeck (New York: Timken, 1992), 142–3.

5 See *The Complete Engravings, Etchings and Drypoints of Albrecht Dürer*, ed. Walter L. Strauss (New York: Dover, 1972), 52, no. 25, *Sol Iustitiæ* or *The Judge*. The Augustinian tradition understood light as indicating intellect in contrast to the 'blind man fumbling along the wall' who, because of a lack of sight, lacked understanding. See Kristin Eldyss Sorensen Zapalac, *'In His Image and Likeness': Political Iconography and Religious Change in Regensburg, 1500–1600* (Ithaca, NY: Cornell University Press, 1990), 15. Further, it 'was believed that God's influence entered the world along rays of light,' as reflected in the illumination of Gothic cathedrals. Theodore K. Rabb, *The Last Days of the Renaissance and the March to Modernity* (New York: Basic Books, 2006), 18–19.

Classical and biblical texts repeatedly cast light as representing truth, darkness as misguidedness and blindness as a disability or punishment.[6] The sighted were *informed* and the blind *limited* in various ways. In both the Hebrew Bible and the New Testament, blindness exemplified ignorance, abandonment or impaired judgment.[7] Blindness precluded a person's entry into holy areas, and blind animals were not to be used as offerings.[8] Further, to be struck blind was a form of punishment.[9]

Canonical stories reiterate these themes. The patriarch Isaac was deceived because, blind, he bestowed his blessing on his son Jacob instead of on his elder son Esau.[10] Isaiah promised 'to open eyes that are blind' and to 'lead blind men on their way'.[11] According to Exodus, 'bribery makes the discerning man blind and the just man give a crooked answer'.[12] At several points, faith cured those who were blind.[13] Imposing blindness was a form of punishment, a theme portrayed repeatedly in Renaissance Town Halls, which showed the Greek lawgiver Zaleucus, ruling around 700 BCE, as having ordered that sanction for his own son but having mitigated it by ordering that both the son and he each lose one eye.[14] In addition, to have 'bandages' placed over one's eyes was to mark an injury. The Book of Job explains: 'The land is given over to the power of the wicked, and the eyes of its judges are

6 For the biblical quotations, we used an English database at Yale at Jeeves Library, which includes many versions. Unless otherwise indicated, quotations come from *The New English Bible with the Apocrypha*, ed. Charles Harold Dodd (Oxford and Cambridge: Oxford and Cambridge University Presses, 1970).

7 See, for example, Isaiah 56: 10 ('Israel's watchmen are blind, all of them unaware. They are all dumb dogs who cannot bark'); Psalms 9–10: 17 ('They rush blindly down to Sheol, the wicked.'); Matthew 23: 17 ('Blind fools! Which is the more important?'); 2 Corinthians 4: 4 ('Their unbelieving minds are so blinded by the god of this passing age, that the gospel of the glory of Christ, who is the very image of God, cannot dawn upon them and bring them light').

8 Leviticus 21: 18 ('No man with a defect shall come, whether a blind man, a lame man, a man stunted or overgrown.'); Leviticus 22: 22 ('You shall present to the Lord nothing blind, disabled, mutilated, with running sore, scab, or eruption, nor set any such creature on the altar as a food-offering to the Lord').

9 Job 11: 20 ('Blindness will fall on the wicked').

10 Genesis 27: 1–38.

11 Isaiah 42: 7, 16.

12 Exodus 23: 8.

13 Psalms 146: 8 ('The Lord restores sight to the blind and straightens backs'); Matthew 12: 22 ('Then they brought him a man who was possessed; he was blind and dumb; and Jesus cured him.').

14 See Resnik and Curtis, *Representing Justice*, 57–8 and fig. 45.

blindfolded.'[15] Jesus himself was made sport of – blindfolded, beaten, and mocked.[16]

Exceptions exist. Blind seers dot epics, as poets famously provided examples – Homer, Milton – of sightless visionaries.[17] Yet generally, blindness was punishment and the blind were portrayed as objects of pity or 'endowed with terrifying power'.[18] Thus, Moshe Barasch concluded in his book devoted to the topic, before the last few centuries, blindness was 'indissolubly linked with distress'.[19]

Mediaeval imagery repeatedly made that point, illustrated here through depictions of Synagoga and Ecclesia, seen in Figure 9.4; this pair of statues, carved around 1230, remains in place on the south portal of Strasbourg Cathedral, France.[20] These two were familiar fixtures, found 'on ivory tablets, in stained-glass windows, on church implements, in manuscript miniatures and in monumental statuary',[21] placed in arenas where marriages were ceremonialized, municipal laws determined, oaths taken, and tributes given.[22]

Synagoga, 'a purely Christian creation', signified the Old Testament (and sometimes Jews in general),[23] while Ecclesia stood for the New Testament (and at times Christianity). Unlike Ecclesia, modelled as a regal woman,

15 Job 9: 24.

16 Mark 14: 65 ('Some began to spit on him, blindfolded him, and struck him with their fists'); Luke 22: 63 ('They beat him, they blindfolded him, and they kept asking him, "Now, prophet, who hit you?"').

17 According to Plato, blindness was Homer's punishment for slandering Helen of Troy. Plato, *Phaedrus*, trans. Robin Waterfield (Oxford: Oxford University Press, 2002), 24. Milton wrote his epic poem *Paradise Lost* after becoming blind. See *John Milton: Complete Shorter Poems*, ed. John Carey (London: Longman, 1971), 'Sonnet XVI' at 327–8. Thus, the 'bard is expected to be blind'. Natalie Kononenko-Moyle, 'Homer, Milton, and Âşık Veysel: The Legend of the Blind Bard', *Harvard Ukrainian Studies*, 3–4/2 (1979–1980) 520–9 at 521.

18 See Moshe Barasch, *Blindness: The History of a Mental Image in Western Thought* (New York: Routledge, 2001) 78.

19 Ibid. at 83.

20 See Nina Rowe, 'Idealization and Subjection at the South Portal of Strasbourg Cathedral', in *Beyond the Yellow Badge: Anti-Judaism and Antisemitism in Medieval and Early Modern Visual Culture*, ed. Mitchell B. Merback (Leiden: Brill, 2008), 179–202.

21 Wolfgang S. Seiferth, *Synagogue and Church in the Middle Ages: Two Symbols in Art and Literature*, trans. Lee Chadeayne and Paul Gottwald (New York: Frederick Ungar, 1970), 96.

22 Bernd Nicolai, 'Orders in Stone: Social Reality and Artistic Approach; The Case of the Strasbourg South Portal', *Gesta*, 41/2 (2002), 111–28 at 112–13.

23 Michael Camille, *The Gothic Idol: Ideology and Image-making in Medieval Art* (Cambridge: Cambridge University Press, 1991), 178.

Figure 9.4 *Ecclesia* (left), circa 1230, and *Synagoga* (right), circa 1230, Strasbourg Cathedral, France (copyright Foto Marburg/Art Resource, New York)

ramrod-straight, crowned and sharp-eyed (the 'bride of Christ'), Synagoga is shown with her eyes covered by a blindfold, slumped and holding a broken rod. Blindfolded, rather than blind, Synagoga was wilfully obstinate, refusing (rather than unable) to comprehend the 'light of redemption'.[24]

Synagoga was not the only embodiment of the harm blindfolds imposed. Renaissance imagery often placed a blindfold on Eros to mark the misguided nature of love, engendering foolishness and confusion.[25] The female image

24 Barasch, *Blindness*, at 79, 83. For example, Giotto showed Synagoga turning her head left toward darkness and away from the 'light that is Christ in the Gospel of John.' Laurine Mack Bongiorno, 'The Theme of the Old and the New Law in the Arena Chapel', *Art Bulletin*, 50 (1968), 11–20, at 13–14.

25 See Edgar Wind, *Orpheus in Praise of Blind Love*, in *Pagan Mysteries in the Renaissance* (London: Faber and Faber, 1968), 53; Erwin Panofsky, 'Blind Cupid', in *Studies in Iconology: Humanistic Themes in the Art of the Renaissance* (New York: Harper and Row, 1962), 95–128.

of Fortuna was shown blindfolded to denote irrationality, randomness and indifference to human suffering.[26] Images of executed criminals showed them hanging, blindfolded and disgraced, as exemplified in one of the great civic frescoes, Ambrogio Lorenzetti's *Allegories of Good and Bad Government* in Siena.[27]

One of the first images known to link blindfolds to the Renaissance Virtue Justice is the 1494 *The Fool Blindfolding Justice* (Figure 9.5).[28] The woodcut, sometimes attributed to Albrecht Dürer, was one of more than 100 illustrations in a book, *The Ship of Fools*[29] by Sebastian Brant, a jurist trained in both civil and canon law. The volume, subsequently printed in many languages and full of 'middle-class moralizing', was well-known through the seventeenth century.[30] This image, placed in the chapter 'Quarreling and Going to Court',[31] reflected Brant's warnings against 'folly, blindness, error and stupidity of all stations and kinds of men.'[32]

Another example of a derisive deployment puts the blindfold on judges, rather than on a Justice. *The Tribunal of Fools* (Figure 9.6)[33] is an illustration in the 1507 volume, *Die Bambergische Halsgerichtsordnung* (also known as the *Bambergensis Constitutio Criminalis*), setting forth the criminal law and

26 See *Cesare Ripa, Baroque and Rococo Pictorial Imagery: The 1758–60 Hertel Edition of Ripa's 'Iconologia' with 200 Engraved Illustrations*, ed. Edward A. Maser (New York: Dover, 1971) (hereinafter Ripa, *Maser* edn), 152 (citing p. 169 of a 1603 edition of Ripa).

27 See Chapter 8 of this work or Randolph Starn, *Ambrogio Lorenzetti: The Palazzo Pubblico, Siena* (New York: George Braziller, 1994), 70–71.

28 Some presume that Dürer was the artist responsible for the woodcuts. See, for example, Theodore Ziolkowski, *The Mirror of Justice: Literary Reflections of Legal Crises* (Princeton: Princeton University Press, 1997), 99, 106. But the illustrations in *Ship of Fools* were not signed, and attributions are questionable. For identifications of this image as one of the first to blindfold a justice, see Wolfgang Pleister and Wolfgang Schild, *Recht und Gerechtigkeit im Spiegel der europäischen Kunst* (*Law and Justice Reflected in European Art*) (Cologne: Dumont Buchverlag, 1988), 206–7, fig. 340; Otto Kissel, *Die Justitia*, 38–55; G. Overdiep, 'Justitia, Waar Is Uw Blinddoek?' ('Justice: Where Is Thy Blindfold?'), *Pro Excolendo Iure Patrio 1761–1961* (Groningen: J. B. Wolters, 1961), 87–122, at 101–3 and n. 1.

29 See Sebastian Brant, *The Ship of Fools*, trans. Edwin H. Zeydel (New York: Columbia University Press, 1944) (hereinafter *Zeydel's Brant*).

30 See John Van Cleve, *Sebastian Brant's The Ship of Fools in Critical Perspective, 1800–1991* (Columbia, SC: Camden House, 1993), 85. At least 70 editions were in circulation, and few modern readers 'would suspect that the work was favorably compared by its contemporaries to Homer's *Odyssey*', Ziolkowski, *The Mirror of Justice*, 98.

31 *Zeydel's Brant*, pp. 236–7 (Chapter 71).

32 Ibid. at 57.

33 This woodcut is one of more than 20 appearing in editions of the *Bambergensis* published in 1507, 1508 and 1510.

Figure 9.5 *The Fool Blindfolding Justice*, sometimes attributed to Albrecht Dürer, 1494, a woodcut illustrating Sebastian Brant's *The Ship of Fools*, printed in Basel, Switzerland (image courtesy of Beinecke Rare Book and Manuscript Library, Yale University)

municipal ordinances of the city of Bamberg.[34] A presiding judge (marked by his clothing, rod of office and enthroned place of honour) and four lay colleagues are all blindfolded and wearing jesters' caps. The scroll above their

34 The *Bambergische Peinliche Halsgerichtsordnung* (*The Penal Code of the Bamberg Criminal Court*) is a legal code in vernacular German, written in 1507 for the Prince-Bishop of Bamberg. Our thanks to Stella Burch Elias for translations. At least eight editions of the *Bambergensis* were printed prior to 1580. Other discussions of *The Tribunal of Fools* include Robert Jacob, *Images de la Justice*, 162, fig. 88; Theodore Ziolkowski, 'The Figure of Justice in Western Art and Literature', *Inmunkwahak, Journal of Humanities*, 75 (1996), at 187.

Abb. 76. Verspottung der ungerechten Richter. Holzschnitt aus: Bambergische Halsgerichtsordnung. Mainz, Joh. Schöffer, 1510.

Figure 9.6 The Tribunal of Fools, from the *Bambergensis* (*Bambergische Halsgerichtsordnung*), 1508 (image reproduced courtesy of the Rare Book Collection, Lillian Goldman Law Library, Yale Law School)

heads reads: 'Out of bad habit these blind fools spend their lives passing judgments contrary to what is right'.[35]

Various hypotheses have been advanced about why judges became the subject of criticism for which the blindfold was enlisted.[36] Scepticism about the authority of law and the quality of judges has been linked to the Reformation, the Inquisition, humanism, the codification of Roman law, the growth of the legal profession and the diversity of universities training new lawyers, as well as to conflicts developing around city-states in their relations

35 Another translation is 'To pass judgments repugnant to what is right and out of sheer bad habit, is the whole life of these blind fools'. See Ziolkowski, 'The Figure of Justice in Western Art and Literature', 207.

36 For example, Kissel argued that the blindfold was emblematic of a growing separation of powers, whereas Christian-Nils Robert posited that the blindfold was bivalent: '*un geste tout à la fois fou et vrai*'. See Otto Kissel, *Die Justitia*; Christian-Nils Robert, *Une allégorie parfaite: La Justice, vertu, courtisane et bourreau*, 88.

to religion and to more distant secular authorities.[37] For example, Sebastian Brant was loyal to Roman law; the fool blindfolding justice reflected his view that the German legal system was plagued by foreign and local advocates able to manipulate lay judges.[38] Writing in the vernacular German to reach lay judges, Brant repeatedly insisted on the 'folly' of blindness, the risks of relying on customary law, and the desirability of reading and following the written law. Thus (and providing the reminder about the polyvocal capacities of imagery), while some theorists argue that adding a blindfold to Justice represented new commitments to positivism and law's rationality, one could – *pace* Brant – read clear-sightedness as the way to mark those very obligations.

Another example of the blindfold as disability comes from *Mundanæ iustitiæ effigies* (*A Portrait [or Effigy] of Worldly Justice*), which is the title placed above an intriguing Janus-faced Justice (Figure 9.7) from a sixteenth-century book, *Praxis rerum civilium* (*Legal Practice in Civil Matters*),[39] published in Latin by 1567 and subsequently in French, Dutch, and German.[40] The author, Joost de Damhoudere, was a Flemish jurist who lived

37 See Gerald Strauss, *Law, Resistance, and the State: The Opposition to Roman Law in Reformation Germany* (Princeton, NJ: Princeton University Press, 1986), 56–95. Europe was a 'mosaic' of many different versions of local practice and a struggle ensued between those customary legal regimes and university-based jurisprudence that aimed to systemize rules that would have binding force. See Constantin Fasolt, 'Hermann Conring and the European History of Law', in *Politics and Reformations: Histories and Reformations (Essays in Honor of Thomas A. Brady, Jr.)*, eds Christopher Ocker, Michael Printy, Peter Starenko and Peter Wallace (Leiden: Brill, 2007), 113–34, at 116–23.

38 *Zeydel's Brant*, 236–7. Chapter 71, illustrated by *The Fool Blindfolding Justice*, includes the verses:

A foreign speaker must be brought
Imported here from far-off port,
That he may well pervert the case
And cheat the judges to their face.

39 The 1567 edition has a few other woodcuts, including a portrait of the author and illustrations of different stages of civil proceedings. We are indebted to Nicholas Salazar for translation of the Latin (hereinafter Damhoudere/Salazar) and to Chavi Keeney Nana for translation of the Dutch. Our quotes come from the Salazar translation. The authorship of the woodcut is not clear but the accompanying text suggests that Damhoudere directed the design.

40 The *Praxis rerum civilium* was subsequently published in Venice in 1568 and in Antwerp in 1569 and 1596 and then republished in 1646 as part of Damhoudere's collected works. Editions were also in French in 1572; in Dutch in 1626, 1646 and 1669, and in German. The figure discussed also appeared in the well-known volume by Damhoudere on criminal practice that was published in 1555. See Valérie Hayaert, *Æquitas, épiéikéïa et pensée symbolique*, in *Éthique et droit du Moyen Âge au siècle des Lumières* (Classiques Garnier, 2012), 169–88.

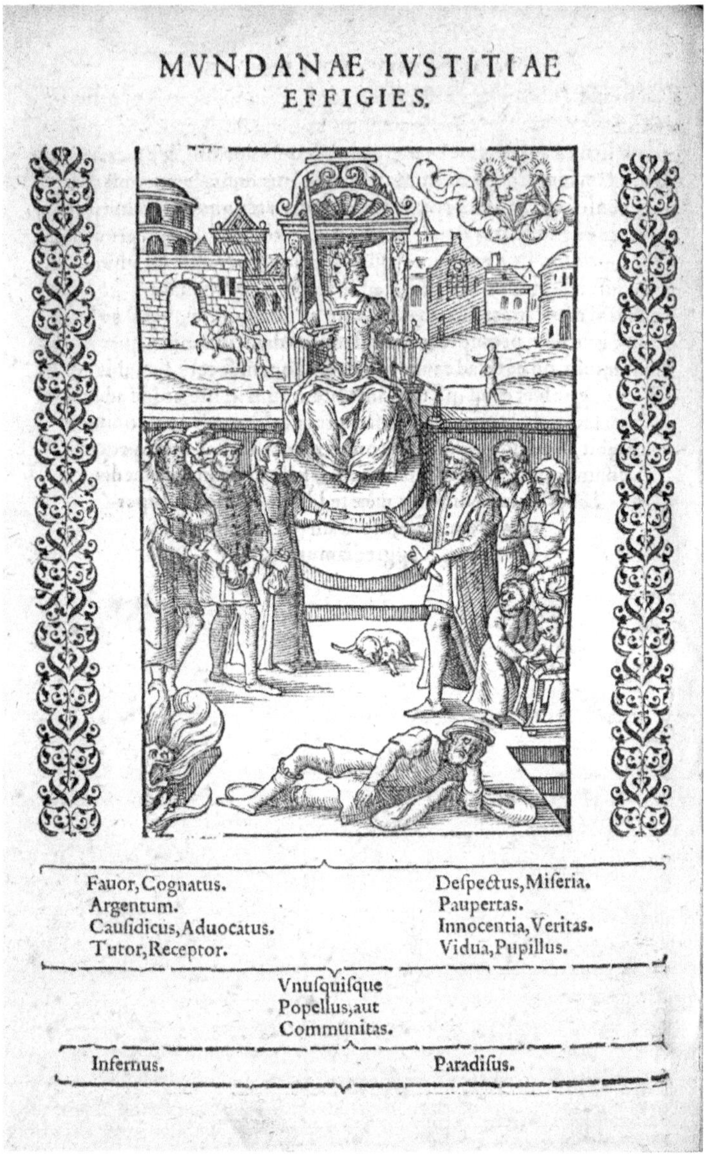

Figure 9.7 *Mundanæ iustitiæ effigies* (A portrait or effigy of worldly justice) in Joost de Damhoudere's *Praxis rerum civilium* (*Legal Practice in Civil Matters*), Antwerp, n.p., 1567 edition (image reproduced with the assistance of Michael Widener, courtesy of the Rare Book Collection, Lillian Goldman Law Library, Yale Law School)

from 1507 to 1581, and who was known for another volume, *Praxis rerum criminalium* (*Legal Practice in Criminal Matters*) that had 'enormous authority and went through over thirty editions in Latin, French, Dutch, and German, the last in 1693'.[41]

The rare depiction puts two faces – one sighted and the other with eyes covered by a blindfold – on to the body of a Justice. The image has drawn the attention of others, who valorize the blindfold's deployment either as reflecting divine justice or discerning law's complexity, yet discussions do not often address the print's labelled figures and its surrounding text (which has not, to our knowledge, been translated into English).[42] Therefore, we pause to detail our argument that this image should be read as akin to the negativity in Brant and in the *Bambergensis.*

The sighted face looks toward Justice's large sword, held upright in her right hand, while the blindfolded face turns toward her left hand, holding tipped scales. Neither face looks at the figures positioned as disputants or supplicants, nor above, where a bird hovers between two men sitting on clouds, one of whom holds a cross – referencing the Holy Trinity. The faces of Justice also appear oblivious to the flaming monster at the bottom left-hand corner, to the dog and the man reclining in the centre foreground and to the background chase scene. Yet those surrounding Justice were not anonymous but personifications, labelled at the bottom of the image.

41 See John H. Langbein, 'The Historical Origins of the Sanction of Imprisonment for Serious Crime', *Journal of Legal History* 5 (1976), 35–60, at 39, n. 21.

42 Kissel provided a picture from a 1596 edition. See Otto Kissel, *Die Justitia* at 120, plate 100 (described as a Janus-faced Justice with sword and scale, 'illustration by Jodocus Damhouder in *Praxis Rerum Civilium* [Antwerp 1596]'); Jacob, *Images de la Justice*, at 230 (fig. 125), identifying the image as '*La Justice aux deux visages, l'un voilé et l'autre aux yeux ouverts* (frontispiece de J. de Damhoudere, *Praxis rerum civilium* … Anvers, 1567)'; Jay, 'Must Justice Be Blind?', at 34–5 (fig. 1.6) (showing a copy described as 'Justice with two faces, one veiled, the other with eyes open, frontispiece of the J. de Damhoudere, *Praxis rerum civilium* … Anvers, 1567'); Goodrich, *Legal Emblems*, at 74–5 (fig. 3.7) (reading the blindfolded face as looking 'to the universal and to the future'). Jay commented that 'the first [face] has eyes that are wide open, able to discern difference, alterity, and nonidentity, looking in the direction of the hand that wields her sword, while the second, facing the hand holding the calculating scales of rule governed impartiality, has eyes that are veiled.' He then posited that 'for only the image of a two-faced deity, a hybrid, monstrous creature that we can in fact see, an allegory that resists subsumption under a general concept, only such an image can do, as it were, justice to the negative, even perhaps aporetic, dialectic that entangles law and justice itself.' Jay, 'Must Justice Be Blind?', at 35. As noted, Hayaert is an exception in her analysis of the image from Damhoudere's work on criminal practice.

The well-clad group on the side where Justice is sighted include Fauor (Favour); Cognatus (Kinsman); Argentum (Money); Causidicus (Lawyer, as in a self-interested pleader of causes); Aduocatus (Advocate in Law, a supporter or witness); Tutor (Guardian), and Receptor (today's Trustee, a person holding and managing property for others). The needy figures on the side where the face is blindfolded are labelled Despectus (Contempt), Miseria (Misery), and Paupertas (Poverty). The children represent Innocentia (Innocence) and Veritas (Truth); one appears either disabled or propped up on some kind of chair. Vidua and Pupillus (Widow and Ward or Orphan) are the woman holding a handkerchief and clutching the hand of a child looking up at her. The phrase beneath the man at the centre foreground reads '*Unusquisque Popellus, aut Communitas*' (Everyone, the Common People). The inscriptions at the bottom label the fire-breathing monster at the left Infernus (Inferno or Hell) and the group in the clouds, Paradisus (Heaven).

The Damhoudere text is an assortment of his commentary and quotes, adapted from the Hebrew Bible, the New Testament, Cicero, Aristotle, St. Augustine and classical poets. Under a heading, '*Divisio*' (Division), the text reads: 'Justice is considered according to the nature, condition, office, state and person of each. Justice is therefore twofold'. We learn that God's justice demonstrated that 'he is not deaf to the cries of the oppressed' and that he judges with equity 'the poor man as for the rich man'. Human justice (which ought to aspire to be like divine justice) is comprised of general justice (loving one's neighbour and treating others as one would want to be treated one's self) and judicial justice (focused on judges, kings, and magistrates 'ordained by God for the regulation of human affairs'). But 'certain unworthy things have crept into human laws and regulations … on account of the blindness of men' that God will need to correct in Heaven and 'remove out of the community tyrannical and stupid princes', some of whom 'reign in blindness and tyranny'.

The 'various persons' before Justice sought to 'win justice itself to their side'. But 'Justice is repeatedly blind and deaf' to those with just causes, while she is more available or attentive to others 'for the most unfair reasons'. Justice is 'two-faced', acting in a manner that appears fair but is dissembling. 'Where she is depicted with eyes', she welcomes 'wealthy persons' and the 'more powerful'. And where she is 'bound by a blindfold', her eyes are shut to 'clemency'. Furthermore, 'because we are showing Justice here as two-faced with eyes on one side and blind on the other, we give an image of worldly justice, certainly corrupt and not at all fair'.

Counterclaims on behalf of the blindfold appear in a few places. For example, Damhoudere noted that portrayals of Justice blindfolded were to represent 'the part of justice to be blind to each party, and to provide a mien either of favor or of hatred to neither'. Damhoudere commented that Justice was 'two-faced' to signify that 'justice's governors must provide a friendly face or intent eyes not only to one of the parties, but also must attend to each of the parties out of fairness'. The few positive implications, however, are overshadowed by the text explicating a scene in which the sighted Justice appears to be corruptible and the blindfolded Justice impervious to the needy before her. In short, the blindfold remained a ready mark of earthly Justice's limitations.

'Acute vision' and judgments not 'against reason'

During the sixteenth century and thereafter, blindfolds or otherwise obscured sight gained another valence – as imposing a positive, disciplinary constraint on the act of judgment. That new proposition can be found in – or read into – two famous compilations of images: the 1531 *Emblematum liber* of Andreas Alciatus and the 1593 *Iconologia* of Cesare Ripa,[43] both of which served as reservoirs from which artists and viewers drew a shared visual vocabulary.[44] In an Alciatus emblem called *The Good Prince in his Council* (Figure 9.8), the central figure was (depending on the edition)

43 See Andreas Alciatus, *The Latin Emblems: Index Emblematicus*, vols. 1 and 2, ed. Peter M. Daly (Toronto: University of Toronto Press, 1985) (hereinafter Alciatus, *Daly* edn) (unpaginated edition with numbered emblems). The spelling of Alciatus varies. A word of explanation is also needed as to the different Ripas and their illustrations. The 1593 Ripa had no drawings; scholars do not believe that Ripa had direct involvement in the drawings used in subsequent editions. See Stefano Pierguidi, 'Giovanni Guerra and the Illustrations to Ripa's Iconologia', *Journal of the Warburg and Courtauld Institutes*, 61 (1998), 158–75, at 167, 174–5. Thereafter, more than 20 editions in about a dozen languages were published. We rely on Cesare Ripa, *Iconologia* ([Padua: Pietro Paolo Tozzi, 1611] New York: Garland, 1976) (hereinafter Ripa, *Padua–1611*); Cesare Ripa, *Iconologia*, vols. 1 and 2 ([Padua: Pietro Paolo Tozzi, 1618] Torino: Fògola Editore in Torino, 1988) (hereinafter Ripa, *Padua–1618*); Cesare Ripa, *Iconologie*, ed. I. Baudoin (Paris: Chez Mathieu Guillemot, 1644) (hereinafter *French Ripa–1644*); Cesare Ripa Van Perugien, *Iconologia, of Uytbeeldingen des Verstands* (Amsterdam: Dirick Pietersz Pers, 1644); Ripa, *Maser* edn; Cesare Ripa, *Iconology London 1779 in Two Volumes by George Richardson* (New York: Garland, 1976) (hereinafter Ripa, *Richardson edn*). The Richardson edition was the 'very last iconology in the tradition of Ripa'; see Thomas Fröschl, 'Republican Virtues and the Free State: Conceptual Frame and Meaning in Early Modern Europe and North America', in *Iconography, Propaganda, and Legitimation*, ed. Allan Ellenius (Oxford: Clarendon, 1998), pp. 255–75, at 263. See also Michael Bath, *Speaking Pictures: English Emblem Books and Renaissance Culture* (London: Longman, 1994), 259–62.

44 See Denis L. Drysdall, 'Emblema Quid? What Is an Emblem?', in *Under the Aegis, The Virtues*, ed. Peter Shand (Auckland: Fortuna, 1997), 137–43; Ernst Gombrich, 'Icones Symbolicae: The Visual Image in Neo-Platonic Thought', *Journal of the Warburg and Courtauld Institutes*, 11 (1948), 163–92.

Figure 9.8 *The Good Prince in his Council,* emblem from the Complete Works of Andreas Alciatus, vol. 4, 1582 (image reproduced courtesy of the Rare Book Collection, Lillian Goldman Law Library, Yale Law School)

shown with covered eyes; he was joined by judges, displayed with their hands cut off, to prevent the receipt of bribes.

That prince (also called a king or a judge in different editions) was described as 'without eyes', 'deprived of his sight', or 'blind'. The explanation (in a 1542 German version) was 'that he may recognise no-one's status and ... judge according to his council'. A French edition of 1536 put it slightly differently: 'Their prince, deprived of his sight, cannot see anybody, and he judges by due sentence according to what is said in his ear'.[45] One could, however, read the image and its texts (as Peter Goodrich does) to be satirical.[46] Moreover, Alciatus's emblems also continued the motif of sightlessness

45 Alciatus, *Daly edn*, vol. 2 at emblem 145 and motto (from the 1536 French).

46 Goodrich, *Legal Emblems*, at 143, also providing another version reproduced by Barthélemy Aneau (fig. 5.7).

and blindness as punishments and profound disabilities. For example, in the emblem called 'Just Vengeance', Ulysses puts his stake into the eye of the Cyclops and blinds him.[47]

Toward the end of the sixteenth century, Ripa reiterated the negativity of blindfolds, while also proffering a positive deployment through one of his seven descriptions of the Virtue Justice. In its first publication in 1593, the *Iconologia* was without illustrations. But in more than forty subsequent versions, drawings and embellishments abound (Figure 9.9). Generally, bandages and blindfolds appear repeatedly as evidence of bad traits. Blindfolds denote arbitrariness (Fortuna), the foolishness of emotions (Eros),

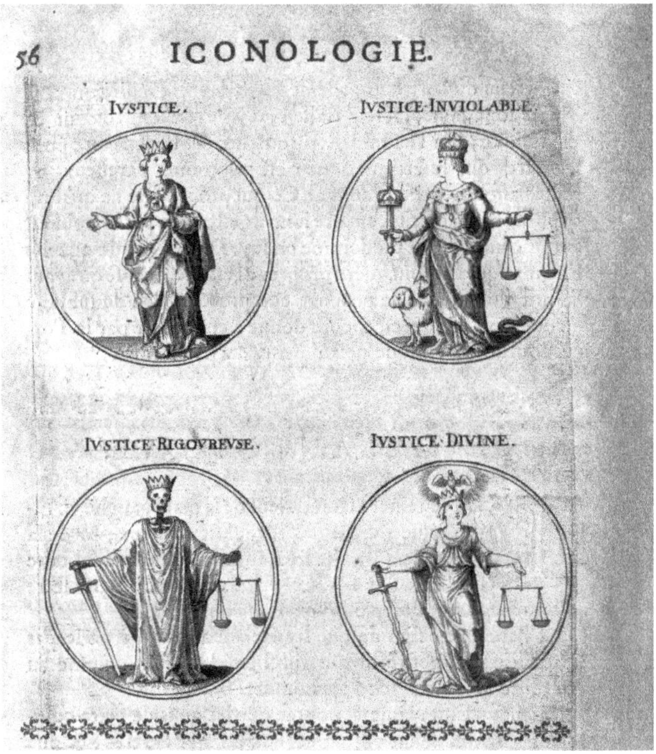

Figure 9.9 *Iconologie*, Cesare Ripa (Paris, Mathieu Guillemot, 1644; reproduced courtesy of the Rare Book Collection, Lillian Goldman Law Library, Yale Law School)

47 Alciatus, *Daly edn*, vol. 2 at emblem 172, 'Just Vengeance'. In 'Mutual Aid,' blindness is an incapacity; a blind man and a lame man each help each other, one providing sight for guidance and the other feet for mobility. Alciatus, *Daly edn*, vol. 2 at emblem 161.

and the indiscriminate force of 'Ambizione' (Ambition).[48] The misguidedness of 'Errore' (Error) was drawn in one edition as a man cloaked and with covered eyes, accompanying 'Ignoranza' (Ignorance).[49] Ripa commended a blindfold for 'Furore' (Furor), a large, angry man holding various weapons.[50] Covered eyes appear for 'Prodigalità' (Prodigality), pouring out the contents of a cornucopia,[51] for 'Simonia' (Simony, the selling of Church offices), enveloped by a black veil,[52] and for Slander, shading her face with a veil.[53] In a later edition of Ripa, Sin was shown as a blindfolded man because 'the blindfold is an obvious allusion to the wilful blindness to God's commandments'.[54] Injustice herself was posited to have one blind eye.[55]

Clear-sightedness, in turn, remained desirable, as illustrated by six of Ripa's seven versions of Justice: Divine Justice ('Giustitia Divina') and six variations on 'Worldly Justices'[56] named Justice ('Giustitia'), Justice According to Aulus Gellius ('*Giustitia … che riferisce Aulo Gellio*'), Principled (or Strict) Justice ('*Giustitia retta*'), Rigorous Justice ('*Giustitia rigorosa*'), Justice of Pausanius in the Eliaci ('*Giustitia di Pausania ne gl'Eliaci*'), and Justice on the medals of Hadrian, Antoninus Pius, and Alexander ('*Giustitia delle Medaglie d'Adriano, d'Antonio Pio, & d'Alessandro*').[57]

48 Ripa, *Padua–1611* at 14; Ripa, *Padua–1618*, vol. 1 at 37–39 (invoking Seneca); Ripa, *Maser edn* at fig. 31.

49 Ripa, *Padua–1611* at 146–7; Ripa, *Padua–1618*, vol. 1 at 145; *French Ripa–1644* at 61.

50 Ripa, *Padua–1611* at 189–90; Ripa, *Padua–1618*, vol. 1 at 178–9.

51 Ripa, *Padua–1618*, vol. 2 at 128.

52 Ripa, *Padua–1618*, vol. 2 at 290–1.

53 Ripa, *Padua–1618*, vol. 1 at 119–20 (invoking St. Thomas Aquinas and the idea of hiding with a veil).

54 See Ripa, *Maser edn* at 164, citing a 1603 edition of Ripa at 383.

55 Injustice ('Ingiustitia') is portrayed in both text and image with one blind eye in Ripa, *Padua–1611* at 250; an identical image and abbreviated text appear in Ripa, *Padua–1618*, vol. 1 at 217. Later editions shift the imagery to the scimitar, turban, and other attributes used to denote justice gone awry—broken tablets, scales, and scrolls. The toad, however, remains as a marker of greed, 'upon which much injustice is founded' (Ripa, *Maser edn* at 117, citing the 1603 edn at 230).

56 Panofsky, 'Blind Cupid', at 109, n. 48.

57 Ripa, *Padua–1611* at 201–4. The Dutch version from 1644 provides the same list of seven as did Ripa, *Padua–1611*. The seven Justices did not, however, reappear in all Ripa editions. In Ripa, *Padua–1618*, for example, only two ('Justice According to Aulus Gellius' and 'Justice') are mentioned. Moreover, slightly different descriptions of various Justices can be found. By the eighteenth century, Justice iconography was compressed into a narrower range; the Ripas of that era offer one description of and one image for Justice. In the 1758 Hertel edition, Justice 'is blindfolded, for nothing but pure reason, not the often misleading evidence of the senses, should be used in making judgments.' Ripa, *Maser edn* at 120. Richardson's 1779 edition retains the blindfold and notes 'She is sitting

Figure 9.10 *Justice According to Aulus Gellius*, Cesare Ripa, 1625 (reproduced courtesy of the Rare Book Collection, Lillian Goldman Law Library, Yale Law School)

In a 1644 edition (Figure 9.9) from Paris, the illustrator drew four open-eyed Justices. In another edition, Ripa's 'Justice According to Aulus Gellius' (Figure 9.10) was shown with 'acute vision' (sometimes translated as 'piercing eyes')[58] and wearing a necklace where 'an eye is portrayed' because

with a bandage over her eyes. The white robes and bandage over her eyes allude to incorrupt justice, disregarding every interested view, by distributing of justice with rectitude and purity of mind, and protecting the innocent.' Ripa, *Richardson edn*, vol. 2 at 21. See also Overdiep, 'Justitia, Waar Is Uw Blinddoek?', at 107 and n. 3.

58 Ripa, *Padua–1611*, at 201; Ripa, *Padua–1618*, vol. 1 at 188.

'Plato said that Justice sees all and that, from ancient times, priests were called seers of all things'.[59]

One of Ripa's Justices was described as having obscured vision. Text from a 1611 version explained:

> A woman dressed in white with bandaged eyes; in her right hand she holds a bundle of rods, with an axe, and in her left hand a fiery flame, together with these things she has an ostrich at her side, and holds a sword and scales.
>
> This is the type of Justice that is exercised in the tribunal of judges and secular executors.
>
> She is wearing white because judges should be without the stain of personal interest or of any other passion that might pervert Justice, and this is also why her eyes are bandaged – and thus she cannot see anything that might cause her to judge in a manner that is against reason. The bundle of rods with the axe, used in ancient times in Rome to show ... that justice must not be remiss in punishing wrongdoing but that justice must also not be precipitous ...
>
> The ostrich teaches us that the things that come before justice, however intricate they may seem, must be tirelessly unraveled with a patient spirit, as the ostrich digests iron, that most durable material, as many authors recount.[60]

A myriad of questions emerges about the sources for various of the attributes, including the blindfold and why it – but not ostriches – gained and retained currency. Where did the idea come from that the blindfold could be

59 Ripa, *Padua–1611*, at 201. Gellius was a Latin grammarian of the second century CE, who authored *Noctes atticae* (*Attic Nights*). The text explains:

> A woman who is a beautiful virgin, crowned and dressed in gold, who, with honesty and discipline, shows herself worthy of reverence, with eyes of the most acute vision and a necklace around her throat that is decorated with an eye.
>
> Plato said that Justice sees all and that from ancient times priests were called seers of all things. From whence Apuleius swore by the eye of the Sun and Justice together to show that one is as insightful as the other ... [and they are] qualities that ministers of Justice must have, because they must also be able to discover truth and, in the manner of virgins, must be exempt from passion, not ... corrupted by flattery, gifts, or anything else ... To indicate Justice and intellectual integrity the ancients used a jug, a basin, a column—as is verified on old marble sepulchers and by diverse antiquities, such that Alciatus said: A good judge must be pure of soul and clean of hands, if he wishes to punish crime and avenge injury.

60 This passage can be found in both the 1611 (at 203) and the 1618 (at 188) editions from Padua under the description of Justice ('Giustitia').

viewed positively? What political and intellectual currents supported its repeated deployment? And how do those rationales relate to the contemporary valorization of blindfoldedness?

At the literal level, Ripa may have drawn on the Alciatus emblem; while not mentioned in connection with blindfolded Justice, Ripa invoked Alciatus for other attributes of Justice – a river and a pillar, purportedly denoting purity and uprightness and therefore appropriate for law and justice.[61] Ripa may also have used the same sources as Alciatus: the 'Egyptian' allegory 'transmitted by Plutarch and Diodorus Sicilus in which the chief justice was shown eyeless in order to illustrate his impartiality, while his colleagues had no hands with which to take bribes'.[62]

Yet Alciatus and Ripa offered somewhat different rationales for the blindfold's deployment. Alciatus commended sightlessness for the prince/judge so 'that he may recognise no-one's status and ... judge according to his council'[63] or 'according to what is said in his ear'.[64] Deprivation of sight may have buffered against status (which could also thus serve as a buffer against soliciting or receiving bribes) and could result in even-handedness. That approach is echoed in maxims repeated elsewhere, as in the inscription from the old Tübingen Town Hall that the Justice's 'eyes are bound [s]o that rich and poor appear the same'.[65]

But what, then, was to be the basis for decision? The answer, at least from Alciatus, was that the judge/prince ought to listen to his advisors. That admonishment may have curbed the absolutism of the power of the judge/prince/king while it also reaffirmed that power rested with ruling authorities (councils). In contrast, by 1593, Ripa suggested that limited sight sharpened analysis. '[Justice's] eyes are bandaged and thus she cannot see anything that might cause her to judge in a manner that is against reason.'[66] The reference to 'against reason' could be akin to the admonition from

61 Ripa, *Padua–1611*, at 202. The Latin version of Alciatus quoted by Ripa – '*Ius hic forma monet dictum sine sordibus esse Defunctum, puras aiq; habuisse mansus*' – can be translated: 'In the image he advises that the Dead Man held court without filth, and that he had clean hands' (translation by Nicholas Salazar). The 1644 Ripa, written in French, could be understood as saying (at 57): 'A good judge must be pure of soul and clean of hands, if he wishes to punish crime and avenge injury'.

62 Panofsky, 'Blind Cupid', at 109, n. 48.

63 Alciatus, *Daly edn*, vol. 2 at emblem 145 and motto (from the 1542 German version).

64 Ibid., with motto (from a French edition of 1536).

65 See Susan Tipton, *Res Publica bene ordinata: Regentenspiegel und Bilder von guten Regiment, Rathausdekorationen in der Fruhen Neuzeit* (*The Well-Ordered Public Sphere: Images of Sovereignty and Pictures of Good Government, Town Hall Decoration in the Early Modern Period*) (Hildesheim: George Olms Verlag, 1996), at 677, fig. 159.

66 Ripa, *Padua–1611*, at 203.

Alciatus not to attend to status or, as some translations of Ripa noted, that the imposition of judgment ought not to come from 'passion'.

Goodrich has argued that blindfolds reference aspirations for divine justice and, further, that blindfolds enjoin viewers from thinking they can see that divine power.[67] Others link the blindfold to the rise of new city-states in which sources of authority were contested, producing complex and ambivalent attitudes towards law.[68] With the expanded use of law and more judges came fears of corruption and struggles for power; blindfolds came to denote the need to impose constraints on judges.[69] Philosophy and theology can also be enlisted. Descartes wrote of the desirability of escaping the confusion of the senses,[70] and Lutheran theology argued that truth came from inner light.[71] The relevance of the Reformation is argued by Martin Jay, who thought that the 'Hebrew interdiction of images' was a way to 'resist what Augustine had famously called the "lust of the eyes;" the blindfold shifted from being a sign of inferiority and became, under this view, a marker of "neutrality".'[72]

But Damhoudere's deployment – as well as images by Peter Bruegel the Elder (not detailed here[73]) and many others – belie reading the blindfold as simply as a positive attribute during these centuries. Moreover, documentation of Justices – such as in the volume by Otto Kissel – show the

67 Goodrich, *Legal Emblems*, at 161–5.

68 Robert, *Justice*, at 118–28.

69 See Strauss, *Law, Resistance, and the State*; Natalie Z. Davis, *The Gift in Sixteenth-Century France* (Oxford: Oxford University Press, 2000).

70 See René Descartes, *Meditations on First Philosophy with Selections from the Objections and Replies*, trans. John Cottingham (Cambridge: Cambridge University Press, 1986).

71 See Kissel, *Die Justitia*, at 90, nn. 155 and 156. Kissel noted that Luther wrote of the 'love of truth' to bring 'light' but also wrote that a judge 'must be blind, his eyes and ears covered'. Ibid., at 90. Luther wrote: 'Therefore he must be quite blind, have his eyes and ears closed, neither see nor hear, but go straight forward in everything that comes before him, and decide accordingly'. Martin Luther, 'The Large Catechism', *Triglot Concordia: The Symbolical Books of the Ev. Lutheran Church*, translated by F. Bente and W. H. T. Dau, (St. Louis: Concordia Publishing House, 1921), p. 565. Yet Luther can also be quoted as stating: '[W]hat kind of judge would he be who should blindly judge matters which he neither heard nor saw?' Martin Luther, 'Secular Authority: To What Extent It Should Be Obeyed', in *Martin Luther: Selections from His Writings*, ed. John Dillenberger (New York: Anchor Books, 1962), 384. Zapalac argued that Lutheranism was a source for the replacement of scenes of the Last Judgment with images of Justice. Zapalac, '*In His Image and Likeness*', at 29, 30, and fig. 3.

72 See Jay, 'Must Justice Be Blind?'; Jacob, *Images de la Justice*, at 234–6.

73 See Resnik and Curtis, *Representing Justice*, at 70–2 and fig. 53.

predominance of open-eyed Justices throughout Europe's town halls.[74] Indeed, as Erwin Panofsky argued, aside from a valorized blindness in Homer and of the blindfolded Justice herself (a 'humanistic concoction of very recent origin'), blindness was 'always associated with evil'.[75] Thus, when blindfolded Justices appeared in town halls, especially in Northern Europe, accompanying inscriptions often explained that addition by either reiterating Ripa's admonition not to judge 'against reason' or referencing obligations to treat disputants evenhandedly.

'If made to see'

A summary of several points spanning centuries is in order before moving forward in time. First, before the sixteenth century, images of Justice were shown with their eyes open. During the Mediaeval and Renaissance periods, the blindfold had a deeply derisive symbolism, which was readily appreciated and regularly reinscribed.

Second, by the seventeenth century and with the influences of Alciatus and Ripa, closed or covered eyes for Justice were uncommon but not unknown, especially in the Netherlands and in Germany.[76] Yet open-eyed Justices continued to mark town halls (including many in Northern Europe)[77] and appeared in a myriad of other depictions, including on tarot cards.[78] Further, the tradition of using images of Justices for the frontispieces of law books. The example included here brings us into the eighteenth century; Figure 9.11 is the frontispiece of Cesare Beccaria's *On Crimes and*

74 Kissel, *Die Justitia*, at 85–92.

75 Panofsky, 'Blind Cupid', at 109, 1100, n. 48.

76 See, for example, Martin Loughlin, *Swords and Scales*, at 96, fig. 40; 98, fig. 42; 99, fig. 43; 120, fig. 67.

77 See, for example, Karl Emil Otto Fritsch, *Denkmaeler Deutscher Renaissance: 300 Tafeln mit Erlaeuternden Text* (*Monuments of the German Renaissance: 300 Plates with Explanatory Text*) (Berlin: Wasmuth, 1891). All came with scales and sword but most did not have blindfolds. Examples include pictures from Bremen, Danzig, Görlitz, Halberstadt, and Wittenberg.

78 See Michael Dummett, *The Visconti-Sforza Tarot Cards* (New York: George Braziller, 1986), 6–11. Card packs had kings, knights, queens, Temperance, Justice, Fortitude, Fortune, and other personifications; Justice is usually shown with sword and scales but not blindfolded. Ibid., at 114–115. On the other hand, the woman at the centre of the 'Wheel of Fortune' is blindfolded. Ibid., at 120–1.

Figure 9.11 Frontispiece, Cesare Beccaria, *Von Verbrechen und Strafen* (Breslau: Johann Friedrich Korn, 1788) (reproduced with the assistance of Michael Widener, courtesy of the Rare Book Collection, Lillian Goldman Law Library, Yale Law School)

Punishment, and the Justice is sighted and shown deliberately turning away from looking at the severed head proffered by an executioner – thereby displaying Beccaria's opposition to capital punishment.[79]

Third, by the eighteenth century, the blindfold on Justice had shed its connections to Synagoga's failing to see the light of Christianity, to jesters made buffoons because they could not see, and to the condemned, blindfolded before execution. Instead, when placed on Justice, the blindfold was turned into a symbol of law's commitment to rationality and even-handedness.[80]

Fourth, the Enlightenment brought other justifications for rethinking the relationship of sight to knowledge and authority, and additional explanations for a blindfolded Justice. Philosophy, science, and political theory all gave rise to epistemological doubt – thereby prompting questions about sight's impact on knowledge.

John Locke's famous inquiry provides a route into the then new puzzles about the relationships among the senses to knowledge. 'Suppose a Man born blind, and now adult, and taught by his touch to distinguish between a Cube, and a Sphere of the same metal … be made to see'.[81] The question

79 This image comes from a 1788 edition of Cesare Beccaria's *On Crimes and Punishment*. Beccaria, an eighteenth-century Italian jurist, philosopher and politician, first published *On Crimes and Punishment* in 1764. The treatise continues to be invoked in discussions of theories of punishment. The illustration, based on a sketch and written description by Beccaria, was engraved by Giovanni Lapi on copperplate and first appeared in a 1765 edition through Livorno publisher Giuseppe Aubert. Franco Venturi, *Utopia and Reform in the Enlightenment* (Cambridge: Cambridge University Press, 1971), 105–6. 'Justice, … portrayed as combining law and wisdom in the features of Minerva … herself recoils from the executioner's offering of three decapitated heads and instead gazes approvingly at various instruments of labor, of measurement, and of detention'. Piers Bierne, 'Inventing Criminology: The "Science of Man", in Cesare Beccaria's *Dei delitti e delle pene* (1764)', in *Criminological Theory*, ed. Marilyn McShane and Frank P. Williams, III (New York: Garland, 1997), 21–65; at 48, 49, n. 40. Additional examples of clear-sighted justices were included in 'The Remarkable Run of a Political Icon: Justice as a Sign of the Law,' an exhibit at the Rare Book Collection, Lillian Goldman Law Library, Yale Law School, curated by Judith Resnik, Dennis Curtis, Allison Tait, and Michael Widener, September 19 – December 16, 2011, available online at http://library.law.yale.edu/justice-sign-law-exhibit (accessed 7 January 2015). See also the 'Justitia: Iconography of Justice' folder at the Yale Law Library Rare Book Collection's Flickr page, available online at www.flickr.com/photos/yalelawlibrary/sets/72157621962572618 (accessed 7 January 2015).

80 A few commentators see the religious imagery surrounding judges in France as signalling some degree of independence from rulers. See Jacob, *Images de la Justice* at 233–7.

81 See John Locke, *An Essay Concerning Human Understanding*, ed. Peter H. Nidditch (Oxford: Oxford University Press, 1975), 146 (italics omitted). Locke identified sight as 'the most comprehensive of all our Senses, conveying to our Minds the Ideas of Light and Colours, which are peculiar only to that Sense'.

of what a newly-sighted person would know has come to be called the 'Molyneux problem', named after Locke's friend William Molyneux, who 'put to him' that issue in 1688.[82] Locke's response was that a person without the experience of seeing the cube and the sphere could not, at first sight, make the judgment required to distinguish and name the two objects.[83]

The Molyneux problem was not only hypothetical. Eighteenth-century physicians were beginning to operate to alleviate the blindness caused by cataracts.[84] Moreover, blindness became a 'subject of intense cultural interest'.[85] In 1749, Diderot published his *Lettre sur les aveugles à l'usage de ceux qui voient* (*An Essay on Blindness in a Letter to a Person of Distinction*),[86] in which he deconstructed (to borrow a term from a later age) Molyneux's problem and Locke's response.

Diderot rebutted the idea that the blind lacked knowledge from experience; he argued instead that those who were blind, like those who see, had understandings informed by their own '*bon sens*' (good sense),[87] even if blindness could inhibit the ability to provide names ('*denomination*')[88] for objects. Diderot posited that preparations before an eye operation would be

82 See William R. Paulson, *Enlightenment, Romanticism, and the Blind in France* (Princeton, NJ: Princeton University Press, 1987), 21–3; Michael J. Morgan, *Molyneux's Question: Vision, Touch and the Philosophy of Perception* (Cambridge: Cambridge University Press, 1977). Molyneux, a member of the Irish Parliament and the author of *The Case for Ireland* (1698) and *Dioptica nova* (1692), lived from 1656 to 1698. His interest in optics may have come in part because his wife was blind. Marjolein Degenaar, *Molyneux's Problem: Three Centuries of Discussion on the Perception of Forms*, trans. Michael J. Collins (Dordrecht: Kluwer Academic, 1996), 17–18, 23, 133.

83 Locke, *An Essay Concerning Human Understanding*, at 146–7. Locke also distinguished between 'primary qualities' that he posited exist independent of a person's observations (shape, for example) and 'secondary qualities' that are artifacts of observation (colour, for example). See Samuel C. Rickless, 'Locke on Primary and Secondary Qualities', *Pacific Philosophical Quarterly*, 78 (1997), 297–319; E. M. Curley, 'Locke, Boyle, and the Distinction between Primary and Secondary Qualities', *Philosophical Review*, 81 (1972), 438–64.

84 In 1728, William Cheselden, a surgeon, published an article describing an account of his operation on a young man who had suffered with cataracts. Degenaar, *Molyneux's Problem* at 52.

85 Paulson, *Enlightenment, Romanticism, and the Blind in France*, at 3.

86 Denis Diderot was born in 1713 and died in 1784. The essay 'ends with a poetic affirmation of our ignorance of ultimate reality. For this Diderot was put into a dungeon in Vincennes'. Morgan, *Molyneux's Question*, at 27–8. Morgan provided an English translation of Diderot's 'letter', at 31–58, and we use his translation for our references to Diderot's argument, which we denote Diderot/Morgan.

87 Diderot/Morgan at 57–8; Paulson, *Enlightenment, Romanticism, and the Blind in France*, at 46.

88 Paulson, *Enlightenment, Romanticism, and the Blind in France* at 48.

relevant to what was reported by the person thereafter, and he disentangled the question of what could be seen immediately (he thought the answer was a multitude of confused sensations) from the question of whether a blind person would be able to distinguish among shapes by naming them.[89]

New sovereignties, veils of ignorance, and color-blind constitutions

As noted at the outset, the roles of judge and ruler were once understood to be deeply and appropriately intertwined. Alciatus's sixteenth-century emblem of the presiding jurist instructed to render judgment according to the advice of his council was one of many images and allegorical stories regularly displayed in rooms where judgments were rendered and teaching norms of judicial *subservience* to rulers and their law.

The idea that judges were deployed by states but yet sat somehow independent of state power came through profound changes in political theory, exemplified by Montesquieu's proposition that 'there is no liberty, if the judicial power be not separated from the legislative and executive'. A yet more radical notion is that judges have the power to sit in judgment of the state, their own employer. A few famous 'folktales of jurisdiction', as Robert Cover called them, can be found in biblical and common law narratives in which brave judges stood their ground against threats of tyrannical kings; those judges insisted on their own authority to 'speak truth to power',[90] even at their own peril. But not until the Enlightenment did the idea become current that ordinary judges were to be insulated from such power and authorized to overturn decisions of other branches of government.

This shift of sovereignty to people, captured by the opening phrase of the American Constitution – 'We the People of the United States' – was accompanied by the protection of an independent sphere for judges. Building on the English Act of Settlement of 1701, the United States Constitution of 1789 required that judges, once appointed, were to keep their jobs 'during good

89 Diderot/Morgan, at 50–5; Degenaar, *Molyneux's Problem*, at 76.

90 Robert Cover, 'The Folktales of Justice: Tales of Jurisdiction', *Capital University Law Review*, 14 (1985), at 179. Cover explored the maxim 'The king does not judge and we do not judge him'. Mishneh Sanhedrin 2: 3, quoted in 'Folktales of Justice' at 183. As Cover related this 'folktale', Simeon ben Shetah, Chief Judge of the Sanhedrin, called on King Yannai to testify in a case involving the King's slave. The King replied that he would do so only if all of the 71 judges would so command him. The judges other than Simeon ben Shetah were intimated by the King and backed away from demanding that he testify. After the King left, Simeon called on God to call the weak judges to account; the Angel Gabriel responded by killing them all. Ibid., at 184.

Behaviour' and to receive salaries that could not be diminished while they served.[91] These new understandings of government produced another explanation for the blindfold – that it marked not only judicial neutrality between parties but also an untethered stance from the government that created the jurisdictional authority for and paid the salaries of judges.[92] A distance attributed to deliberate restrictions on sight continues to be invoked, as illustrated by a 2004 volume entitled *The Blindfold of Lady Justice: Judicial Independence and Impartiality in Light of the Requirements of Article 6 ECHR [European Convention on Human Rights]*.[93]

Democratic processes are also linked to imagery of obscured sight, as famously proffered by John Rawls, describing the import of a 'veil of ignorance' in his 1971 book *A Theory of Justice*.[94] Rawls argued that principles of justice had to be developed behind such a veil so as to ensure that no one would be 'advantaged or disadvantaged in the choice of principles by the outcome of natural chance or the contingency of social circumstances'.[95] Rawls used the veil to put one in an 'original position', without 'knowledge of those contingencies which sets men at odds and allows them to be guided by their prejudices'.[96] Fair – rather than self-serving – decisions could therefore be made as long as one did not know the personal consequences that could be derived from one's class, social status, abilities, intelligence, life plan, and the surrounding social, economic or political order.[97] Such levelling and equality created the possibility for 'a unanimous choice of a particular conception of justice',[98] achieved by reasoning in stages about principles of justice.

A 1997 steel sculpture, *Lady Justice* (Figure 9.12), by Diana Moore, could be read as a visual translation of this stance. This statue is at the centre of the entry to the renovated Warren B. Rudman United States Courthouse in Concord, New Hampshire. The United States General Services Administration, the entity in charge of federal buildings, described the 'highly original interpretation' as focused on the 'action of blindfolding as an

91 US Constitution Art. III, sec. 1.

92 Justice blindfolded could not see the signals a sovereign might have sent about how to decide a case. Kissel, *Die Justitia* at 82–92.

93 Martin Kuijer, *The Blindfold of Lady Justice: Judicial Independence and Impartiality in Light of the Requirements of Article 6 ECHR* (Leiden: Wolf Legal Publishers, 2004).

94 John Rawls, *A Theory of Justice* (Cambridge: Belknap/Harvard University Press, 1971), 12.

95 Ibid., at 12.

96 Ibid., at 19.

97 Ibid., at 136–7.

98 Ibid., at 140.

Figure 9.12 *Lady Justice*, Diana K. Moore, 1996; Warren B. Rudman, Jr. Federal Courthouse, Concord, New Hampshire. Photographer: Nick Wheeler (reproduced courtesy of the artist, Diana Moore, and with the permission of the architectural firm of Shepley Bulfinch Richardson and Abbott)

emblem of clear and impartial judgment'.[99] This volitional blindfolding (a 'self-imposed neutrality ... repeated in her unadorned robe')[100] uses a diaphanous cloth, suggestive of a mask.[101]

The tropes of sight and blindness have also become central to intense constitutional debates in the United States. More than 100 years ago, in 1896, when protesting the Supreme Court's approval of segregated railway cars, Justice John Marshall Harlan spoke of the 'eye of the law' as he insisted that

99 General Service Administration, *Justice: A Justice for Concord – Forging Together the Ancient and the Modern* (undated and unpaginated monograph from about 1997, published to recognize the renovation of the courthouse and the installation of the art).

100 Ibid. The GSA further explained that the blindfold 'is not an imposed hindrance, through which she struggles to see. Rather, it is a sign that she draws upon an inner source of wisdom, to allow for a fair and prudent administration of the law'.

101 Ibid.

the United States was a place without caste; the country had no 'superior, dominant, ruling class of citizens' because 'Our Constitution is color-blind'.[102]

At that time, 'colored' referenced dark skin, reflected in the name of the National Association for the Advancement of Colored People, chosen in 1909 for an organization devoted to the rights of African Americans.[103] Similarly, in 1925, when twelve black lawyers met in Des Moines, Iowa, and formed the National Bar Association, they explained they were a group of 'practicing attorneys of the Negro race'[104] aiming to eradicate the second-class citizenship of 'the American of Color'.[105]

Only much later, in part as critical theorists explored the social constructions solidifying the relevance and content of the meaning of race, did the idea develop that everyone has a 'color' – whether white, black, or part of a 'rainbow' in between. Toward the end of the twentieth century, white students, white employees and white contractors went to courts to advance what are called 'reverse discrimination' claims; they argued that they had been subjected to unfair treatment based on their whiteness.

In 1896, when Justice Harlan aspired that the law's 'eye' be 'blind', he knew that, were the law to 'see', it would (and did) discriminate against dark-skinned peoples. But, in 2007, on behalf of a majority of five, Chief Justice John Roberts relied on Justice Harlan's metaphor to invalidate an affirmative action plan that had taken into account the races and ethnicities of schoolchildren so that the lower schools in Seattle, Washington, and St. Louis, Missouri might be somewhat diverse.[106]

102 *Plessy v. Ferguson*, 163 US 537, 559 (1896) (Harlan, J., dissenting). Harlan continued that the Constitution 'neither knows nor tolerates classes among citizens'.

103 August Meier and John H. Bracey Jr, 'The NAACP as a Reform Movement, 1909–1965: "To Reach the Conscience of America"', *Journal of Southern History*, 59 (1993), at 8.

104 Elmer C. Jackson Jr and Jacob U. Gordon, *A Search for Equal Justice by African-American Lawyers: A History of the National Bar Association* (New York: Vantage Press, 1999), at 16, quoting Raymond Pace Alexander. In the late 1990s, the objectives were to 'improve economic conditions (of all American citizens) regardless of race, sex or creed in their efforts to secure a free and untrammeled use of the franchise'. Ibid., at 141. In the original constitution of 1926, there was no mention of race in the section on objectives.

105 Ibid., at xi, quoting an inaugural address given in 1948 by President Thurman L. Dodson.

106 See *Parents Involved in Community Schools v. Seattle School District No. 1*, 551 US 701 (2007). Chief Justice John Roberts's opinion for the five-person majority quoted from the *Plessy* opinion (ibid. at 731), while the concurrence by Justice Clarence Thomas used the phrase 'color-blind' several times (ibid., at 772, 780, 782). The impassioned dissent by Justice Stephen Breyer argued that no case had followed the version of color-blindness proposed by Justice Thomas but rather had attended to the 'asymmetry between that which seeks to *exclude* and that which seeks to *include* members of minority races.' Ibid., at 830 (emphasis in the original).

The trope of a 'color-blind' constitution and the image of a blindfolded justice could both be read as universalizing one particular stance, rather than focusing on context. In contrast, some justices have discussed the choices available to courts in terms of what they can look at, or not. In 1950, Justice Felix Frankfurter concurred in the decision that the Equal Protection Clause of the Fourteenth Amendment prohibited racial discrimination in the selection of grand jurors, authorized to indict criminal defendants. The Supreme Court's ruling found illegal the process for choosing grand jurors in Dallas County, Texas. Although a large number of black people were eligible for service, none had ever sat. Frankfurter explained that if 'one factor is uniform in a continuing series of events that are brought to pass through human intervention, the law would have to have the blindness of indifference rather than the blindness of impartiality not to attribute the uniform factor to man's purpose'.[107]

Justice Frankfurter's distinction (the blindness of indifference, the blindness of impartiality) did not totally reject the imagery of blindness. In contrast, a keen sense of law's unfairness has propelled objections to such tropes as serving to sustain a claim of innocence from inequality's perpetuation that law does not deserve. This position is eloquently explained by Langston Hughes in his poem *Justice*, first published in the *Amsterdam News* in 1923 and later included in a 1932 collection called *Scottsboro Limited*.[108]

> That Justice is a blind goddess
> Is a thing to which we black are wise.
> Her bandage hides two festering sores
> That once perhaps were eyes.

The title is a reference to the convictions of nine young black men ('the Scottsboro Boys') who had been taken from a freight train, charged in Alabama courts, found guilty of raping two young white women and sentenced to death in 1931.[109] Hughes visited the prisoners while they were

107 *Cassell v. Texas*, 339 US 282, 293 (1950) (Frankfurter, J., concurring, joined by Justices Burton and Minton).

108 See Hans Ostrom, *A Langston Hughes Encyclopedia*, Westport, CT: Greenwood Press, 2002 (hereinafter Hughes *Encyclopedia*), 195; Joseph McLaren, *Langston Hughes: Folk Dramatist in the Protest Tradition, 1921–1943* (Westport, CT: Greenwood Press, 1997), 33–40. Hughes republished *Justice* in 1938 in a book of poems entitled *A New Song*. There, the phrase 'we black' in the second line of the poem became 'we poor'. See Langston Hughes, *The Collected Works of Langston Hughes, Vol. 1: The Poems, 1921-1940*, ed. Arnold Rampersad (Columbia, MO: University of Missouri Press, 2001), 133.

109 Dan T. Carter, *Scottsboro: A Tragedy of the American South* (Baton Rouge, LA: Louisiana State University Press, 1979), 3–48.

on death row.[110] He sparked and joined a chorus of protests, national and international, about their treatment. In 1937, Alabama released four of the nine and, in 1976, Alabama's Governor George Wallace pardoned the last living defendant, then still in prison.[111]

Langston Hughes' critique of the blindfold is echoed in the logo chosen by a group of black jurists, formed in 1971 as a part of the National Bar Association, founded (as noted earlier) in the 1920s for the advancement of black lawyers.[112] These judges argued that 'the quality of justice in America has always been and is now directly related to the color of one's skin as well as to the size of one's pocket book'.[113] Given that courts had been a significant source of unfairness,[114] judges had a special obligation to respond.[115]

This group chose as their pledge: 'Let us remove the blindfold from the eyes of American justice'. For an emblem, they selected a regal depiction of a Justice taking off a blindfold (Figure 9.13). One of the group's leaders explained:

> Justice is supposed to be blind. It treats all individuals alike – rich or poor, black or white, male or female. Well, it's time to remove the blindfold that gives the illusion of fair treatment. We want to expose to the full glare of reality the inequities superimposed on that great but unrealized objective.[116]

Breaking the visual plane and multiplying the vantage points

John Rawls and Diana Moore suggest donning a blindfold to constrain the bases for fair decision-making. Langston Hughes, the Judicial Council of the

110 Ibid., at 166.

111 In 2013, 'three black men received posthumous pardons' absolving 'the last of the 'Scottsboro Boys' of criminal misconduct. See Alan Blinder, 'Alabama Pardons 3 Scottsboro Boys after 80 Years', *NY Times* (21 Nov. 2013).

112 By the late 1990s, more than 18,000 black lawyers, judges, legal scholars and students were members, and six women had served among the 56 presidents. See President Beverly McQueary Smith, who served in 1998–1999, quoted in Jackson and Gordon, *A Search for Equal Justice by African-American Lawyers*, at xii. At the time, of about 12,500 judges nationwide in state and federal courts, some 325 were black. See George W. Crockett Jr, 'Racism in the Courts', *Journal of Public Law*, 20 (1971), at 388–9.

113 Honorable George W. Crockett Jr, quoted by Gilbert Ware, *Introduction, Proceedings: Founding Convention of the Judicial Council of the National Bar Association*, ibid., at 371, 372.

114 The group identified judicial discretion and courts as sources of 'racism,' including differential treatment by police and prosecutors, exclusion from juries, inattentive witnesses, and abuse from lawyers. Ibid., at 388.

115 Ibid., at 371.

116 Crockett, 'Racism in the Courts', at 389.

Figure 9.13 Logo of the Judicial Council of the National Bar Association, 1971; the facsimile by Yale University Press is reproduced with the permission of the Honorable Michael Bagneris, 2006 Chair of the Judicial Council of the National Bar Association, and with the assistance of Maurice Foster of that organization

National Bar Association, and many critical theorists argue that the failure to see pre-existing conditions of inequality renders judgment unfair. That debate is replayed as Chief Justice Roberts invokes the trope of a 'color-blind

Constitution', while some of his colleagues insist that race matters and needs to be seen and taken into account. These exchanges exemplify why the imagery of a blindfolded – or sighted – Justice may mark a building as a courthouse but does not reflect aspirations of democratic and critical theories about how judges ought to do their work.

A return to Diderot's critique of Locke's resolution of the Molyneux problem is in order. Recall that Diderot thought that how a blind person was prepared would affect whether, if 'made to see', that person would 'know' a cube from a sphere. (The question continues to prompt inquiries about, in today's terms, the rapidity of 'cross-modal' transfers, as knowledge moves from the sense of touch to that of sight).[117] As Diderot understood, the exchanges between the subject of any such experiment and the observer would be a variable affecting the outcome, not only because preparations could skew results but also because observers were not themselves 'dispassionate'.[118] Moreover, Diderot insisted that the blind comprised a diverse set, not to be used as 'univocal symbols … for any single position'.[119] The more general proposition was that no 'single discursive mode of understanding or communication [was] common to all individuals'.[120]

The complexities Diderot identified have only deepened. As Jonathan Crary explained, the view of 'knowledge of space and depth [as] built up out of an orderly accumulation and cross-referencing of perceptions on a plane independent of the viewer' was an eighteenth-century attitude assuming that the senses were an 'adjunct of a rational mind'.[121] Yet, by the nineteenth century, the camera obscura had 'collapse[d] … as a model for the condition of the observer'. Instead of one fixed source of light, there were many vantage points from which to look. The result was a 'rupture with renaissance or *classical* models of vision',[122] and with it, the hegemony of a single meta-narrative confidently promulgated by one authoritative voice.[123]

Contemporary critical theory, both reflected and produced through the multiplication of images and texts, makes palpable the subjectivity of what

117 See, for example, Richard Held, Uyri Ostrovsky, Beatrice de Gelder, Tapan Ghandi, Suma Ganesh, Umang Mathur, and Pawan Sinha, 'The Newly Sighted Fail to Match Seen with Felt', *Nature: Neuroscience*, 14 (2001), 551–3.

118 Diderot/Morgan at 33–40; see also Degenaar, *Molyneux's Problem*, at 73–5; Diderot/Morgan, at 50–5; Degenaar, *Molyneux's Problem*, at 76.

119 Paulson, *Enlightenment, Romanticism, and the Blind in France*, at 52.

120 Ibid., at 47.

121 Jonathan Crary, *Techniques of the Observer: On Vision and Modernity in the Nineteenth Century* (Cambridge, MA: MIT Press, 1990) (hereinafter Crary, *Techniques*), 59–62.

122 Ibid., at 3.

123 Ibid., at 1–4.

is seen. Borrowing again from Crary (as well as extrapolating from Diderot), 'observers' are not autonomous (their eyes are not 'innocent')[124] but they (we) are 'embedded in a system of conventions and limitations',[125] situated to see 'within a prescribed set of possibilities'.[126] Whether using illustrations of sighted or blindfolded eyes, locating aspirations for Justice in a single positioned personification ignores that embeddedness, just as talking about a 'color-blind' Constitution obscures the question of law's relationship to the results of past harms.[127] The issue for constitutional law is not about *seeing* race but about what meaning *to make* of racialized categories and histories.

Yet another problem with the blindfold comes from Peter Goodrich's argument that it served as 'an injunction not to look'.[128] Public observation – looking – is at the heart of democratic adjudicatory processes. As Jeremy Bentham put it long ago, 'Publicity is the very soul of justice ... It keeps the judge himself, while trying, under trial'.[129] Writing in 1812, Bentham explained: 'Without publicity all other checks are insufficient: in comparison with publicity, all other checks are of small account'.[130] Bentham's claims about why courts ought to be public are, although not often directly cited, echoed regularly in case law on rights of access to courts. Bentham believed that, when rendering decisions in public, it would be 'natural' for judges to adopt 'the habit of giving reasons from the bench'.[131] Courts were therefore 'schools' – teaching the public about the rules of law.

Famously (as underscored by Michel Foucault), observation brings with it disciplinary power. Bentham urged that ordinary spectators ('auditors')[132] be permitted to make notes that could be distributed widely. These 'minutes' could serve as insurance for the good judge and as a corrective against 'misrepresentations' made by 'an unrighteous judge'.[133] By suggesting that trials put the state (through its representative, the judge) on display, Bentham raised the specter that both judges and the state were to be

124 Ibid., at 95, citing *The Works of John Ruskin*, vol. 15 at 27.

125 Ibid., at 6.

126 Ibid., at 6.

127 See, generally, Reva Siegel, 'The Supreme Court, 2012 Term, Foreword: Equality Divided', *Harvard Law Review*, 127 (2013), 1–94.

128 Goodrich, *Legal Emblems*, at 161.

129 See Jeremy Bentham, 'Rationale of Judicial Evidence' (1827) (hereinafter Bentham, 'Rationale'), in 6 *The Works of* Jeremy *Bentham*, ed. John Bowring (Edinburgh: William Tait, 1843) (hereinafter Bowring/Works), at bk. II, ch. X at 355.

130 Bentham, 'Rationale' in 6 *Bowring/Works* at bk. II, ch. X, at 351, 355.

131 Ibid., at 357.

132 Ibid., at 355.

133 Ibid., at 355.

subjected *to* judgment. Bentham's commitment to auditors parallels Jonathan Crary's rejection of the term 'spectators', passive in the face of authority, and Crary's insistence on the active posture to be taken by 'observers', engaging in critique as part of their exercise of authority.[134]

Law ought not to reify a single point of view from which to see, nor assume that screening out a person's race depends only on sight. Rather, the meaning of race crosses many modalities to construct its import. Just as a focus on eyes suggests some unity about what information is requisite for judgment or obscures what democratic polities endow the public with the right to see, personifications of a single Virtue miss what judging now requires.[135]

How might one materialize commitments to the multiplicity of vantage points legitimately to be taken into account? In closing, and with appreciation for emblem traditions, we offer the reminder that Justice was once part of a foursome, the Cardinal Virtues, regularly discussed and viewed together because the composite representation provided a collective set of ideal attributes.

Plato is often identified as the source, setting out the qualities – 'wise, brave, moderate, and just'[136] – that 'would eventually be called cardinal virtues', whose interconnections achieved 'a kind of unity of function'.[137] By the fourth century, these attributes became nested in Christian theology; St. Ambrose's funeral oration for his brother analogized the four Platonic virtues to periods within the Old and New Testaments and denominated them 'cardinal' to capture their moral freight and cosmological significance.[138]

134 See Crary, *Techniques*, at 6. Another challenge, given the competition for attention in a world rich with or overwhelmed by visual materials, is actually engaging people in such observations. See, generally, Jonathan Crary, *Suspensions of Perception: Attention, Spectacle, and Modern Culture* (Cambridge, MA: MIT Press, 1999).

135 This point is akin to that made by Uriel Procaccia, that the project of codification (a term coined by Bentham) has ended.

136 See Plato, *The Republic*, trans. G. M. A. Grube (Indianapolis, IN: Hackett, 1974,) at IV, 427e, 93. We use the lower case for these virtues and capitalization when discussing their personifications.

137 R. E. Houser, 'Introduction', *The Cardinal Virtues: Aquinas, Albert, and Philip the Chancellor*, trans. R. E. Houser (Toronto: Pontifical Institute of Medieval Studies, 2004), (hereinafter Houser, 'Introduction'), 1, 9–11. These virtues also overlapped with other sets, such that Fortitude was both a 'Gift Virtue' and a Cardinal Virtue. See Helen North, *Sophrosyne: Self-Knowledge and Self-Restraint in Greek Literature* (Ithaca, NY: Cornell University Press, 1966) (hereinafter North, *Sophrosyne*), at 186–7.

138 See Houser, 'Introduction', at 32–5. Ambrose spoke of the Virtues as 'born together and perfected together'. See Ambrose, *De excessu fratris Satyri*, 1.57, CSEL 73: 239, as translated by Houser. Ibid., at 33.

Thomas Aquinas brought the four down to earth, for he argued that what made them 'cardinal' was not that they 'were more perfect than all the other virtues, but because human life more principally turns on them'.[139] Aquinas cited Pope Gregory I for the proposition that unless

> prudence is just and temperate and brave, it is not true prudence, nor is there perfect temperance which is not brave, just, and prudent, nor complete fortitude which is not prudent, temperate and just, nor true justice which is not prudent, brave and temperate.[140]

Moreover, 'all virtues must, simply speaking, be equal for the same reason that they are connected, since equality is a kind of connection in quantity'.[141] Artists, in turn, regularly displayed them as a set, deployed with other Virtues in various epic battles against a host of Vices and placed in buildings of import, such as the Vatican, other rulers' palaces, and town halls. Figure 9.14 draws in part on Raphael to provide a compendium of the four.

How does such imagery resonate with contemporary adjudication and expand the associations beyond those produced by Justice, with scale, sword and blindfold, or not? Classical and Renaissance literature linked prudence, a habit 'obtained and perfected through practice in deliberation and action',[142] to good governance. Cicero saw prudence as 'the first of the virtues possessed by the ideal statesman and the wise man'.[143] Commentators speak of prudence as 'the humility … of unbiased perception; the trueness-to-being of memory; the art of receiving counsel; alert, composed readiness for the unexpected'.[144] Aquinas is cited for the idea that prudence requires careful

139 Thomas Aquinas, *Disputed Questions on Virtue*, trans. Ralph McInerny (South Bend, IN: St. Augustine's Press, 1999), 112.

140 Ibid., at 105, citing to *Morals on Job*, 22. See Gregory the Great, *Morals on the Book of Job*, vol. 2 (Oxford: John Henry Parker, 1845), 547. Gregory stated that 'Blessed Job' himself displayed the unity of virtues 'viz. prudence, temperance, fortitude, and justice' that were 'mutually joined to one another' and 'separated they can never be perfect'. Ibid., at 547.

141 Aquinas, *Disputed Questions* at 130–1.

142 Daniel Mark Nelson, *The Priority of Prudence: Virtue and Natural Law in Thomas Aquinas and the Implications for Modern Ethics* (University Park, PA: Pennsylvania State University Press, 1992), 79.

143 Robert Cape, Jr, 'Cicero and the Development of Prudential Practice at Rome', *Prudence: Classical Virtue, Postmodern Practice*, ed. Robert Harriman (University Park, PA: Pennsylvania State University Press, 2003), 51–2.

144 Josef Pieper, *The Four Cardinal Virtues: Prudence, Justice, Fortitude, Temperance* (Notre Dame, IN: University of Notre Dame Press, 1966), 22.

Figure 9.14 *Iusticia* (*Justice*), Cornelis Matsys, circa 1543–1544; *Prudence*, Agostino Veneziano, 1516. Bottom: *Temperance*, Agostino Veneziano, 1517; *Fortitudo* (*Fortitude*), Marcantonio Raimondi, circa 1520 (copyright Warburg Institute, University of London); the composite is drawn from images that are reproduced courtesy of the Warburg Institute and with the assistance of Elizabeth McGrath; details about each can be found in Resnik and Curtis, *Representing Justice*, at 8–12, 344–7

inquiry producing wise judgment ('rightly to counsel, judge and command concerning the means of obtaining a due end').[145] 'Sympathetic understanding' is how one modern commentator put it.[146]

Ralph Waldo Emerson described prudence as central to human flourishing because it entailed 'the art of securing a present well-being'.[147] Contemporary legal literature invokes prudence as the embodiment of a 'tradition of statecraft' that has a 'normative' rather than a 'value-free' content.[148] Thus, the relevance of prudence for judges comes not only from the association with the investigation of situations and deliberation about action (for Aquinas, 'prudence is in reason', while justice was 'in will'[149]) but also because prudence was seen as related to the auxiliary virtue, *synesis* or understanding.[150]

Temperance, in turn, moderated the desires and appetites of both the gods and humankind. Helen North provided a history of the development from the Greek term *sophrosyne* to the Roman temperance or 'soundness of mind' and self-knowledge.[151] The '*polis* by its very nature required a much greater exercise of restraint' than had a more loosely organized society,[152] making *sophrosyne* a socio-political attribute as well as an internally desirable mode of conducting one's own life. Temperance, the opposite of hubris ('considered a characteristic vice of tyrants') produced balance for both persons and social orders.[153]

Fortitude (sometimes equated with courage) came to denote strength and endurance, as well as the virtues of perseverance, patience, loyalty, and magnanimity.[154] Cicero described fortitude as the virtue through which one

145 Nelson, *The Priority of Prudence*, at 81.

146 Alberto R. Coll, 'Normative Prudence as a Tradition of Statecraft', *Ethics and International Affairs*, 5 (1991), pp. 33–51, at 38.

147 Ralph Waldo Emerson, 'Prudence', *in Essays: first and second series* (New York: Vintage Books, Library of America, 1990), 227.

148 See, for example, Coll, 'Normative Prudence as a Tradition of Statecraft', at 35; Anthony J. Kronman, 'Alexander Bickel's Philosophy of Prudence', *Yale Law Journal*, 94 (1985), 1567–616. See, generally, Douglas J. Den Uyl, *The Virtue of Prudence* (New York: Peter Lang, 1991).

149 Aquinas, *Disputed Questions*, at 109.

150 Houser, 'Introduction', at 74.

151 See North, *Sophrosyne*, at 1.

152 Ibid., at 9–12.

153 Ibid., at 14–19, 268–85.

154 Pieper, *The Four Cardinal Virtues* at 122–33. See R. E. Houser, 'The Virtue of Courage', in *The Ethics of Aquinas*, ed. Stephen J. Pope (Washington DC: Georgetown University Press, 2002), at 308–11.

undertakes dangerous tasks that impose hardships.[155] St. Ambrose is quoted for the proposition that 'Fortitude without justice is a lever of evil'.[156]

Like Justice, her sibling Cardinal Virtues also had their objects, with a motley array of items sometimes affixed to more than one Virtue and varying as well across time, place and setting.[157] As for their eyes, as Figure 9.14 shows, the tradition was to show them sighted. Indeed, Prudence often had a mirror, said to capture self-knowledge. Her depiction commends her as the most post-modern of the four Cardinal Virtues – representing the need for multiple and potentially conflicting perspectives through a mirror and, upon occasion, two heads so as to look both forward and backwards, and a third eye to watch the present as well.

Given the many complaints leveled against courts for having an impoverished range of remedies, discussions of adjudication are oddly devoid of this richer array of virtues. The language and theory of rights, liabilities, sanctions, and sentencing make few references to prudence, endurance or steadfastness. To the extent that temperance or restraint is called for, it is usually a code for cutting off judicial power, rather than carefully deploying it. And the various legal doctrines that may embody self-abnegation (such as not ordering monetary sanctions against sovereigns or deferring to administrators or other courts) are typically explained as self-protective of judges, aiming to avoid the risk of being disobeyed.

The visual reductionism yielding the singular icon Justice thus reflects a contraction of both theory and practice about the breadth of qualities needed for the tasks asked of courts. This brief excursion back to the four Cardinal Virtues is but a glimpse at a much richer normative and didactic account that could be provided in the doctrine, practice, and imagery of adjudication, once one turns to look beyond a single personification of Justice.

155 See Rosemond Tuve, *Allegorical Imagery: Some Medieval Books and Their Posterity* (Princeton, NJ: Princeton University Press, 1966), 59.

156 Pieper, *The Four Cardinal Virtues*, at 125.

157 How these connections were forged is something of a puzzle. '[T]he issue is whether the emblem depends on the invention of original but arbitrary connections between image and meaning, or whether the relation between sign and referent depends on some deeper and more intrinsic ('natural') affinity.' Michael Bath, *Speaking Pictures*, 3. Further, given the diversity of codification systems, Bath contested the conception of them as 'a single, unitary genre.' Ibid., at 280.

CHAPTER 10

Crime shows: CSI in Hapsburg Spain

William Egginton

The European sixteenth century witnessed an extraordinary expansion of the state and its bureaucracy. In Spain, especially, this expansion led to an explosion in legislation and litigation, and increased awareness and reflection on criminality and society's responses. Writers in general and playwrights in particular strove to *show* criminality, delinquency, guilt and the procedures for determining and controlling these, to a public ever more eager to consume such representations and make sense of these changes. The state, meanwhile, exercised increasing measures of censorship of and influence over cultural production to control the message and to ensure the dissemination of an image of criminality that implicitly justified the criminal justice system and its bureaucracy. In the face of rampant corruption, the monarchy and its defenders likewise sought means of both cementing a public perception of justice as flowing directly from the king's authority and disseminating an image of virtue as rooted in self-discipline, abnegation and an internalization of duty.

In this chapter, I propose for the reception of early modern Spanish jurisprudence an analogue to what has been called the 'CSI effect' (crime scene investigation) in contemporary criminological research, according to which the prevalence in popular culture of certain models of investigation, evidence, innocence and guilt alter the predisposition of juries to convict or acquit. While the Hapsburg State had no juries, it was attuned to public opinion to a degree that had few precedents, which was itself precedential for the modern era that it helped inaugurate. The legitimacy of the state in the eyes of the public was a matter of consistent and pressing concern for the king and his bureaucracy, and this legitimacy rested in large part on the claim that the government and its judicial representatives exercised *justice* and not merely capricious coercion in matters of law and order. Thus were the tools of visual media, from emblems to the massively popular theatre industry, co-opted for the purpose of training popular conceptions and expectations to conform to the state's version of justice. To use Peter

Goodrich's term, emblem books and the theatre constituted essential tools in Hapsburg Spain's *visiocracy*, the medial and visual foundation of its rule.[1]

The CSI effect

Despite her proverbial, principled and stonily sculpted veil, we now know that justice is far from blind.[2] In so many cases, so many instances, we learn that the very standards that juries are asked to apply uniformly are themselves subject to multiform interpretations and applications, such that even those most offended by the travesty of the acquittal of George Zimmerman in the slaying of Treyvon Martin had to stay their gut instinct to condemn a jury that had been asked to apply the letter and spirit of a Florida law and question the reasonableness of a neighbourhood watchman's behaviour under the jurisdiction of that law. As Cardozo's Ekow N. Yankah wrote in August 2013, 'What is reasonable to do, especially in the dark of night, is defined by preconceived social roles that paint young black men as potential criminals and predators'.[3]

How those roles become preconceived is, of course, *the* question. And there is a good deal of evidence that at least one of the media for conveying and colouring our preconceptions – for priming our reception of notions of the reasonableness of others' behaviour but also of what constitutes evidence, proof, guilt or innocence and justice itself – is, well, 'the media' and, perhaps specifically, *crime shows*. Donald Shelton has conducted research into the potential veracity of at times conflicting claims around the influence on juries, either bending them to acquit or to convict, of frequently watching the popular contemporary crime show *CSI: Crime Scene Investigation*, in any of its urban variants.

The commonplace complaint, at least as the term 'CSI effect', began to make the rounds of criminal jurisprudence, was that such an evening pastime did much to inculcate in viewers an unreasonable expectation for scientifically derived forensic evidence. In the words of one frustrated prosecutor, 'I once heard a juror complain that the prosecution had not done a

1 Peter Goodrich, 'Visiocracy: On the Futures of the Fingerpost', *Critical Inquiry* 39/3 (2013), 498–531, 508.

2 As Goodrich puts it, 'The blindness of justice is emblematic ... The simple point is that the eye of the spirit, the interior eye, has precedence over the exterior'; Goodrich, *Legal Emblems and the Art of Law* (Cambridge: Cambridge University Press, 2014), 16.

3 Ekow N. Yankah, 'The Truth About Trayvon', *New York Times*, (15 July 15 2013). Available online at www.nytimes.com/2013/07/16/opinion/the-truth-about-trayvon.html?_r=0 (accessed 7 January 2015).

thorough job because "they didn't even dust the lawn for fingerprints"'.[4] Nevertheless, it is important to note that the outcome of the research was a little deflating:

> Although *CSI* viewers had higher expectations for scientific evidence than non-*CSI* viewers, these expectations had little, if any, bearing on the respondents' propensity to convict. This, we believe, is an important finding and seemingly very good news for our Nation's criminal justice system: that is, differences in expectations about evidence did *not* translate into important differences in the willingness to convict.[5]

Despite what appears to be exculpatory evidence in the case of *CSI*, the general case for a special relationship between juror priming and visuality or, specifically, the ability to imagine specific scenarios, has been forcefully defended. As Kevin Jon Heller puts in an article explaining jurors' tendency to undervalue circumstantial evidence and overvalue direct evidence, 'jurors decide whether to acquit not through mechanical probability calculations, but on the basis of their ability to imagine a scenario in which the defendant is factually innocent'.[6] As Goodrich argues in his book *Legal Emblems and the Art of Law*, such focus on the power of the imagination and specifically the visual was recognized by early modern jurists as well: 'to believe, according to the emblematist Matthaeus Merian, you have first to see, because "men believe much more in the eyes than in the ears"' and he continues "it is through the eyes that the great truths are imprinted upon the human soul"'.[7] Given this implicit and even unconscious reliance on scenarios, scenographies or in general an imagination of the scene of the crime, it behoves us to be ever-vigilant of those shortcircuits between word and image that replace the veil of justice with a print, screen or stage on which a certain judgment has already played itself out.

4 Donald E. Shelton, 'The "CSI Effect": Does It Really Exist?' *NIJ Journal*, no. 259 (March 2008). Available online at www.nij.gov/journals/259/pages/csi-effect.aspx (accessed 7 January 2015).

5 Ibid.

6 Kevin Jon Heller, 'The Cognitive Psychology of Circumstantial Evidence', *Michigan Law Review*, 106 (2006), 241–306, at 245–6.

7 Peter Goodrich, *Legal Emblems*, xvii.

Emblems

In his article coining the aforementioned term, 'visiocracy', Goodrich cites a New York University study in which groups of first-year law students argued cases, some in classrooms dressed in street clothes, others in formal courtrooms before judges who had donned the full regalia of the legal profession. The study concluded that the latter group was 'significantly more likely to view the procedure as more legitimate, the judgment as more authoritative, and the judge as more learned in law than those who appeared in the makeshift informal auditoria'. The students, Goodrich argues, 'apprehended ... that there was more to the theater of justice than can be captured by reason and reduced to the page'.[8] Goodrich finds precedent in the emblematic tradition for this essentially visual aspect of the practice of law, this tendency for legality to find illegitimate legitimacy in a kind of imagination of justice that grounds authority in an unexamined visual realm or 'visiocracy'. As he puts it, 'The visual is in classical emblematic terms universal, undivided, free of the chaos that Babel inflicted upon language. The visual is the primary means and medium for transmitting law because, like law, it touches all'.[9]

Support for this thesis comes from realms other than the legal. Bradley Nelson has dedicated a study to emblematics in early modern Spanish literature, from which he derives similar conclusions regarding the efficacy of emblems and emblematic tropes in 'the collective interpellation of the audience into foundational narratives of monarchical unity'. Nelson identifies both in emblem books published at the time as well as in such emblematic cultural genres as the theatre, which we turn to as well, a disposition toward the 'guidance of the spectator toward a "correct" interpretation [that] necessitates his or her engagement in a conflict between deviant and correct discursive and moral models'.[10]

In a few of the emblems that I discuss here, we can see precisely such a modelling of desirable behaviour; but I am even more interested in how the modelling in this selection of emblems engages and guides popular ideas of sovereignty and authority in relation to individual freedom and pleasure. Specifically, I argue that the emblematic tradition contains at least one stream dedicated to rationalizing the exertion of power, of punishment, of corrective violence as a personal hardship and hence sacrifice, even on an

8 Goodrich, 'Visiocracy', 499.
9 Goodrich, 'Visiocracy', 508.
10 Bradley J. Nelson, *The Persistence of Presence: Emblem and Ritual in Baroque Spain* (Toronto: University of Toronto Press, 2010), 24.

implicitly religious register, for the sovereign. This equation, in turn, informs an ancillary discourse of self-discipline and punishment as the inherent justification or redemption of fears and suspicions, rampant in a society steeped in the corruption of legality and abuse of authority for the personal gain and pleasure of those in positions of power. In other words, what the emblems do is to fuse an image of righteous suffering with the idea of legality that had been hijacked in the public imagination by stories of graft and corruption to create an image of justice, a visiocracy, in which potentially arbitrary violence is seared into the public imagination as the justified exertion of a higher law felt equally by all, the sovereign included.

As Susan Byrne, Richard Kagan and others have shown, the evolution of the legal tradition in Hapsburg Spain was characterized by ever-increasing confusion and the generalized sense that laws were there to be broken or ignored by anyone with the power or wherewithal to do so. In Kagan's words, 'Castilian justice in the sixteenth and seventeenth centuries was a hodgepodge of confused laws and competing jurisdictions that crafty litigants exploited to their own advantage'.[11] Such complaints rose through the chain of command, infecting public confidence in the legitimacy of authority at the local and even national level, leading even to innuendos of kings themselves not obeying the law, together with counter examples such as that of Cabrera de Córdoba, who protests too much that:

> the dresses and adornments worn by their Royal Highnesses and the happy couple were in conformity with the pragmatic, without any gold in the embroidery or passementerie trim, or any other thing of gold, although the gentlewomen and men who attended the ceremony wore much that had hold embroidery or passementerie.[12]

So it is that Sebastián de Covarrubias, in his popular and widely diffused *Emblemas morales* of 1610 (Figure 10.1), portrays the lion of royalty fused with the aged and bony body of a steer, and asks the question, 'What do you think it means to rule? To serve, dying' (Figure 10.2).

The emblem turns the table on the common complaint of abuse of power: to wield power is to suffer abuse in the service of the common good; it is to give up all pleasure and selfish desires, to be consumed by sacrifice. The face of the lion, like the steer's body, is sagging, the skin loose and hanging, aged

11 Richard Kagan, *Lawsuits and Litigants*, 31; quoted in Susan Byrne, *Law and History in Cervantes' Don Quixote* (Toronto: University of Toronto Press, 2013), 49.

12 Quoted in Byrne, *Law and History in Cervantes' Don Quixote*, 49.

EMBLEMAS MORALES
DE DON SEBASTIAN DE
Couarrubias Orozco, Capellan del Rey N.S. Maestrescuela,
y Canonigo de Cuenca, Consultor del
santo Oficio.
DIRIGIDAS A DON FRANCISCO GOMEZ DE
Sandoual y Roxas, Duque de Lerma, Marqs de Denia, Sumiller de Corps
Cauallerizo mayor del Rey N.S. Comendador mayor de Castilla,
Capitan General de la caualleria de España.

Attingit à fine vsque ad finem.

Neque enim micuerunt frustra.

CON PRIVILEGIO,
En Madrid, Por Luis Sanchez: Año 1610.

Figure 10.1 Frontispiece to Sebastián de Covarrubias, *Emblemas morales* (Madrid, 1610) (courtesy of the George Peabody Library, Sheridan Libraries, Johns Hopkins University)

CENTVRIA. I. 84

EMBLEMA 84.
Que pẽsais q̃ es reynar? seruir muriẽ-
Los dias, y las noches trabajando, (do,
Y quãdo vos comeis, ó estais durmiẽdo,
No comer, ni dormir, y estar velando:
El Rey, parte es leon, feroz, y horrẽdo,
De quien el mũdo todo està temblãdo,
Y manso buey, del medio cuerpo abajo,
Nacido para el yugo, y el trabajo.
Mar-

Figure 10.2 Covarrubias, *Emblemas morales* (Madrid, 1610), 34 (courtesy of the George Peabody Library, Sheridan Libraries, Johns Hopkins University)

early by the cares of office. The front right paw, placed in paternal protection on the orb of the world, is devoid of the violence and fear that great beast's claws would normally project and radiates instead a father's benevolence.

Covarrubias then shifts the suffering of sovereignty inward in an emblem depicting the fatal outcome of the easy road of self-fulfilment as a wide-open net of pleasure, or *gusto*, that narrows into the deathtrap of the great Satanic fisher of souls (Figure 10.3). Just as a people's proper protection requires the self-sacrifice of the sovereign, this emblem directs it reader toward a sacrifice of his own pleasure, linking as it does all pleasure to damnation. A watchful, prudent eye must be watchful first and foremost of its own desires.

We can see a positive counterpart to this admonition in the 1665 festival book *Luces de la aurora* or *Lights of Dawn*. In this emblem, we are treated to an inversion of the traditional moral of Phaeton's fall. Rather than a cautionary tale of the dangers of uninhibited ambition, of leaving one's natural station in life and flying too high, Francisco de la Torre reads Phaeton as morally exemplary, a self-sacrificing model of altruism, whose flaming fate is worthwhile suffering as long as the intent was noble (Figure 10.4).

CENTVRIA. III. 204

NO ES·TAN·FACIL·LA·SALIDA

EMBLEMA 4.

En las coſas de propio guſto entramos
Para prouar, ſi en la preſente vida
En alguna manera le hallamos,
Quãdo ocaſiõ nos llama, y nos cõbida:
Porque no ſucediendo, confiamos
Eſtar en nueſtra mano la ſalida,
Mas el gran peſcador Satã maldito,
No ſuelta al q̃ ha cogido en el garlito.

Dd 4 El

Figure 10.3 Sebastián de Covarrubias, *Emblemas morales* (Madrid, 1610), 204 (courtesy of the George Peabody Library, Sheridan Libraries, Johns Hopkins University)

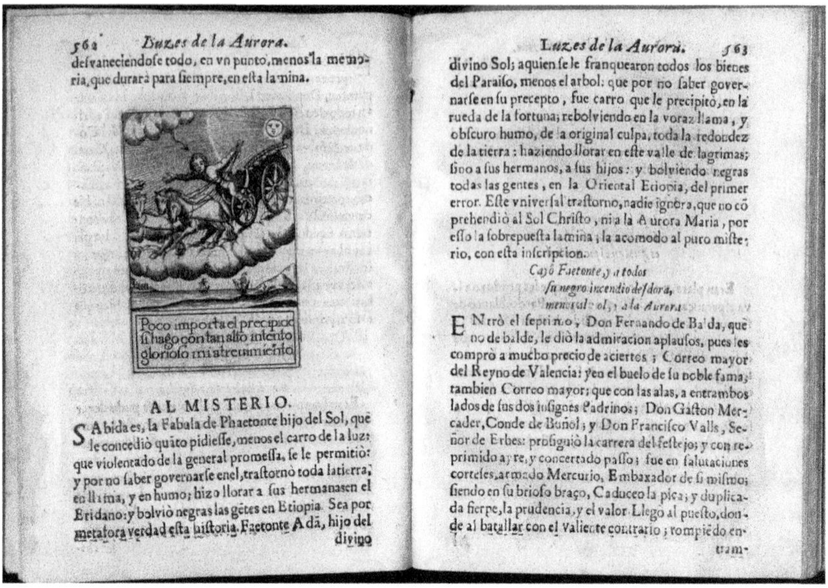

562 Luzes de la Aurora.

desvaneciendose todo, en vn punto, menos la memoria, que durarà para siempre, en esta lamina.

Poco importa el precipicio
si hago con tan alto intento
glorioso mi atrevimiento

AL MISTERIO.

SAbida es, la Fabula de Phaetonte hijo del Sol, que le concediò quāto pidiesse, menos el carro de la luz: que violentado de la general promessa, se le permitiò: y por no saber governarse en el, trastornò toda la tierra, en llama, y en humo; hizo llorar a sus hermanas en el Eridano: y bolviò negras las gētes en Etiopia. Sea por metafora verdad esta historia. Faetonte Adā, hijo del divino

Luzes de la Aurora. 563

divino Sol; a quien se le franquearon todos los bienes del Paraiso, menos el arbol: que por no saber governarse en su precepto, fue carro que le precipitò, en la rueda de la fortuna; rebolviendo en la voraz llama, y obscuro humo, de la original culpa, toda la redondez de la tierra: haziendo llorar en este valle de lagrimas; sino a sus hermanos, a sus hijos: y bolviendo negras todas las gentes, en la Oriental Etiopia, del primer error. Este vniversal trastorno, nadie ignora, que no cō prehendiò al Sol Christo, ni a la Aurora Maria, por esso la sobrepuesta lamina; la acomodo al puro misterio, con esta inscripcion.

Cayò Faetonte, y a todos
su negro incendio desdora,
menos al Sol, y a la Aurora

ENtrò el septimo, Don Fernando de Balda, que no de balde, le diò la admiracion aplausos, pues les comprò a mucho precio de aciertos; Correo mayor del Reyno de Valencia: y en el buelo de su noble fama; tambien Correo mayor; que con las alas, a entrambos lados de sus dos insignes Padrinos; Don Gaston Mercader, Conde de Buñol; y Don Francisco Valls, Señor de Erbes: prosiguiò la carrera del festejo; y con reprimido ayre, y concertado passo; fue en salutaciones corteses, armado Mercurio, Embaxador de si mismo; siendo en su brioso braço, Caduceo la pica; y duplicada sierpe, la prudencia, y el valor. Llegò al puesto, donde al batallar con el valiente contrario; rompiēdo entram-

Figure 10.4 Francisco de la Torre, *Luces de la aurora* (Valencia, 1665), 562–3 (courtesy of the George Peabody Library, Sheridan Libraries, Johns Hopkins University)

The theme of self-directed suffering in the service of a greater morality is rampant in Covarrubias, especially in the realm of education, where the whip is shown in several cases as being essential to the civilization of students, to their happiness, and even, as in this personalization of the pedagogy of violence, to life itself (Figure 10.5).

'Dolor les doy, y juntamente vida – pain I give them, and at the same time, life', says the whip, but it also specifies the kind of student who will benefit from its rigor: the *lerdos*, the oafs and the slow-witted. Those, in other words, who have not the self-discipline to tame themselves will benefit and even gain life from punishment. But not all students need to be shaped in this way. As Covarrubias writes in another emblem dedicated to the theme of education, teachers should spare the whip on well-born children, for whom its rigours are more likely to cause their generous spirits to cower and make them waste their time in useless exercises (Figure 10.6).

The comparison between these two views on corporal punishment is eye-opening: in agreement with the tendency of his age, Covarrubias accepts a foundational distinction between kinds of men, already present in their children. There are those whose blood destines them to be leaders, whose

Figure 10.5 Sebastián de Covarrubias, *Emblemas morales* (Madrid, 1610), 237; courtesy of the George Peabody Library, Sheridan Libraries, Johns Hopkins University

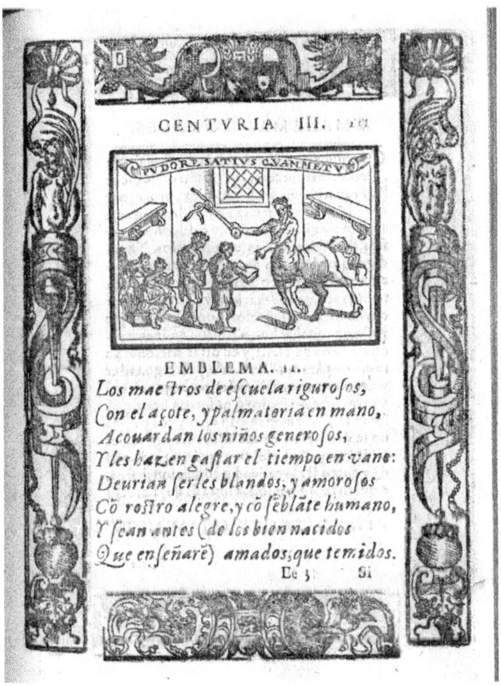

Figure 10.6 Sebastián de Covarrubias, *Emblemas morales* (Madrid, 1610), 21 recto (courtesy of the George Peabody Library, Sheridan Libraries, Johns Hopkins University)

natural generosity makes the imposition of suffering unnecessary and even potential detrimental; for these 'sons of something' as the base term for the gentry, hidalgo, literally signified, already have in them a proclivity to choose suffering over pleasure. It is meanwhile the oafish, the weak, those lacking such lineage who should not be spared the lash, if only out of duty and compassion for their likely fate free from its guard.

Theatre

What were the crimes shows, the *CSIs*, the *Law and Orders*, the *Tatorts*, of the burgeoning urban populace under the Spanish Hapsburgs? Certainly not emblem books themselves, which, while popular enough were expensive and rare, showpieces of wealth and learning and hardly the equivalent of a working man's Sunday night *Krimi*. No, the *comedia de capa y espada*, the *comedia de honor*, these were Hapsburg Madrid's crime shows, drawing thousands to the corrales – the open public theatres set up in the courtyards between buildings – week after week, irrespective of class or literacy, to flood their eager brains with freshly wrought versions of largely the same tale: someone gives in to temptation; someone loses his honour; someone must pay the price. A favourite variant was to have the source of dishonour be noble or, in a few cases, even royal, and the victim a loyal and honourable commoner who ends the play dispensing outlaw justice of the bloodiest sort, an unforgivable crime in the eyes of the law, but one that suddenly finds a rationalizing image of justice in the emblematic tableau's suggested by the comedia's denouements.

In Calderón de la Barca's *El alcalde de Zalamea* or *The Alderman of Zalamea*, the wealthy and honourable Pedro Crespo is forced by law and custom, together with his fellow townspeople, to billet the king's troops as they pass through Zalamea. When an officer abuses his privilege and rapes Pedro's daughter Isabel, the scene is set for that classic conflict, honour versus duty. It is honour, of which Pedro famously says it is 'the patrimony of the soul, and the soul belongs to God', that wins out.[13] Rather than hide his dishonor or – more incomprehensibly to us but not to societies still clapped in the irons of that code – cleanse the stain with his daughter's blood, Pedro becomes judge, juror and executioner to Isabel's rapist, sentencing him to the ignominious death of a commoner. The withdrawn curtains of the '*apariencia*' that so often served on the Spanish stage to 'reveal a marvelous scene in one of the niches at the back of the stage',[14] in this case presents the

13 Cálderon de la Barca, *El alcalde de Zalamea*, I, 857.

14 Nelson, *The Persistence of Presence*, 149.

audience with a scene of horror, the garroted body of the captain, still bound to a chair. As Cull says of this and other such dramatic tableaus,

> the combination of striking visual motifs (*pictura*) with the commentary in the form of dramatic dialogue (*subscription*) imitated the structure of the emblem ... These scenes, designed to provoke *admiratio* in the spectators, often embodied the play's central message or moral.[15]

Indeed, the emblem itself was designed to function in the same way as the theatrical *apariencia*, revealing a hidden truth via the short-circuit between image and subscript, igniting the wonder of sudden insight much as the stage machinery that could make a character or body suddenly materialize. As Covarrubias notes in the entry he composes for *emblema* in the dictionary he published one year after his *Emblemas morales*, the *Tesoro de la lengua castellana o española* that would be his greatest claim to posterity, among the terms related to and easily confused with the emblem is *pegma*, the name for the moveable stage machinery used to enable pageants, which itself had descended etymologically from its classical usage to denote a scaffold, frame or structure meant to hold an ancestor's death mask.

The revelation of the innermost space in the comedia's stage architecture had another, indeed perhaps more profound, impact. Akin to the position of the altar over a tomb in mediaeval church architecture, the last interior space opened by the *apariencia* at the denouement of a *comedia* tapped into a powerful experience of *presence* on the part of contemporary observers. Rather than referring to a next act for their eventual interpretation, such dramatic tableaus depicting bodies in pain or at the very moment of their deaths, acted as a full stop to the otherwise highly fungible, metonymic gliding of empty theatrical space from one represented place to another. In this way, the final tableau could insert in the place of a meaning, a feeling, a physical impact, as if the audience were touching something beyond mere human capacities for explanation.[16]

This tableau is not the last, however, for like others in its genre, the *comedia* must resolve the conflict between Pedro's undeniable crime, the law and the justice for which it stands. And only one figure could perform this slight of hand: the king. As Nelson writes, 'Felipe II's *apariencia* on stage

15 John T. Cull, '*Hablan poco y dicen mucho*: The Function of Discovery Scenes in the Drama of Tirso de Molina', *Modern Language Review* 91 (1996), 619–34, 620; quoted in Nelson, 149.

16 For a fuller discussion see my *How the World Became a Stage* (Albany: SUNY Press, 2003).

configures yet another emblematic moment in the *comedia*, in which the king embodies the presence of a transcendental *deus ex machina* who restores order by invoking a superior idea of … "poetic justice"'.[17] For faced with this undeniable violation of the dimension of the law, the king nevertheless bows to Pedro's invocation of justice, of *the king's own* justice: '*Toda la justicia vuestra es un cuerpo, no más* – all your justice is one body, no more'[18] and, hence, whether I, Pedro Crespo, have been his executioner, or any other of your subjects, the fact remains that justice was served. Perhaps the best way we can imagine such a visual embodiment of justice is to compare the moment in the play with an image of Saint Ferdinand III, the thirteenth-century king canonized some nine years before Calderón's death in 1680, taken from the Festival book published in honour of that canonization in Seville that very year (Figure 10.7).

An earlier play by the great playwright Felix Lope de Vega y Carpio embodies the *deus ex machina* of justice in the figures of the historical founders of Spain's unified monarchy, Isabel and Ferdinand. Moreover, it does so in a way that explicitly draws a border between prior, mediaeval (explicitly denigrated as capricious and violent) forms of judgment and Lope's imagining of a universal, quasi-divine justice meted out by the Catholic monarchs. In what some consider his greatest play, *Fuenteovejuna*, published in 1619 but likely performed between 1612 and 1614, the entire eponymously named town comes together to avenge the rape of its women by its feudal lord. When they are one by one submitted to trial by ordeal by the examining judge, they all hold to the story that 'Fuenteovejuna did it' and refuse to single anyone out. At this moment, the monarchs arrive, to the delight of all, especially the townspeople – who apparently shed the recent trauma of their torture with some ease once bathed in the glow of the royal aura, for their first words are expressions of awe at the monarchs' beauty:

> Laurencia: Those are the monarchs?
> Frondoso: And powerful over all of Castille!
> Laurencia: By my faith are they beautiful!
> May Saint Anthony bless them![19]

And yet it is clear that their beauty and, from the staging of the scene, their *presence*, grounds something else, something missing from the application

17 Nelson, *The Persistence of Presence*, 149.

18 Calderón de la Barca, *El alcalde de Zalamea*, III, 937–8; quoted in Nelson, *The Persistence of Presence*, 153.

19 Lope de Vega, *Fuenteovejuna*, v, 736–9.

Figure 10.7 *Fiestas dela santa iglesia de Sevilla al culto nuevamente concedido al Señor Rei San Fernando III de Castilla i Leon* (Seville, 1671) (courtesy of the George Peabody Library, Sheridan Libraries, Johns Hopkins University)

of the letter of the law by the examining magistrate, namely, justice. For upon hearing their enumerated pleas, Fernando finally speaks and cites the very absence of a written confession as the justification for his overstepping traditional hierarchies and taking the township under his direct governance, in so doing absolving the township and its people of any guilt.

While there are a number of sources from which Lope may have taken his inspiration for the composition of his greatest play, there can be no doubt that he knew of Covarrubias's emblem book and that he had seen in it Covarrubias's own reference to 'the case of Fuente Ovejuna'. As in many such references, the emphasis of Covarrubias's emblematic analysis is on the moral dilemma of the moment of justice, when the judge, faced with the town's insistence that '*Fuente Ovejuna* did it', must decide between exonerating them all or condemning an entire populace to death (Figure 10.8).

Here the emblematist fiercely condemns the mob rule as 'atrocious', without God, King, or Law'[20] and yet, as Dixon points out in his analysis of the scene and its relation to Covarrubias's emblem, both the playwright and

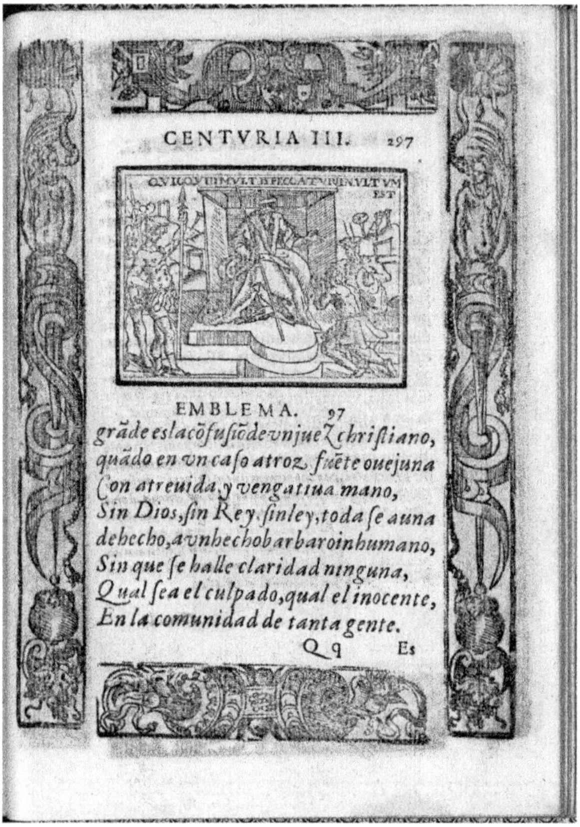

CENTVRIA III. 297

EMBLEMA. 97

grãde es la cõfusiõ de vn juez christiano,
quãdo en vn caso atroz, Fuẽte ouejuna
Con atreuida, y vengatiua mano,
Sin Dios, sin Rey, sin ley, toda se auna
de hecho, a vn hecho barbaro inhumano,
Sin que se halle claridad ninguna,
Qual sea el culpado, qual el inocente,
En la comunidad de tanta gente.

Qq Es

Figure 10.8 Sebastián de Covarrubias, *Emblemas morales* (Madrid, 1610), 297 (courtesy of the George Peabody Library, Sheridan Libraries, the Johns Hopkins University)

20 See Alexander Samson and Jonathan Thacker's discussion in their chapter 'Three Canonical Plays', in *A Companion to Lope de Vega* (London: Tamesis, 2008), 119–30, at 122.

the emblematist fixate their attention on this moment of unanimity of the people and the inherent selflessness of justice. As Covarrubias explains on the verso page to this emblem, justice so favours the innocent that it will prefer to let the guilty go free than to risk punishing the innocent. Thus, while executing an entire village was in fact not outside the realm of possible outcomes given the real system of justice at the time, both representations also point to a new world order, carved into the theatrical emblem of a people who unanimously cashed in their suffering for the authority of a universal sovereign.[21]

In a lecture delivered at Cardozo Law School under the auspices of Drucilla Cornell's conference on 'Deconstruction and the Possibility of Justice', Jacques Derrida posed the problem of justice in terms of speech act theory, arguing that 'as a performative cannot be just, in the sense of justice, except by grounding itself on conventions and so on other performatives, buried or not, it always maintains itself with some irruptive violence'.[22] The visual dimension of law, its visiocracy, serves at least in part to tame and focus, to justify that irruptive violence. In Goodrich's words,

> What is significant, because the genealogy and especially the philology can become tedious, is that in looking at law, in appearing before the court in its glory, the student sees not law but justice, not rule but principle, not force but flowers, in the garments of justice. Justice is a matter of faith, of belief in what is not and has no being ... and so a matter of parabolic appearances and of the enigmatic signs that form the secrets of government.[23]

On the one hand, then, is the plague of corruption, the evident absence of anything approaching a justifying justice behind the self-serving abuse of the law. On the other, an opposing and desperate discourse, evident in these emblematic structures, in which the violence and coercion of the law is equated with the common good, by way of its being wielded ultimately by a selfless and suffering, even a saintly sovereign whose own embrace of pain in turn justifies and redeems the apparent abuses at all levels below him. This emblematic structure creates an *image of justice* in which the force of law is cured of its seemingly arbitrary application and identified with a legitimate, because universal, suffering anchored ultimately in the sovereign's

21 Victor Dixon, '*Su majestad habla, en fin, como quien tanto ha acertado*': *la conclusión ejemplar de Fuente Ovejuna*', *Criticón* 42 (1988), 157–68, at 159.

22 Derrida, *Acts of Religion* (London: Routledge, 2001), 256.

23 Goodrich, 'Visiocracy', 516.

own self-abnegation: it is right that we all suffer because no one, not even the king, not even modern day priests of the law, those suffering poet-detectives of hard-boiled and police procedural fame is exempt from that suffering. In J. Madison Davis's words, the police hero:

> is a man of common background in quest of justice, but can only exact a small portion of it out of the unfragrant world we live in. Usually, the police hero is also as scarred as the hard-boiled private eye in his battles to make something, anything, right. Sam Spade pays an emotional price for turning Brigid O'Shaughnessy over to the police. There's an ongoing ruefulness in Philip Marlowe's loneliness. All this is in contrast to the joyful revelations that characterize the traditional puzzle-solving detectives of Agatha Christie, S. S. Van Dine, and Arthur Conan Doyle.[24]

Is it a stretch to see in the modern detective, with his suffering etched like an emblem into the care-worn lines of his all-too human face, a direct descendent of Covarrubias's suffering sovereign, united in their noble quest for a justice that anchors the apparent caprice of the law? For ours is a universal empire of pain; with the movement toward interiority and intent in the rereading of Phaeton's fall, we are asked to replace the evident injustice of the legal system with the assumption of a greater or real justice that we can only assume, trust or have faith exists in the heart of the other, for, in Aquinas's words, 'Man, the framer of human law, is competent to judge only of outward acts; because man seeth those things that appear … while God alone, the framer of the divine law, is competent to judge the inward movement of wills'.[25]

24 'He Do the Police in Different Voices: The Rise of the Police Procedural', *World Literature Today*, 86/1 (2012), 9–11, at 9.

25 Quoted in Kevin Jon Heller, 'The Cognitive Psychology of Mens Rea', 99 *Journal of Criminal Law and Criminology*, 317 (2008–2009), 1.

Bibliography

Primary sources

Alciato, Andrea (= Alciat, André), *Les Emblemes d'Alciat de nouveau translatez en françois vers pour vers jouxte les latins* ... (Lyon: Guillaume Rouillé, 1549).
—— *De Verborum Significatione* (Lyon: Sébastien Gryphe, 1530).
—— *Emblematum liber* (Augsburg: Steyner, (1531).
—— *Parergôn juris libri tres* (Lyon: Sébastien Gryphe, 1538).
—— *Emblematum libellus* (Venice: Aldus Manutius, 1546).
—— *Omnia Andreae Alciati ... Emblemata cum commentariis ... per Claudium Minoem Divionensem*, Claude Mignault (Antwerp: Christophe Plantin, 1577).
—— *Opera Omnia* (Basel: Thomas Guarin, 1582).
—— 'Oratio in laudem juris civilis' in *Opera Omnia* (Basel: Thomas Guarin, 1582), IV, col. 1022–31.
—— *Emblematum cum commentariis Cl. Minois I.C., Francisci Sanctii Brocensis et notis Laurentii Pignorii Patavinii*, J. Thuilii Mariaemontani (Padua: Petro Paulo Tozzi, 1621).
Allestree, Richard, *Government of the Tongue* (Oxford: At the Theater, 1674).
Aneau, Barthélemy, *Imagination Poétique* (Lyon: Macé Bonhomme, 1552).
—— *Picta Poesis. Ut Pictura Poesis erit* (Lyon: Macé Bonhomme, 1552).
—— *Iurisprudentia a primo et divino sui ortu ad nobilem Biturigem Academiam deducta* (Lyon: A l'enseigne du Sagittaire, 1554).
Apollo, Orus, *De la signification des notes hiéroglyphiques des Ægyptiens* (Paris: Jacques Kerver, 1543).
Bambergische Peinliche Halsgerichtsordnung, *Bambergische Peinliche Halsgerichtsordnung* [*The Penal Code of the Bamberg Criminal Court*] (Bamberg, 1507).

Bateman, Stephen, *A Christal Glasse of Christian Reformation* (London: John Day, 1569).
Beccaria, Cesare, *Von Verbrechen und Strafen* [*On Crimes and Punishment*: 1st edn 1764] (Breslau: Johann Friedrich Korn, 1788).
Boissard, Jean-Jacques, *Emblemes latins* (Metz: Abraham Faber, 1588).
Brèche Jean (Ioannes Brechaeus), *Ad Titulum Pandectarum De verborum et rerum significatione commentarii* (Lyon: Jean Temporal, 1556).
Bruck, Jacob, *Emblemata politica* (Cologne: Jan van der Heyden et Abraham Hogenberg, 1618).
Buck, Sir George, 'The Third Universitie of England' in John Stow, *The Annales. Or Generall Chronicle of England* (London: Thomas Adams, 1615).
Budé, Guillaume, *Annotationes in XXIV Pandectarum libros* (Paris: Josse Bade, 1508).
—— *Annotationes in XXIV Pandectarum libros* (Paris, 1514).
—— *Opera Omnia*, Cœlius Secundus Curio (Basel: Nicolas Episcopius, 1557).
Caepolla, Bartholomaeus, *In titulum de verborum et rerum significatione doctissima commentaria* (Lyon: Jacques, Jean et Claude Senneton, 1551).
Castejon y Fonseca, Diego de, *Odorico Rinaldi, Fiestas dela santa iglesia de Sevilla al culto nuevamente concedido al Señor Rei San Fernando III de Castilla i Leon* (Seville, 1671).
Caussin, Nicolas, *De symbolica Ægyptiorum* (Cologne: Ioannes Kinckius, 1623).
Chasseneuz, Barthélemy, *Catalogus gloriæ mundi* (Venice: Heirs of Vincenzo Valgrissi, 1576).
Coke, Edward, *Postnati. Calvin's Case, 7 Reports*, 1608.
—— *The Fourth Part of the Institutes of the Laws of England: Concerning the Jurisdiction of Courts* (London: M. Flesher, 1644).
—— *The Reports of Sir Edward Coke, Knt In English*, ed. George Wilson (London: J. Rivington, 1777).
Coke, Roger, *Justice Vindicated from the False Fucus put upon it by Thomas White Gent, Mr Thomas Hobbes and Hugo Grotius* (London: Thomas Newcomb, 1660).
Combe, Thomas, *The Theatre of Fine Devices* (London: Richard Field, 1593, 1614).
—— *Theatre of Fine Devices* (London, Field, 1614).
Corrozet, Gilles, *Hecatomgraphie* (Paris: Denis Janot, 1540).
Corvinus van Belderen, Arnold, *Digesta per Aphorismos strictim explicata* (Amsterdam, 1656).
Coustau, Pierre (Petrus Costalius/ Petrus Costus), *Le Pegme ... avec les narrations philosophiques, mis de latin en français par Lanteaume de Romieu* (Lyon: Macé Bonhomme, 1560).
—— (= Petrus Costalius/ Petrus Costus), *Pegma cum narrationibus philosophicis* (Lyon: Macé Bonhomme, 1555).
Cowell, John, *The Interpreter: or Booke containing the signification of words wherein is set foorth the true meaning of all, or the most part of such words and termes, as are mentioned in the law writers* (Cambridge: John Legate, 1607).
Damhoudere, Joost, *Praxis rerum civilium* (Antwerp: Joannes Bellarus, 1567).
Davies, Sir John, *Le premier report des cases et matters en ley resolves and adiudges en les courts del Roy en Ireland* (Dublin: John Franckton, 1615).
de Covarrubias, Sebastián, *Emblemas morales* (Madrid: Sanchez, 1610).
de Hooghe, Romeyn, *Ars magna et admirabilis. Speciminibus variis confirmata, qua Pandectarum Tituli, eorumque praecipua materia, ope Figurarum Emblematicarum*

brevissime, jucunde et tenaciter, memoriae imprimi, firmiter contineri et opportune in usum transferre possunt: In maximum commodum Legis Studiosi (Leiden: Johannes Luchtmans, 1695).
de Montenay, Georgette, *Emblematum Christianorum centuria* (Zurich: Christoph Froschover, 1584).
Dodderidge, Sir John, *The English Lawyer: Describing a Method for the managing of the Lawes of this Land* (London: John More, 1631).
Dugdale, Sir William, *Origines Juridiciales or Historical Memorials of the English Laws* (London: F. & T. Warren, 1666).
Earne, Thomas, *A Collection of Curious Discourses, Written by Eminent Antiquaries Upon Several Heads in our English Antiquities* (Oxford: Thomas Earne, 1720).
Finch, Sir Henry, *Law or a Discourse thereof (1627)* (London: Henry Lintot, 1759).
Fortescue, John, *De Laudibus Legum Angliæ*, ed. John Selden, London, R. Gosling, 1737.
Goodyere, Sir Henry, *The Mirrour of Maiestie: or, the Badges of Honour Conceitedly Emblazoned: with Emblems Annexed, Poetically Unfolded* (London: W. Jones, 1618).
Gravelot et Charles-Nicolas Cochin, Hubert-François, *Iconologie par figures ou traité complet des allégories, emblèmes etc. Ouvrage utile aux artistes, aux amateurs et pouvant servir à l'éducation des jeunes personnes* (Paris: Lattré, [1791]).
Horace, *Art of Poetry made English by the Right Honourable the Earl of Roscommon* (London: H. Herringman, 1680).
Hugo, Herman. *Pia Desideria Emblematis Elegiis & affectibus S.S. Patrum illustrata*, Antwerp: Henri Aertssen, 1624.
Junius, Hadrianus. *Emblemata* (Antwerp: Christophe Plantin, 1565).
Justinian, *Corpus juris civilis* (Lyon: Jacques, Jean et Claude Senneton, 1548-1550), I–V.
La Perrière, Guillaume, *Le Theatre des bons engins* (Paris: Denis Janot, 1540).
—— *La Morosophie* (Lyon: Macé Bonhomme, 1553).
Ménestrier, Claude-François, *L'art des emblèmes* (Lyon: Benoist Coral, 1662).
Mignault, Claude, *Omnia Emblemata cum luculenta enarratione* (Paris: Denis Du Pré, 1571).
Paradin, Claude, *Symbola heroica* (Antwerp: Christophe Plantin, 1583).
Père Le Moyne, *De l'art des devises* (Paris: Sébastien Cramoisy, 1666).
Perkins, William, *A Discourse of Conscience* (Cambridge, John Legate, 1608).
Puttenham, George, *The Arte of English Poesie* (London: Richard Field, 1589).
Rastell, John, *An Exposition of Certaine Difficult and Obscure Words and Termes of the Laws of this Realme (1526)* (London: T. Wright, 1602).
Ripa, Cæsar (Cesare), *Iconologia or Moral Emblems* (London: Benjamin Motte, 1709).
Rollenhagen, Gabriel, *Nucleus emblematum selectissimorum* (Cologne: Crispijn van de Passe, 1613).
Scarlatini, Ottavio, *Homo et eius partes figuratus & symbolicus, anatomicus, rationalis, moralis, mysticus, politicus, & legalis, collectus et explicatus cum figuris, symbolis, anatomiis, factis, emblematibus* (Augsburg/ Dillingen: Johann Kaspar Bencard, 1695).
Schoonhovius, Florentius, *Emblemata partim Moralia partim etiam Civilia* (Gouda. Andreas Burier, 1618).
Selden, John, *The Reverse or Back-Face of the English Janus*, trans. Redman Westcot (London: Thomas Basset & Richard Chiswell, 1682).
Sidney, Sir Philip, *The Defence of Poesie* (London: W. Ponsonby, 1595).

Van Haeften, Benedictus, *Schola cordis sive aversi a Deo Cordis ad eumdem reductio et instructio* (Antwerp: Jerome Verdussen, 1629).
Whitehouse, Edward, *Fortescutus Illustratus, or a Commentary on that Nervous Treatise De Laudibus Legum Angliæ* (London: Thomas Roycroft for Thomas Dicas, 1663).
Wither, George, *A Collection of Emblemes Ancient and Moderne* (London: Robert Allot, 1635).
Zincgref, Julius Wilhem, *Emblematum Ethico Politicorum Centuria* (Frankfurt am Main: Johann Theodor de Bry, 1619).

Secondary sources

Abbondanza, Roberto, '*A proposito dell' epistolario dell' Alciato*', *Annali di storia del diritto*, 1 (1957), 467–500.
—— 'Alciati', in *Dizionario biografico degli Italiani*, ed. Codier Corvo (Rome: Istituto della Enciclopedia italiana, 1983), I, p. 69–77.
Adams, Alison, Stephen Rawles, and Alison Saunders, *Bibliography of French Emblem Books of the Sixteenth and Seventeenth Century* (Geneva: Droz, 1999).
Agamben, Giorgio, *The Kingdom and the Glory. For a Theological Genealogy of Economy and Government* (Palo Alto, CA: Stanford University Press, 2011).
Alciat, André, *Index Emblematicus*, ed. S. Hirsch Cuttler and P. Daly (Toronto: Toronto University Press, 1985).
—— *Il libro degli Emblemi, secondo le edizioni del 1531 e del 1534*, (Mino Gabriele, Milan: Adelphi, 2009).
Arabeyre, Patrick, Jean-Louis Halpérin, and Jacques Krynen, eds, *Dictionnaire historique des juristes français* (Paris: Presses universitaires de France, 2007).
Archer, E., E. Goldring, S. Knight, eds, *The Intellectual and Cultural World of the Early Modern Inns of Court* (Manchester: Manchester University Press, 2001).
Aristotle, *The Poetics*, trans. Malcom Heath (London: Penguin, 1996).
—— *Nicomachean Ethics*, trans. J. A. K. Thomson (London: Penguin, 2004).
Bacon, Francis, *The Works of Francis Bacon*, ed. James Spedding, Robert L. Ellis, and Douglas D. Heath (London: Longmans, 1857–74).
Baker, John Hamilton, *An Introduction to English Legal History* (4th edn, London: Butterworths, 2002).
Balavoine, Claudie, '*Le classement thématique des emblèmes d'Alciat: recherches en paternité*', in *The Emblem in Renaissance and Baroque Europe: Tradition and Variety. Selected Papers of the Glasgow Emblem Conference, 13–17 August 1990*, ed. A. Adams, A. J. Harper, and E. J. Brill (Leiden: Brill, 1992).
—— '*La manipulation des images symboliques à la Renaissance: Démocrite entre rire et folie*', in *Florilegio de estudios de Emblemàtica, Actas del VI Congreso Internacional de Emblemàtica de 'The Society for Emblem Studies'* (Corunna: Ferrol, 2004), 167–75.
Barasch, Moshe, *Blindness: The History of a Mental Image in Western Thought* (Abingdon: Routledge, 2001).
Barni, Gian Luigi, *Le lettere di Andrea Alciato Giuresconsulto* (Florence: Le Monnier, 1953).
Baschet, Jérôme, *Les justices de l'au-delà. Les représentations de l'enfer en France et en Italie (XIIè–XVè siècle)* (Rome: École française de Rome, Bibliothèques des écoles françaises de Rome et d'Athènes, 1993), no. 279.

Bate, Jonathan, *Shakespeare and Ovid* (Oxford: Clarendon Press, 1993).
Bath, Michael, *Speaking Pictures: English Emblem Books and Renaissance Culture* (London: Longman, 1994).
Bennett Capers, I., 'Blind Justice', *Yale Journal of Law and Humanities*, 24/1 (2012), 179–90.
Behrmann, Carolin, 'Metrics of Justice. A Sundial's Nomological Figuration', *Nuncius*, 30/1 (2015), 161–94.
Blackstone, William, *Commentaries on the Laws of England* (Chicago, IL: Chicago University Press, 1979).
Blumenberg, Hans, *Paradigms for a Metaphorology* (Ithaca, NY: Cornell University Press, 2010).
—— *Paradigmen zu einer Metaphorologie (1960)*, ed. von Anselm Haverkamp (Berlin: Suhrkamp, 2013).
Boureau, Alain, 'État moderne et attribution symbolique: emblèmes et devises dans l'Europe des XVIè et XVIIè siècles', in *Culture et idéologie dans la genèse de l'État moderne: actes de la table ronde, Rome, 15–17 octobre 1984* (Rome: École française de Rome, 1985), 155–78.
—— *L'Aigle. Chronique politique d'un emblème* (Paris: Éditions du Cerf, 1985).
—— '*Le livre d'emblèmes sur la scène publique. Côté jardin et côté cour*', in Roger Chartier, *Les usages de l'imprimé (XVè-XIXè)* (Paris: Fayard, 1987), 343–79.
—— 'Books of Emblems on the Public Stage: *Côté jardin and côté cour*', in Roger Chartier, *The Culture of Print. Power and the Uses of Print in eraly Modern Europe*, (Cambridge: Polity Press, 1989), 261–89.
——'*L'image comme pièges à énoncés. La leçon de Kantorowicz*', in S. Dümmchen and M. Nerlich, *Texte-image. Bild-Text* (Berlin: Technische Universität, 1990), 107–14.
——'*La preuve par le cadavre qui saigne au XIIIè siècle, entre expérience commune et savoir scolastique*', *Micrologus*, 7 (1999), 247–81.
Bossuat, R., '*Jean de Rouvroy, traducteur des Stratagèmes de Frontin*', *Bibliothèque d'humanisme et renaissance*, 22/3 (1960), 273–86, 469–89.
Bowen, Barbara C., '*Lingua Quo Tendis?* Speech and Silence in French Renaissance Emblems', *French Forum*, 4/3 (1979), 249–60.
Boyer, Allen D., *Sir Edward Coke and the Elizabethan Age* (Stanford, CA: Stanford University Press, 2003).
Brandt, Sebastian, *The Ship of Fools*, trans. Edwin H. Zeydel (New York: Columbia University Press, 1944).
Brissaud, Yves-Bernard, '*Pistes pour une histoire de l'édition juridique française sous l'Ancien Régime*', in *Histoire et civilisation du livre*, Frédéric Barbier (Geneva: Droz, 2005), 1, 85–187.
Brooks, Douglas A., ed. *Printing and Parenting in Early Modern England* (Aldershot: Ashgate, 2005).
Burgess, Glenn, *Absolute Monarchy and the Stuart Constitution* (New Haven, CT: Yale University Press, 1996).
Byrne, Susan, *Law and History in Cervantes' Don Quixote* (Toronto: Toronto University Press, 2013).
Campe, Rüdiger, 'Questions of Emblematic Evidence: Phaeton's disaster, with Reference to Pierre Legendre's Theory of Emblems', in *New Directions in Emblem Studies*, 4 (1999), 1–25

Cassirer, Ernst, *Individuum und Kosmos in der Philosophie der Renaissance. Die Platonische Renaissance in England und die Schule von Cambridge (1927)* (Hamburg: Felix Meiner Verlag, 2002).

Cazals, Géraldine, *Une civile société. La République selon Guillaume de la Perrière (1499–1554)* (Toulouse: Presses de l'Université des sciences sociales de Toulouse, 2008).

Christin, Olivier, *Une révolution symbolique. L'iconoclasme huguenot et la reconstruction catholique* (Paris: Minuit, Le sens commun, 1991).

—— *Les Yeux pour le croire. Les dix commandements en images, XVè-XVIIIè siècle* (Paris: Seuil, 2003).

Christin, Olivier, *Vox Populi: Une histoire du vote avant le suffrage universel* (Paris: Seuil, 2014).

Cicero, *On the Republic: On the Laws*, trans. C. W. Keyes (Cambridge, MA: Harvard University Press, 1928).

—— *On Duties*, trans. E. M. Atkins and M. T. Griffin (Cambridge: Cambridge University Press, 1991).

Coquillette, Daniel R. 'Legal Ideology and Incorporations I: The English Civilian Writers, 1523–1607', *Boston University Law Review*, 61 (1981), 1–89.

Cover, Robert, 'The Folktales of Justice: Tales of Jurisdiction', *Capital University Law Review*, 14 (1985).

Crary, Jonathan, *Techniques of the Observer: On Vision and Modernity in the Nineteenth Century* (Cambridge, MA: MIT Press, 1990).

Cristaudo, Wayne, Paul Caringella, and Glenn Hughes, 'History, theology and the relevance of the *translatio imperii*', *Thesis Eleven*, 116 (2013), 5–18.

Curtius, Ernst, *Europäische Literatur und Lateinisches Mittelalter*, Bern, A. Francke, 1948, trans. Willard Trask as *European Literature and the Latin Middle Ages* (London: Routledge and Kegan Paul, 1991).

Daly, Peter, *Emblem Theory: Recent German Contributions to the Characterization of the Emblem Genre* (Nendeln-Liechtenstein: KTO, 1979).

de Lubac, Henri, *Exégèse médiévale: les quatre sens de l'Écriture* (Paris, Aubier, 1959–1964).

de Ville, Jacques, 'Mythology and the Images of Justice', *Law and Literature*, 23/3 (2011), 324–64.

Debaecque, Antoine, 'The Allegorical Image of France, 1750–1800: A Political Crisis of Representation', *Representation. Special Issue: National Cultures before Nationalism*, no. 47 (Summer 1994), 111–43.

Demonet, Marie-Luce, *Les voix du signe. Nature et origine du langage à la Renaissance (1480–1580)* (Paris: Champion, 1992).

Derrida, Jacques, 'The Force of Law: The Mystical Foundation of Authority', *Cardozo Law Review*, 11/5–6 (1990), 919–1045.

Didi-Hubermann, Georges, 'Ressemblance mythifiée et ressemblance oubliée chez Vasari: la légende du portrait "sur le vif"', *Mélanges de l'École française de Rome, Italie et Méditeranée*, 106/2 (1994), 383–432.

—— *L'image survivante: Histoire de l'art et temps des fantômes selon Aby Warburg* (Paris: Minuit, 2002).

—— *L'Image ouverte* (Paris : Gallimard, 2007).

Dorsett, Shaunnagh, and Shaun McVeigh, 'The *Persona* of the Jurist in Salmond's Jurisprudence: On the Exposition of "What Law is…"', *Victoria University of Wellington Law Review*, 38 (2007), 771–96.

Drysdall, Denis L., 'A Lawyer's Language Theory: Alciato's *De verborum significatione*', *Emblematica*, 9/2 (1995), 269–92.

—— 'Hieroglyphs, Speaking Pictures and the Law: The Context of Alciato's Emblems', *Glasgow Emblem Studies*, 16 (2013).

Ebel, Friedrich, Andreas Fijal, and Gernot Kocher, *Römisches Rechtsleben im Mittelalter. Miniaturen aus den Handschriften des* Corpus Iuris Civilis (Heidelberg: C. F. Müller, 1988).

Edgerton, Samuel Y., *Pictures and Punishment: Art and Criminal Prosecution during the Florentine Renaissance* (Ithaca, NY: Cornell University Press, 1985).

Eisenstein, Elizabeth L., *The Printing Press as an Agent of Change: Communications and Cultural Transformations in Early-Modern Europe* (Cambridge: Cambridge University Press, 1979).

Enenkel, Karl, 'Florentius Schoonhovius's *Emblemata partim moralia, partim etiam civilia*', in Karel Porteman, Marc Van Vaeck, John Manning, *The Emblem Tradition in the Low Countries, 4th International Emblem Conference, 1996* (Turnhout: Brepols, 1999), 177–95.

Érasme, *Les Silènes d'Alcibiade, traduction, introduction et notes de Jean-Claude Margolin* (Paris: Belles Lettres, 1998).

Fischer-Taylor, Katherine, *In the Theater of Criminal Justice: The Palais de Justice in Second Empire Paris* (Princeton, NJ: Princeton University Press, 1993).

Fortescue, Sir John, 'On the Nature of the Law of Nature', in Shelley Lockwood, *On the Laws and Governance of England* (Cambridge: Cambridge University Press, 1997).

Foster, E. R., ed., *Proceedings in Parliament, 1610* (New Haven, CT: Yale University Press, 1966).

Foucault, Michel, *The History of Sexuality*, trans. Robert Hurley, 3 vols. (London: Allen Lane, 1978–1984).

—— *Aesthetics, Method and Epistemology: Essential Works of Foucault, 1954–1984*, ed. James D. Faubion (London: Penguin, 2000).

Fox-Davies, Arthur Charles, *A Complete Guide to Heraldry* (London: Studio Editions, 1993).

Fraunce, Abraham, *The Arcadian Rhetoric (1588)* (Menston: Scolar Press, 1969).

Frank, Jerome, *Courts on Trial: Myth and Reality in American Justice* (Princeton, NJ: Princeton University Press, 1973).

Fröschl, Thomas, 'Republican Virtues and the Free State: Conceptual Frame and Meaning in Early Modern Europe and North America', in Allan Ellenius, ed., *Iconography, Propaganda, and Legitimation* (Oxford: Clarendon, 1998), 255–75.

Fumaroli, Marc, 'Rhetorics, Politics and Society: From Italian Ciceronianism to French Classicism', in James. G. Murphy, *Renaissance Eloquence. The Theory and Practice of Renaissance Rhetoric* (Berkeley, CA: University of California Press, 1983), 253–71.

Garapon, Antoine, *L'Âne portant des reliques. Essai sur le rituel judiciaire* (Paris: Centurion, 1985).

—— *Bien juger. Essai sur le rituel judiciaire* (Paris: Odile Jacob, 2001).

Garapon Antoine, and Valérie Hayaert, *Allégories de Justice: le décor de la Grand' chambre du Parlement de Flandre*, foreword Robert Badinter (Abbeville: Paillart, 2014).

Garden Barnes, Thomas, *Shaping the Common Law: From Glanwill to Hale, 1188–1688*, ed. Allen D. Boyer (Redwood City, CA: Stanford University Press, 2008).

Geoffrey of Monmouth, *The History of the Kings of Britain*, trans. Lewis Thorpe (London: Penguin, 1966).

Gibb, Sir Hamilton, *The Life of Saladin: From the Works of 'Imad Ad-Din and Baha' Ad-Din'* (Oxford: Clarendon, 1973).

Ginzburg, Carlo, *Miti, emblemi, spie* (Torino: Einaudi, 1986).

Girard, P. F., 'Alciat et la *notitia dignitatum*', in *Studi in onore di S. Perozzi* (Palermo: Castiglia, 1925) 59–87.

Girard, René, *La Violence et le Sacré* (Paris: Grasset, 1973).

Godin, André, *Érasme, lecteur d'Origène*, Genève, Droz, 1982.

Gombrich, Ernst H., '*Icones symbolicæ, l'image visuelle dans la pensée néo-platonicienne*', in *Symboles de la Renaissance* (Paris: Presses de l'ENS, 1976) 17–30.

Goodrich, Peter, *Languages of Law: From Logics of Memory to Nomadic Masks* (London: Weindenfeld and Nicolson, 1990).

—— 'Eating Law: Commons, Common Land, Common Law', *Journal of Legal History*, 12 (1991), 246–67.

—— 'Poor Illiterate Reason: History, Nationalism and Common Law', *Social and Legal Studies*, 1 (1992), 7–29.

—— *Law in the Courts of Love. Literature and other Minor Jurisprudences* (London: Routledge, 1996).

—— 'Signs Taken for Wonders: Community, Identity, and "A History of Sumptuary Law"', *Law and Social Inquiry*, 23 (1998), 707–28.

—— 'The Theatre of Emblems; On the Optical Apparatus and the Investiture of Persons', *Law, Culture and the Humanities*, 8 (2012), 47–61.

—— 'Visiocracy: On the Futures of the Fingerpost', *Critical Inquiry*, 39/3 (2013), 498–531.

—— *Legal Emblems and the Art of Law.* Obiter depicta *as the Vision of Governance* (Cambridge: Cambridge University Press, 2014).

Goyet, Francis, *Le sublime du lieu commun: l'invention rhétorique dans l'Antiquité et à la Renaissance* (Paris: Champion, 1996).

Guiderdoni, Agnès, '*Les figures angéliques dans les recueils de méditation emblématiques des XVIè et XVIIè siècles*', in *La parte dell' angelo- Documents de travail et pré-publications* (Urbino: Centro Internazionale de Semiotica e Linguistica, 2008), D 370–2, 18–29.

Guy, John, 'The Elizabethan Establishment and the Ecclesiastical Polity', in *The Reign of Elizabeth I: Court and Culture in the Last Decade* (Cambridge: Cambridge University Press, 1995).

Habermas, Jürgen, *The Structural Transformation of the Public Sphere: An Inquiry into a Category of Bourgeois Society*, trans. Thomas Burger and Frederick Lawrence (Cambridge, MA: MIT Press, 1989).

Hamlin, Cyrus, and John Michael Krois, eds, *Symbolic Forms and Cultural Studies, Ernst Cassirer's Theory of Culture* (New Haven, CT: Yale University Press, 2004).

Haverkamp, Anselm, *Figura cryptica: Theorie der literarischen Latenz* (Frankfurt: Suhrkamp, 2002).

—— 'To Conceive of, in Pictures: Antonello da Messina, August Sander', *Res: Aesthetics and Anthropology*, 59–60 (2011) 266–82.

Hayaert, Valérie, 'Pierre Coustau's *Pegma* (1555): Emblematics and legal humanism', *Emblematica*, 14 (2005), 55–99.

—— Mens emblematica *et humanisme juridique. Le cas du* Pegma cum narrationibus philosophicis *de Pierre Coustau (1555)* (Geneva: Droz, 2008).

—— '*Calumnia,* De Famosis libellis *et ripostes aux attaques injurieuses: la verve satirique de l'emblème*', *Revue Textimage*, no. 2 (Summer 2010).

—— '*Emblemata, greffes ou entregectz? Botanique et poésie dans la section Arbores du recueil d'Alciat*', in Alison Adams and Philip Ford, eds, *Le Livre demeure: Studies in Book History in Honour of Alison Saunders*, vol. 97 (Geneva, Droz, 2011), p. 62–77.

—— '*Æquitas, Épiékéia et littérature emblématique: une continuité d'invention*', in Bruno Méniel and Bénédicte Boudou, *Droit et Éthique*, (Paris: Garnier, 2012), 88–92.

—— '*De l'art de la jurisprudence à celui de l'emblème chez André Alciat et Pierre Coustau: œquiparatio, acumen et satire*', in Alexandre Vanautgaerden and Max Engammare, eds, *L'Intime du droit à la Renaissance, Cahiers d'Humanisme et de Renaissance*, 117 (2014), 19–41.

—— '*Du manuscrit juridique à l'édition ornée d'emblèmes et de 'hiéroglyphes': le cas de l'Archion Avenionense ca 1475 et de la Sennetoniana-Lyon, 1548–1550*', in Olivier Leplatre, ed. *Les détours de l'illustration*, Genève, Droz, Cahiers du Gadges, 2014.

Heckscher, William S., *The Princeton Alciati Companion: a Glossary of Neo-Latin Words and Phrases used by Andrea Alciato and the Emblem Book Writers of his Time. Including a Bibliography of Secondary Sources relevant to the Study of Alciato's Emblems* (New York: Garland, 1989).

Heidegger, Martin, *The Principle of Reason*, trans. Richard Rojcewicz (Bloomington, IN: Indiana University Press 1991).

Heller, Kevin Jon, 'The Cognitive Psychology of Circumstantial Evidence', *Michigan Law Review*, 106 (2006), 241–306.

Höltgen, Karl Josef, 'The Ruler between Columns: Imperial Aspirations and Political Iconography from the Emperor Charles V to William of Orange', in Michael Bath, Pedro F. Campa, and Daniel S. Russell, eds, *Emblem Studies in Honour of Peter M. Daly* (Baden-Baden: Verlag Valentin Koerner, 2002), 143–68.

Hooper, Wilfrid, 'The Tudor Sumptuary Laws', *English Historical Review*, 30/119 (1915), 433–49.

Hunt, Alan, *Governance of the Consuming Passions: A History of Sumptuary Law* (Basingstoke: Macmillan, 1996).

Hunter, Ian, *The Secularization of the Confessional State: The Political Thought of Christian Thomasius* (Cambridge: Cambridge University Press, 2007).

Jacob, Robert, '*Le jugement de Dieu et la formation de la fonction de juger dans l'histoire européenne*', *Histoire de la Justice*, 4 (1991), 53–78.

—— *Images de la Justice. Essai sur l'iconographie judiciaire du Moyen-Âge à l'âge classique* (Paris. Le Léopard d'Or, 1994).

Jacobs, E. F., *Sir John Fortescue and the Law of Nature* (Manchester: Manchester University Press, 1934).

Jeanneret, Michel, *Perpetuum mobile. Métamorphoses des corps et des œuvres de Vinci à Montaigne* (Paris: Macula, Argô, 1997).

Justinian, *Institutes*, trans. Peter Birks and Grant McLeod (London: Duckworth, 1994).
Kaiserliche Notariatsordnung, *Kaiserliche Notariatsordnung von 1512*, ed. Herbert Grziwotz (Munich: Beck Verlag, 1995).
Kantorowicz, Ernst, *The King's Two Bodies: A study in medieval political theology* (Princeton, NJ: Princeton University Press, 1957).
—— 'The Sovereignty of the Artist: A note on Legal Maxims and Renaissance Theories of Art', in Millard Meiss, *De artibus opuscula XL, Essays in honor of Erwin Panofsky* (New York: New York University Press, 1961), vol. 1, art. no. 22, 267–79.
—— *Selected Studies* (New York: Augustin, 1965).
Kelley, Donald R., 'Legal Humanism and the Sense of History', *Studies in the Renaissance* 13 (1966), 184–99.
—— *Foundations of Modern Historical Scholarship. Language, Law and History in the French Renaissance* (New York: Columbia University Press, 1970).
—— '*Vera Philosophia*: The Philosophical Significance of Renaissance Jurisprudence', *Journal of the History of Philosophy*, 14 (1976), 267–79.
—— '*Jurisconsultus perfectus:* the lawyer as Renaissance man', *Journal of the Warburg and Courtauld Institutes*, 51 (1988), 84–102.
King James VI and I, *King James VI and I: Political Writings*, ed. Johann P. Sommerville (Cambridge: Cambridge University Press, 1994).
Kissel, Otto Rudolf, *Die Justitia. Reflexionen über ein Symbol und seine Darstellung in der bildenden Kunst* (Munich: C. H. Beck, 1997).
Klecker, Elisabeth, '*Des signes muets aux emblèmes chanteurs: les Emblemata d'Alciat et l'emblématique*', *Littérature*, 145/1 (2007).
Klein, Robert, '*La théorie de l'expression figurée dans les traités italiens sur les Imprese*, 1555-1612', in *La forme et l'intelligible. Écrits sur la Renaissance et l'art moderne* (Paris: Gallimard, 1970), 320–41.
Kocher, Gernot, '*Sachsenspiegel, Institutionen, Digesten, Codex- Zum Aussagewert mittelalterlicher Rechtillustrationen*', *Forschungen zur Rechtarchäologie und Rechtlichen Volkskunde*, 3 (1985), 5–34.
Kononenko-Moyle, Natalie, 'Homer, Milton, and A ik Veysel: The Legend of the Blind Bard', *Harvard Ukrainian Studies*, 3–4/2 (1979–1980), 520–9.
Kuijer, Martin, *The Blindfold of Lady Justice: Judicial Independence and Impartiality in Light of the Requirements of Article 6 ECHR* (Leiden: Wolf Legal, 2004).
La Justice en ses temples. Regards sur l'architecture judiciaire en France, foreword, Robert Badinter (Paris-Poitiers: Brissaud, 1992).
Lacan, Jacques, *The Seminar of Jacques Lacan*, Jacques-Alain Miller, ed., *Book XI The Four Fundamental Concepts of Psychoanalysis*, trans. Alan Sheridan (New York: Norton, 1978).
Langum, V. E., 'Sins of Tongues, Pain of Members; Speech and Sacrament in late Medieval *Exempla*', *Marginalia*, 6 (2006–2007), 1–12.
Laurens, Pierre, and Florence Vuilleumier, '*De l'archéologie à l'emblème: la genèse du Liber alciati*', *Revue de l'Art*, 101/4 (1993), 45–51.
—— '*Entre Histoire et Emblème: le recueil des inscriptions milanaises d'André Alciat*', *Revue des études Latines*, 72 (1994), 218–37.
—— '*L'invention de l'emblème par André Alciat et le modèle épigraphique*', in *L'âge de l'inscription. La rhétorique du monument en Europe du XVIè au XVIIè siècle* (Paris: Les Belles Lettres, 2010).

Lee, Rensselaer W., *Ut Pictura Poesis: The Humanistic Theory of Painting* (New York: Norton, 1967).
Lefèvre d'Étaples, Jacques, *Quincuplex Psalterium, fac-similé de l'édition de 1513*, ed. Guy Bedouelle (Genava: Droz, 1979).
Legendre, Pierre, *Le Dossier occidental de la parenté. Textes juridiques indésirables sur la généalogie* (Paris: Fayard, 1988).
Legendre, Pierre, *Le Désir politique de Dieu* (Paris: Fayard, 1988).
—— *Les enfants du texte* (Paris: Fayard, 1992).
—— *Law and the Unconscious: A Legendre Reader*, trans. Peter Goodrich, with Alain Pottage and Anton Schütz (Basingstoke: Macmillan, 1997).
Levack, Brian P., *The Civil Lawyers in England, 1603–1641: A Political Study* (Oxford: Clarendon, 1973).
Lévy-Bruhl, Henri, *La Preuve judiciaire. Étude de sociologie juridique* (Paris: Librairie Marcel Rivière, 1964).
Longfield Carr, Susan, *Self and History in the Works of Guillaume Budé, Andreas Alciato and Zasius, A Study of the Role of Legal Humanism in Western Natural Law* (Chicago: University of Chicago Press, 2008).
Maclean, Ian, *Interpretation and meaning in the Renaissance: The Case of Law* (Cambridge: Cambridge University Press, 1992).
—— 'Legal fictions and Fictional Entities in Renaissance Jurisprudence', *Legal History*, 20/3 (1999), 1–24.
Maitland, Frederic W., *English Law and the Renaissance* (Cambridge: Cambridge University Press, 1901).
Maser, Edward A., ed., *Baroque and Rococo Pictorial Imagery: The 1758–60 Hertel Edition of Ripa's 'Iconologia' with 200 Engraved Illustrations* (New York: Dover, 1971).
Massing, Jean-Michel, *Du texte à l'image, la Calomnie d'Apelle et son iconographie* (Strasbourg: Presses universitaires de Strasbourg, 1990).
Matthieu-Castellani, Gisèle, 'Le défi de l'emblème', *Revue de littérature comparée*, 69/4 (1990), 597–603.
Mazzio, Carlo, 'Sins of the Tongue in Early Modern England', *Modern Language Studies*, 28/3–3 (1998), 95–124.
Merleau-Ponty, Maurice, *The Visible and the Invisible*, trans. Alphonso Lingis (Evanston, IL: Northwestern University Press, 1968).
Meyer, August, *Die Notariatsordnungen von 1512 und 1871 als Beiträge zur Rechtssicherheit. Festschrift des Delegiertentages der österreichischen Notariatskammern* (Salzburg: Residenz Verlag, 1971).
Michaud, Yves, '*Des modes de subjectivation aux techniques de soi: Foucault et les identités de notre temps*', *Cités*, 2000, 2 (*Michel Foucault: de la guerre des races au biopouvoir*), 11–39.
Miedema, Hessel, 'The Term Emblema in Alciati', *Journal of the Warburg and Courtauld Institutes*, 31 (1968), 234–50.
Mommsen, Theodor E., 'Petrarch and the Story of Hercules', *Journal of the Warburg and Courtauld Institutes*, 16 (1953), 178–92.
Monheit, Michael L., 'Guillaume Budé, Andrea Alciato, Pierre de l'Estoile: Renaissance Interpreters of Roman Law', *Journal of the History of Ideas*, 58/1 (1997), 21–40.
Nelson, Bradley J., *The Persistence of Presence: Emblem and Ritual in Baroque Spain* (Toronto: University of Toronto Press, 2010).

Nietzsche, Friedrich, *The Birth of Tragedy*, ed. Michael Tanner, trans. Shaun Whiteside (Harmondsworth: Penguin, 1993).

Nils-Robert, Christian, *Une allégorie parfaite. La justice, vertu, courtisane et bourreau* (Geneva: Georg, 1993).

—— *La Justice dans ses décors (XVè-XVIè siècles)* (Geneva: Droz, 2006).

Nitschke, August, *Kunst und Verhalten: Analoge Konfigurationen* (Stuttgart: Fromann Holzboog, 1975).

Nussbaum, Martha, *Poetic Justice: the Literary Imagination and Public Life* (Boston:, Beacon, 1995).

Walter Ong, *Orality and Literacy. The Technologizing of the Word* (London: Routledge, 1988).

Ordine, Nuccio, *Trois couronnes pour un roi. La devise d'Henri III et ses mystères*, trans. L. Hersant (Paris: Les Belles Lettres, 2011).

Panofsky, Erwin, *Gothic Architecture and Scholasticism*, trans. Pierre Bourdieu (Latrobe, PA: Archabbey, 1951).

—— *Studies in Iconology: Humanistic Themes in the Art of the Renaissance* (New York: Harper and Row, 1962).

Panofsky, Erwin, *Hercules am Scheideweg und andere antike Bildstoffe in der Neueren Kunst*, afterword on new edn, David Wuttke (Berlin: Gebr. MannVerlag, 1997).

Pastoureau, Michel, *L'étoffe du Diable. Une histoire des rayures et des tissus rayés* (Paris: Seuil, Points Histoire, 2007).

Pedullà, Gabriele, *In Broad Daylight. Movies and Spectators After the Cinema* (London : Verso, 2012).

Peil, Dietmar, 'Emblem Types in Gabriel Rollenhagen's Nucleus Emblematum', *Emblematica*, 6/2 (1992), 255–82.

Peters, Julie Stone, 'Theatrocracy Unwired: Legal Performance in the Modern Mediasphere', *Law and Literature*, 26/1 (2014), 31–64.

Pitlo, A., *Enkele mnemotechnische juridica. Ad personam. Opstellen aangeboden aan Prof. Mr Ch. J. Enschedé*, Zwolle, 1981.

Praz, Mario, *Studies in Seventeenth Century Imagery* (Rome: Edizioni di storia e letteratura, 1964).

Prest, Wilfrid R., *The Rise of the Barristers: A Social History of the English Bar 1590–1640* (Oxford: Clarendon, 1991).

Pross, Wolfgang, '*Le péché et la constitution du sujet à la Renaissance*', in *Dispositifs du sujet à la Renaissance, Rue Descartes*, 27 (2000), 79–116.

Raffield, Paul, 'Bodies of Law: The Divine Architect, Common Law and the Ancient Constitution', *International Journal for the Semiotics of Law*, 13 (2000), 333–56.

—— *Images and Cultures of Law in Early Modern England: Justice and Political Power, 1588–1660* (Cambridge: Cambridge University Press, 2004).

—— *Shakespeare's Imaginary Constitution. Late Elizabethan Politics and the Theatre of Law* (Oxford: Hart, 2010).

—— 'The Elizabethan Rhetoric of Signs: Representation of *Res Publica* at the Early Modern Inns of Court', *Law, Culture and the Humanities*, 7 (2011), 244–63.

—— 'The Dramatic Imagination and the Dream of Law', in Marco Wan, ed., *Reading the Legal Case: Cross-Currents between Law and the Humanities* (Abingdon: Routledge, 2012).

Rancière, Jacques, *Le partage du sensible: esthétique et politique* (Paris: La Fabrique, 2000).
—— *The Future of the Image*, trans. G. Elliott (London: Verso, 2009).
Rawles, Stephen, 'Layout, Typography and Chronology in Chrétien Wechel's Editions of Alciato', in David Graham, ed., *An Interregnum of the Sign: the Emblematic Age in France* (Glasgow: Glasgow Emblem Studies, 2001), 49–71.
Rawls, John, *A Theory of Justice* (Cambridge, MA: Belknap/Harvard University Press, 1971).
Resnik, Judith, and Dennis Curtis, *Representing Justice: Invention, Controversy and Rights in City-States and Democratic Courtrooms* (New Haven, CT: Yale University Press, 2011).
Rigolot, François, '*Nicomaque et la règle de plomb, fictions légitimes et illégitimes de la justice montaignienne*', in *La Justice, Bulletin de la Société des Amis de Montaigne*, 8/21–22 (2001), 87–97.
Roberts, Hugh, Guillaume Peureux and Lise Wajeman, eds, *Obscénités renaissantes*, foreword Michel Jeanneret, Travaux d'Humanisme et Renaissance, no. 473 (Geneva: Droz, 2011).
Rubinstein, Nicolai, 'The Piazza della Signoria', in *The Palazzo Vecchio, 1298–1532* (Oxford: Oxford University Press, 1995).
Russell, Daniel, *The Emblem and Device in France* (Lexington: French Forum, 1985).
—— 'The emblem and authority', *Word and Image*, 4 (1988), 81–7.
—— *Emblematic Structures in Renaissance French Culture* (Toronto: Toronto University Press, 1995).
Russell, M. J., 'Trial by Battle in the Court of Chivalry', *Journal of Legal History*, 29 (2008), 335–57.
Saunders, David, 'The Critical Jurist and the Moment of Theory', *Postcolonial Studies*, 10/1 (2007), 77–92.
Sbriccioli, Mario, 'La triade, le bandeau, le genou. Droit et procès pénal dans les allégories de Justice du Moyen-Âge à l'âge moderne', *Crime, Histoire et Sociétés*, 9/1 (2005), 33–78.
Schmidt-Wiegand, Ruth, 'Text und Bild in der *Codices picturati* des Sachsenspiegels. überlegungen zur Fonktion der Illustration', in *Text-Bild Interpretation. Untersuchungen zu den Bilderhandschiften des Sachsenspiegels* (Munich: Fink, 1986).
Schmitt, Jean-Claude, *La raison des gestes dans l'Occident médiéval* (Paris: Gallimard, 1990).
Scholz, Bernard, '*Libellum composui epigrammaton cui tituli feci Emblemata:* Alciato's Use of the Expression *Emblema* Once Again', *Emblematica*, 1/2 (1986) 213–26.
Schopenhauer, Arthur, *The World as Will and Idea*, trans. R. B. Haldane and John Kemp (London: Kegan Paul, Trench, Trübner, 1906).
Screech, Michael, 'Emblems and colours: the controversy over Gargantua's colours and devices (Gargantua, 8, 8, 10)', in *Mélanges d'histoire du XVIè siècle offerts à Henri Meylan* (Geneva: Droz, 1970).
Sharpe, Kevin, *Politics and Ideas in Early Stuart England* (London: Pinter, 1989).
Sherry, Richard, *Treatise of the Figures of Grammar and Rhetoric Profitable for all that be Studious of Eloquence* (1560) (University Park, PA: Pennsylvania State University, 1994).
Silcox, Mary V., 'The translation of La Perrière's *Le Theatre des bons engins* into Combe's *The Theatre of Fine Devices*', *Emblematica*, 2/1 (1987).

Spruit, J. E., *Le droit romain, sujet d'une décoration murale du 17è siècle. Carreaux émaillés illustrant les Pandectes de Justinien* (Arnhem: Gouda Quint BV, 1989).
Starn, Randolph, *Ambrogio Lorenzetti: The Palazzo Pubblico, Siena* (New York: George Braziller, 1994).
Stolleis, Michael, *The Eye of the Law* (Abingdon: Birkbeck Law Press, 2004).
Strauss, Gerald, *Law, Resistance, and the State: The Opposition to Roman Law in Reformation Germany* (Princeton, NJ: Princeton University Press, 1986).
Taylor, Anthony Brian, 'Golding's Ovid, Shakespeare's 'Small Latin', and the Real Object of Mockery in *Pyramus and Thisbe*', *Shakespeare Survey*, 42 (1990), 53–64.
Teissier-Ensminger, Anne, 'Formules en forme(s): les adages juridiques illustrés', *Revue de la Recherche juridique*, 2 (2007), 1081–104.
—— 'Le sanctuaire du droit visité par l'image: à propos de la thèse de V. Hayaert, *Mens emblematica et humanisme juridique*', *Revue historique de droit français et étranger*, 86/3 (2008), 383–95.
—— 'La juridicité au bonheur de l'emblématique: à propos d'André Laingui, Curiosités de l'histoire du droit, grandes dates, faits notables', *Revue de la Recherche juridique*, 4 (2008), 2275–96.
Tipton, Susan, *Res Publica bene ordinata: Regentenspiegel und Bilder von guten Regiment, Rathausdekorationen in der Fruhen Neuzeit* (Hildesheim: George Olms Verlag, 1996).
Tournon, André, *Montaigne, la glose et l'essai* (Paris: Editions Honoré Champion, 1983).
—— 'La plasticité des énoncés selon le *De verborum significatione* d'Alciat', *Les commentaires et la naissance de la critique littéraire XIVè-XVIè siècles* (Paris: Aux amateurs de livres, 1990), 157–63.
Trachtenberg, Marvin, *Dominion of the Eye* (Cambridge: Cambridge University Press, 1997).
Usher, Roland G., *The Rise and Fall of the High Commission* (Oxford: Clarendon Press, 1913).
Valla, Lorenzo, *On the Donation of Constantine (1440)*, trans. G. W. Bowersock (Cambridge, MA: Harvard University Press, 2008).
Van Vliet, Muriel, ed., *Ernst Cassirer et l'art comme forme symbolique* (Rennes: Presses universitaires de Rennes, Aesthetica, 2010).
Viard, Paul-Emile, *André Alciat (1492–1550)* (Paris: Sirey, 1926).
Vincent, Susan, *Dressing the Elite: Clothes in Early Modern England* (Oxford: Berg, 2003).
Vivanti, Corrado, 'Henri IV, the Gallic Hercules', *Journal of the Warburg and Courtauld Institutes*, 30 (1967), 176–97.
Volkmann, L., *Ars memorativa*, in *Jahrbuch der Kunsthistorischen Sammlungen in Wien*, 1929, N.F. III, 180–4.
Webbe, George, 'The Arraignment of the Unruly Tongue' (1619), in *The Unruly Tongue in Early Modern England. Three Treatises*, Nathalie Vienne-Guérin (Plymouth: Rowman, 2012).
Wesphal, Bertrand, ed., *Le rivage des mythes: une géocritique méditerranéenne, le lieu et son mythe*, *Espaces Humains* no. 2 (Limoges: Presses Universitaires de Limoges, 2001).
Willson, D. H., *King James VI and I* (London: Johnathan Cape, 1959).
Wind, Edgar, 'Hercules and Orpheus: Two Mock-Heroic Designs by Dürer', *Journal of the Warburg Institute*, 2/3 (1939), 206–18.

—— 'Orpheus in Praise of Blind Love', in *Pagan Mysteries in the Renaissance* (London: Faber and Faber, 1968), 57–78.

Woods Callahan, Virginia, 'Andreas Alciatus and Boniface Amerbach: The chronicle of a Renaissance friendship', in *Acta Conventus Neo-Latini Guelpherbytani* (Binghamton, NY: Medieval and Renaissance Text and Studies, 1988).

—— 'Proto-Emblematica in Andrea Alciati's *Oration in Praise of Civil Law* (Avignon, 1520)', *Emblematica*, 4/1 (1989), 3–13.

Woolrych, H. W., *The Life of the Right Honourable Sir Edward Coke, Knt, Lord Chief Justice of the King's Bench, & co* (London: J & W.T. Clarke, 1826).

Yates, Frances Amelia, *Giordano Bruno and the Hermetic Tradition* (Chicago, IL: University of Chicago Press, 1964).

—— *The Art of Memory* (Chicago: University of Chicago Press, 1966).

—— *Astrea: The Imperial Theme in the Sixteenth Century* (London: Routledge and Kegan Paul, 1975).

Zemon Davis, Natalie, *The Gift in Sixteenth-Century France* (Oxford: Oxford University Press, 2000).

Ziolkowski, Theodore, 'The Figure of Justice in Western Art and Literature', *Inmunkwahak, Journal of Humanities*, 75 (1996).

—— *The Mirror of Justice: Literary Reflections of Legal Crises* (Princeton, NJ: Princeton University Press, 1997).

Index